target zone

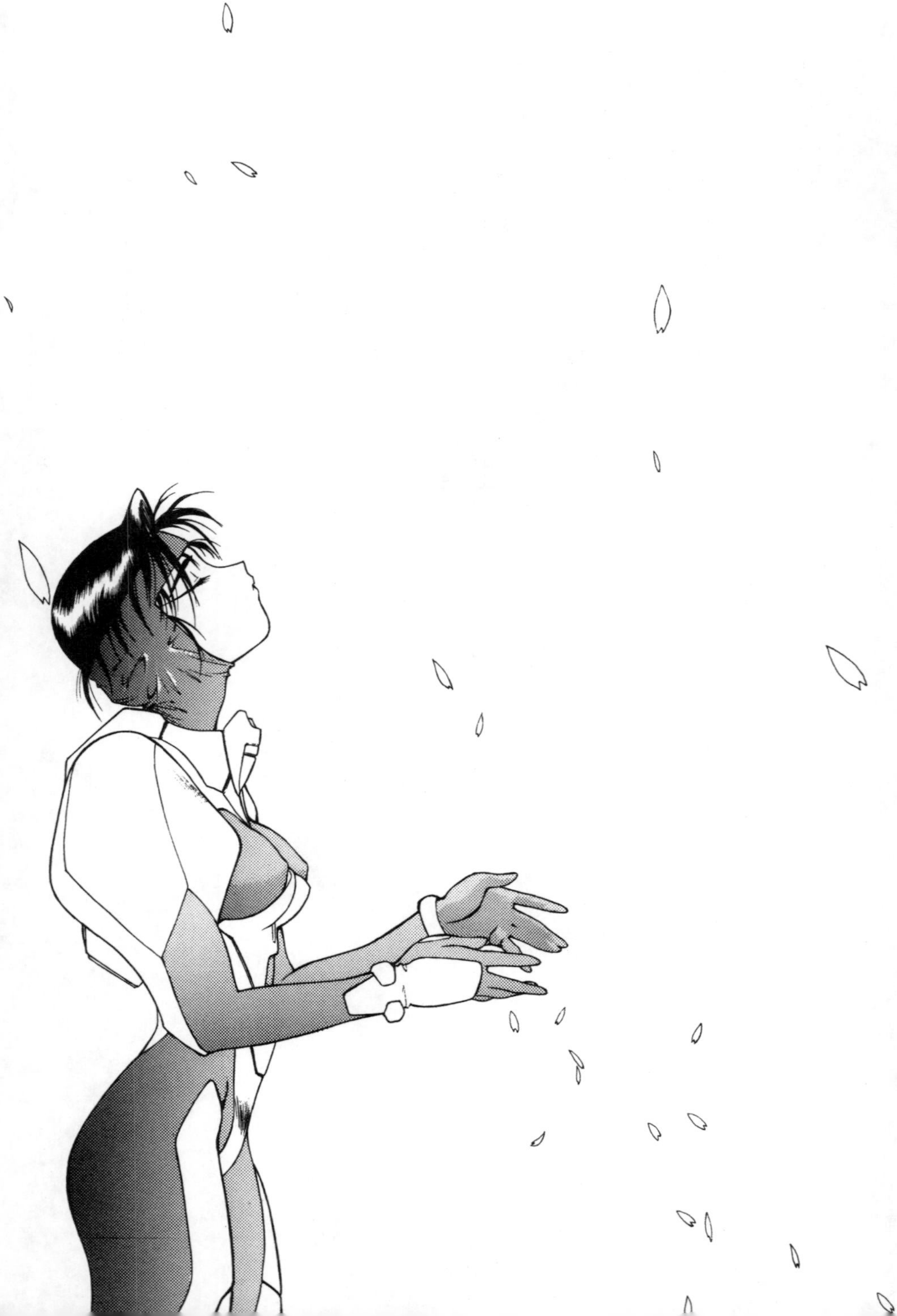

SERAPHIC FEATHER

Target Zone

art and story
HIROYUKI UTATANE
and
TOSHIYA TAKEDA

translation
DANA LEWIS *and* ADAM WARREN

lettering and touch-up
PAT L. DUKE

DARK HORSE COMICS™

publisher
MIKE RICHARDSON

series editor
TIM ERVIN-GORE

series executive editor
TOREN SMITH *for* STUDIO PROTEUS

collection editor
CHRIS WARNER

collection designer
DARIN FABRICK

art director
MARK COX

English-language version produced by STUDIO PROTEUS,
and DARK HORSE COMICS, INC.

SERAPHIC FEATHER VOL. III: TARGET ZONE

THIS VOLUME COLLECTS SERAPHIC FEATHER STORIES FROM ISSUES NINETEEN THROUGH TWENTY-FIVE OF THE DARK HORSE COMIC-BOOK SERIES SUPER MANGA BLAST!

PUBLISHED BY
DARK HORSE COMICS, INC.
10956 SE MAIN STREET
MILWAUKIE, OR 97222

WWW.DARKHORSE.COM

TO FIND A COMICS SHOP IN YOUR AREA, CALL THE COMIC SHOP
LOCATOR SERVICE TOLL-FREE AT 1-888-266-4226

FIRST EDITION: MARCH 2003
ISBN: 1-56971-912-8

1 3 5 7 9 10 8 6 4 2

PRINTED IN CANADA

SERAPHIC
FEATHER

ACT 18

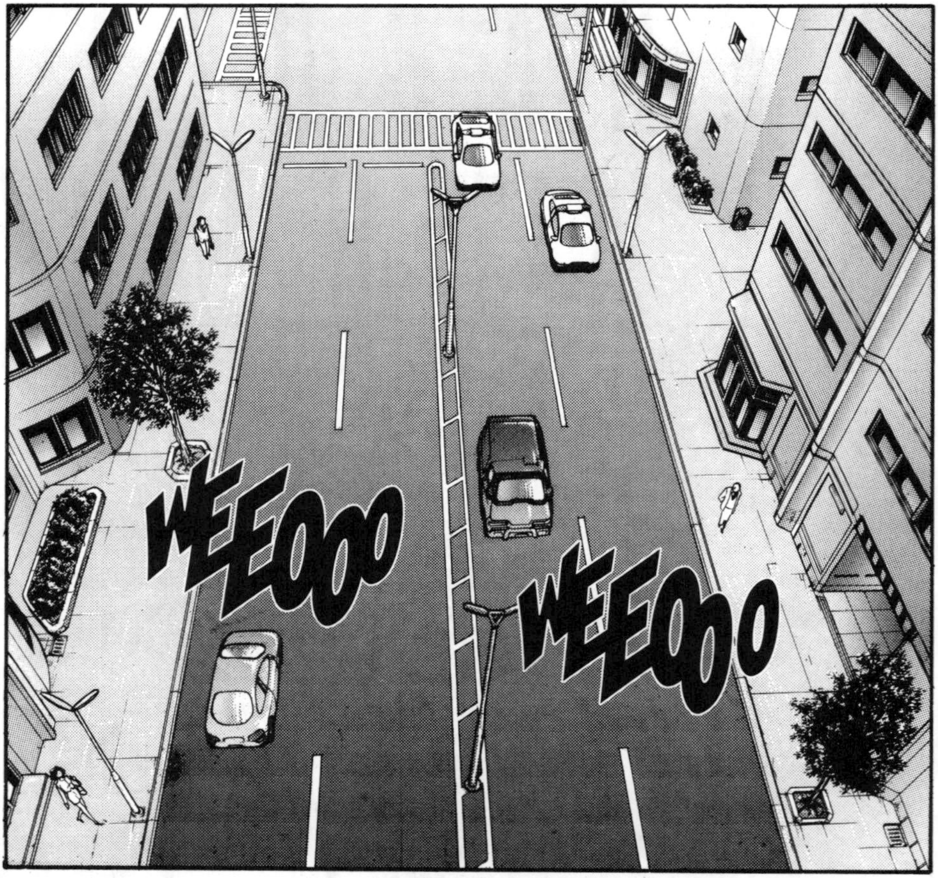
WEEOOO
WEEOOO
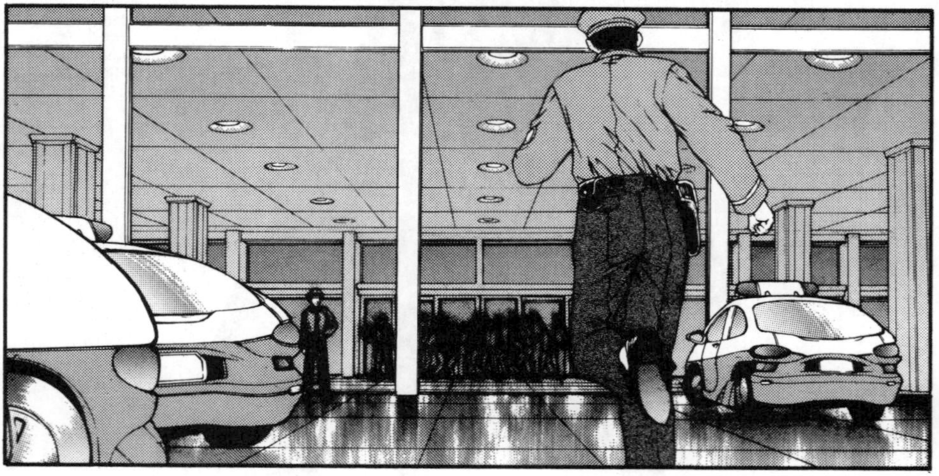

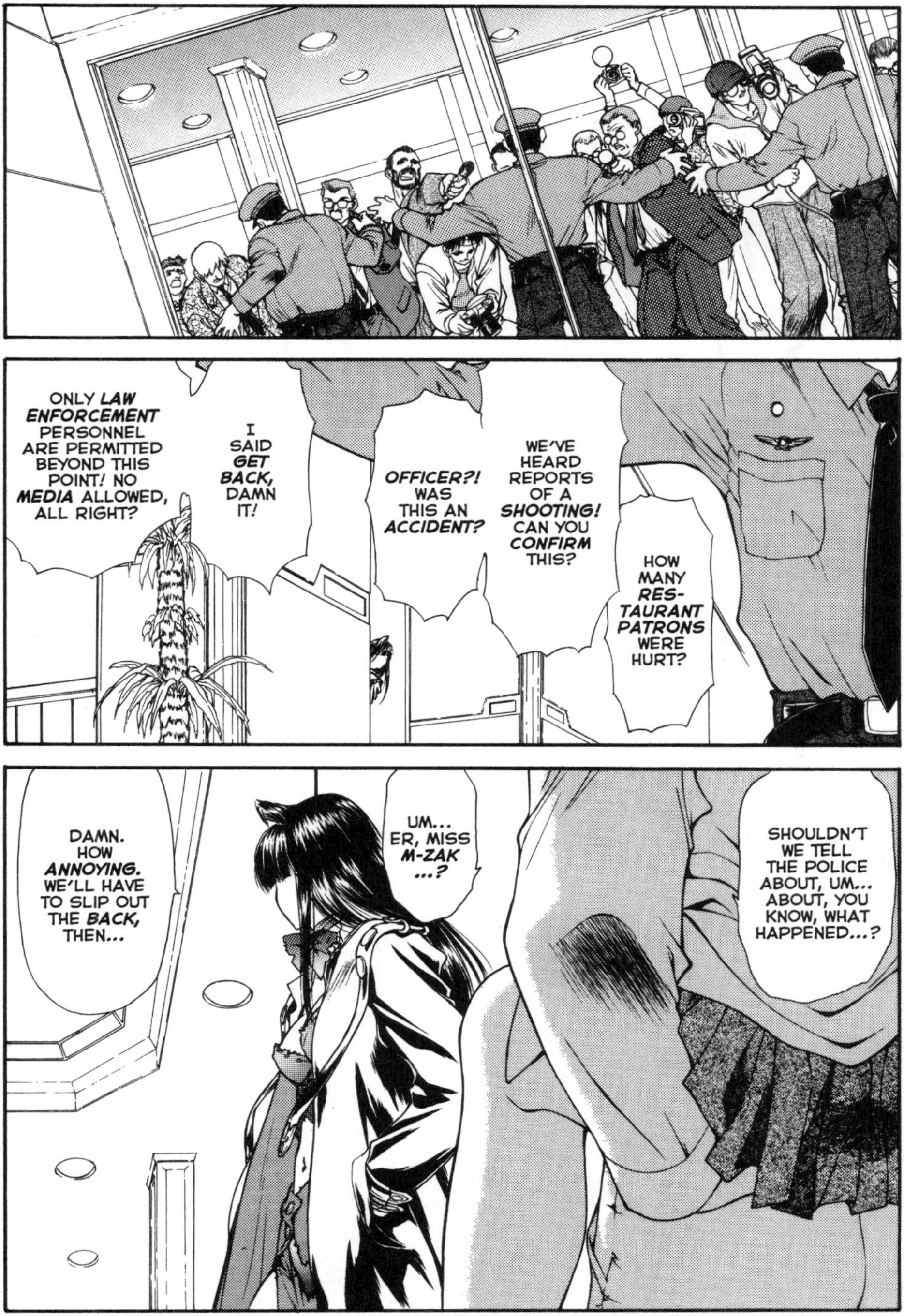
ONLY LAW ENFORCEMENT PERSONNEL ARE PERMITTED BEYOND THIS POINT! NO MEDIA ALLOWED, ALL RIGHT?
I SAID GET BACK, DAMN IT!
OFFICER?! WAS THIS AN ACCIDENT?
WE'VE HEARD REPORTS OF A SHOOTING! CAN YOU CONFIRM THIS?
HOW MANY RES-TAURANT PATRONS WERE HURT?
DAMN. HOW ANNOYING. WE'LL HAVE TO SLIP OUT THE BACK, THEN...
UM... ER, MISS M-ZAK ...?
SHOULDN'T WE TELL THE POLICE ABOUT, UM... ABOUT, YOU KNOW, WHAT HAPPENED...?

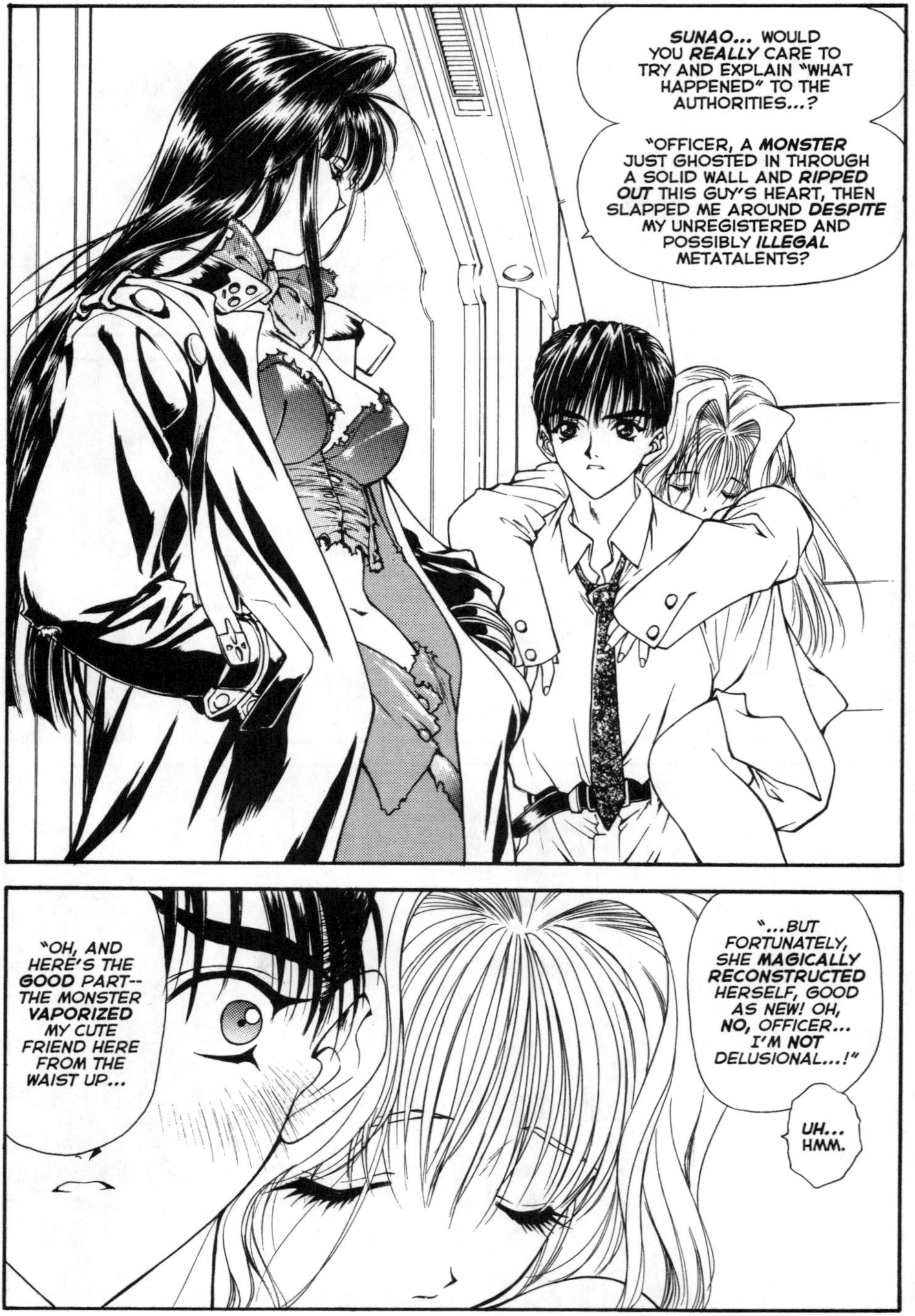
SUNAO... WOULD YOU REALLY CARE TO TRY AND EXPLAIN "WHAT HAPPENED" TO THE AUTHORITIES...?
"OFFICER, A MONSTER JUST GHOSTED IN THROUGH A SOLID WALL AND RIPPED OUT THIS GUY'S HEART, THEN SLAPPED ME AROUND DESPITE MY UNREGISTERED AND POSSIBLY ILLEGAL METATALENTS?
"OH, AND HERE'S THE GOOD PART-- THE MONSTER VAPORIZED MY CUTE FRIEND HERE FROM THE WAIST UP...
"...BUT FORTUNATELY, SHE MAGICALLY RECONSTRUCTED HERSELF, GOOD AS NEW! OH, NO, OFFICER... I'M NOT DELUSIONAL...!"
UH... HMM.

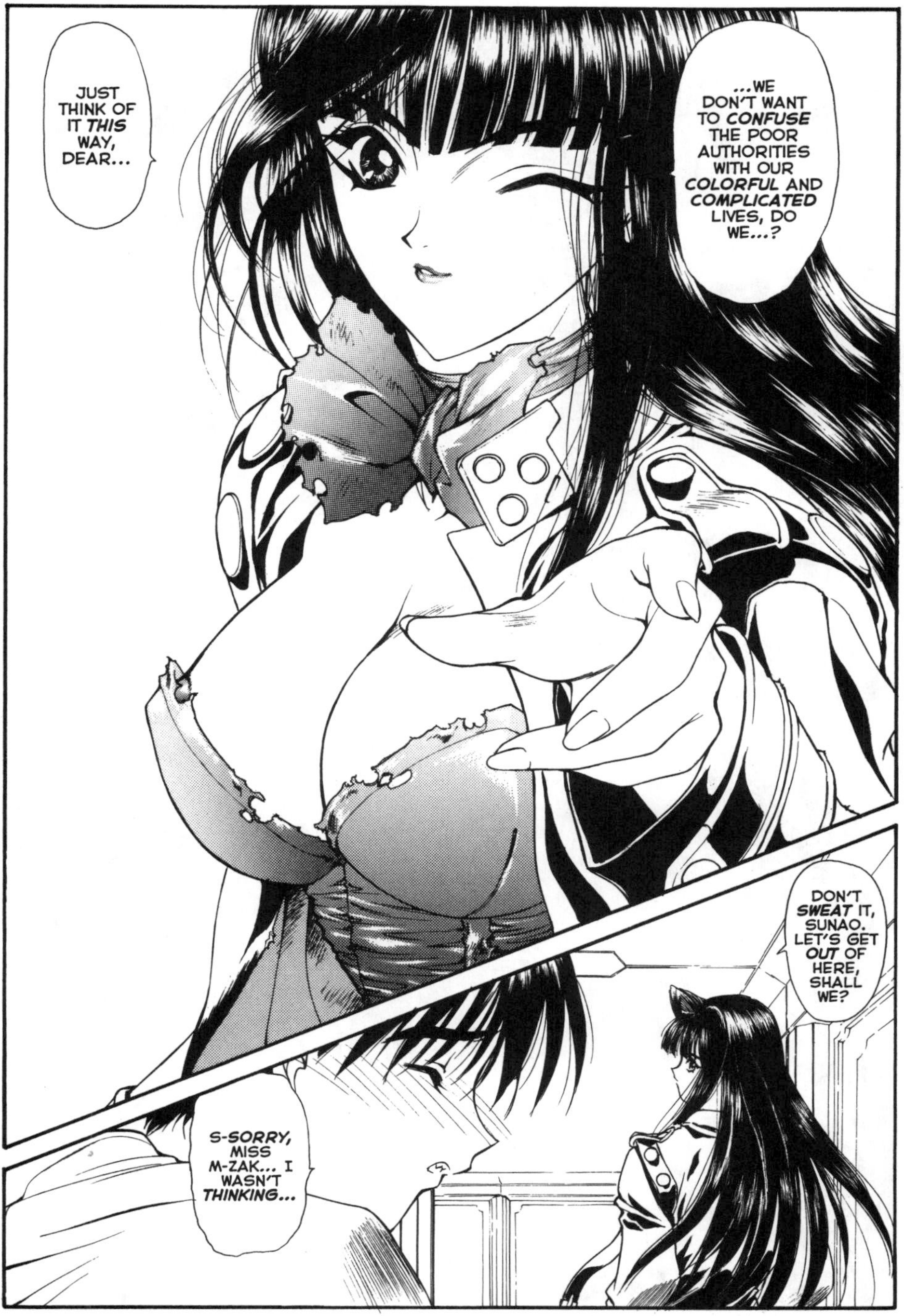
JUST THINK OF IT THIS WAY, DEAR...
...WE DON'T WANT TO CONFUSE THE POOR AUTHORITIES WITH OUR COLORFUL AND COMPLICATED LIVES, DO WE...?
S-SORRY, MISS M-ZAK... I WASN'T THINKING...
DON'T SWEAT IT, SUNAO. LET'S GET OUT OF HERE, SHALL WE?

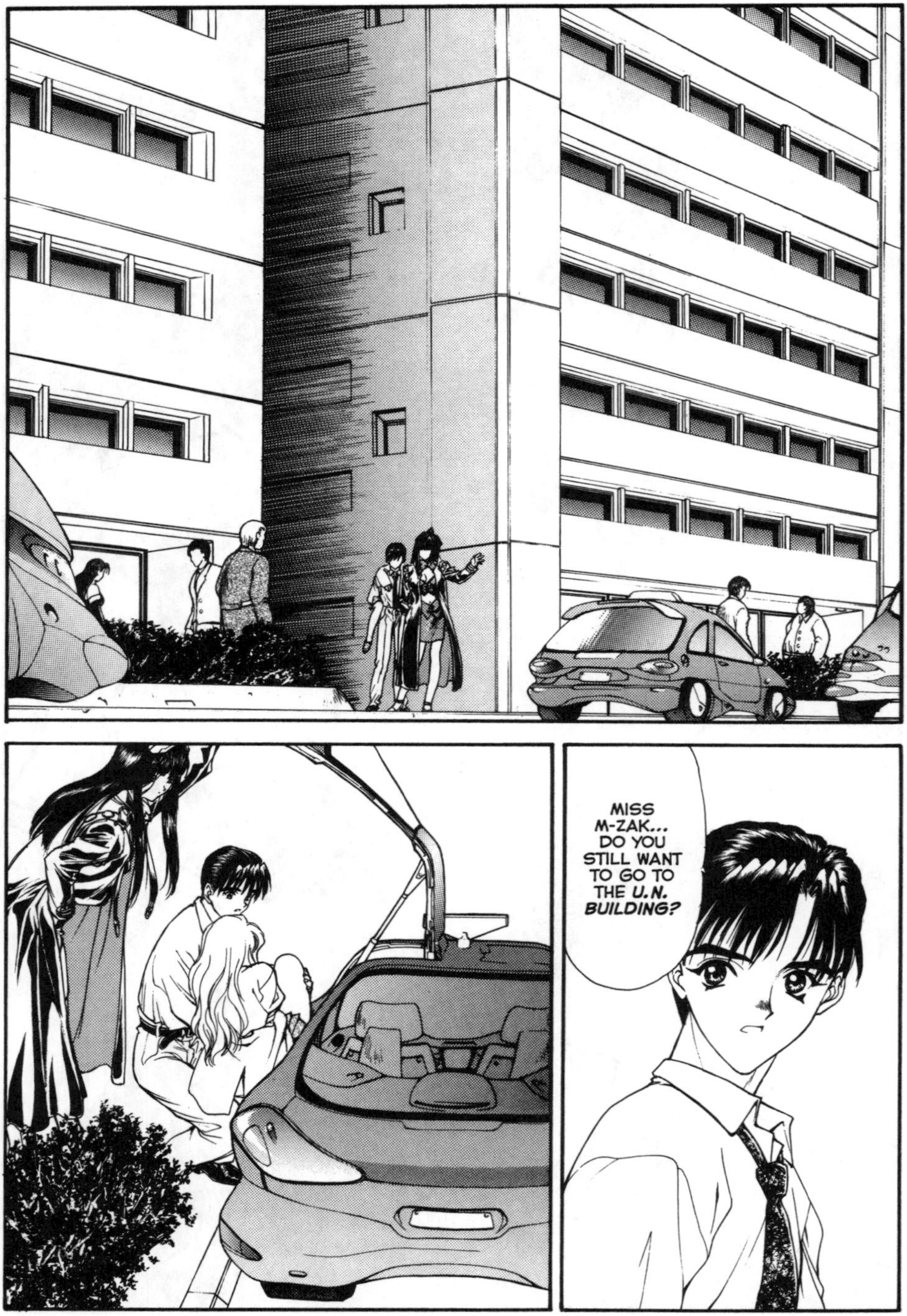
MISS M-ZAK... DO YOU STILL WANT TO GO TO THE U.N. BUILDING?

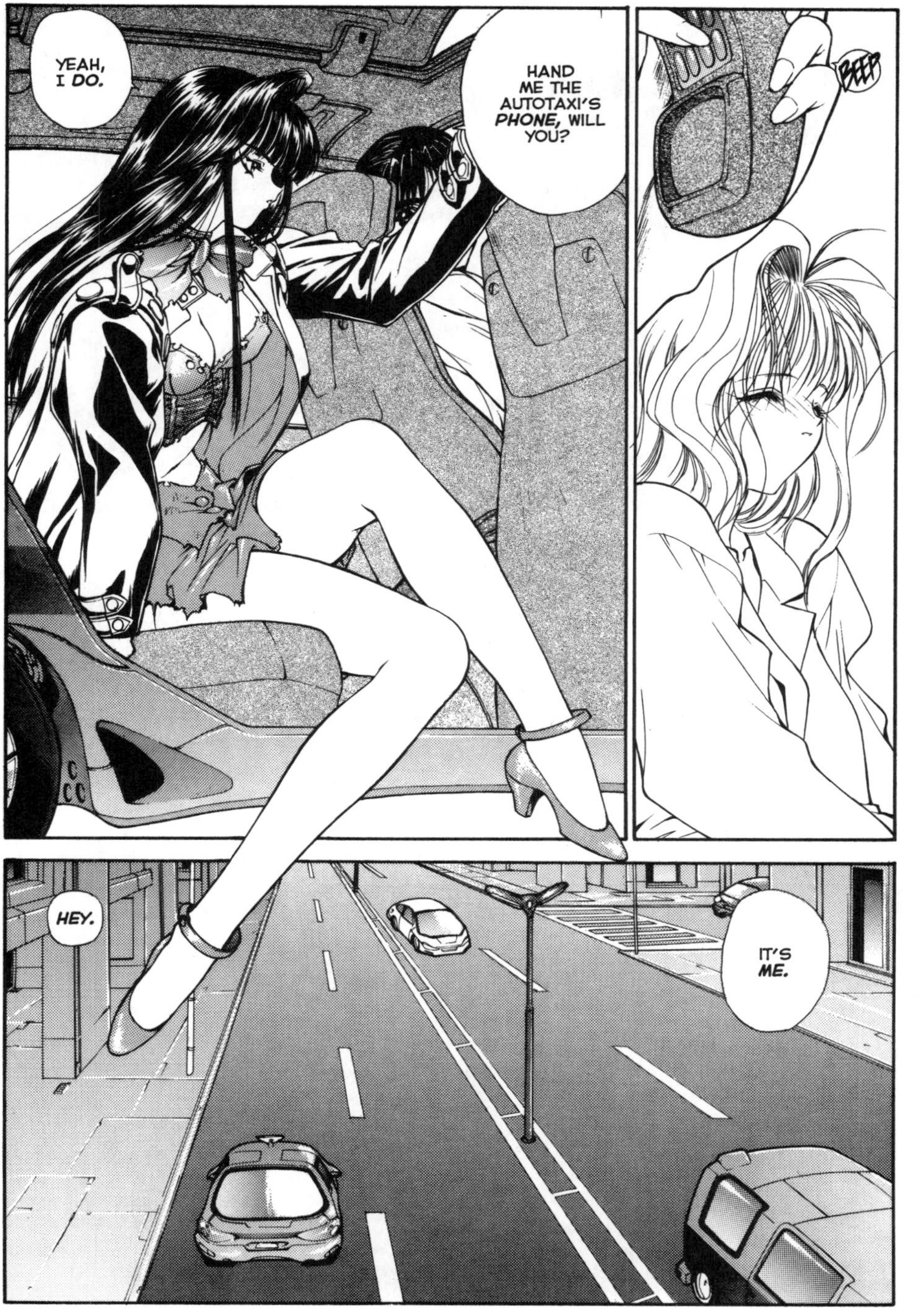
YEAH, I DO.
HAND ME THE AUTOTAXI'S PHONE, WILL YOU?
BEEP
HEY.
IT'S ME.

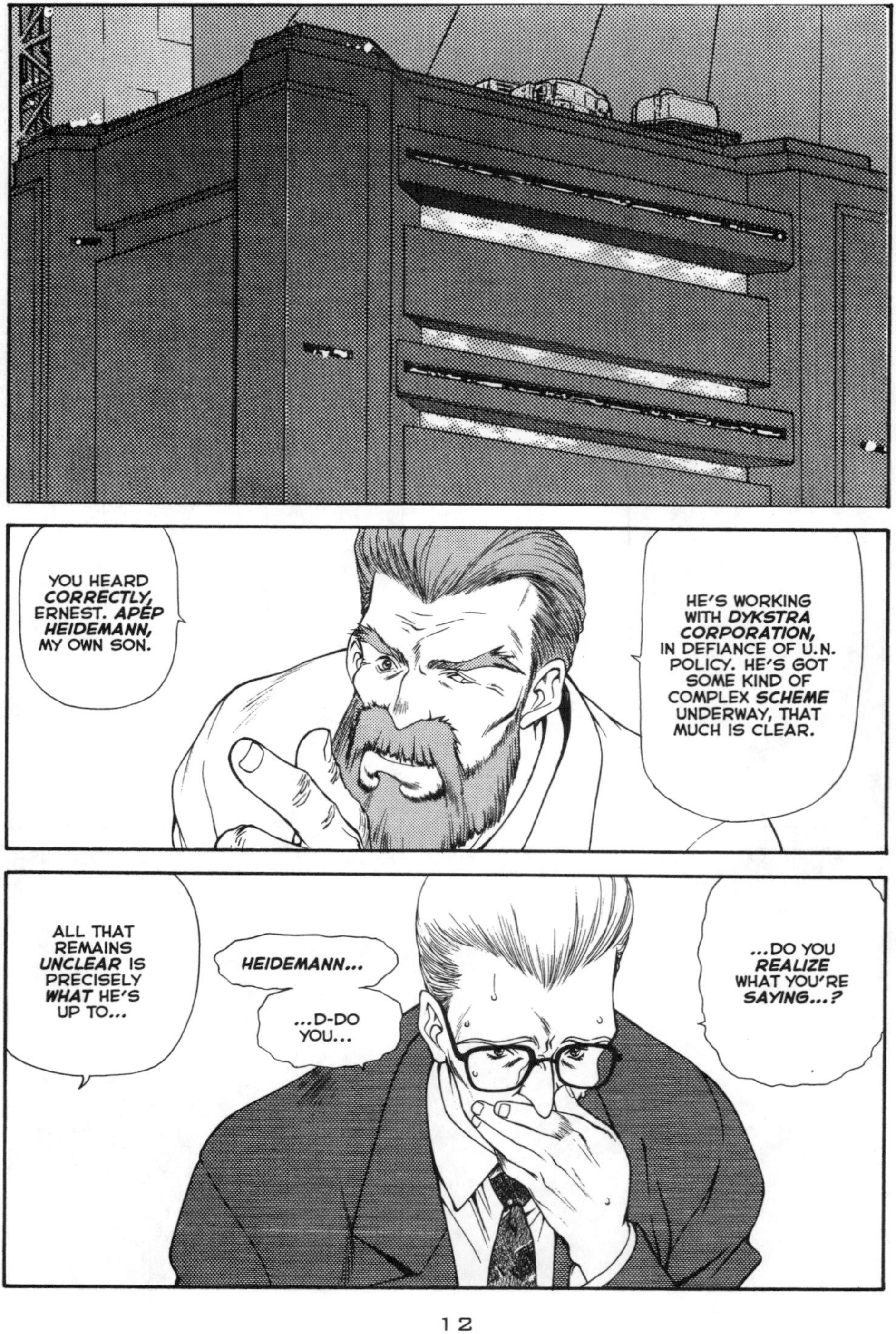

YOU HEARD CORRECTLY, ERNEST. APEP HEIDEMANN, MY OWN SON.
HE'S WORKING WITH DYKSTRA CORPORATION, IN DEFIANCE OF U.N. POLICY. HE'S GOT SOME KIND OF COMPLEX SCHEME UNDERWAY, THAT MUCH IS CLEAR.
ALL THAT REMAINS UNCLEAR IS PRECISELY WHAT HE'S UP TO...
HEIDEMANN...
...D-DO YOU...
...DO YOU REALIZE WHAT YOU'RE SAYING...?

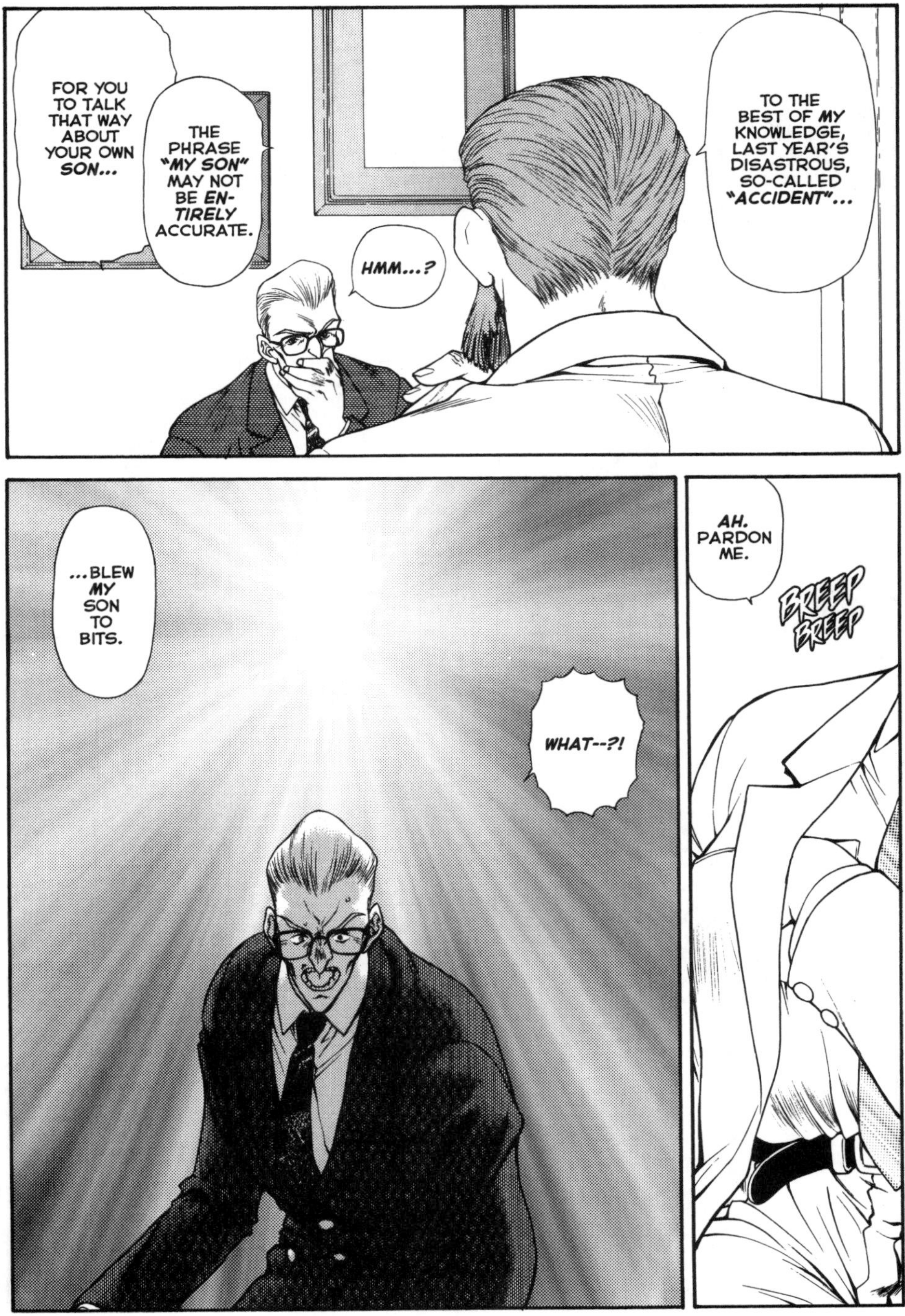
FOR YOU TO TALK THAT WAY ABOUT YOUR OWN SON...
THE PHRASE "MY SON" MAY NOT BE EN-TIRELY ACCURATE.
HMM...?
TO THE BEST OF MY KNOWLEDGE, LAST YEAR'S DISASTROUS, SO-CALLED "ACCIDENT"...
...BLEW MY SON TO BITS.
WHAT--?!
AH. PARDON ME.
BREEP BREEP

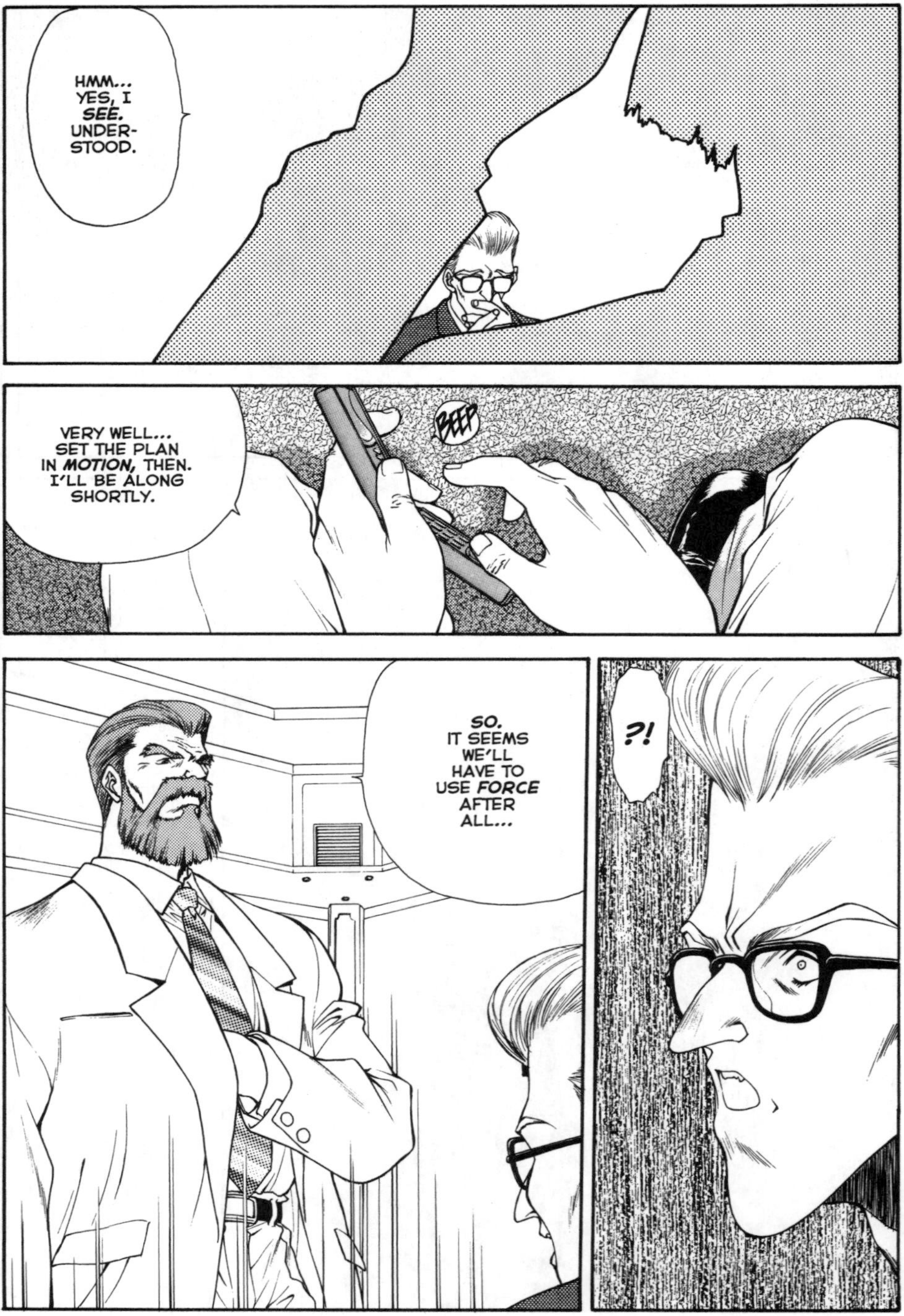
HMM... YES, I SEE. UNDER-STOOD.
VERY WELL... SET THE PLAN IN MOTION, THEN. I'LL BE ALONG SHORTLY.
BEEP
SO. IT SEEMS WE'LL HAVE TO USE FORCE AFTER ALL...
?!

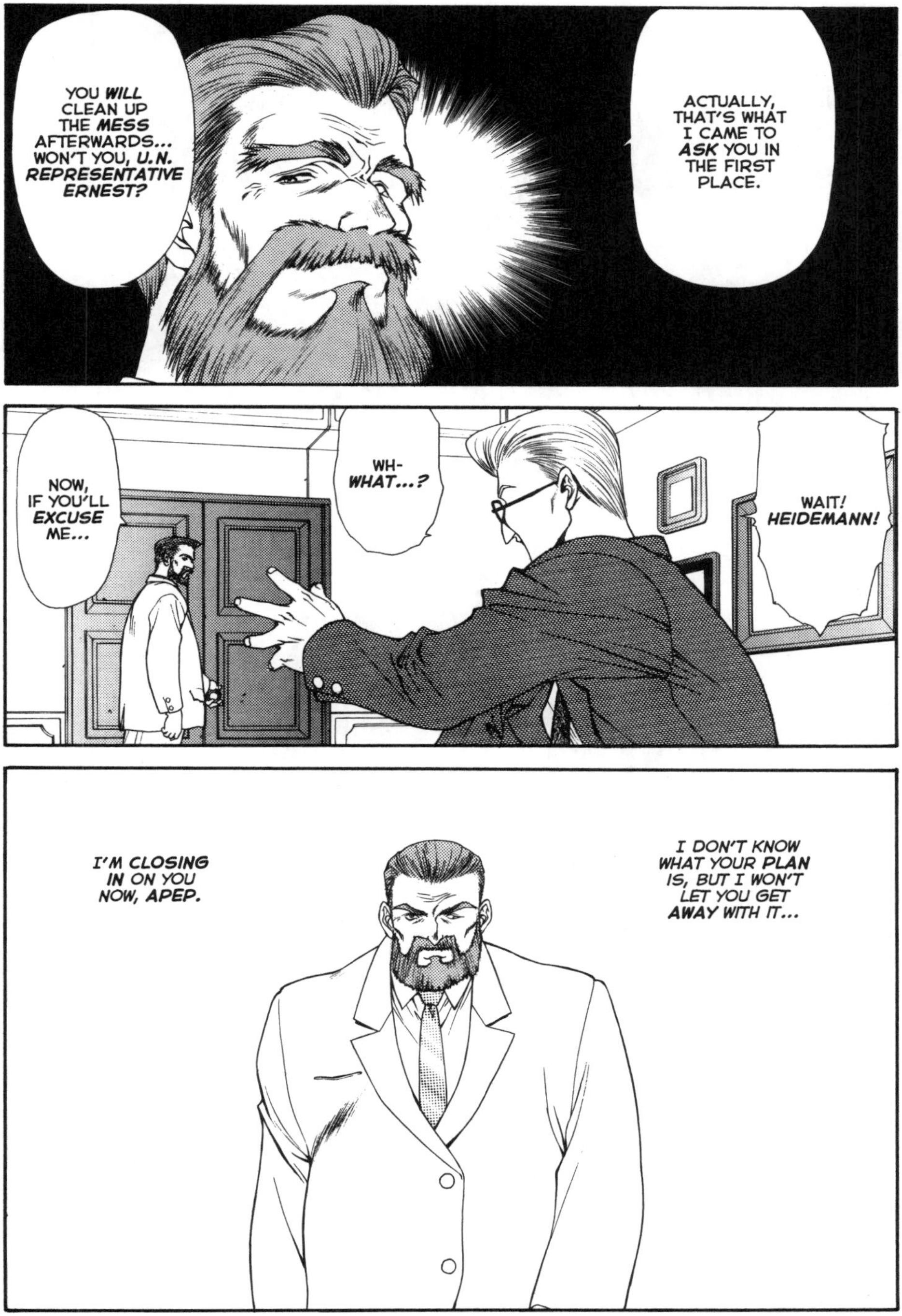
YOU WILL CLEAN UP THE MESS AFTERWARDS... WON'T YOU, U.N. REPRESENTATIVE ERNEST?
ACTUALLY, THAT'S WHAT I CAME TO ASK YOU IN THE FIRST PLACE.
NOW, IF YOU'LL EXCUSE ME...
WH- WHAT...?
WAIT! HEIDEMANN!
I'M CLOSING IN ON YOU NOW, APEP.
I DON'T KNOW WHAT YOUR PLAN IS, BUT I WON'T LET YOU GET AWAY WITH IT...

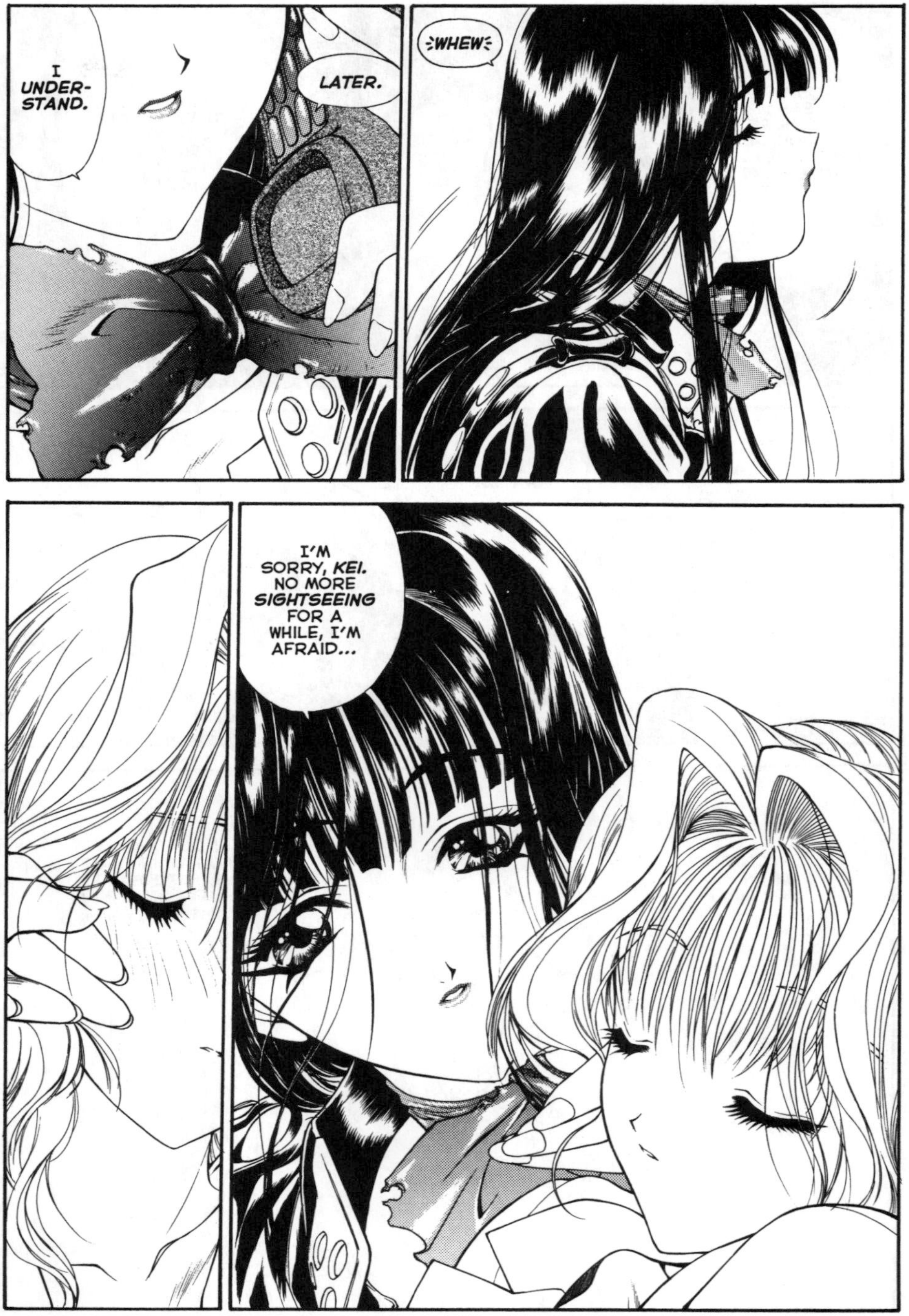
I UNDERSTAND.
LATER.
WHEW
I'M SORRY, KEI. NO MORE SIGHTSEEING FOR A WHILE, I'M AFRAID...

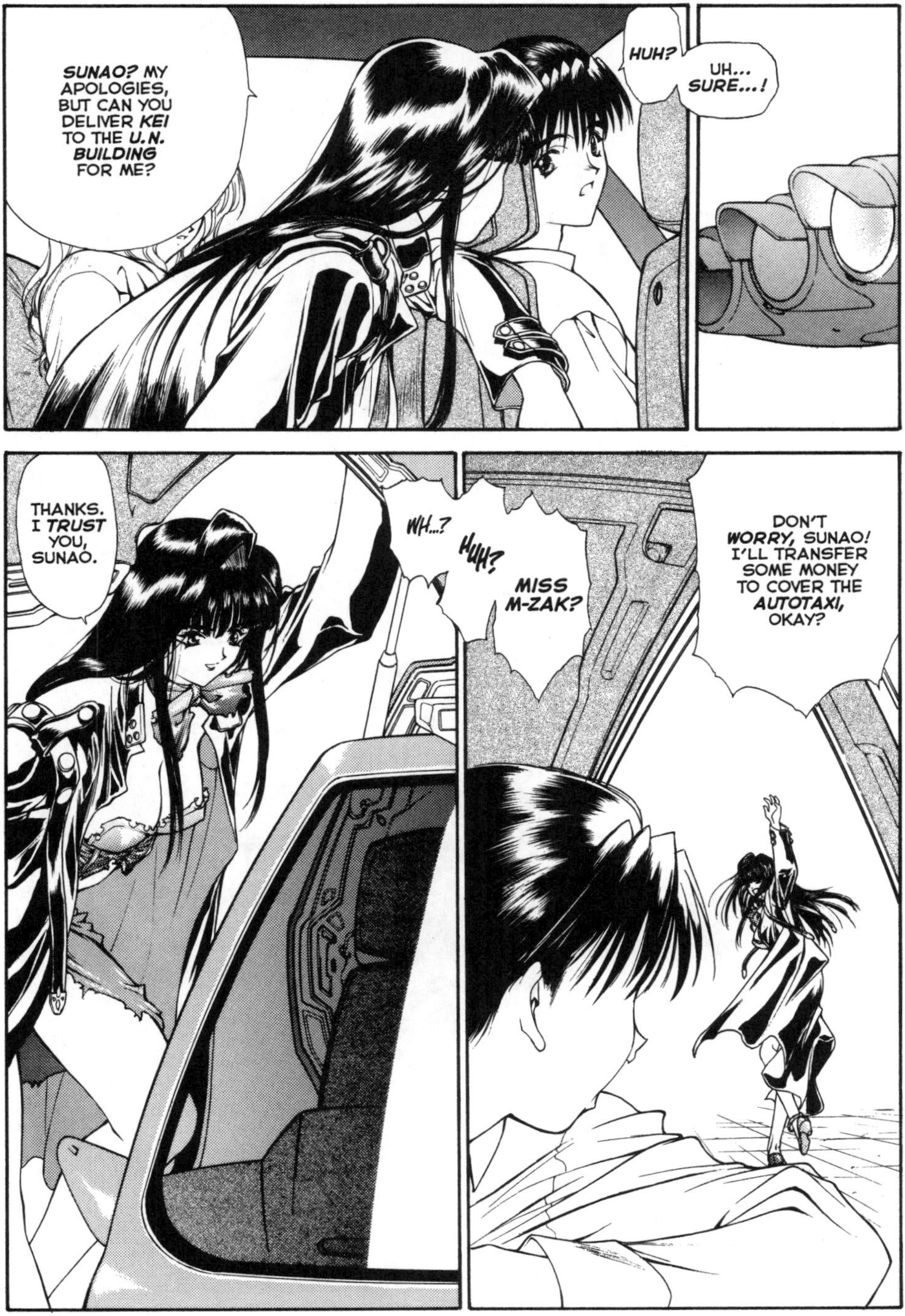
SUNAO? MY APOLOGIES, BUT CAN YOU DELIVER KEI TO THE U.N. BUILDING FOR ME?
HUH?
UH... SURE...!
THANKS. I TRUST YOU, SUNAO.
WH...?
HUH?
MISS M-ZAK?
DON'T WORRY, SUNAO! I'LL TRANSFER SOME MONEY TO COVER THE AUTOTAXI, OKAY?

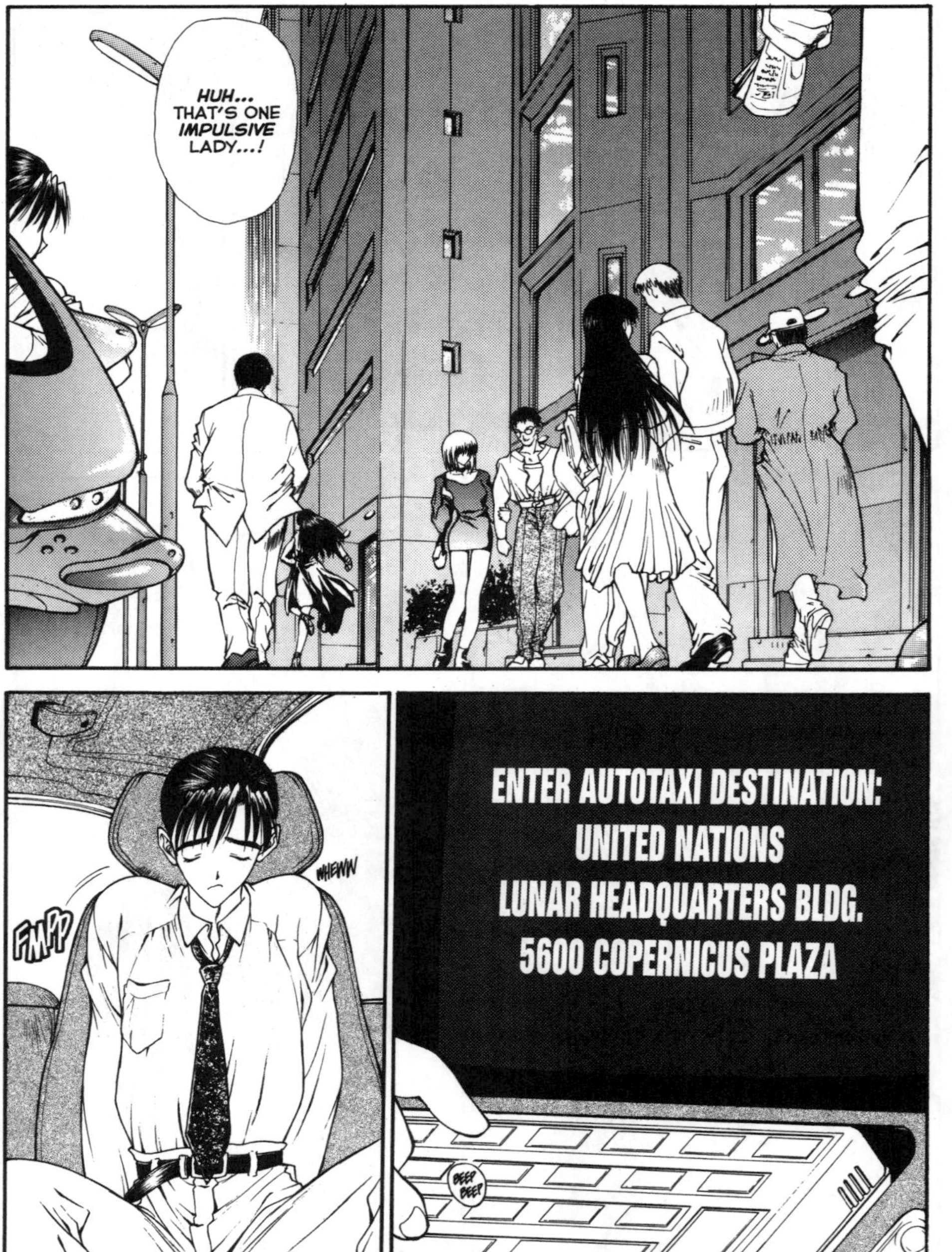
HUH... THAT'S ONE IMPULSIVE LADY...!
FMPP
WHEWW
ENTER AUTOTAXI DESTINATION:
UNITED NATIONS
LUNAR HEADQUARTERS BLDG.
5600 COPERNICUS PLAZA
BEEP BEEP

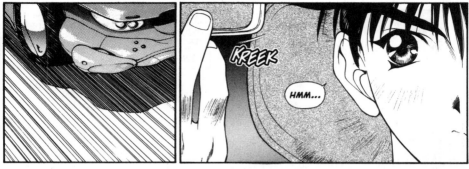

KREEK

HMM...

THANK GOD SHE'S *ALL RIGHT*...!

HAHH...

BUT *STILL*...

19

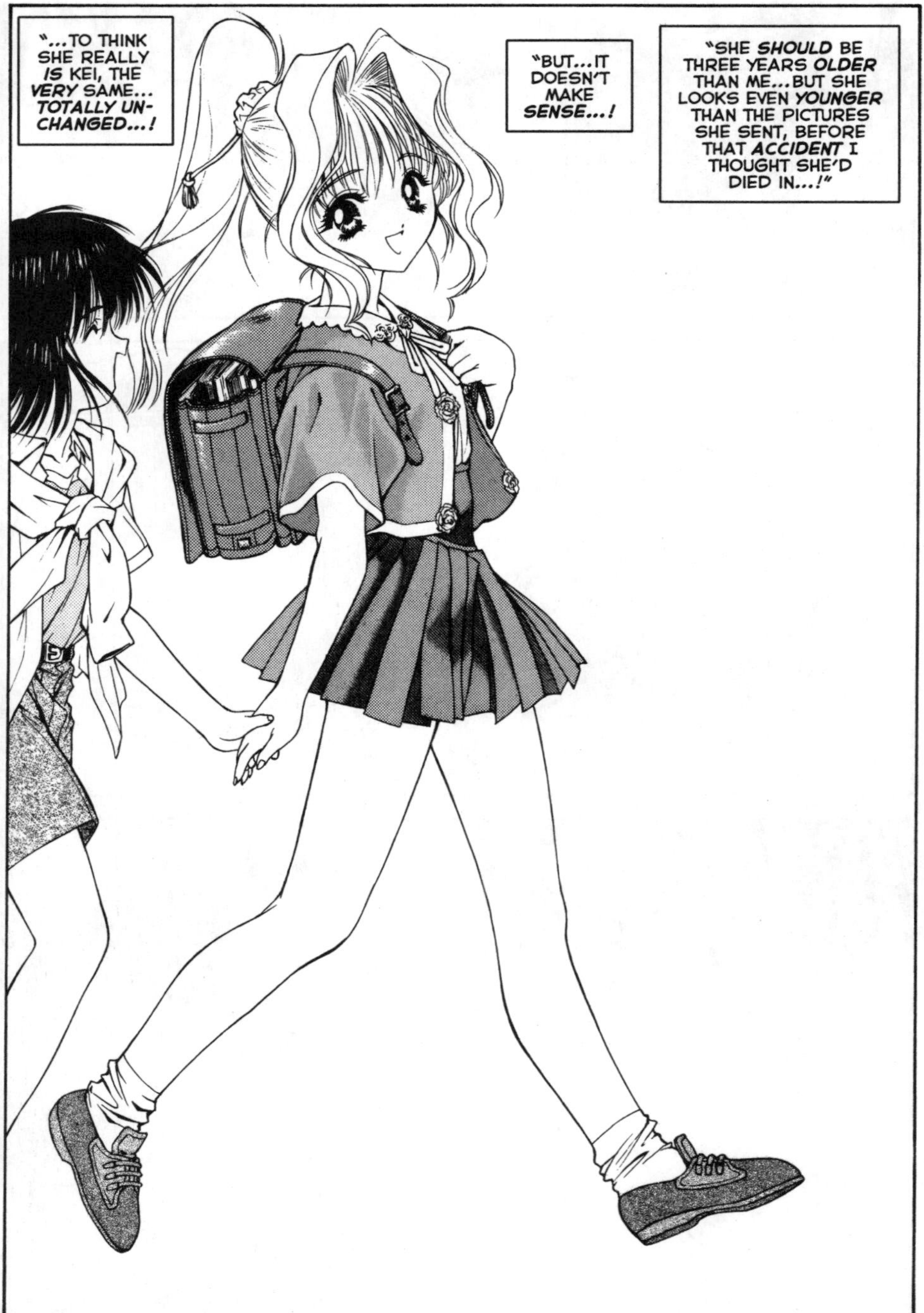
"...TO THINK SHE REALLY IS KEI, THE VERY SAME... TOTALLY UN-CHANGED...!
"BUT...IT DOESN'T MAKE SENSE...!
"SHE SHOULD BE THREE YEARS OLDER THAN ME...BUT SHE LOOKS EVEN YOUNGER THAN THE PICTURES SHE SENT, BEFORE THAT ACCIDENT I THOUGHT SHE'D DIED IN...!"

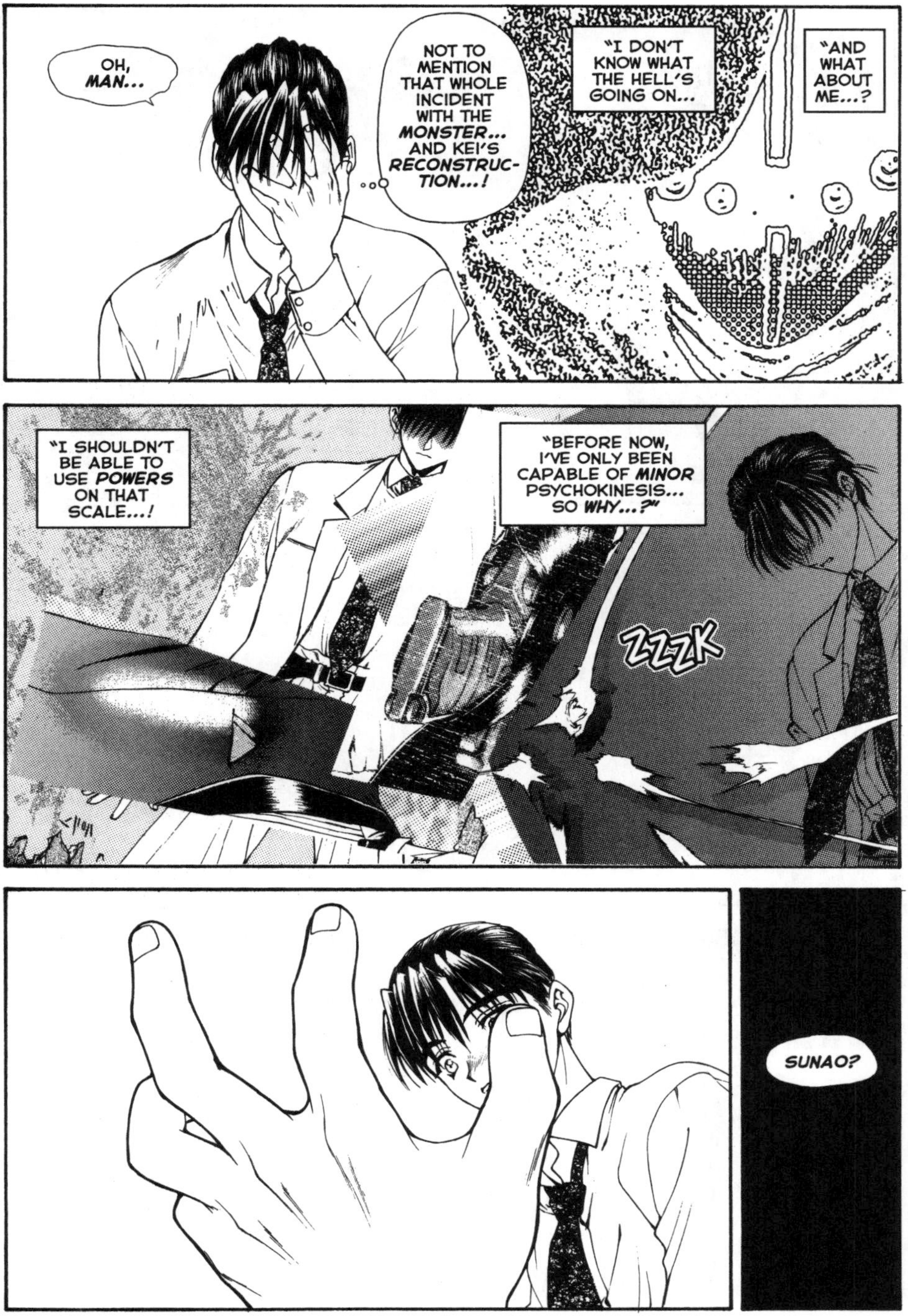
OH, MAN...
NOT TO MENTION THAT WHOLE INCIDENT WITH THE MONSTER... AND KEI'S RECONSTRUCTION...!
"I DON'T KNOW WHAT THE HELL'S GOING ON...
"AND WHAT ABOUT ME...?
"I SHOULDN'T BE ABLE TO USE POWERS ON THAT SCALE...!
"BEFORE NOW, I'VE ONLY BEEN CAPABLE OF MINOR PSYCHOKINESIS... SO WHY...?"
ZZZK
SUNAO?

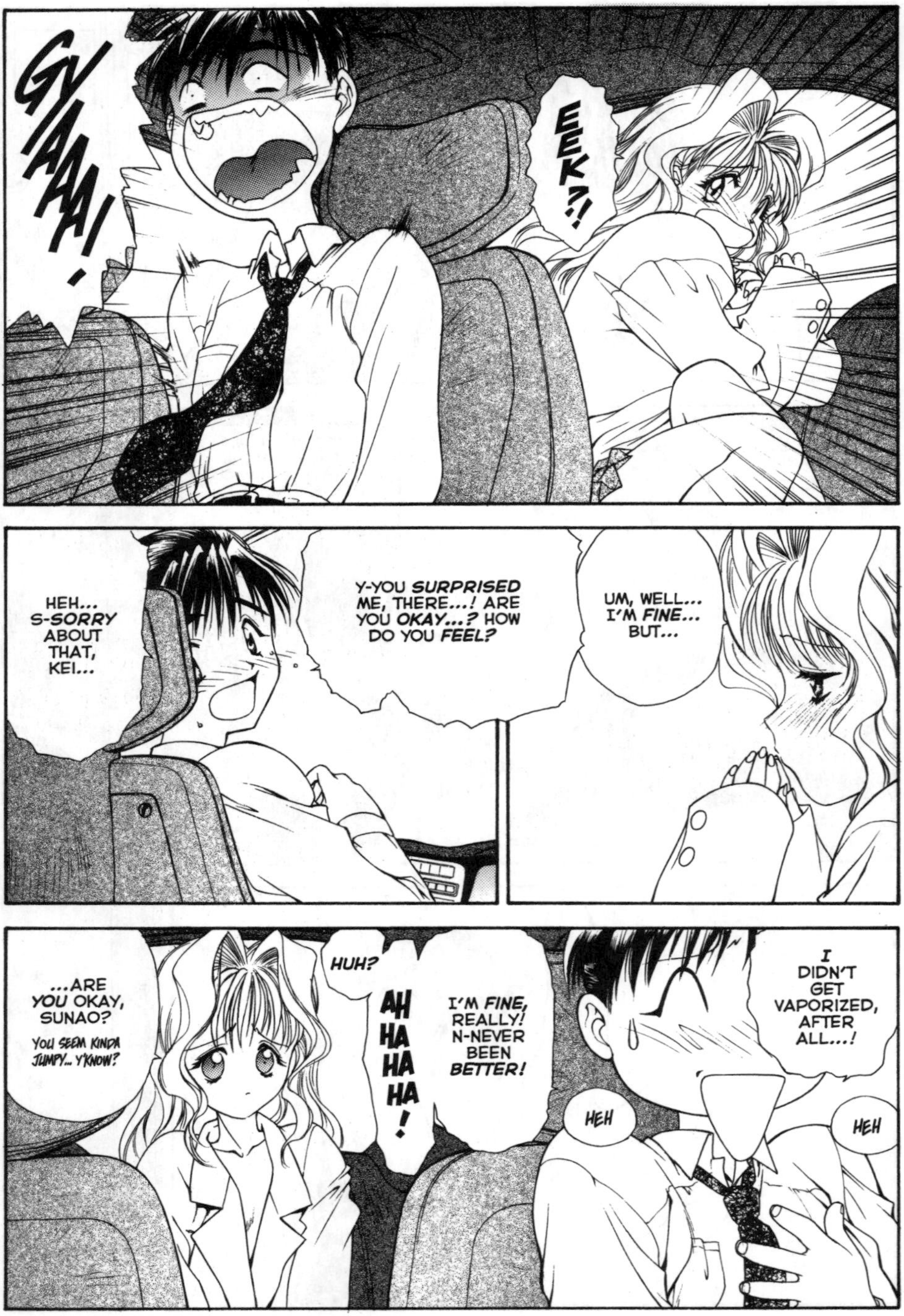
GYAAAA!!
EEK?!!
HEH... S-SORRY ABOUT THAT, KEI...
Y-YOU SURPRISED ME, THERE...! ARE YOU OKAY...? HOW DO YOU FEEL?
UM, WELL... I'M FINE... BUT...
...ARE YOU OKAY, SUNAO?
YOU SEEM KINDA JUMPY... Y'KNOW?
HUH?
AH HA HA HA!
I'M FINE, REALLY! N-NEVER BEEN BETTER!
I DIDN'T GET VAPORIZED, AFTER ALL...!
HEH
HEH

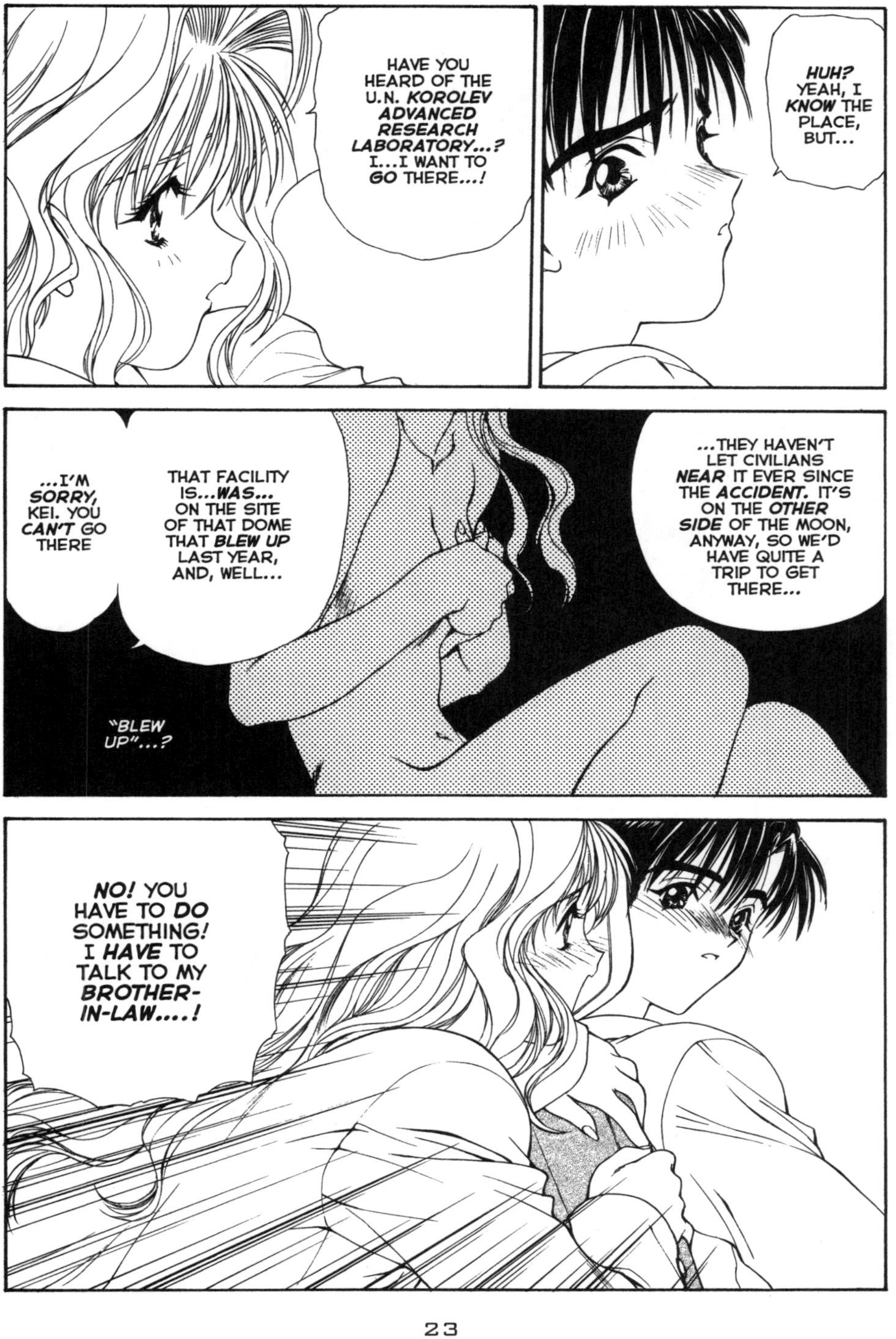
HAVE YOU HEARD OF THE U.N. KOROLEV ADVANCED RESEARCH LABORATORY...? I...I WANT TO GO THERE...!
HUH? YEAH, I KNOW THE PLACE, BUT...
...I'M SORRY, KEI. YOU CAN'T GO THERE
THAT FACILITY IS...WAS... ON THE SITE OF THAT DOME THAT BLEW UP LAST YEAR, AND, WELL...
...THEY HAVEN'T LET CIVILIANS NEAR IT EVER SINCE THE ACCIDENT. IT'S ON THE OTHER SIDE OF THE MOON, ANYWAY, SO WE'D HAVE QUITE A TRIP TO GET THERE...
"BLEW UP"...?
NO! YOU HAVE TO DO SOMETHING! I HAVE TO TALK TO MY BROTHER-IN-LAW....!

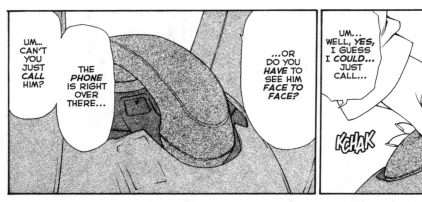

UM... CAN'T YOU JUST **CALL** HIM?

THE **PHONE** IS RIGHT OVER THERE...

...OR DO YOU **HAVE** TO SEE HIM **FACE** TO **FACE**?

UM... WELL, **YES**, I GUESS I **COULD**... JUST CALL...

KCHAK

BROTHER-IN-LAW...? I DIDN'T KNOW SHE HAD **ANY** SIBLINGS, LET ALONE **MARRIED** ONES...!

OH, WELL... JUST THE **LATEST** OF KEI'S **MYSTERIES**, I GUESS...!

...
...

?

NO ONE'S ANSWERING?

N-NO.

THIS LINE IS TEMPORARILY OUT OF SERVICE. WE WILL RESTORE SERVICE AS SOON AS--

24

UM, *SUNAO...?* ISN'T THERE *ANYTHING* YOU CAN DO?!

WELL... UM...

SAY, WEREN'T YOU SUPPOSED TO *MEET* SOMEONE AT *U.N. HEAD-QUARTERS* ...?

OH!

KOVAK

THAT'S *RIGHT!* MY *FATHER-IN-LAW!*

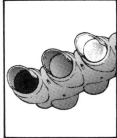

NO LUCK.

THEY SAY HE *TOOK OFF* ON SOME SORT OF BUSINESS. THEY DON'T KNOW *WHEN* HE'LL BE BACK...

÷SIGH÷

SUNAO! DO SOME-THING! YOU'RE A *GUIDE,* RIGHT?

ACK!

WHDD

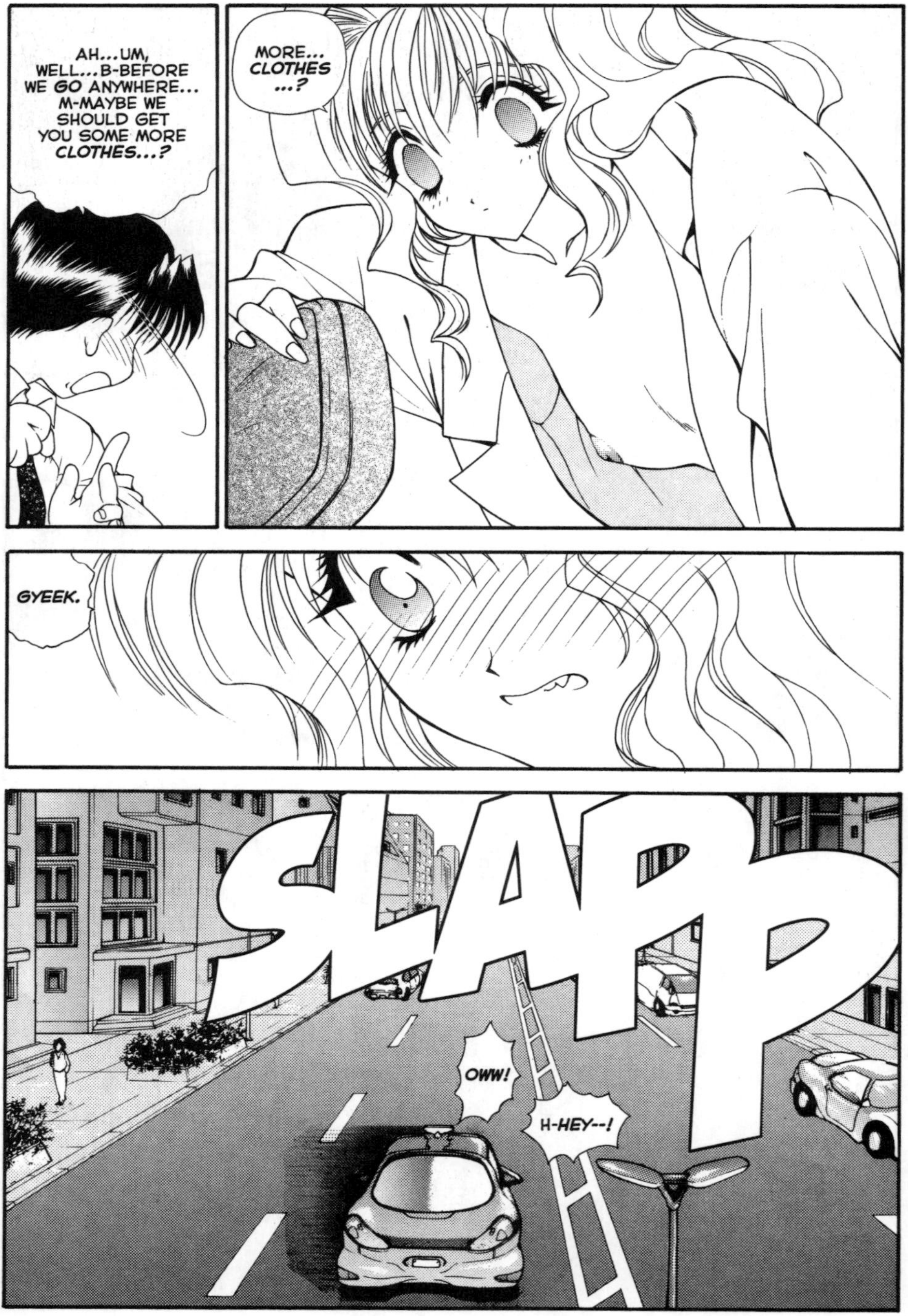
AH...UM, WELL...B-BEFORE WE GO ANYWHERE... M-MAYBE WE SHOULD GET YOU SOME MORE CLOTHES...?
MORE... CLOTHES ...?
GYEEK.
SLAPP
OWW!
H-HEY--!

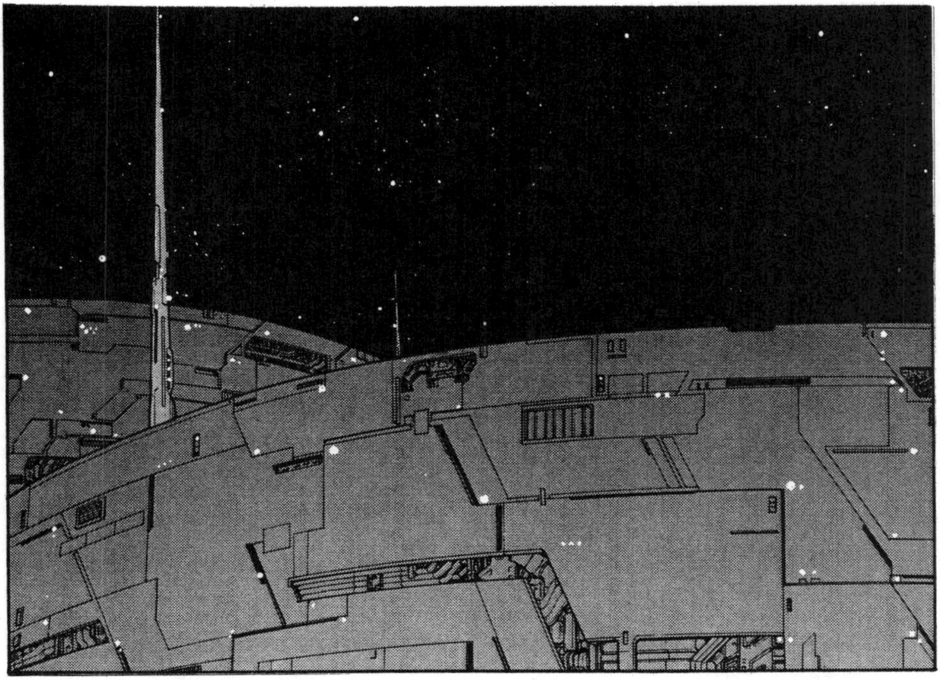

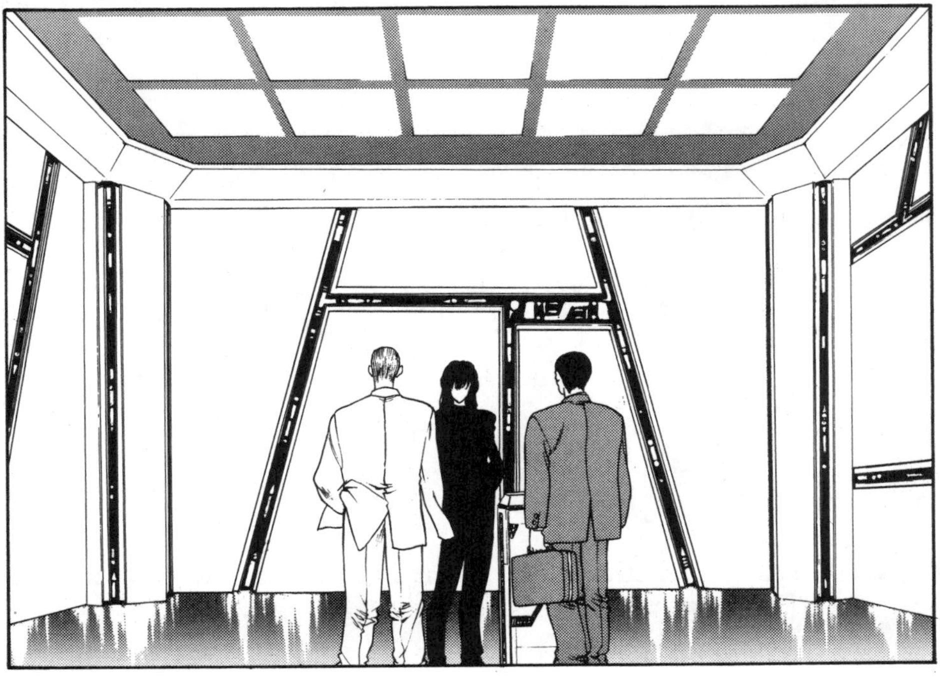

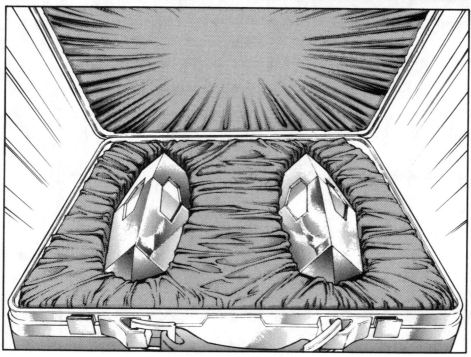

ACT 19

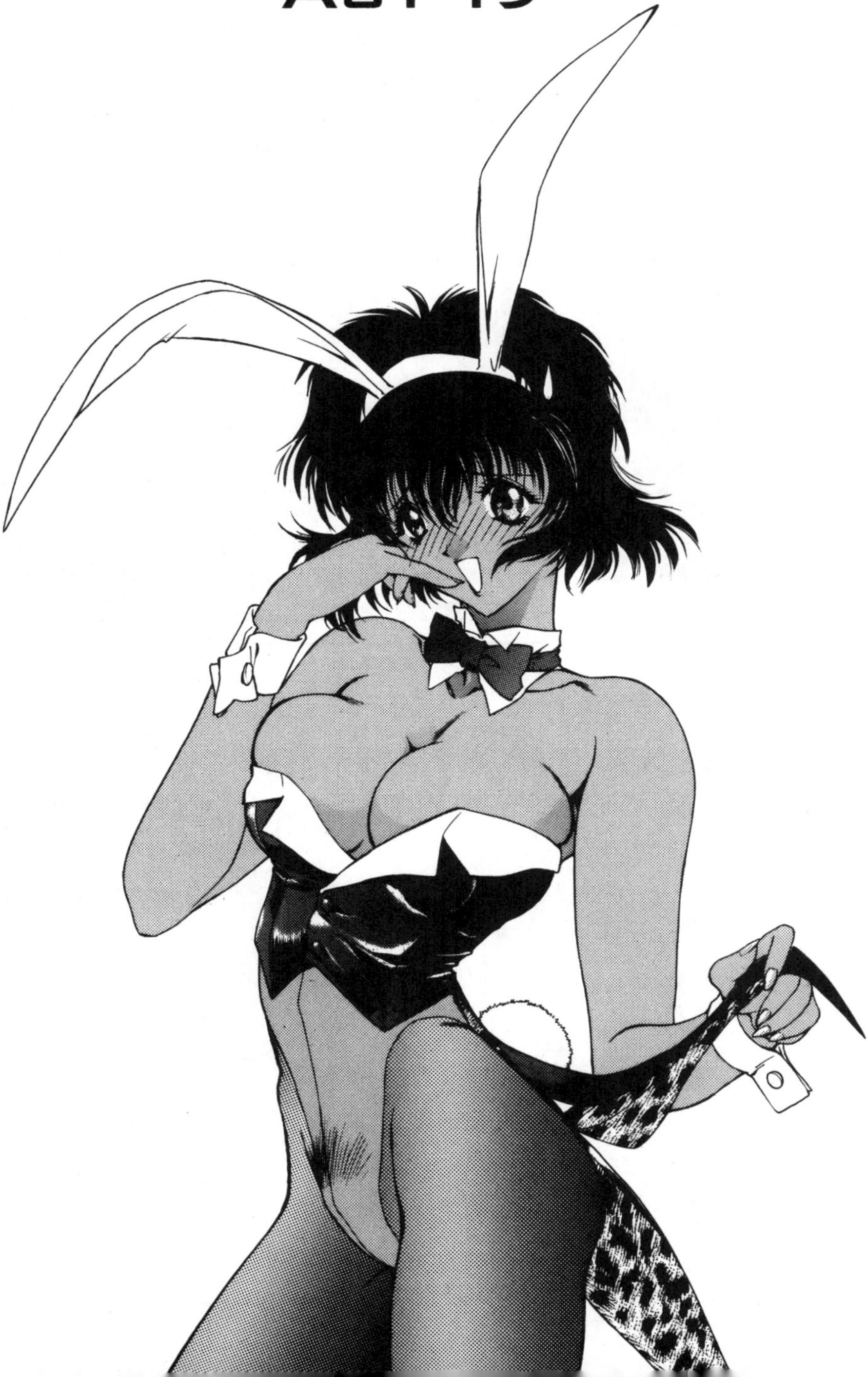

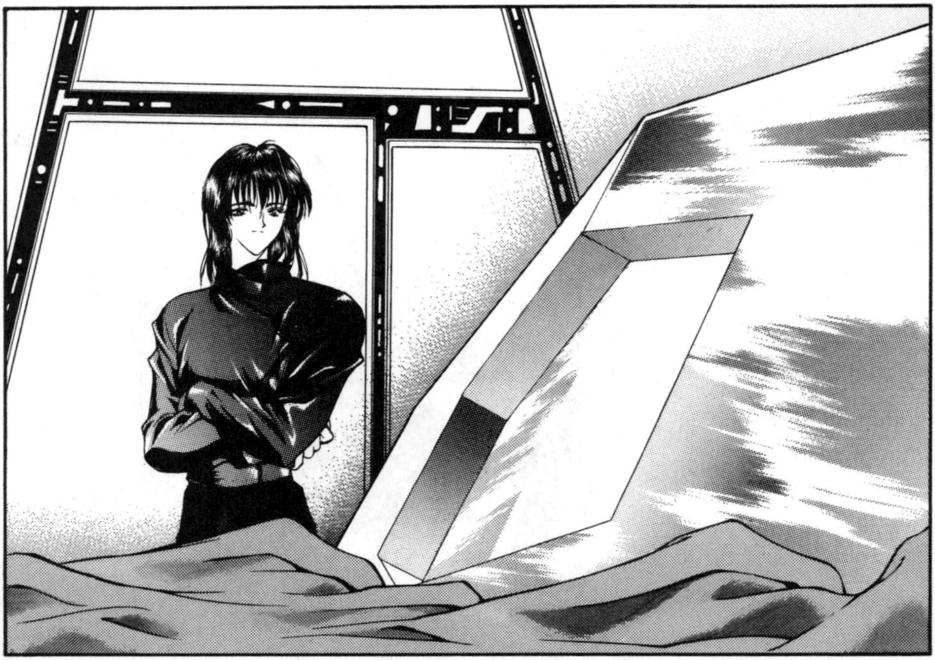

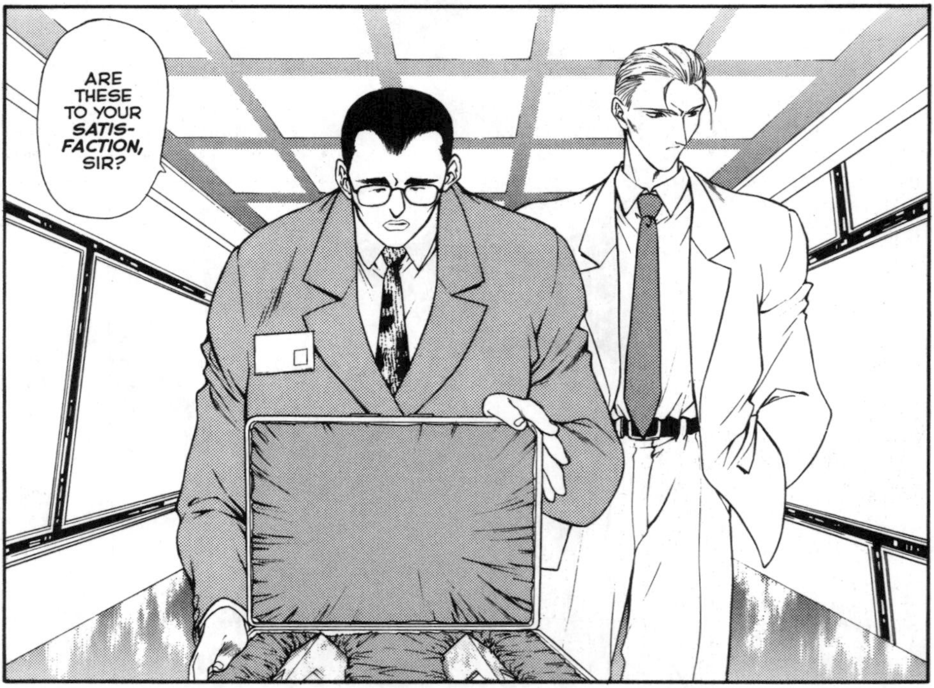
ARE THESE TO YOUR SATIS- FACTION, SIR?

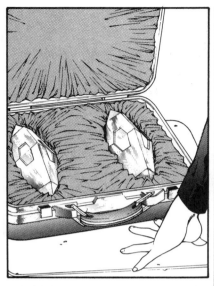

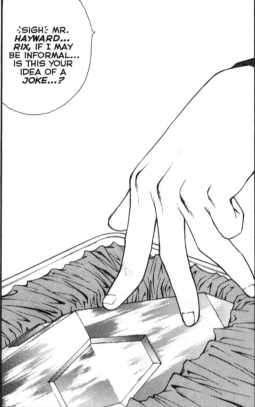

≍SIGH≍ MR. *HAYWARD*... *RIX*, IF I MAY BE INFORMAL... IS THIS YOUR IDEA OF A *JOKE*...?

HAHH...

WH-WHAT THE HELL ARE YOU *TALKING* ABOUT--?!

I LOST *TWO* OF MY MEN... AND MY GOD-DAMNED *ARM*... AND YOU THINK IT'S A *JOKE?*

YOU GOD-DAMNED LITTLE *PUNK--!*

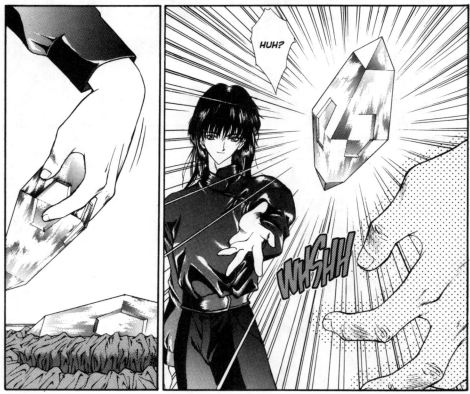

HUH?

WHSHH

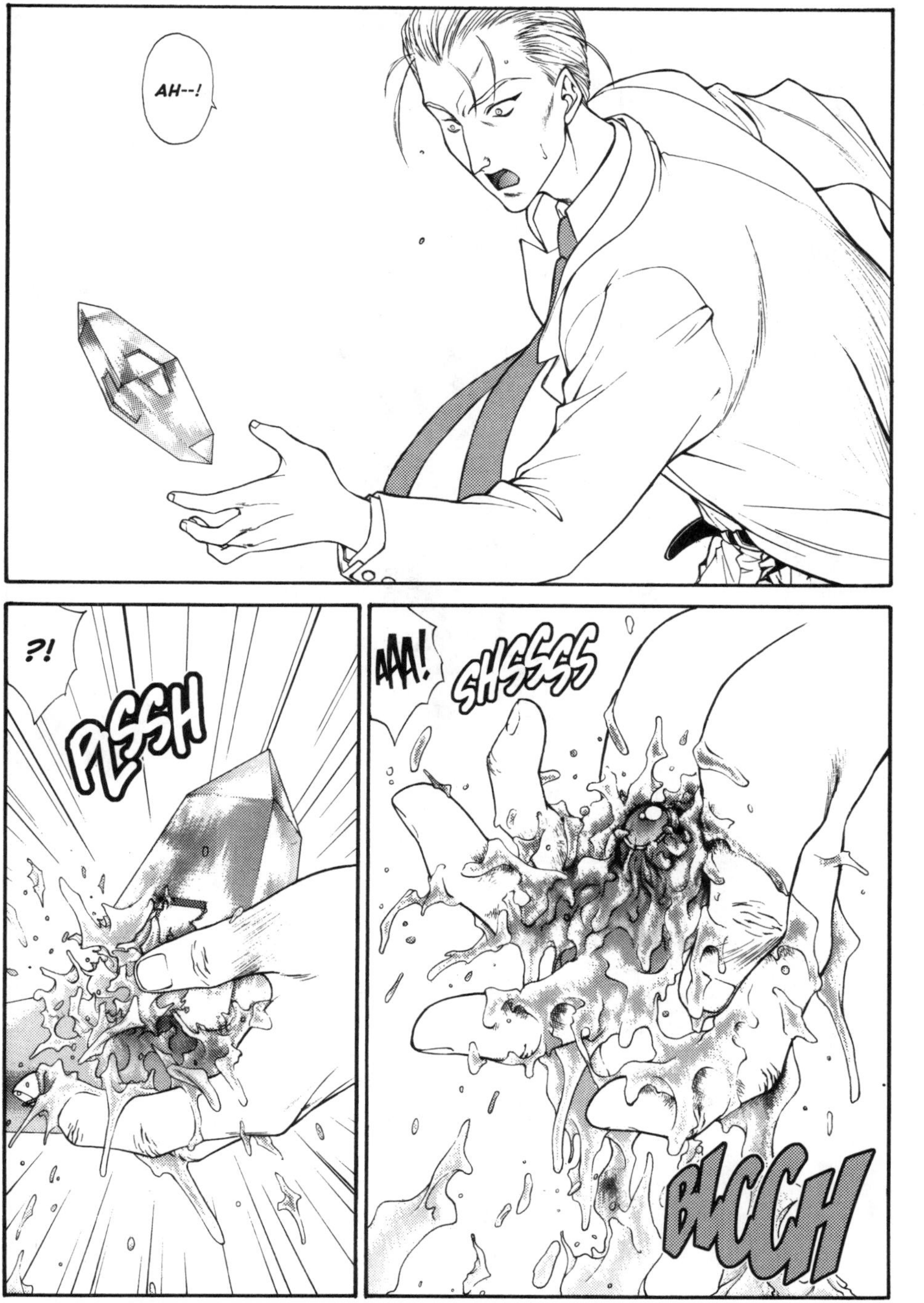
AH--!
?!
PLSSH
AAA!
SHSSSS
BLCCH

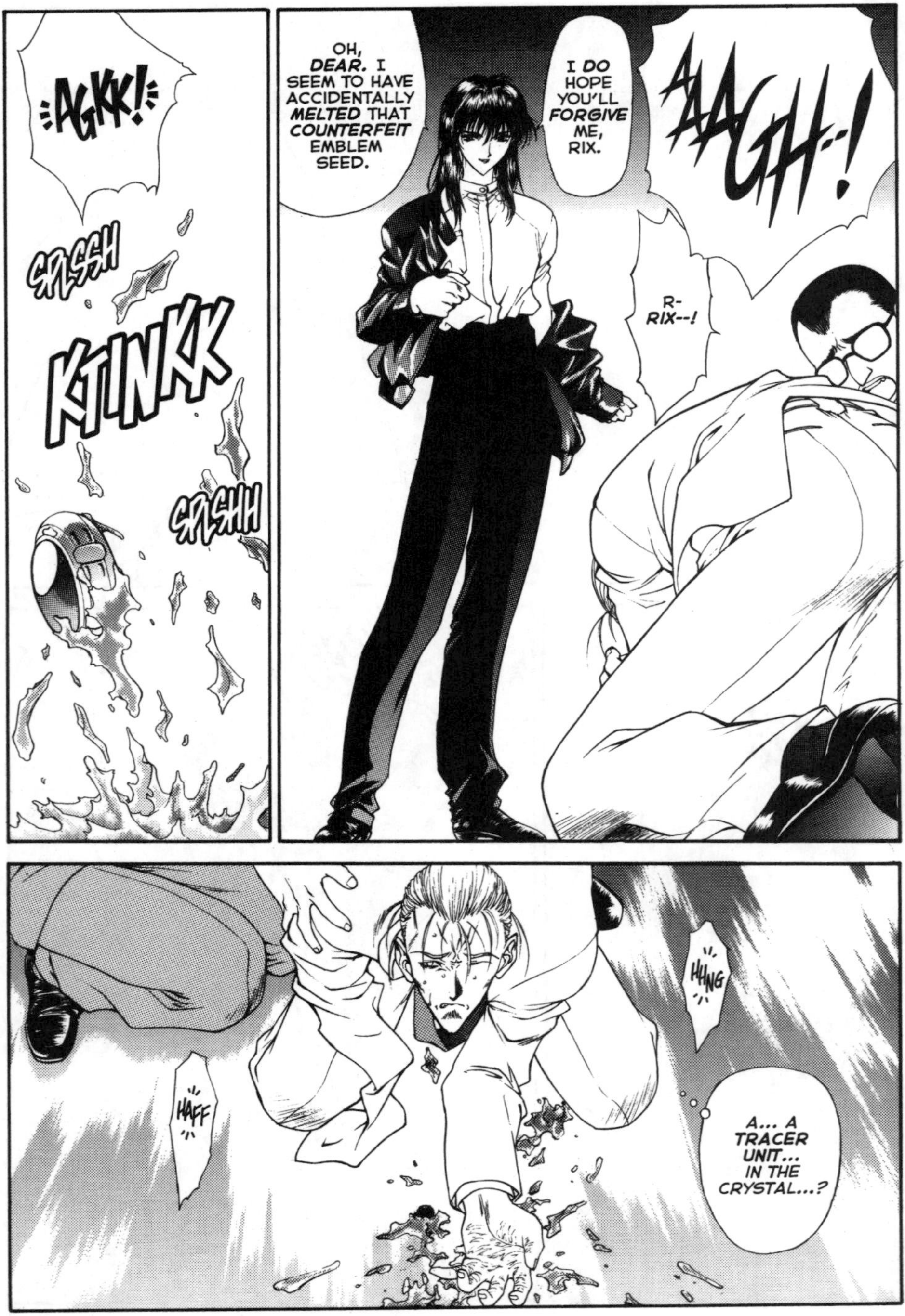
AGKK!
SPLSSH
KTINKK
SPLSHH
OH, DEAR. I SEEM TO HAVE ACCIDENTALLY MELTED THAT COUNTERFEIT EMBLEM SEED.
I DO HOPE YOU'LL FORGIVE ME, RIX.
AAAGH--!
R-RIX--!
HHNG
HAFF
A... A TRACER UNIT... IN THE CRYSTAL...?

NOT A VERY IMPRESSIVE *TRADE*, RIX.

YOU LOST YOUR *MEN*, AND YOUR *ARM*, IN EXCHANGE FOR A PAIR OF *TRACER-EQUIPPED FAKES*.

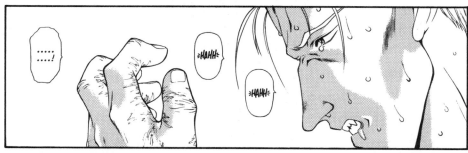

.....!

HAHH

HAHH

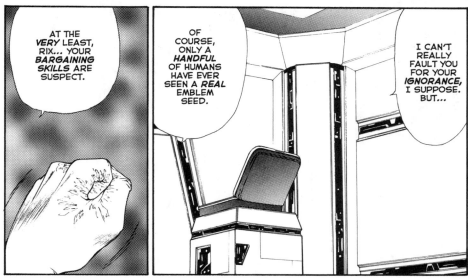

AT THE *VERY* LEAST, RIX... YOUR *BARGAINING SKILLS* ARE SUSPECT.

OF COURSE, ONLY A *HANDFUL* OF HUMANS HAVE EVER SEEN A *REAL* EMBLEM SEED.

I CAN'T REALLY FAULT YOU FOR YOUR *IGNORANCE*, I SUPPOSE. BUT...

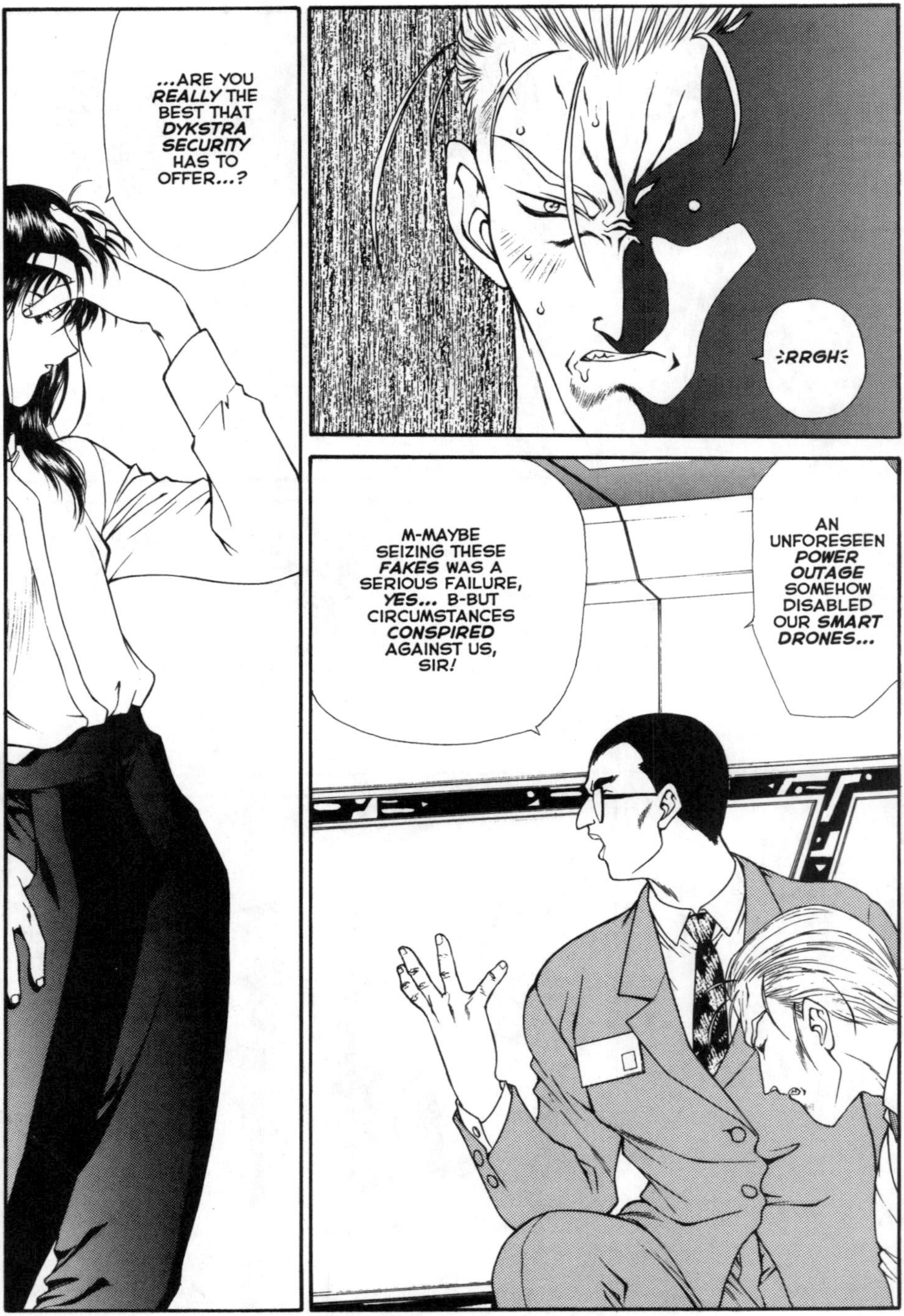
...ARE YOU *REALLY* THE BEST THAT *DYKSTRA SECURITY* HAS TO OFFER...?
RRGH
M-MAYBE SEIZING THESE *FAKES* WAS A SERIOUS FAILURE, *YES...* B-BUT CIRCUMSTANCES *CONSPIRED* AGAINST US, SIR!
AN UNFORESEEN *POWER OUTAGE* SOMEHOW DISABLED OUR *SMART DRONES...*

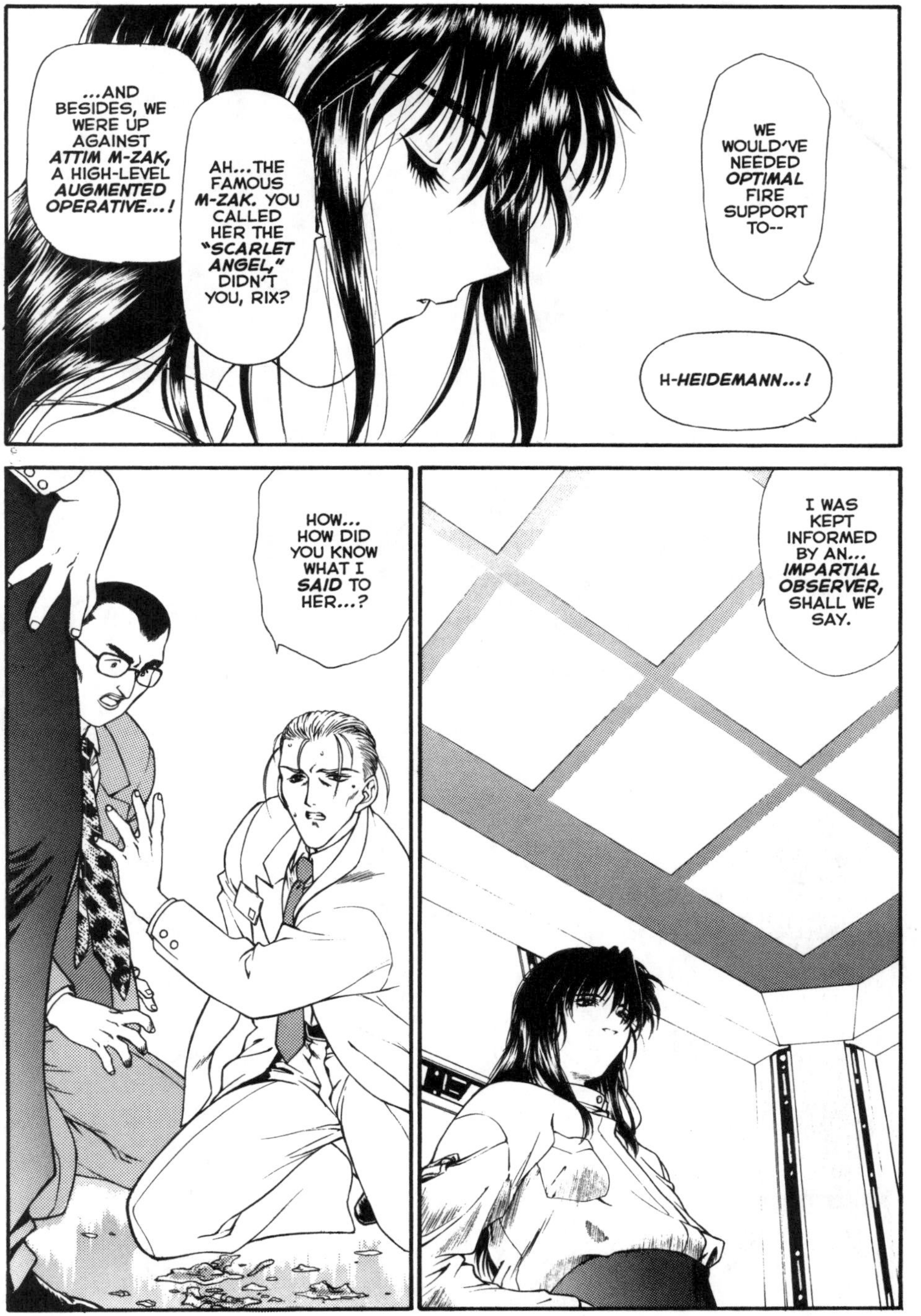
...AND BESIDES, WE WERE UP AGAINST ATTIM M-ZAK, A HIGH-LEVEL AUGMENTED OPERATIVE...!
AH...THE FAMOUS M-ZAK. YOU CALLED HER THE "SCARLET ANGEL," DIDN'T YOU, RIX?
WE WOULD'VE NEEDED OPTIMAL FIRE SUPPORT TO--
H-HEIDEMANN...!
HOW... HOW DID YOU KNOW WHAT I SAID TO HER...?
I WAS KEPT INFORMED BY AN... IMPARTIAL OBSERVER, SHALL WE SAY.

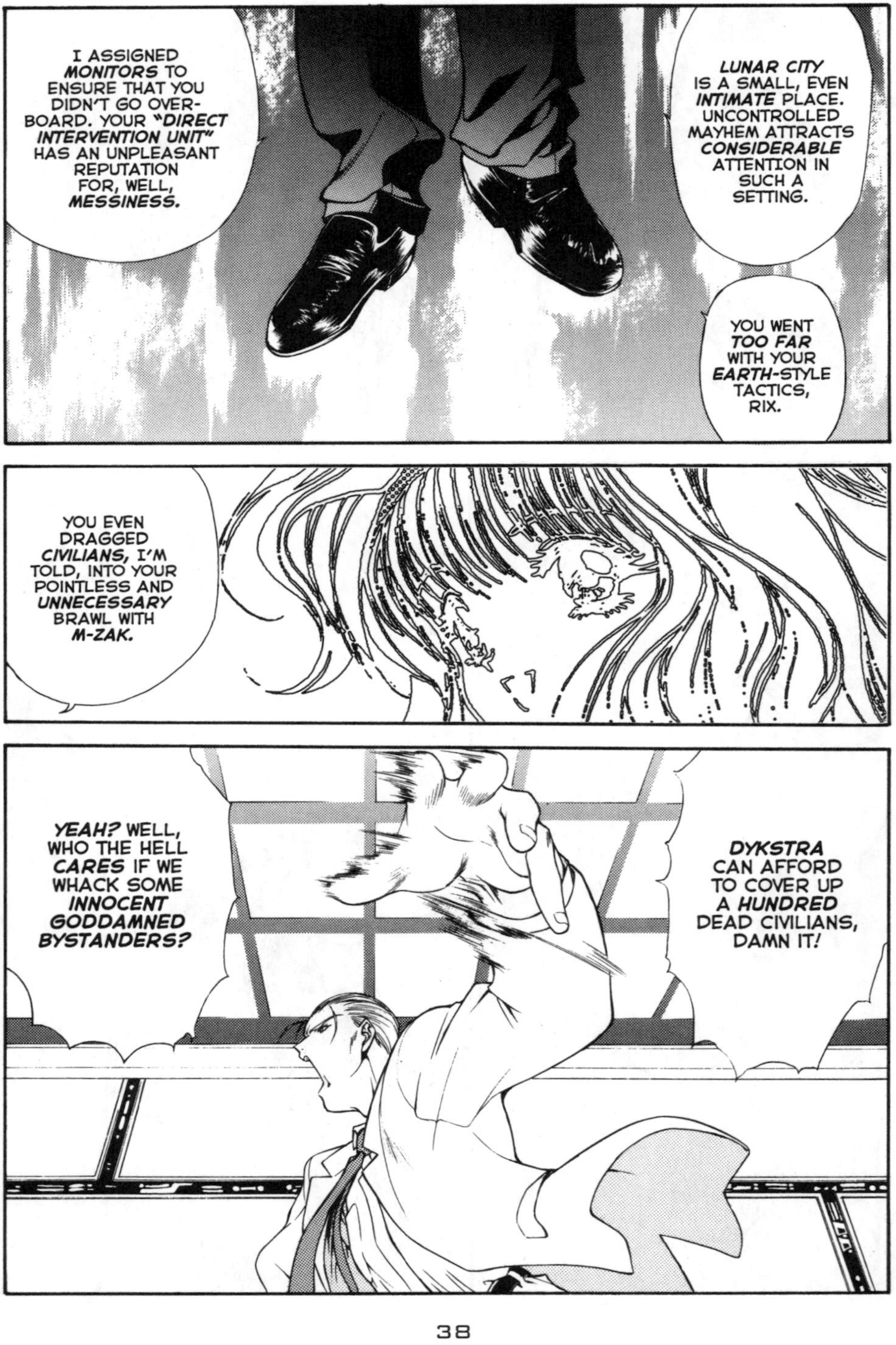
I ASSIGNED MONITORS TO ENSURE THAT YOU DIDN'T GO OVER-BOARD. YOUR "DIRECT INTERVENTION UNIT" HAS AN UNPLEASANT REPUTATION FOR, WELL, MESSINESS.
LUNAR CITY IS A SMALL, EVEN INTIMATE PLACE. UNCONTROLLED MAYHEM ATTRACTS CONSIDERABLE ATTENTION IN SUCH A SETTING.
YOU WENT TOO FAR WITH YOUR EARTH-STYLE TACTICS, RIX.
YOU EVEN DRAGGED CIVILIANS, I'M TOLD, INTO YOUR POINTLESS AND UNNECESSARY BRAWL WITH M-ZAK.
YEAH? WELL, WHO THE HELL CARES IF WE WHACK SOME INNOCENT GODDAMNED BYSTANDERS?
DYKSTRA CAN AFFORD TO COVER UP A HUNDRED DEAD CIVILIANS, DAMN IT!

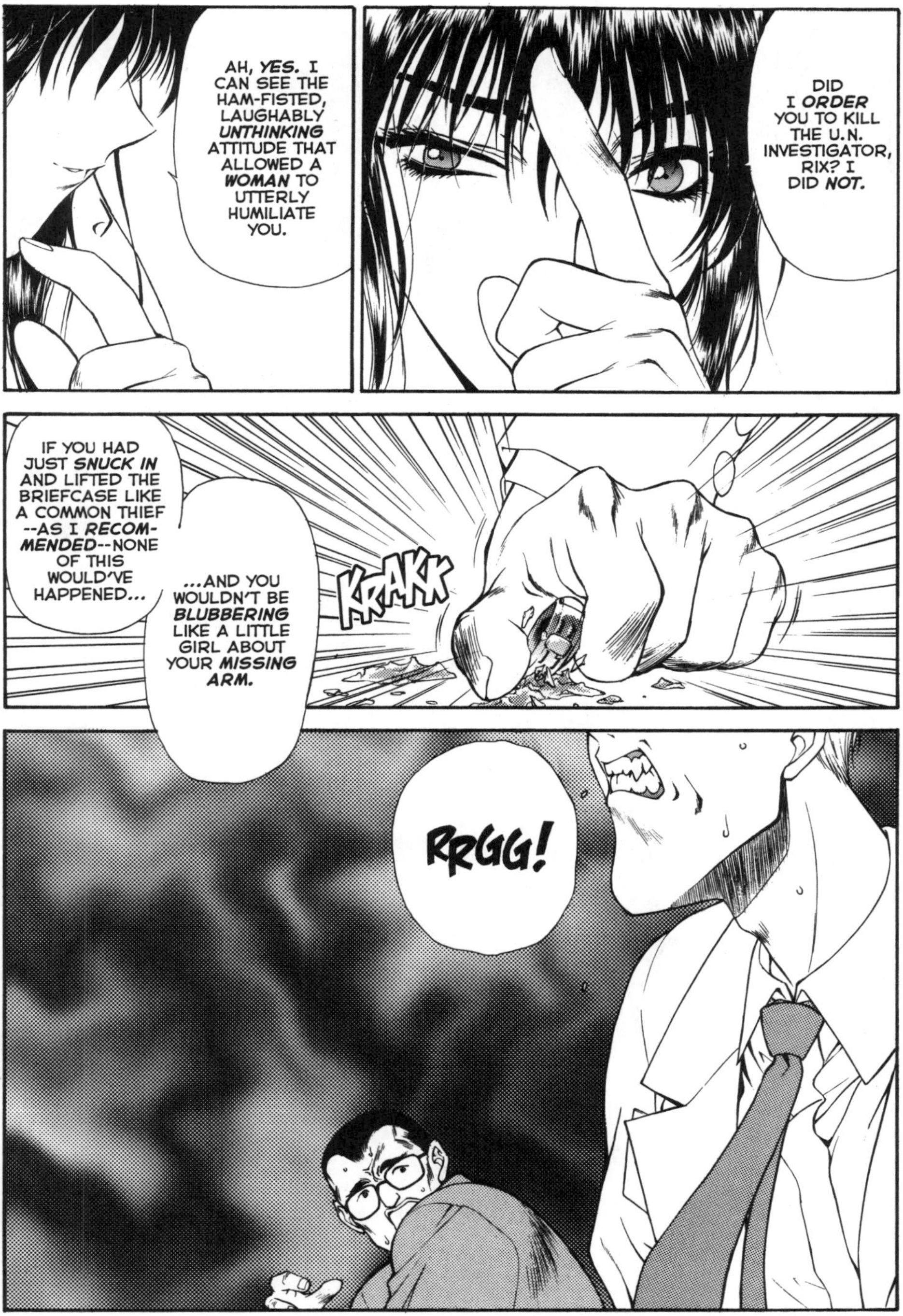
AH, YES. I CAN SEE THE HAM-FISTED, LAUGHABLY UNTHINKING ATTITUDE THAT ALLOWED A WOMAN TO UTTERLY HUMILIATE YOU.
DID I ORDER YOU TO KILL THE U.N. INVESTIGATOR, RIX? I DID NOT.
IF YOU HAD JUST SNUCK IN AND LIFTED THE BRIEFCASE LIKE A COMMON THIEF --AS I RECOMMENDED--NONE OF THIS WOULD'VE HAPPENED...
...AND YOU WOULDN'T BE BLUBBERING LIKE A LITTLE GIRL ABOUT YOUR MISSING ARM.
KRAKK
RRGG!

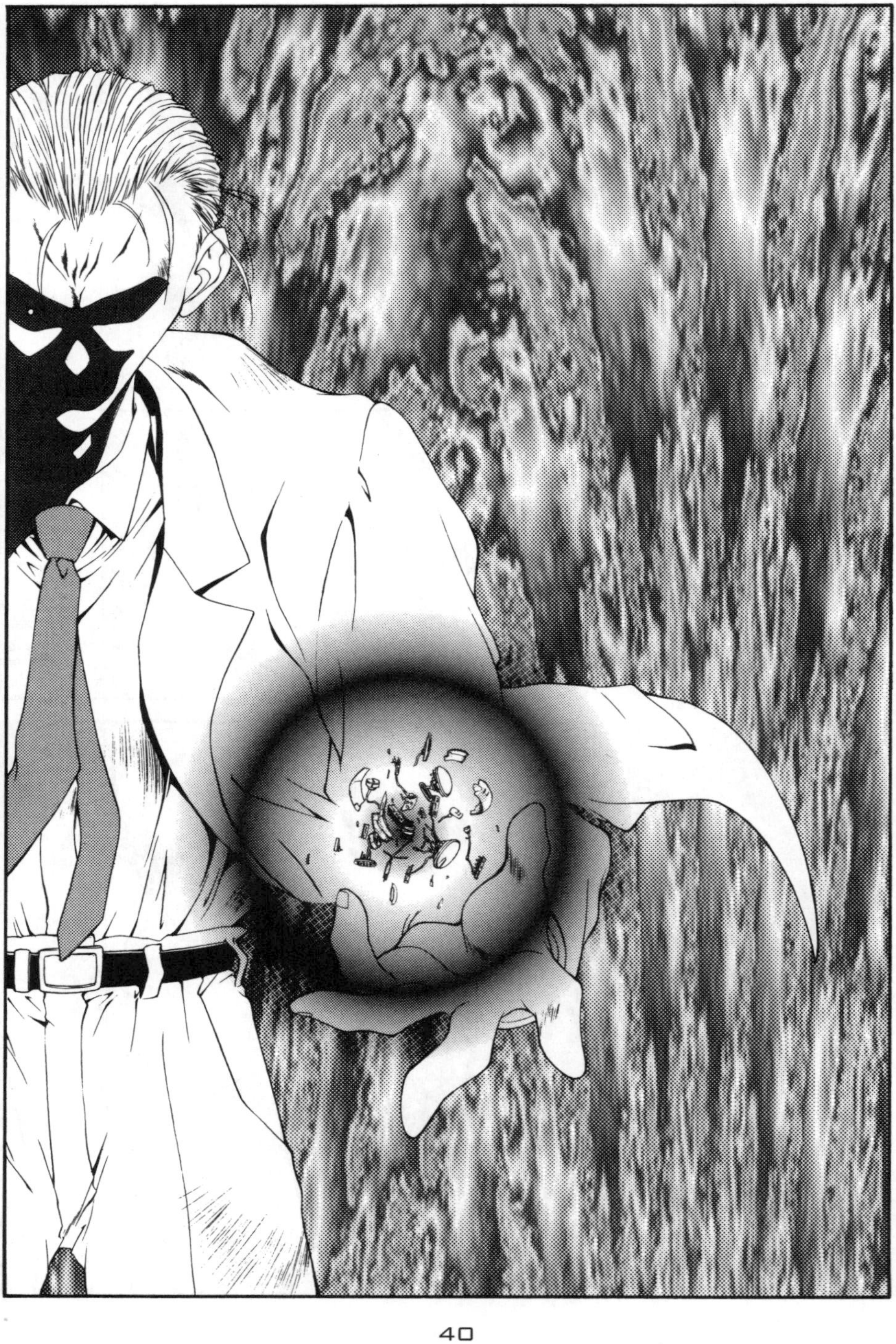

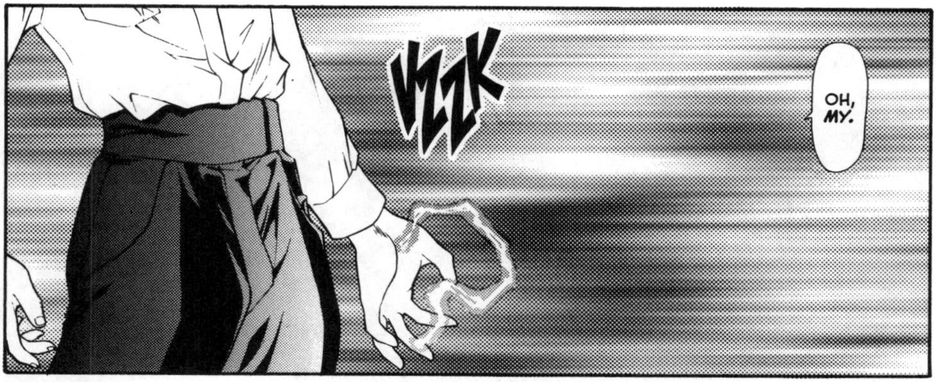
VZZK
OH, MY.

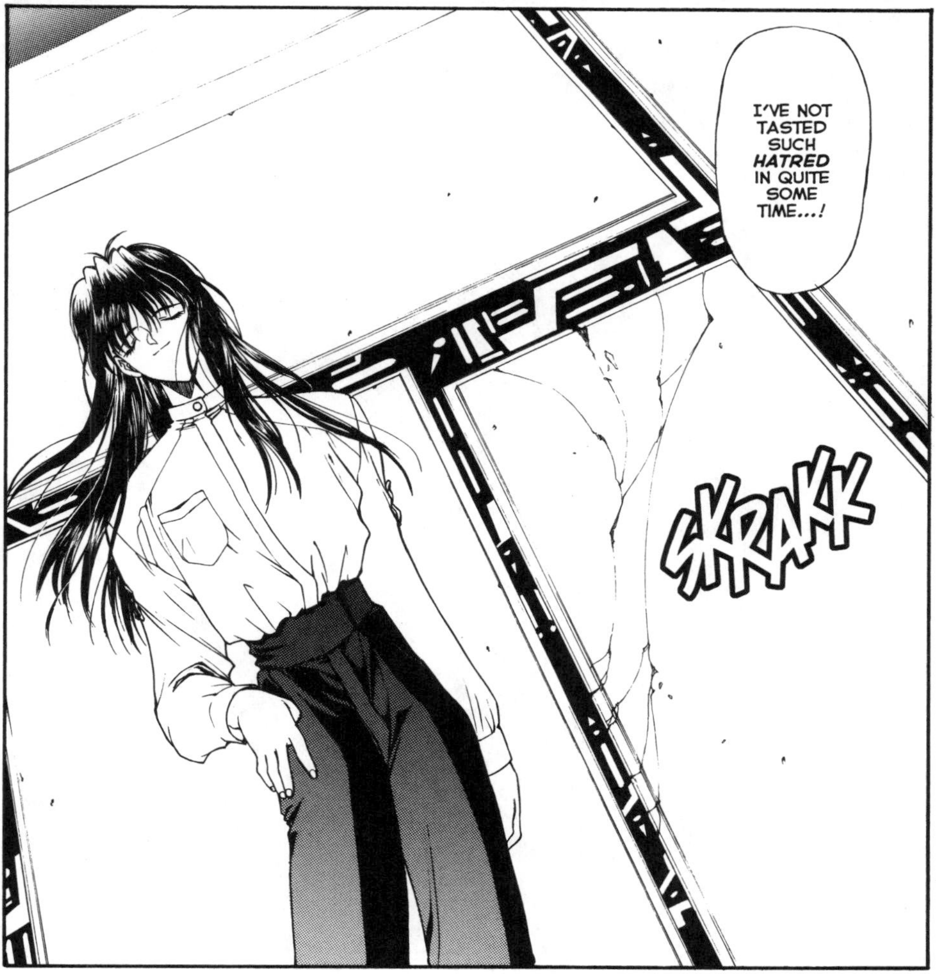
I'VE NOT TASTED SUCH HATRED IN QUITE SOME TIME...!
SKRAKK

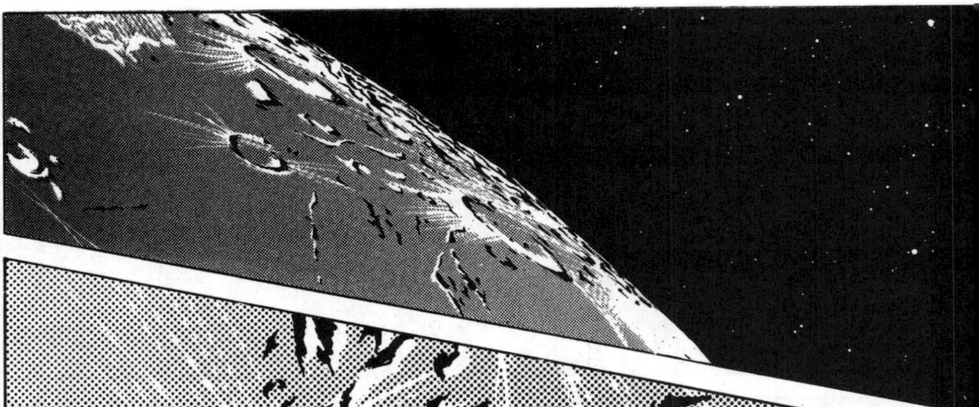

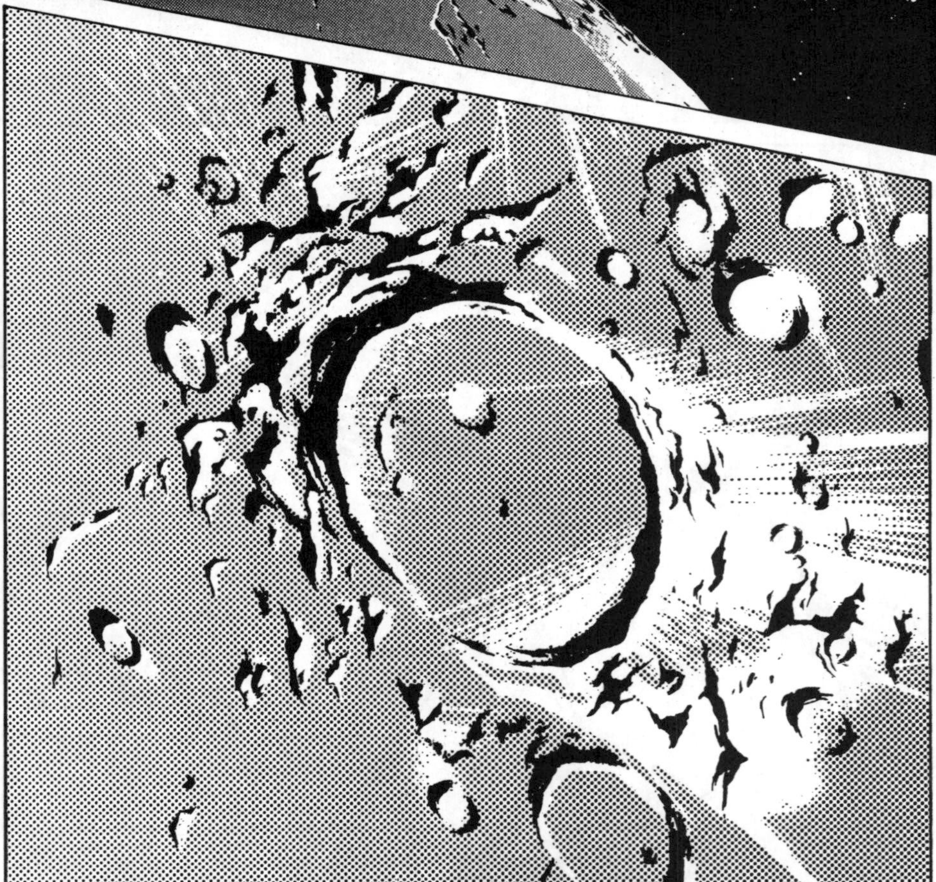

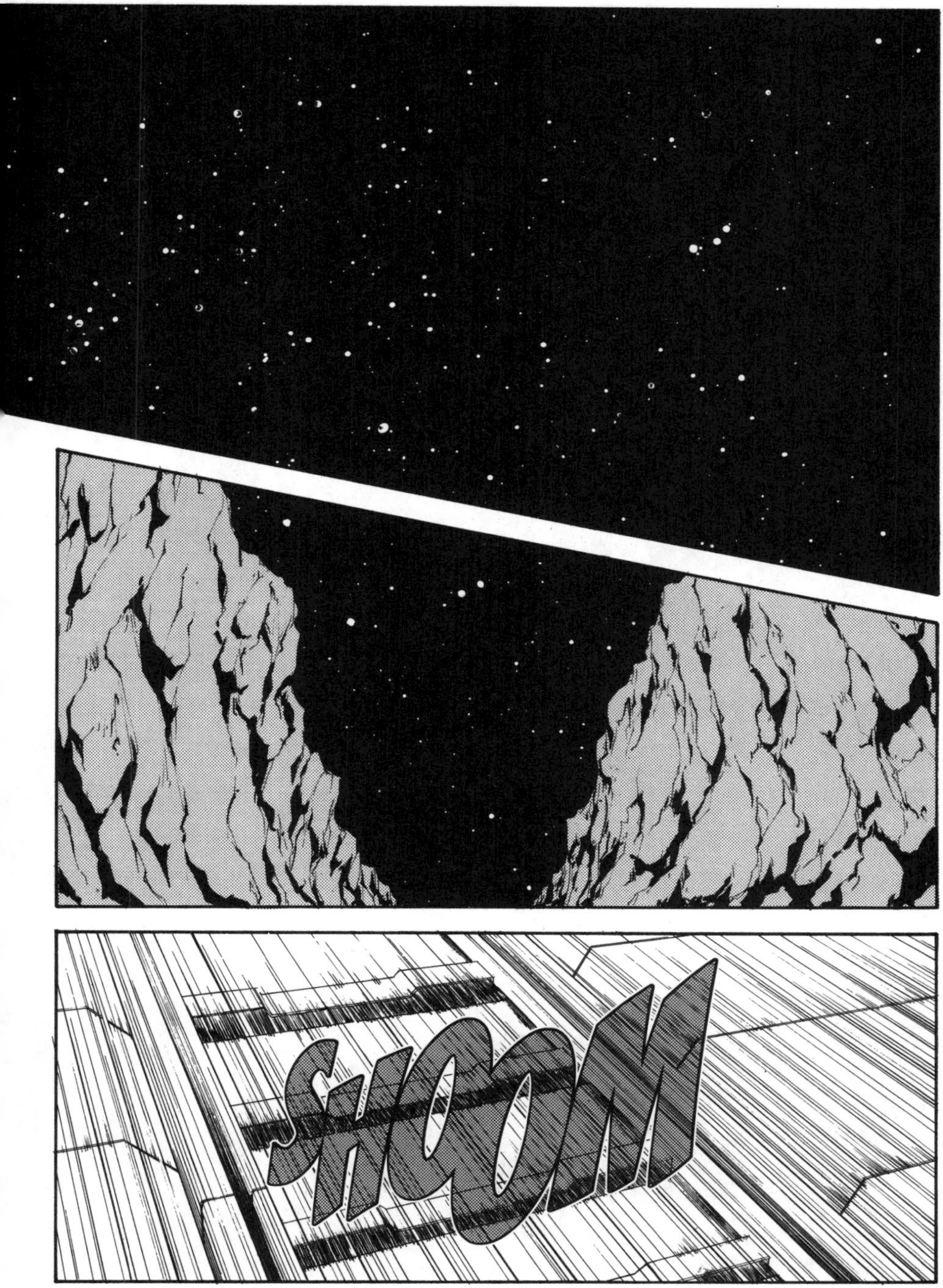
SHOOM

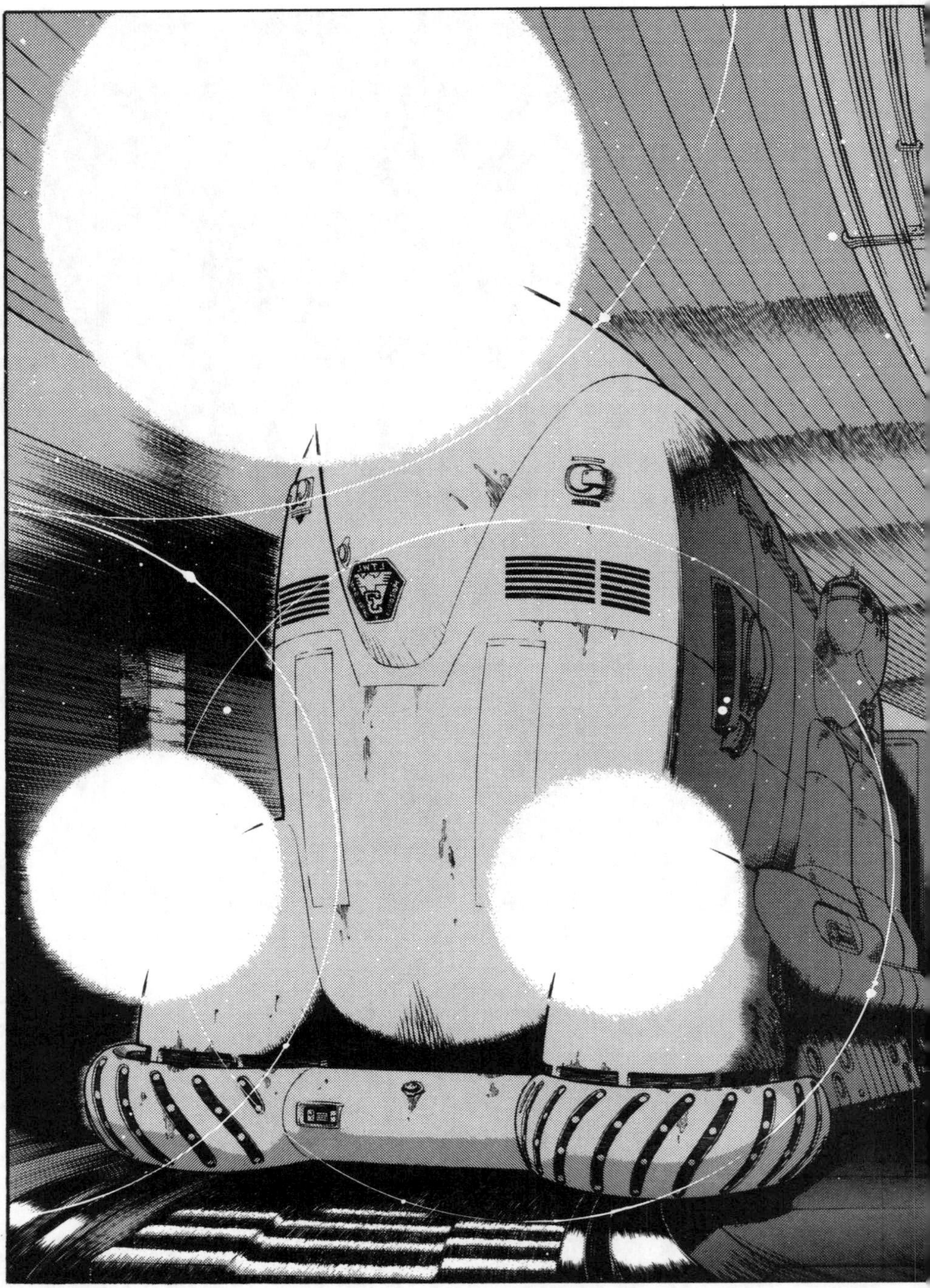

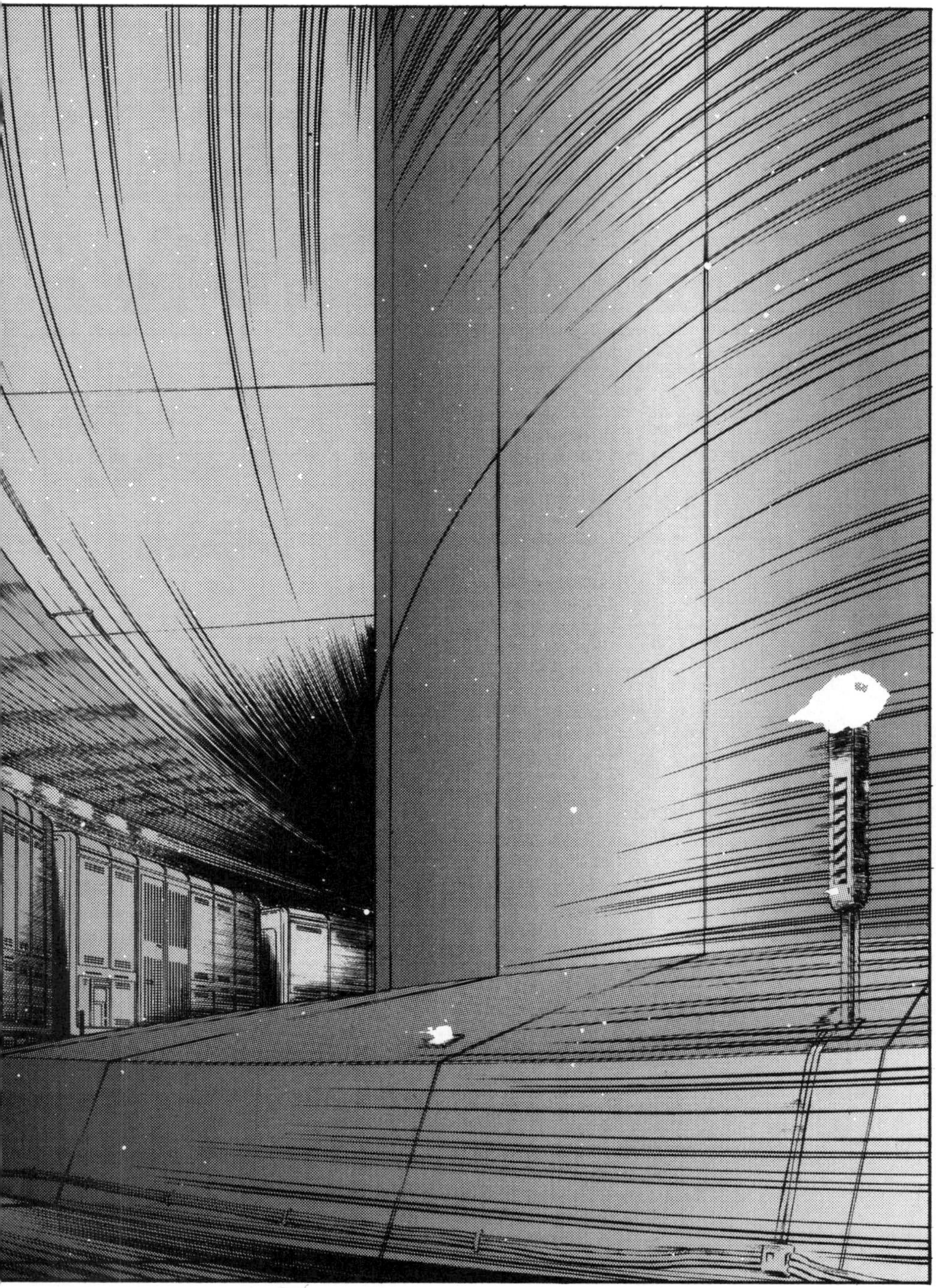

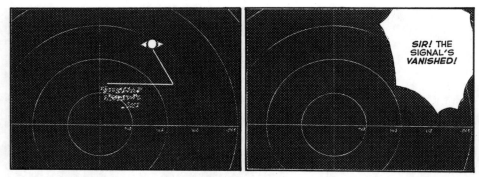

SIR! THE SIGNAL'S VANISHED!

HAH! THEY FOUND THE TRACER TOO *LATE!* THE PROSECUTOR'S OFFICE HAS *CONFIRMED* THAT IT REACHED THE *KOROLEV ADVANCED RESEARCH LABORATORY!*

THEY WON'T *SPIN* THEIR WAY OUT OF *THIS* ONE!

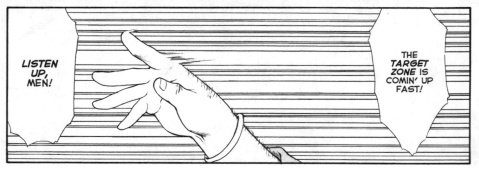

LISTEN UP, MEN!

THE *TARGET ZONE* IS COMIN' UP FAST!

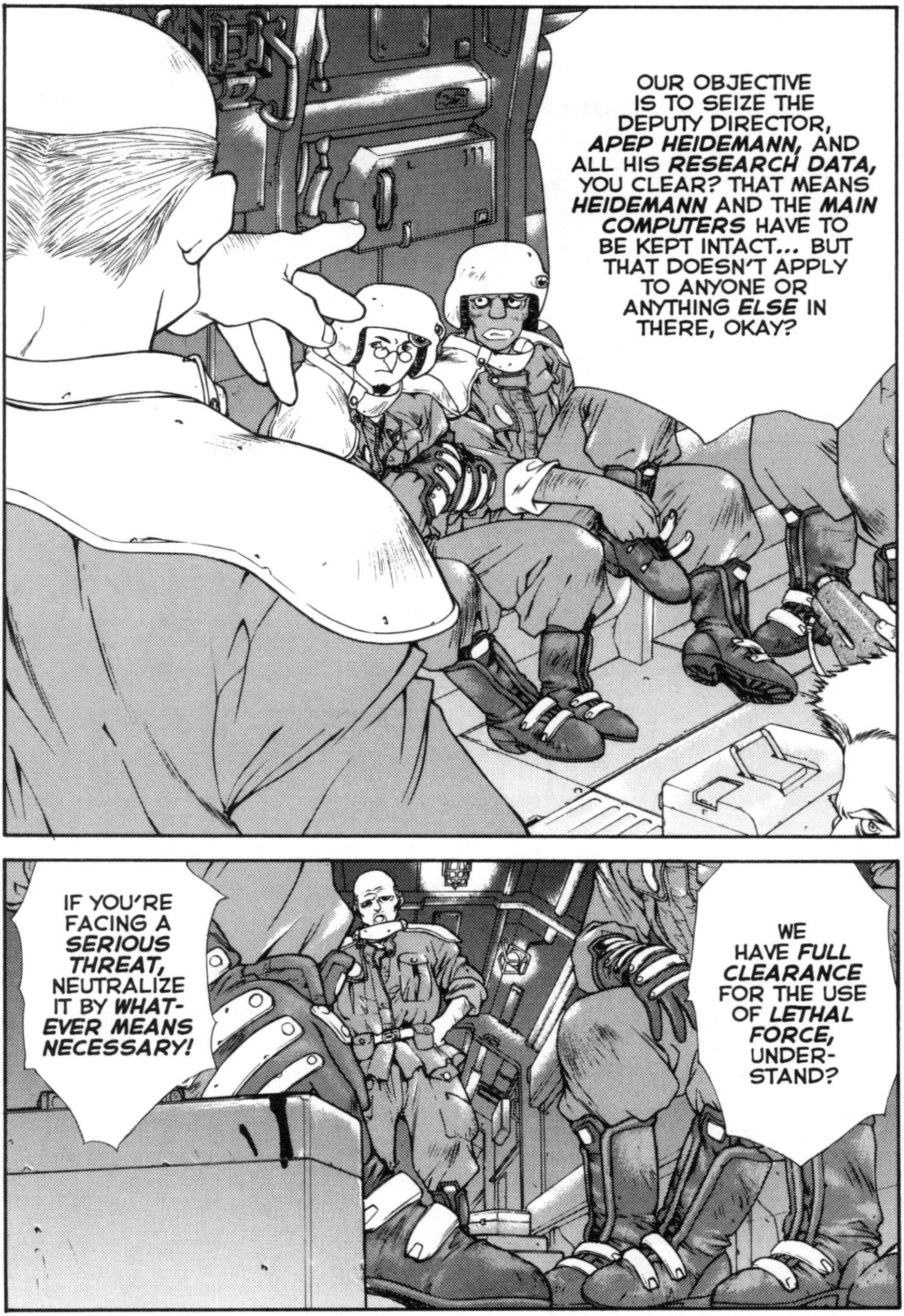
OUR OBJECTIVE IS TO SEIZE THE DEPUTY DIRECTOR, *APEP HEIDEMANN,* AND ALL HIS *RESEARCH DATA,* YOU CLEAR? THAT MEANS *HEIDEMANN* AND THE *MAIN COMPUTERS* HAVE TO BE KEPT INTACT... BUT THAT DOESN'T APPLY TO ANYONE OR ANYTHING *ELSE* IN THERE, OKAY?
IF YOU'RE FACING A *SERIOUS THREAT,* NEUTRALIZE IT BY *WHAT-EVER MEANS NECESSARY!*
WE HAVE *FULL CLEARANCE* FOR THE USE OF *LETHAL FORCE,* UNDER-STAND?

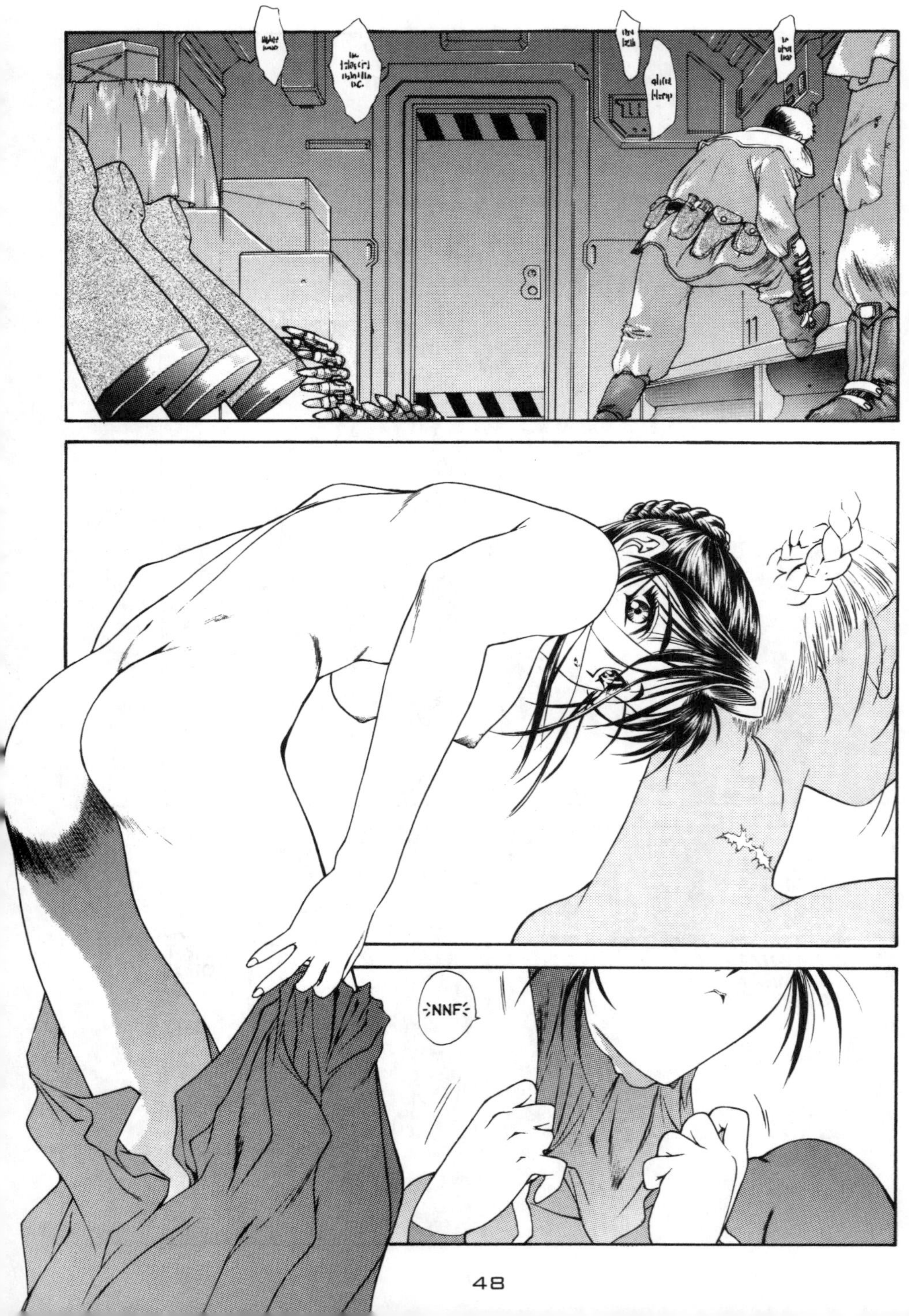
NNF

KCHAK
KSHHHT
!

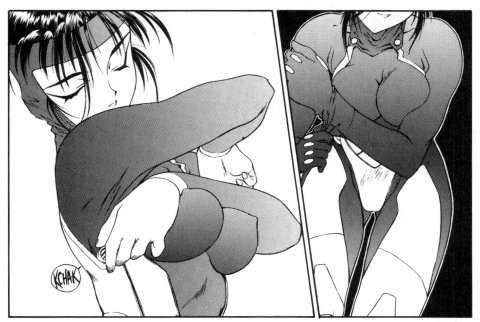

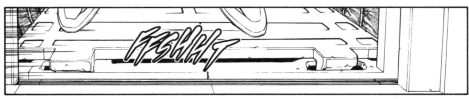

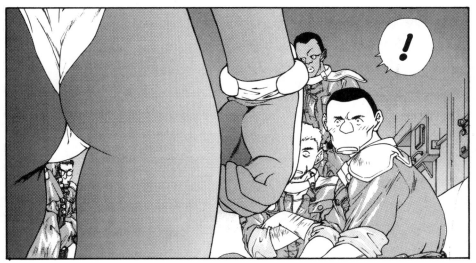

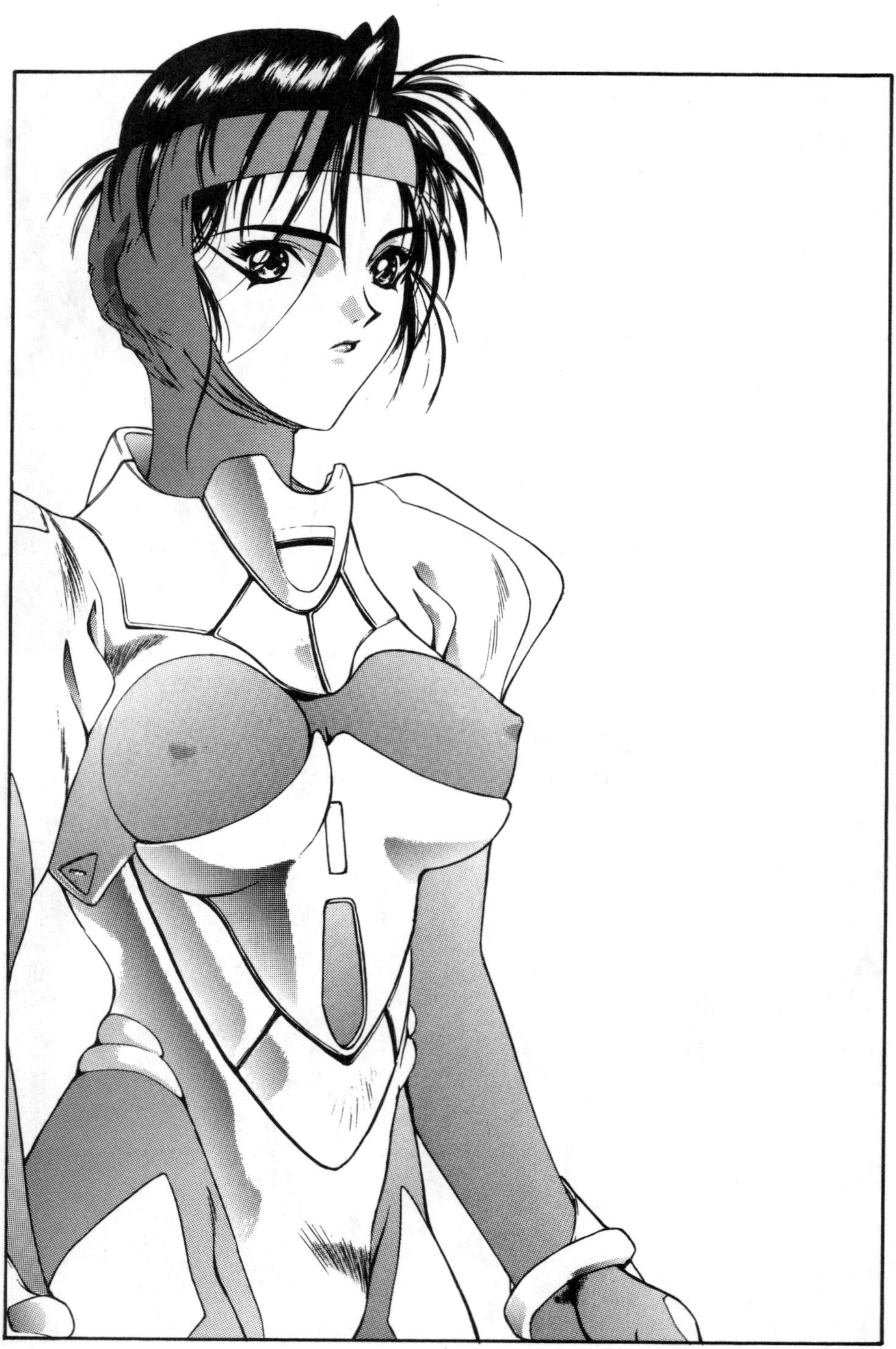

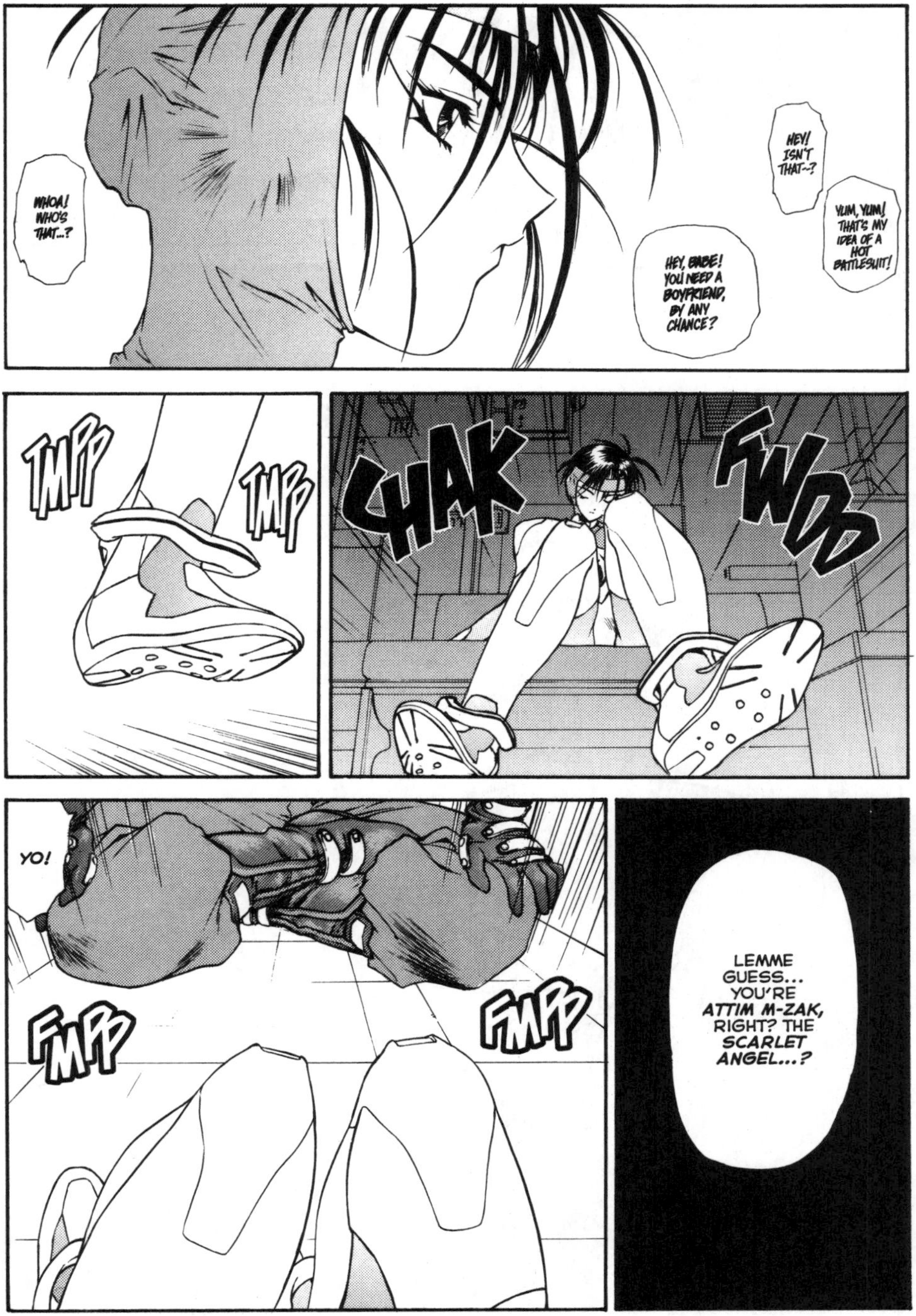

WHOA! WHO'S THAT...?
HEY, BABE! YOU NEED A BOYFRIEND, BY ANY CHANCE?
HEY! ISN'T THAT--?
YUM, YUM! THAT'S MY IDEA OF A HOT BATTLESUIT!
TMPP
TMPP
CHAK
FWDD
YO!
FMPP
FMPP
LEMME GUESS... YOU'RE ATTIM M-ZAK, RIGHT? THE SCARLET ANGEL...?

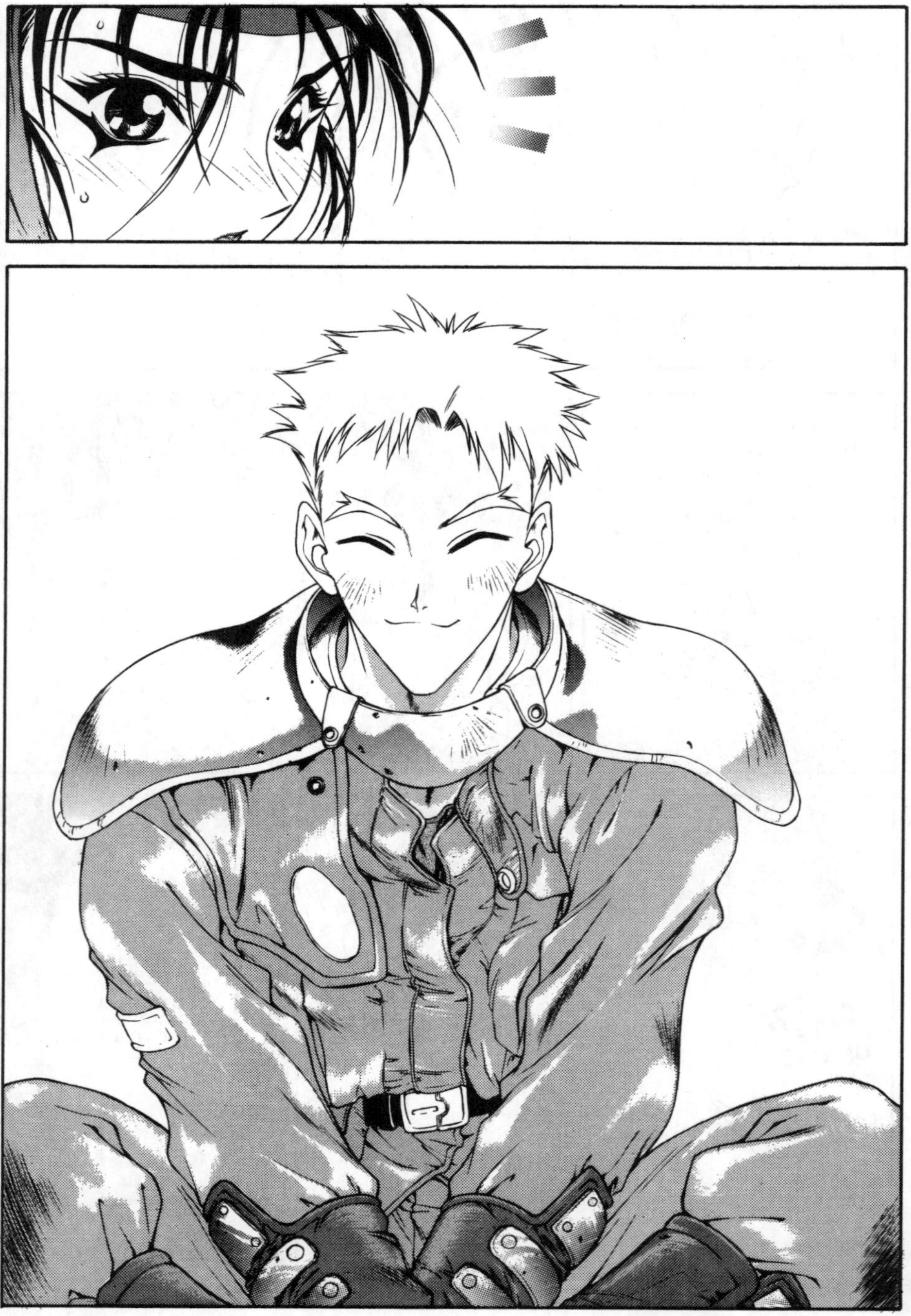

ACT 20

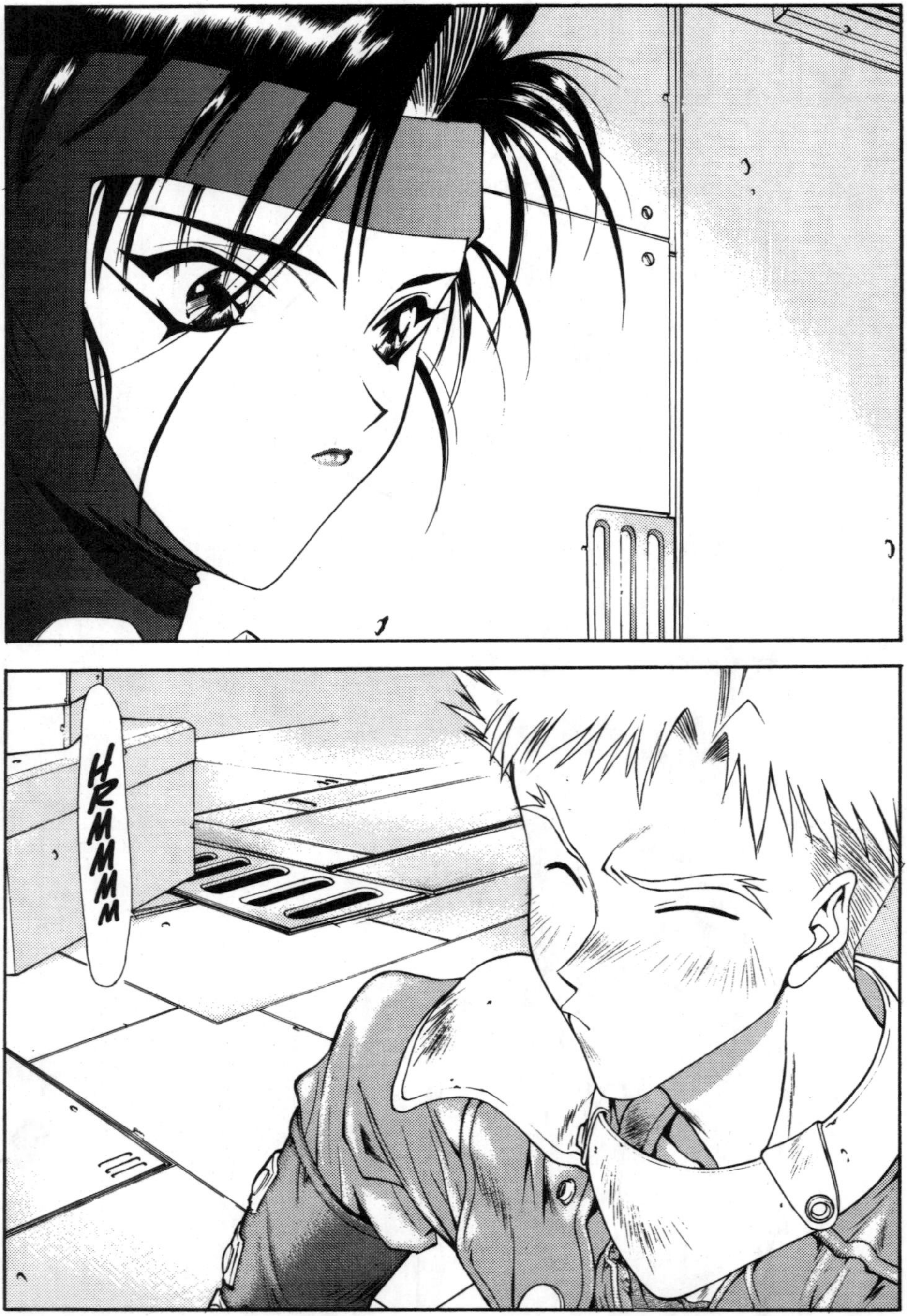
HRMMMM

DAMN! YOU'RE *KILLIN'* ME WITH THAT *GRIM OL'* FACE, GIRL!

SMAK

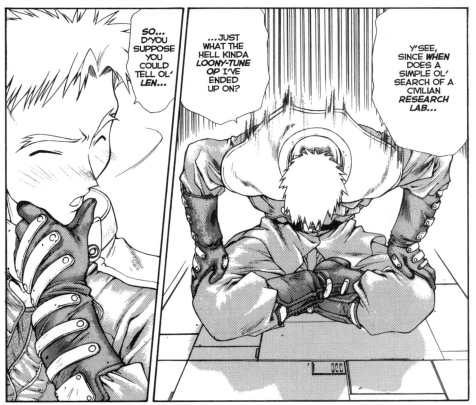

SO... D'YOU SUPPOSE YOU COULD TELL OL' *LEN*...

...JUST WHAT THE HELL KINDA *LOONY-TUNE* OP I'VE ENDED UP ON?

Y'SEE, SINCE *WHEN* DOES A SIMPLE OL' SEARCH OF A CIVILIAN *RESEARCH LAB*...

...REQUIRE THE FOLLOWIN' *UNUSUAL* ITEMS...?

ONE, A FULL *BATTALION'S* WORTH OF BADASS ELITE SPECIAL-OPS TROOPS!

WHKSH

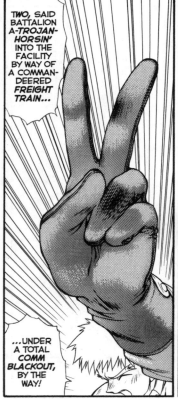

TWO, SAID BATTALION A *TROJAN-HORSIN'* INTO THE FACILITY BY WAY OF A COMMANDEERED *FREIGHT TRAIN...*

...UNDER A TOTAL *COMM BLACKOUT*, BY THE WAY!

AND *THREE*, THE SCARY OL' *SCARLET ANGEL* TAGGING ALONG!

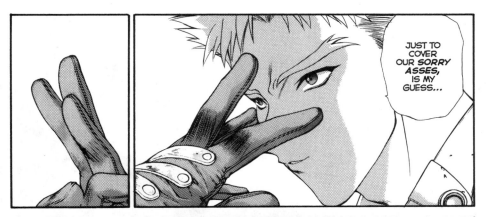

JUST TO COVER OUR *SORRY ASSES,* IS MY GUESS...

CLEARLY, THESE ARE ALL SIGNS OF HOW *IMPORTANT* THIS MISSION HAPPENS TO BE.

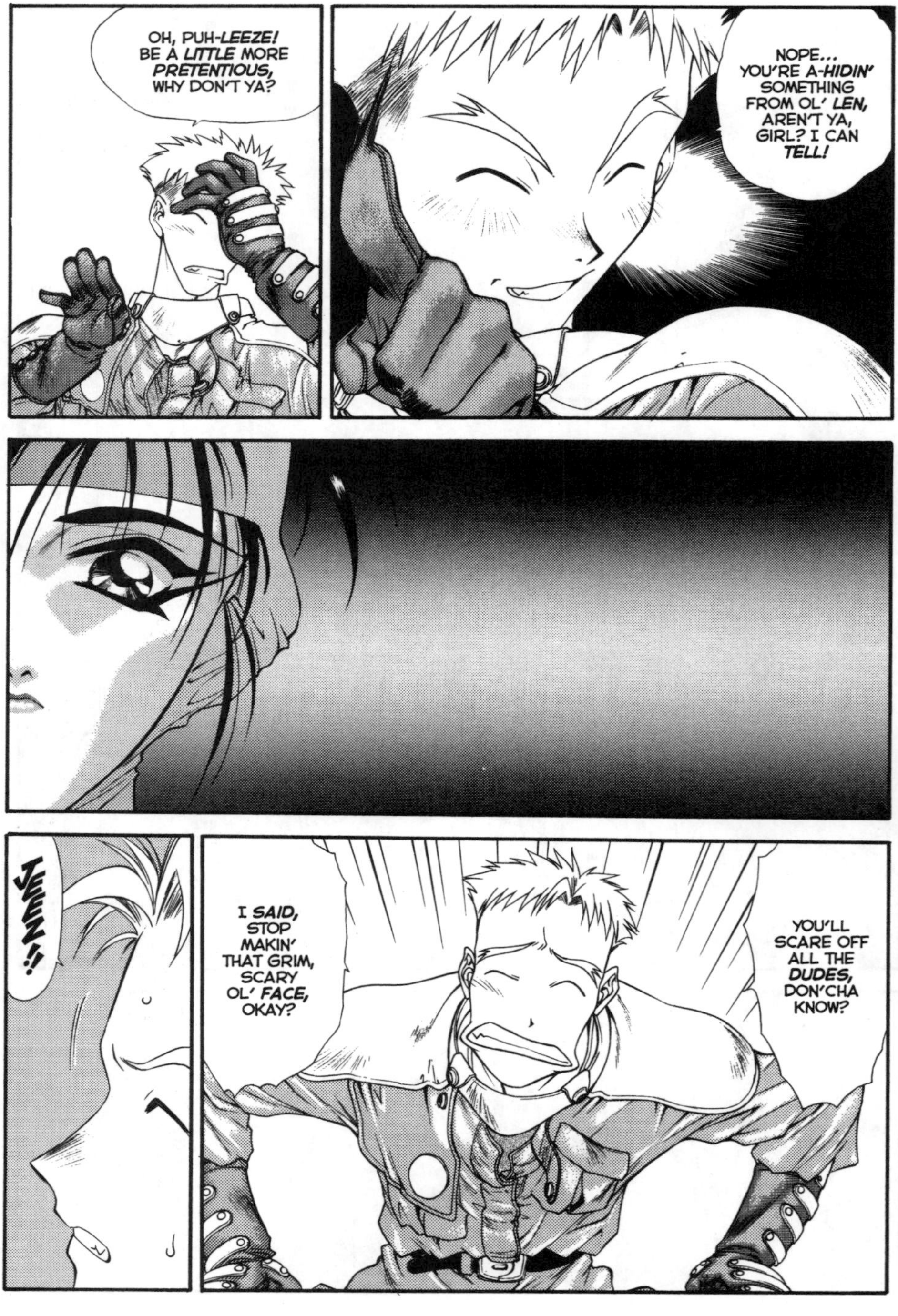
OH, PUH-LEEZE! BE A LITTLE MORE PRETENTIOUS, WHY DON'T YA?
NOPE... YOU'RE A-HIDIN' SOMETHING FROM OL' LEN, AREN'T YA, GIRL? I CAN TELL!
JEEZ!!
I SAID, STOP MAKIN' THAT GRIM, SCARY OL' FACE, OKAY?
YOU'LL SCARE OFF ALL THE DUDES, DON'CHA KNOW?

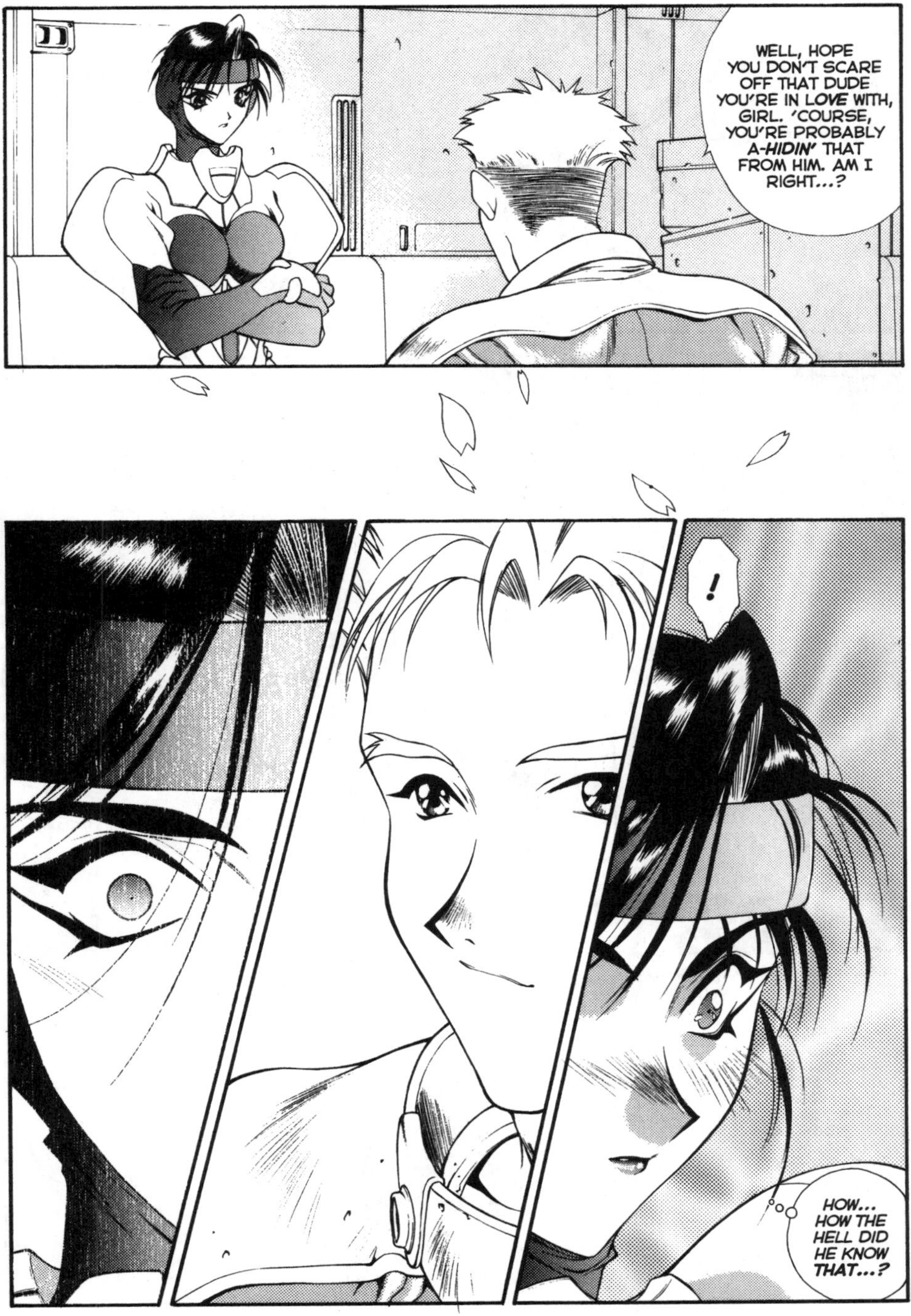
WELL, HOPE YOU DON'T SCARE OFF THAT DUDE YOU'RE IN LOVE WITH, GIRL. 'COURSE, YOU'RE PROBABLY A-HIDIN' THAT FROM HIM. AM I RIGHT...?
!
HOW... HOW THE HELL DID HE KNOW THAT...?

YOUR FACE *CAN'T* BE READ, CAN IT?

HAHH...?

BECAUSE YOUR EXPRESSIONS KEEP *CHANGING,* LIKE A PACK OF *CARDS* CONSTANTLY BEING SHUFFLED. SHIFTING SO FAST THAT THEY HIDE THE *REAL YOU.*

WELL, I CAN'T DO THAT.

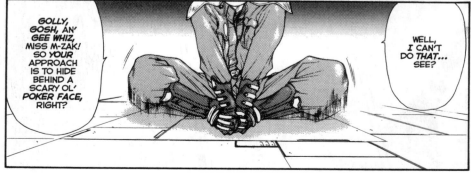

GOLLY, GOSH, AN' *GEE WHIZ,* MISS M-ZAK! SO *YOUR* APPROACH IS TO HIDE BEHIND A SCARY OL' *POKER FACE,* RIGHT?

WELL, I CAN'T DO *THAT...* SEE?

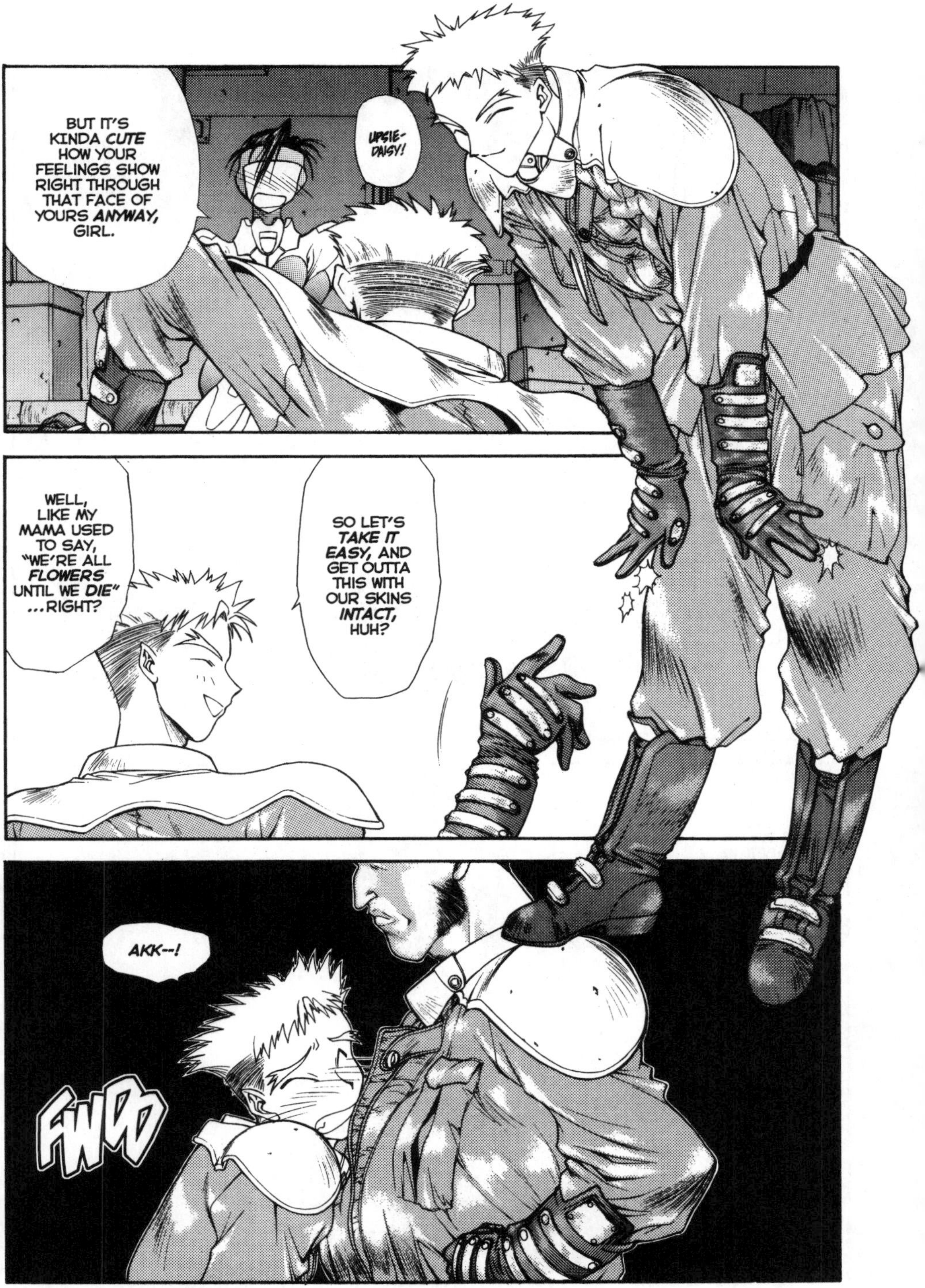
BUT IT'S KINDA CUTE HOW YOUR FEELINGS SHOW RIGHT THROUGH THAT FACE OF YOURS ANYWAY, GIRL.
UPSIE-DAISY!
WELL, LIKE MY MAMA USED TO SAY, "WE'RE ALL FLOWERS UNTIL WE DIE" ...RIGHT?
SO LET'S TAKE IT EASY, AND GET OUTTA THIS WITH OUR SKINS INTACT, HUH?
AKK--!
FWOOD

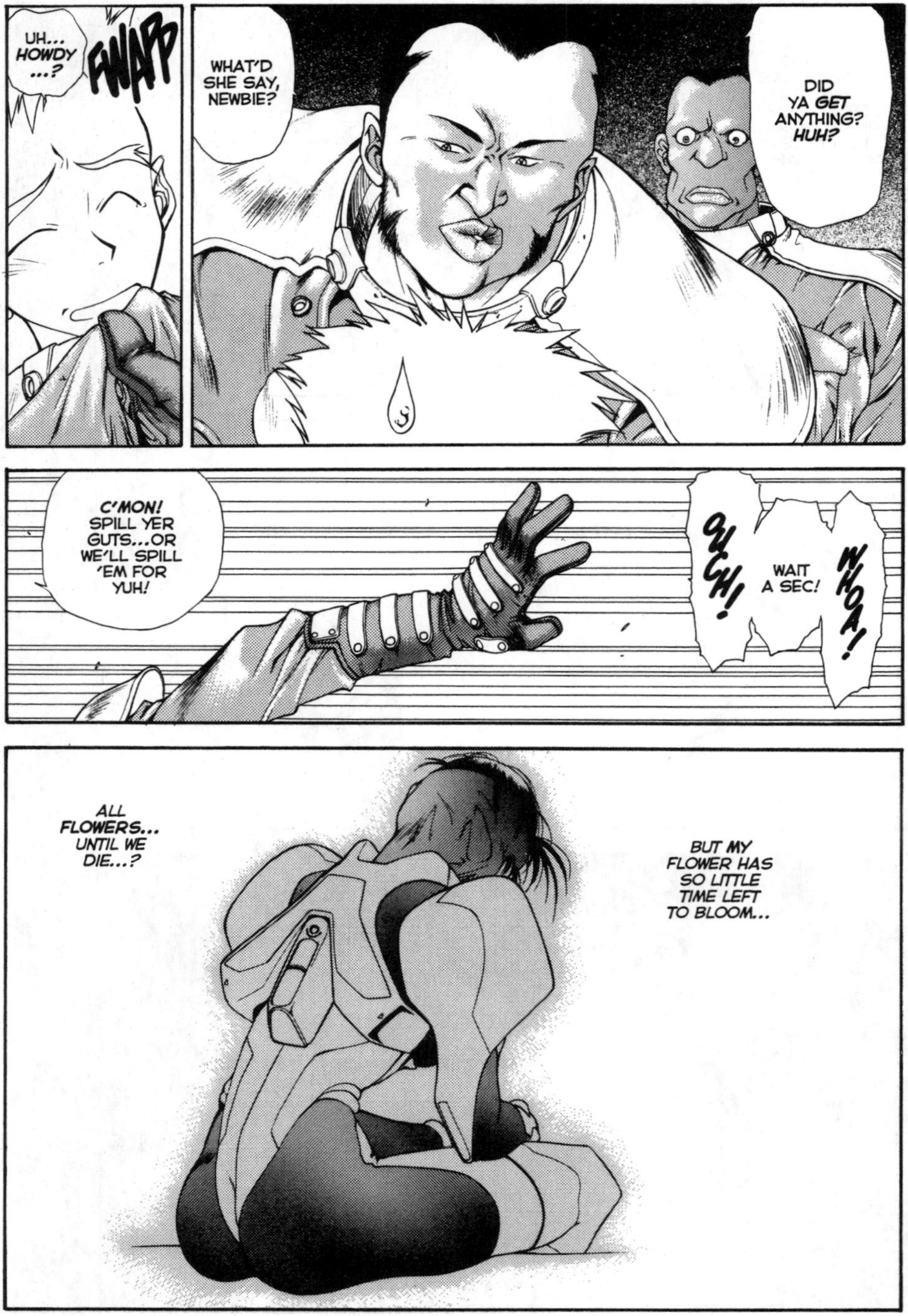
UH... HOWDY ...?
FWAPP
WHAT'D SHE SAY, NEWBIE?
DID YA GET ANYTHING? HUH?
C'MON! SPILL YER GUTS...OR WE'LL SPILL 'EM FOR YUH!
OUCH!
WAIT A SEC!
WHOA!
ALL FLOWERS... UNTIL WE DIE...?
BUT MY FLOWER HAS SO LITTLE TIME LEFT TO BLOOM...

...SOON THE PETALS WILL FALL, LIKE THOSE FLOWERS...

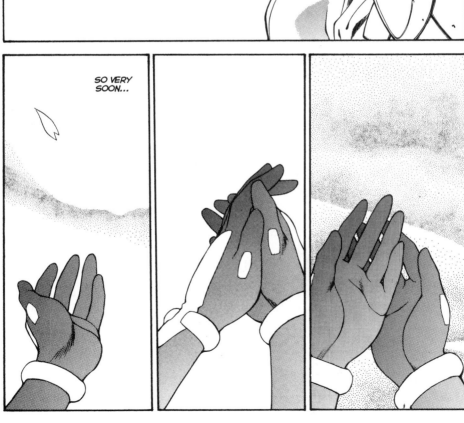

SO VERY SOON...

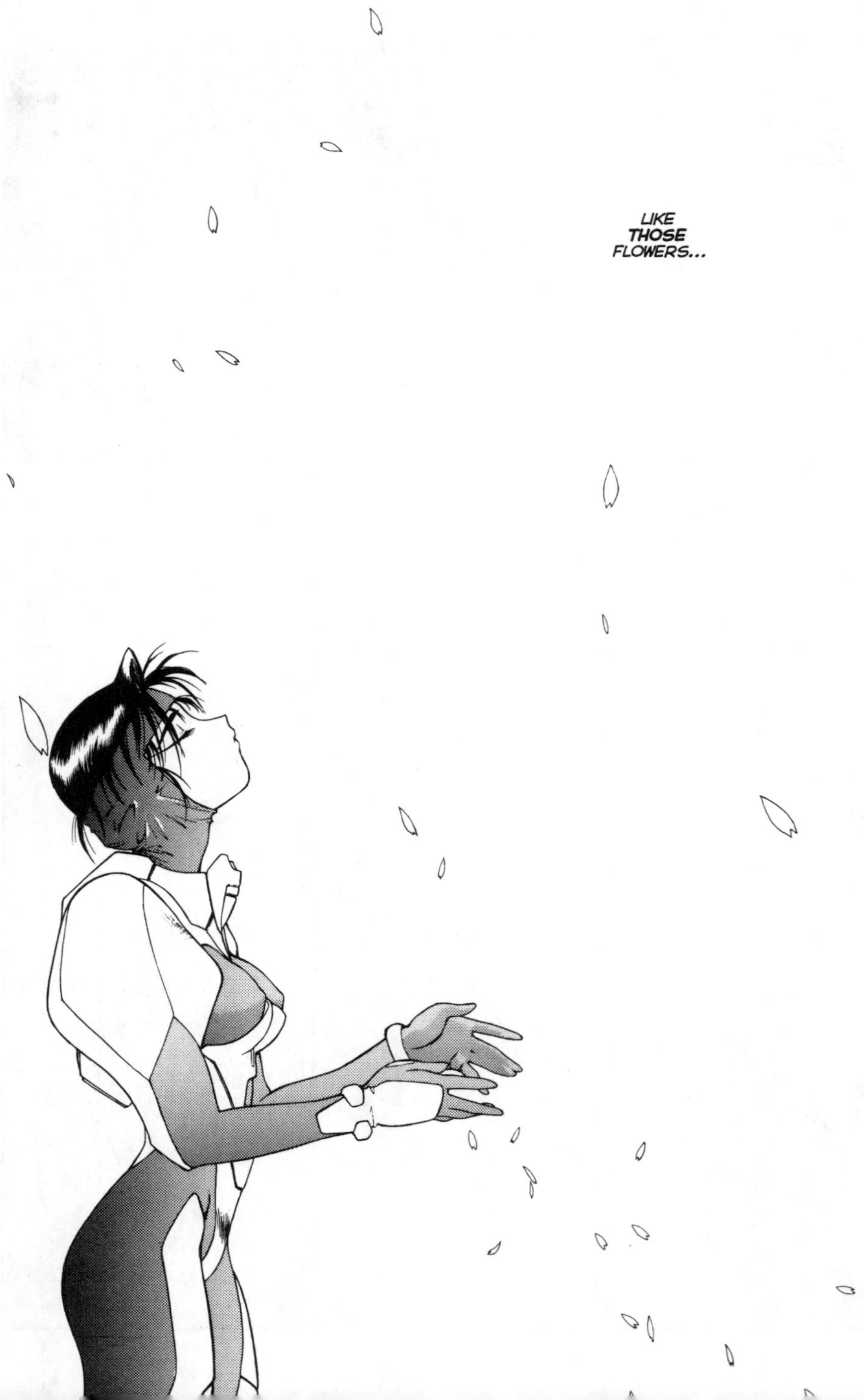
LIKE THOSE FLOWERS...

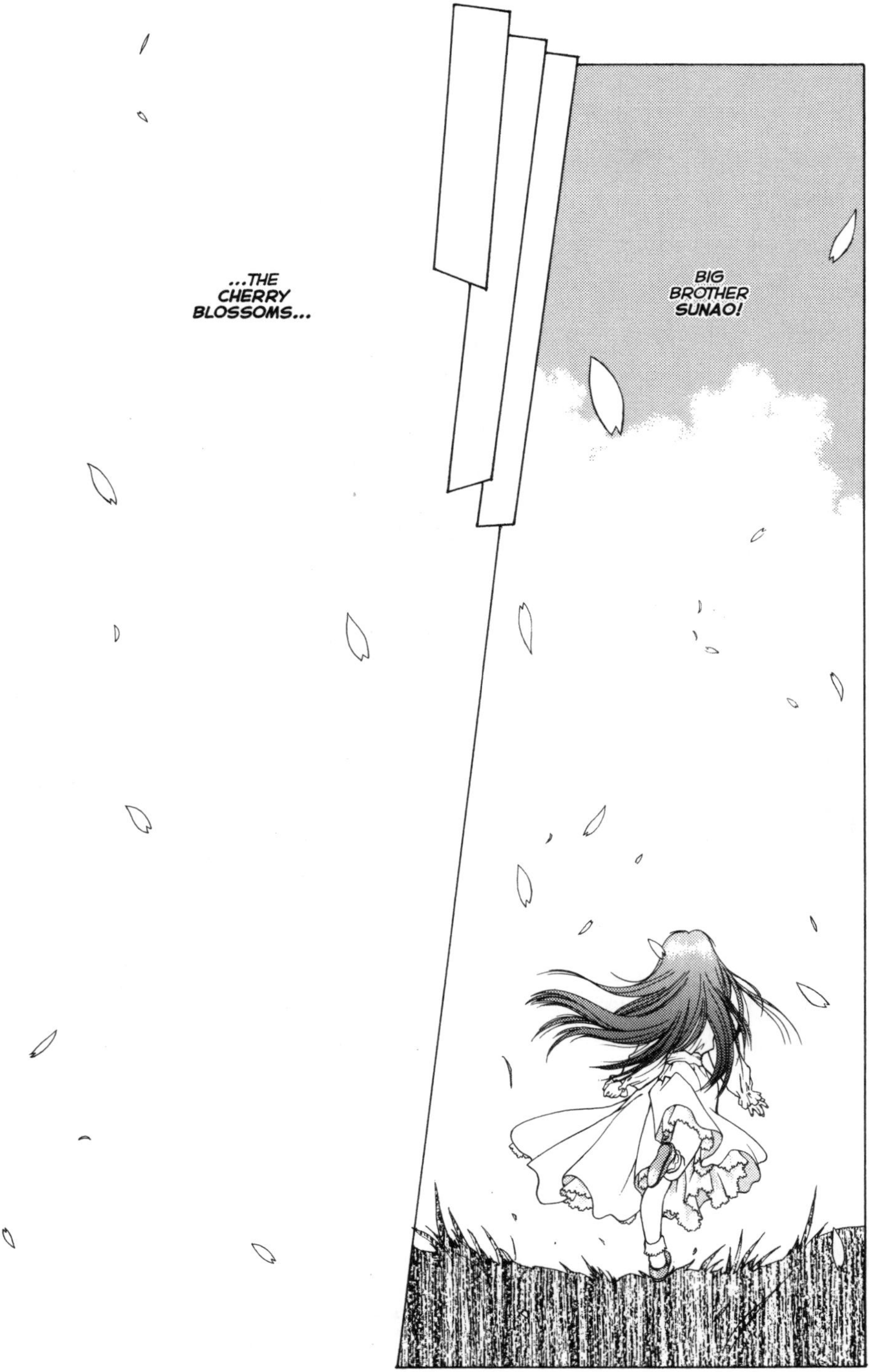
...THE CHERRY BLOSSOMS...
BIG BROTHER SUNAO!

WHEEE!

H-HEY!
BE **CAREFUL**,
OKAY?

TELL ME!
TELL ME!

WHAT
ARE THESE
FLOWERS
CALLED,
AGAIN?

MMM?

DON'T
YOU
REMEMBER?

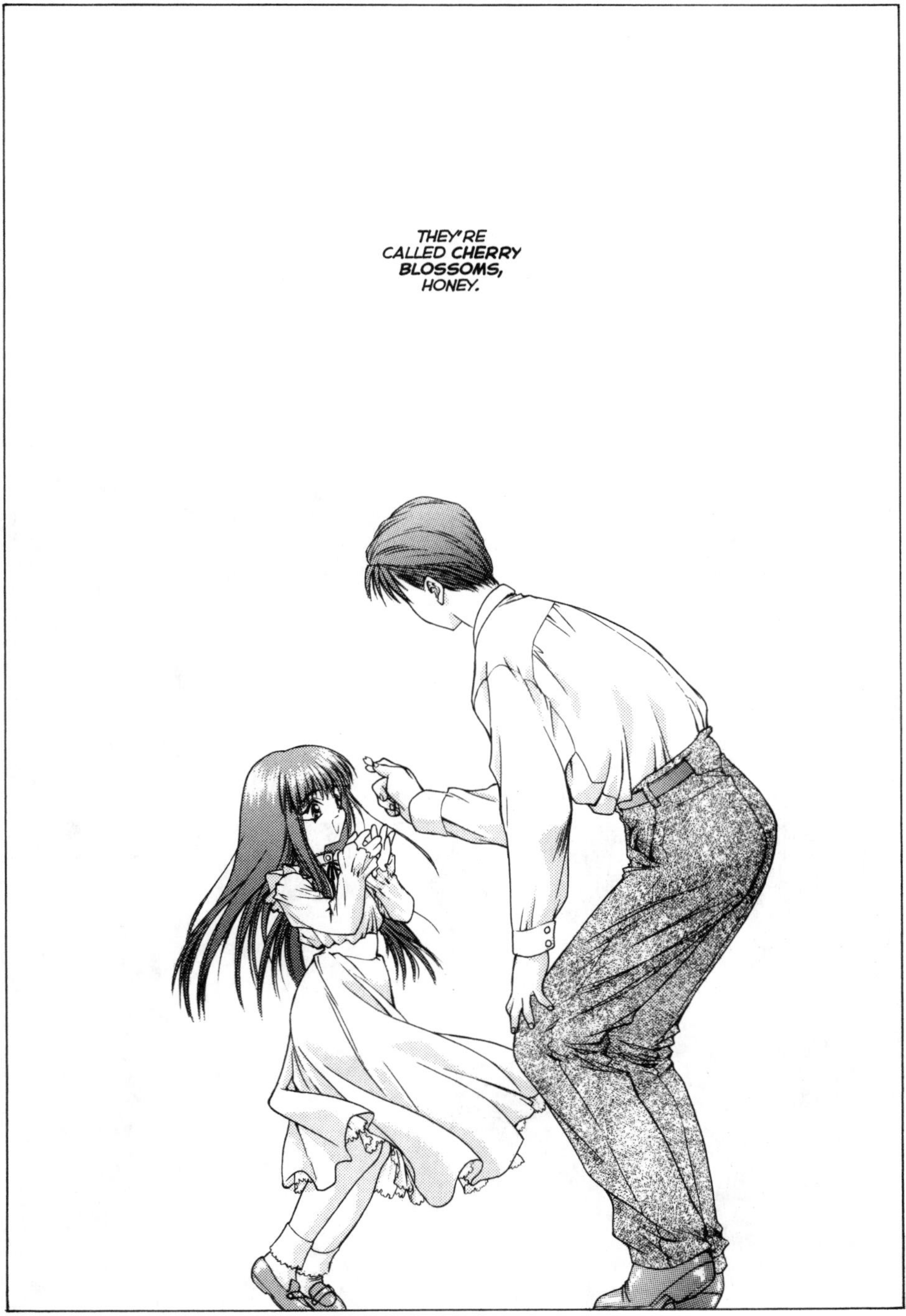
THEY'RE CALLED CHERRY BLOSSOMS, HONEY.

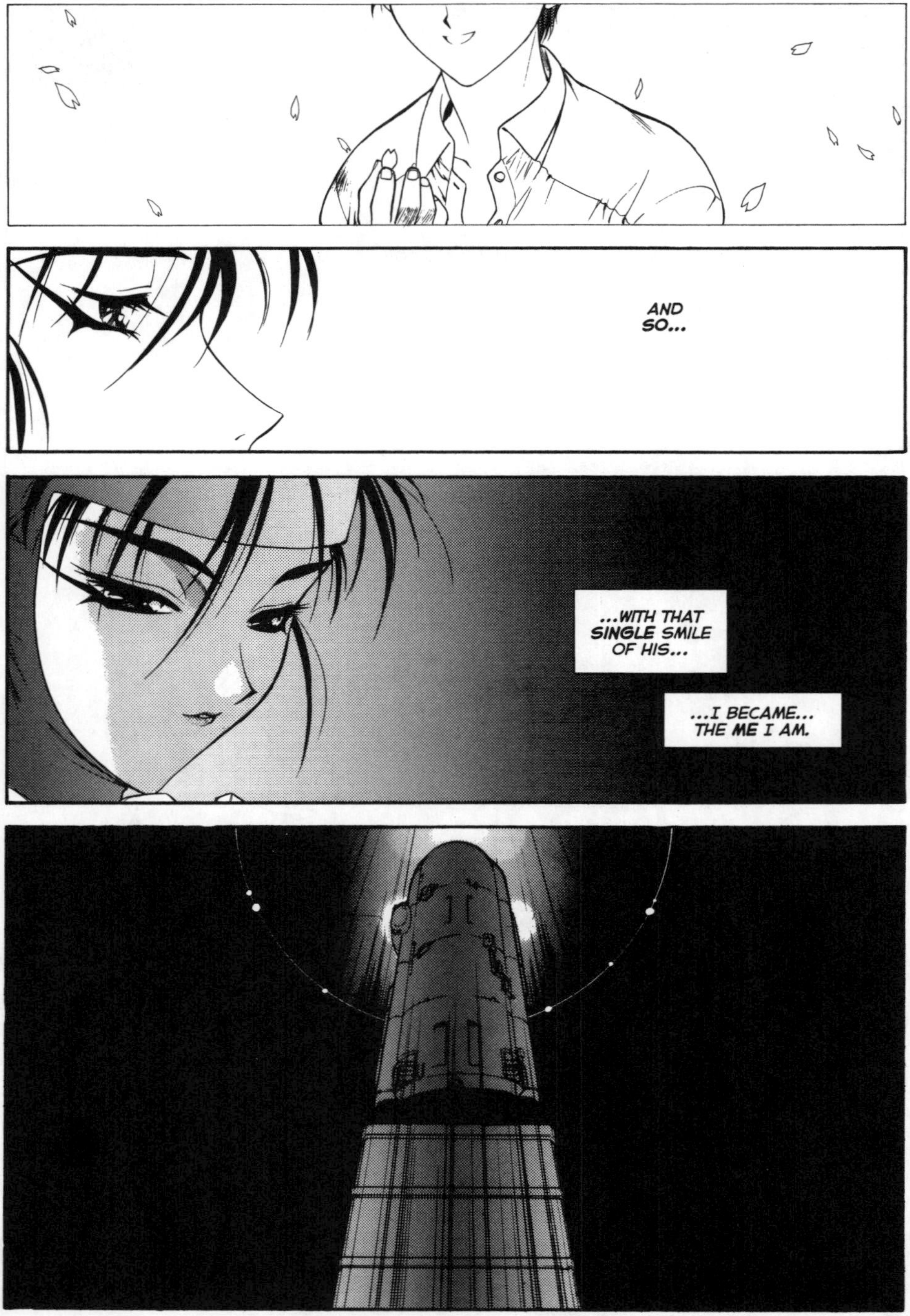
AND SO...
...WITH THAT SINGLE SMILE OF HIS...
...I BECAME... THE ME I AM.

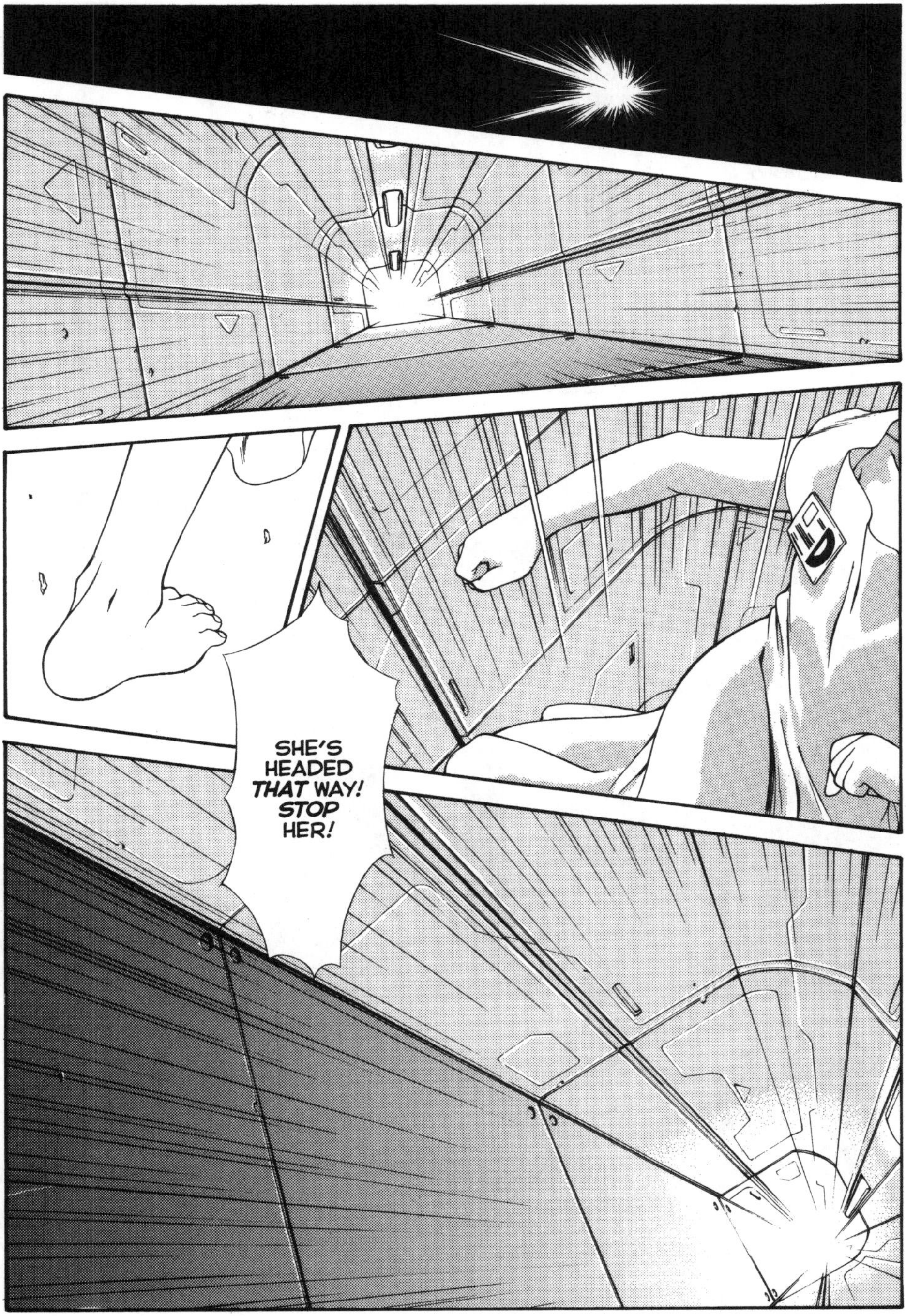
SHE'S HEADED THAT WAY! STOP HER!

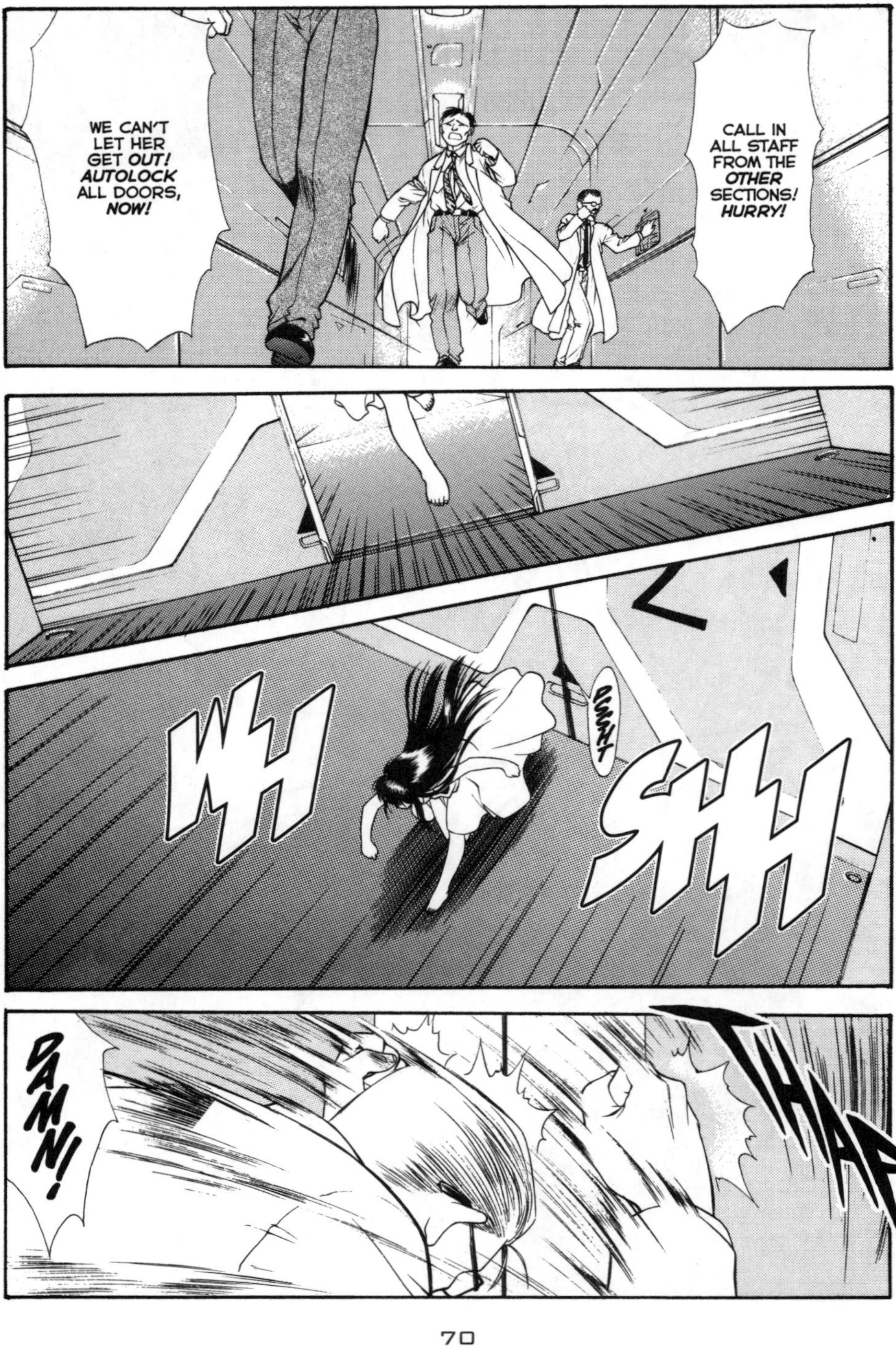
WE CAN'T LET HER GET OUT! AUTOLOCK ALL DOORS, NOW!
CALL IN ALL STAFF FROM THE OTHER SECTIONS! HURRY!
WH
SHH
DAMN!
THAP

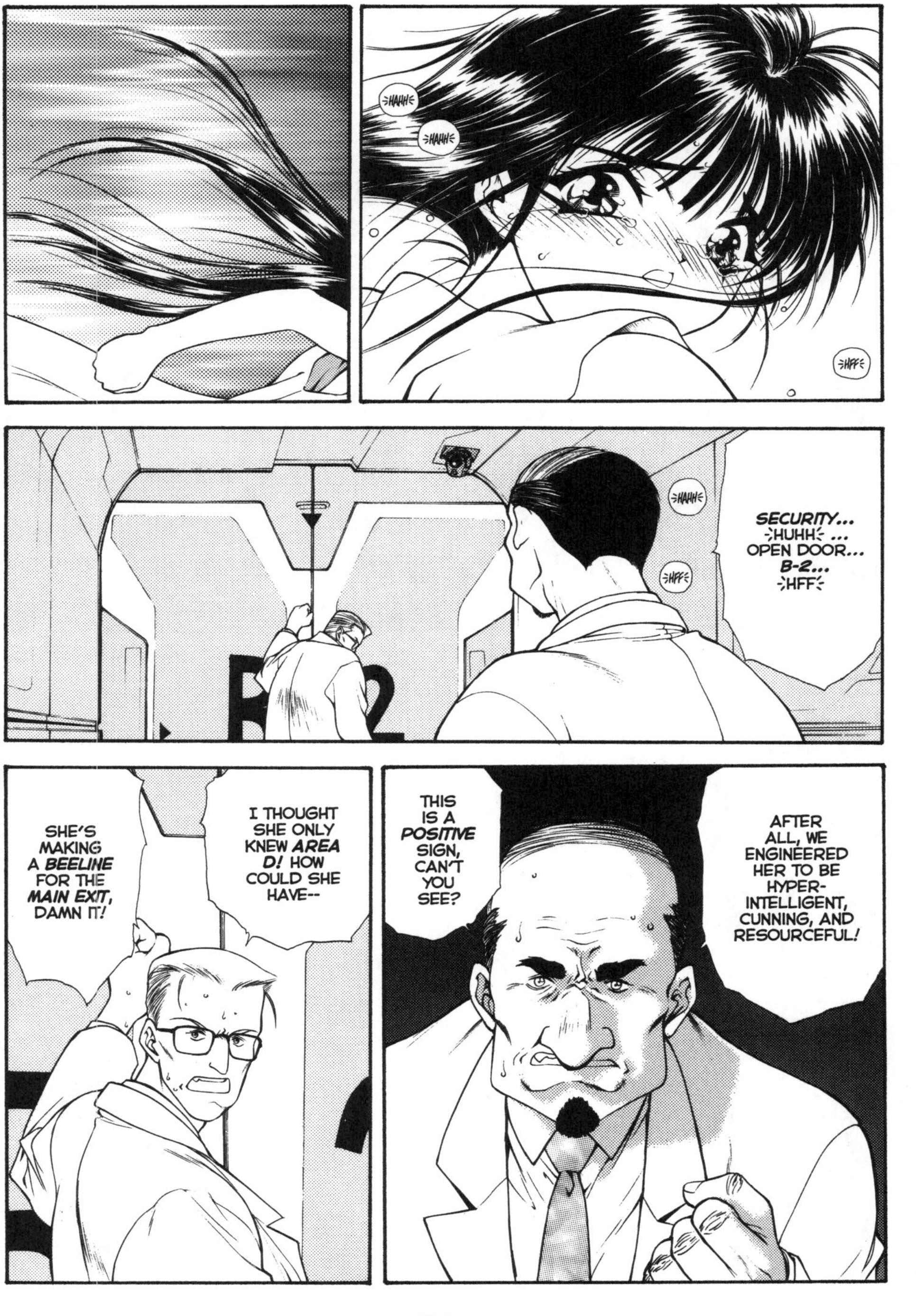
HAHH
HAHH
HFF
HAHH
HFF
SECURITY... HUHH ... OPEN DOOR... B-2... HFF
SHE'S MAKING A BEELINE FOR THE MAIN EXIT, DAMN IT!
I THOUGHT SHE ONLY KNEW AREA D! HOW COULD SHE HAVE--
THIS IS A POSITIVE SIGN, CAN'T YOU SEE?
AFTER ALL, WE ENGINEERED HER TO BE HYPER-INTELLIGENT, CUNNING, AND RESOURCEFUL!

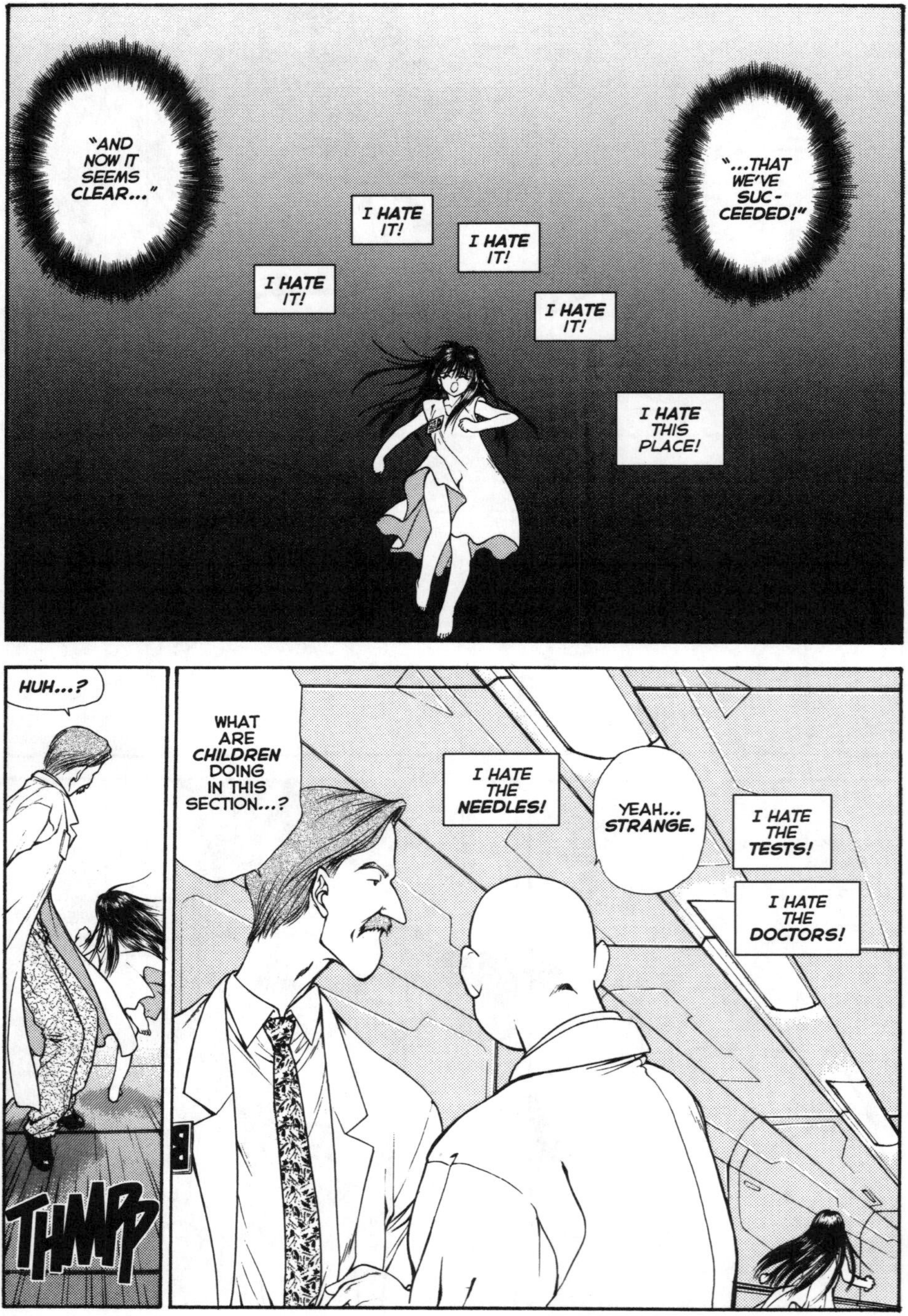
"AND NOW IT SEEMS CLEAR..."
I HATE IT!
I HATE IT!
I HATE IT!
I HATE IT!
"...THAT WE'VE SUC-CEEDED!"
I HATE THIS PLACE!
HUH...?
THMPB
WHAT ARE CHILDREN DOING IN THIS SECTION...?
I HATE THE NEEDLES!
YEAH... STRANGE.
I HATE THE TESTS!
I HATE THE DOCTORS!

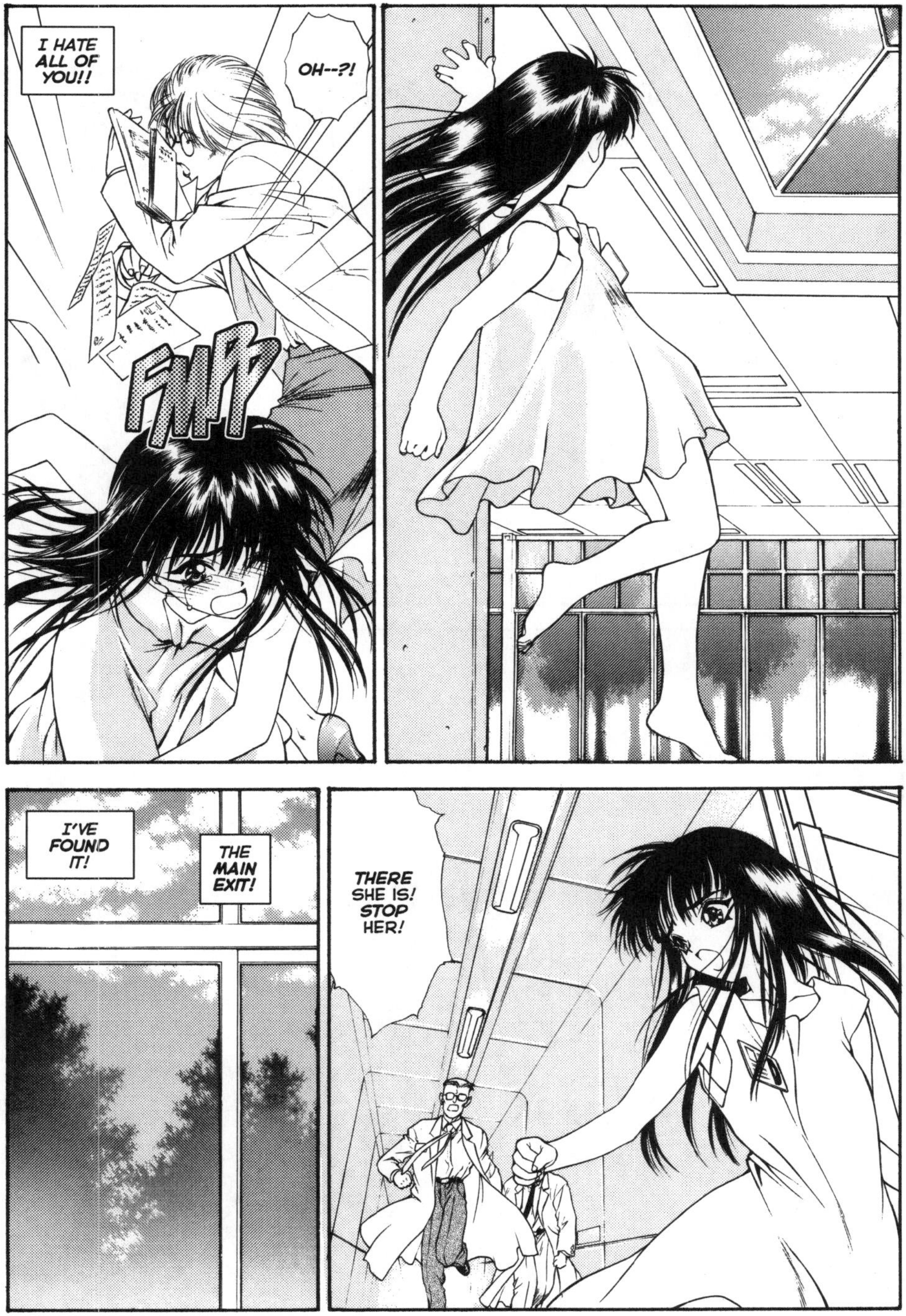
I HATE ALL OF YOU!!
OH--?!
FWP
I'VE FOUND IT!
THE MAIN EXIT!
THERE SHE IS! STOP HER!

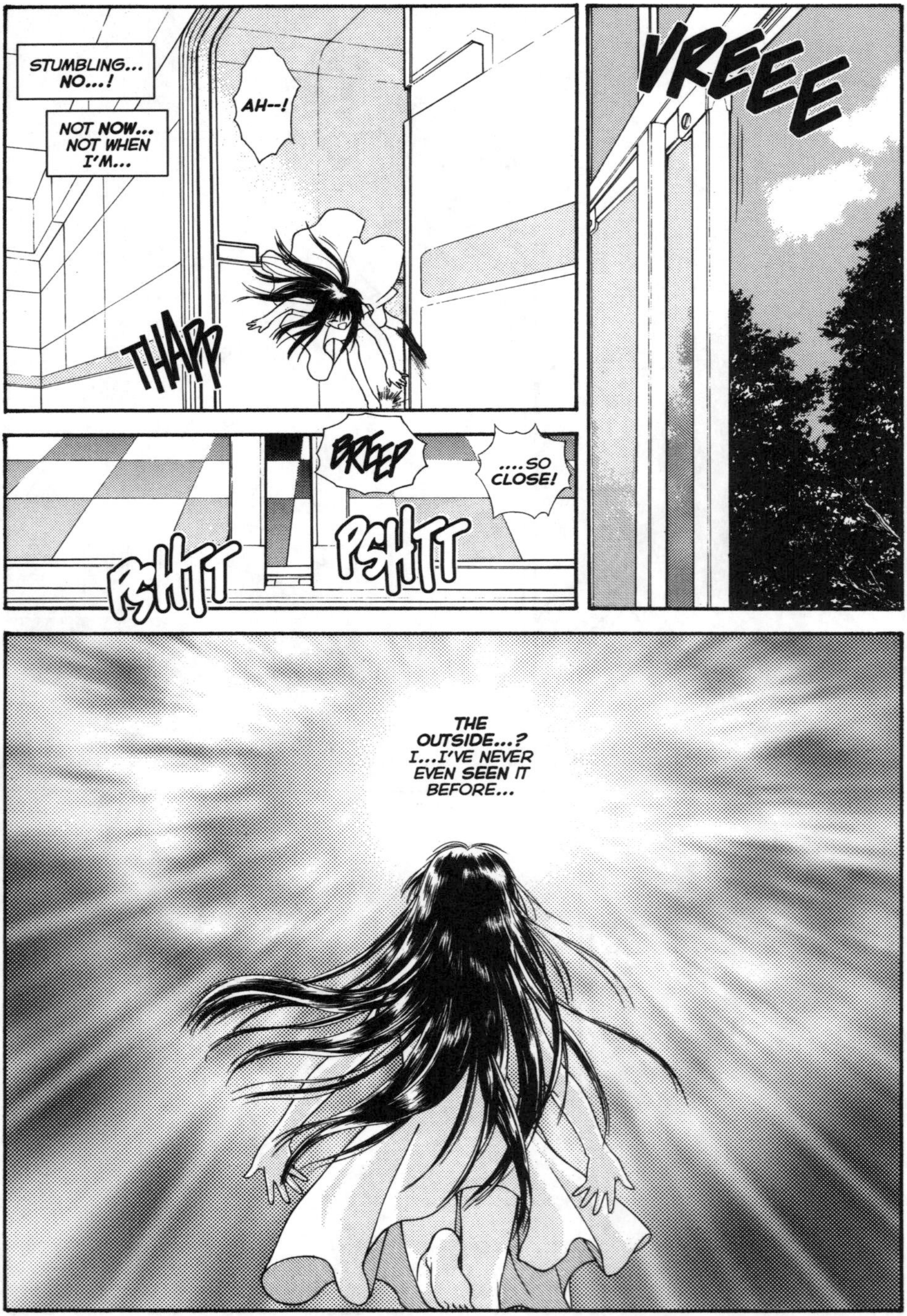
STUMBLING... NO...!
NOT NOW... NOT WHEN I'M...
AH--!
THAPP
BREEP
....SO CLOSE!
PSHTT
PSHTT
VREEE
THE OUTSIDE...? I...I'VE NEVER EVEN SEEN IT BEFORE...

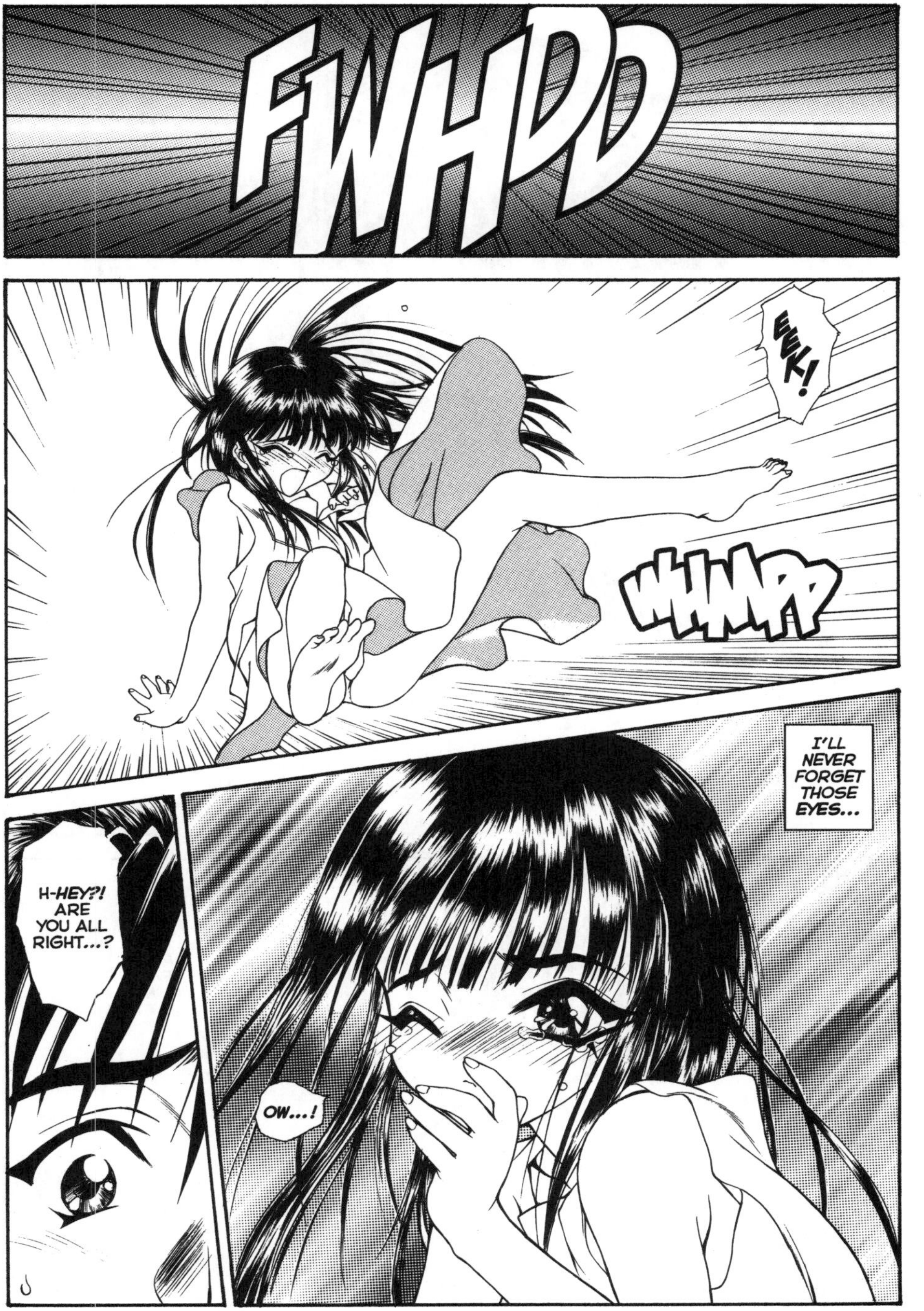
FWHDD
EEEK!
WHAPP
H-*HEY?!* ARE YOU ALL RIGHT...?
I'LL NEVER FORGET THOSE EYES...
OW...!

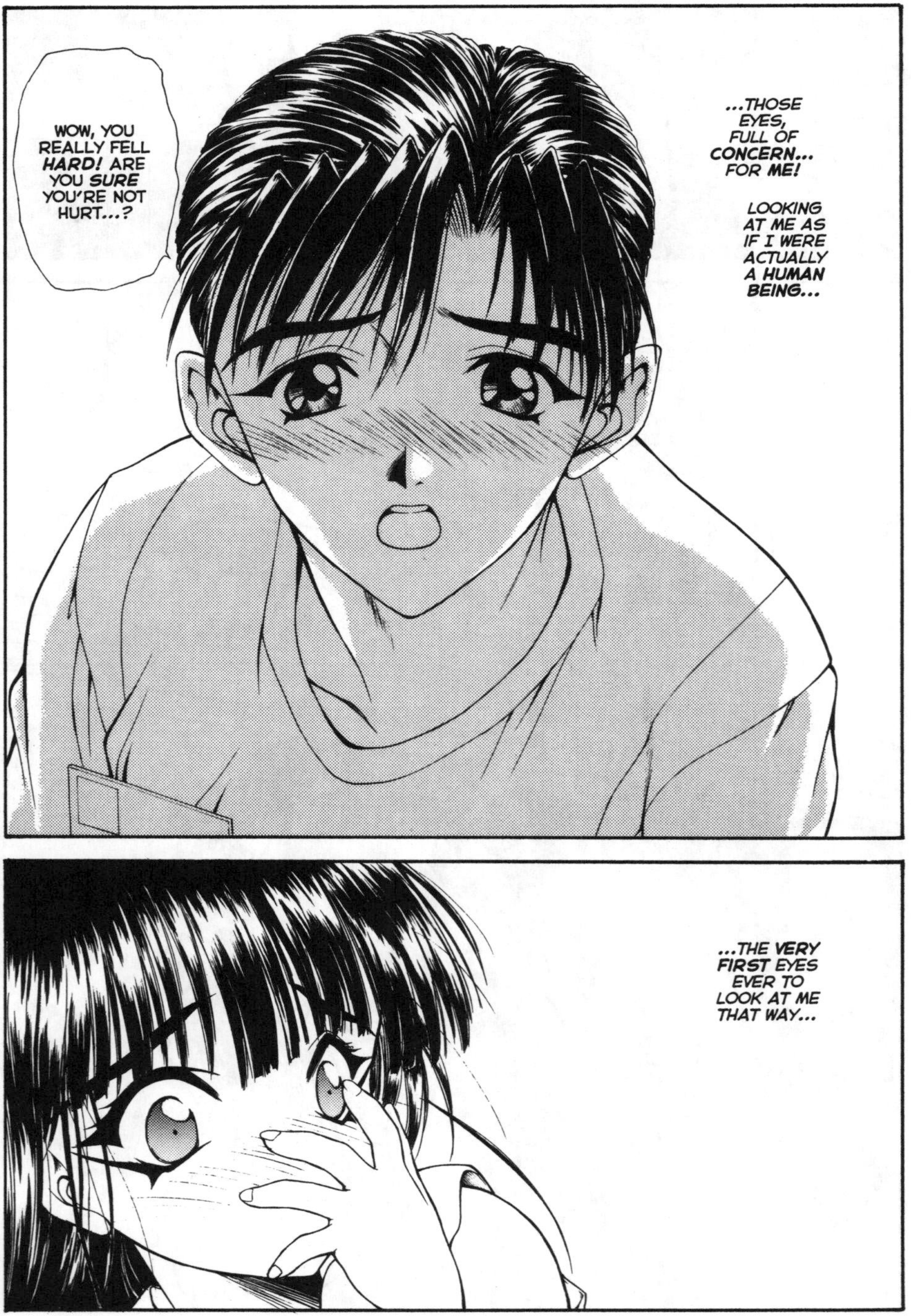
WOW, YOU REALLY FELL *HARD!* ARE YOU *SURE* YOU'RE NOT HURT...?
...THOSE EYES, FULL OF **CONCERN...** FOR **ME!**
LOOKING AT ME AS IF I WERE ACTUALLY A **HUMAN BEING...**
...THE **VERY FIRST** EYES EVER TO LOOK AT ME THAT WAY...

ACT 21

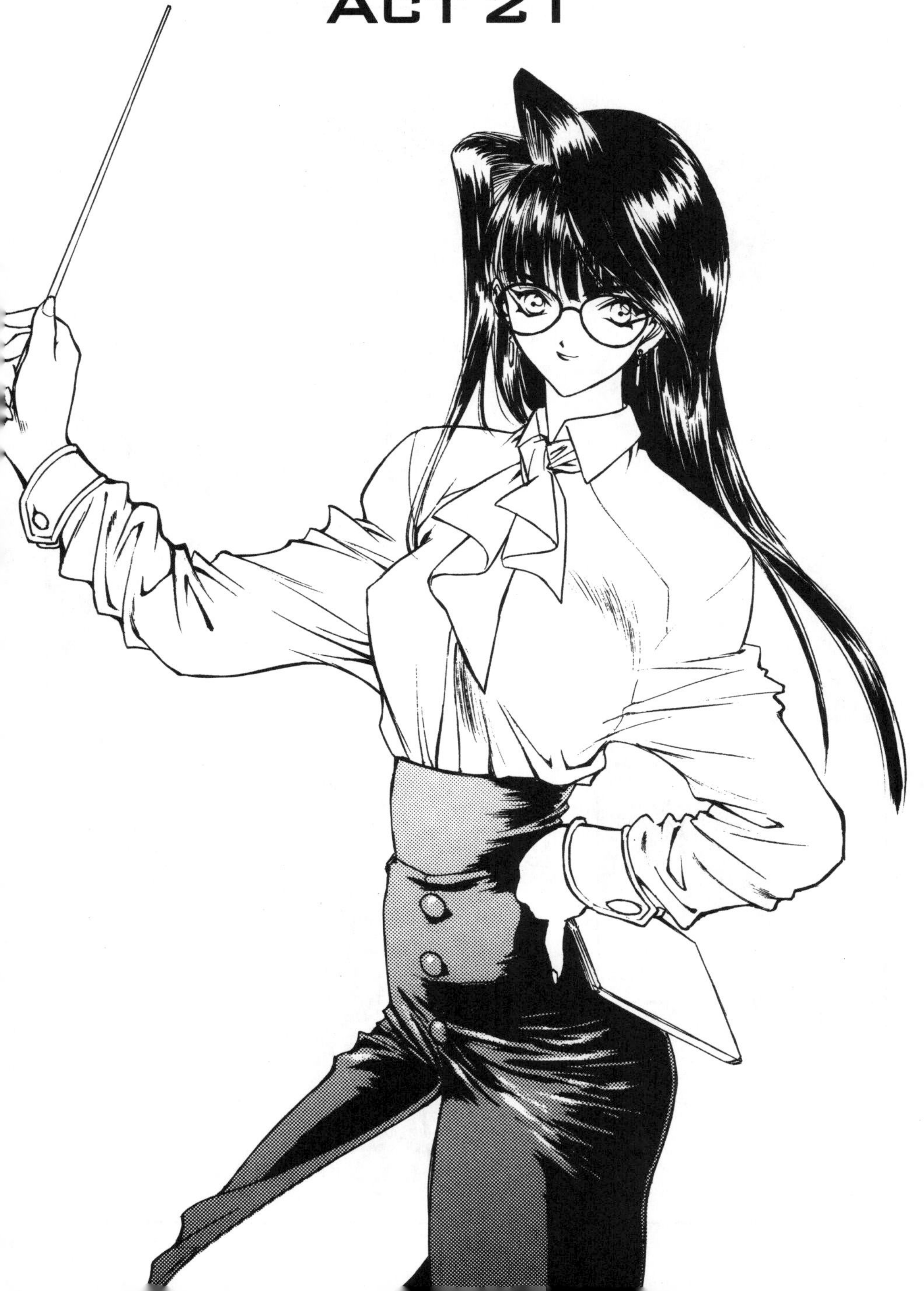

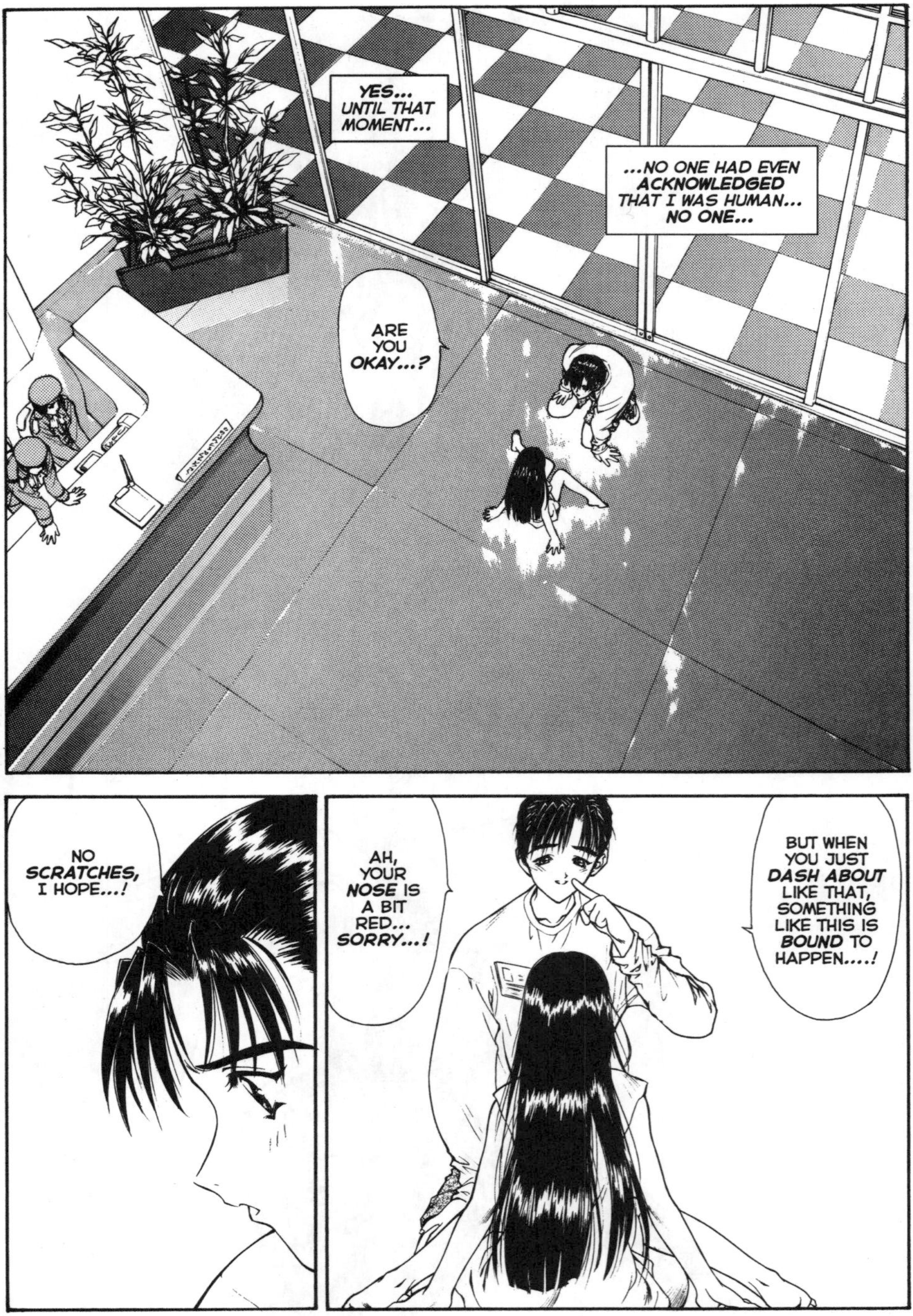
YES... UNTIL THAT MOMENT...
...NO ONE HAD EVEN ACKNOWLEDGED THAT I WAS HUMAN... NO ONE...
ARE YOU OKAY...?
NO SCRATCHES, I HOPE...!
AH, YOUR NOSE IS A BIT RED... SORRY...!
BUT WHEN YOU JUST DASH ABOUT LIKE THAT, SOMETHING LIKE THIS IS BOUND TO HAPPEN....!

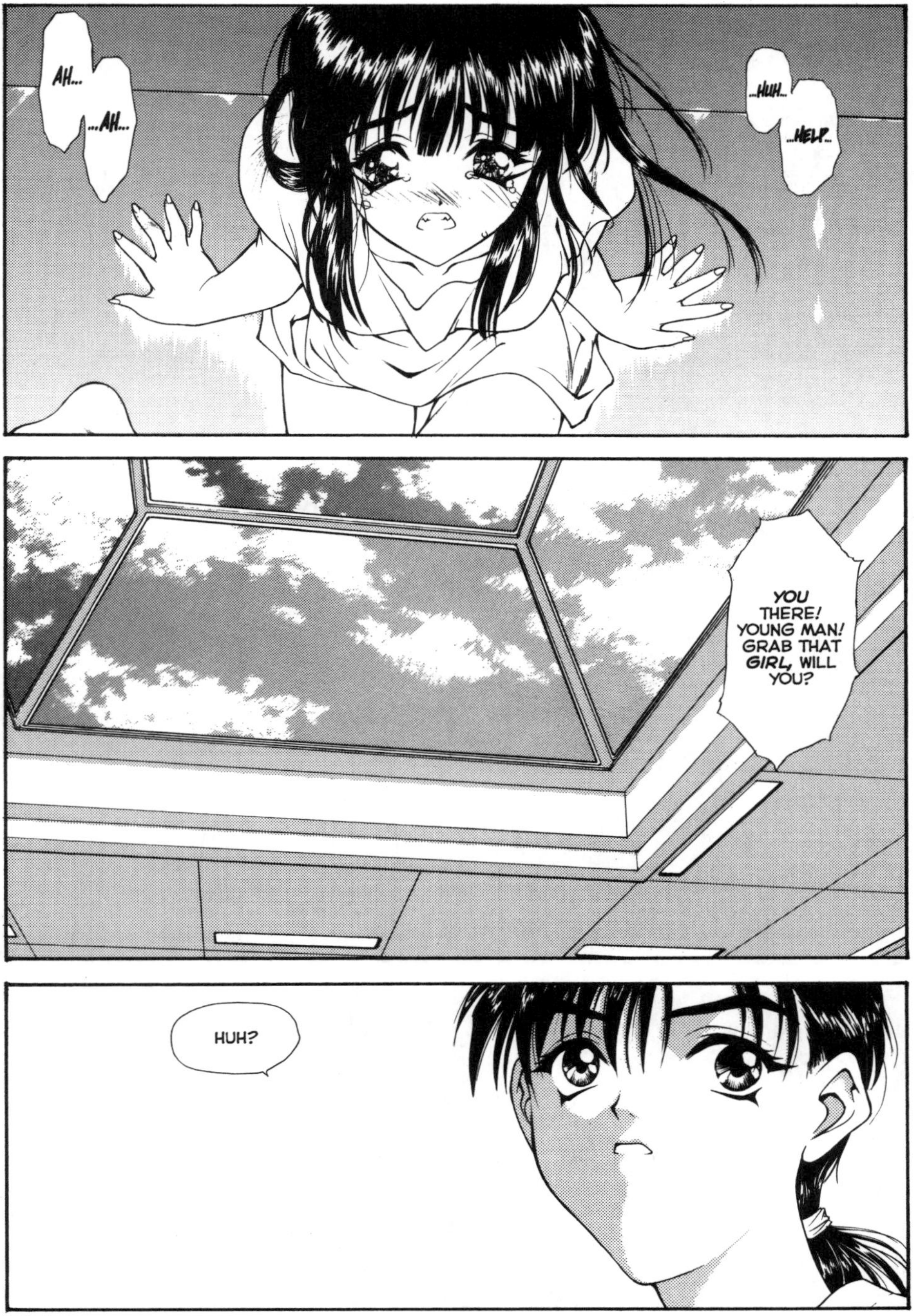
AH...
...AH...
...HUH...
...HELP...
YOU THERE! YOUNG MAN! GRAB THAT GIRL, WILL YOU?
HUH?

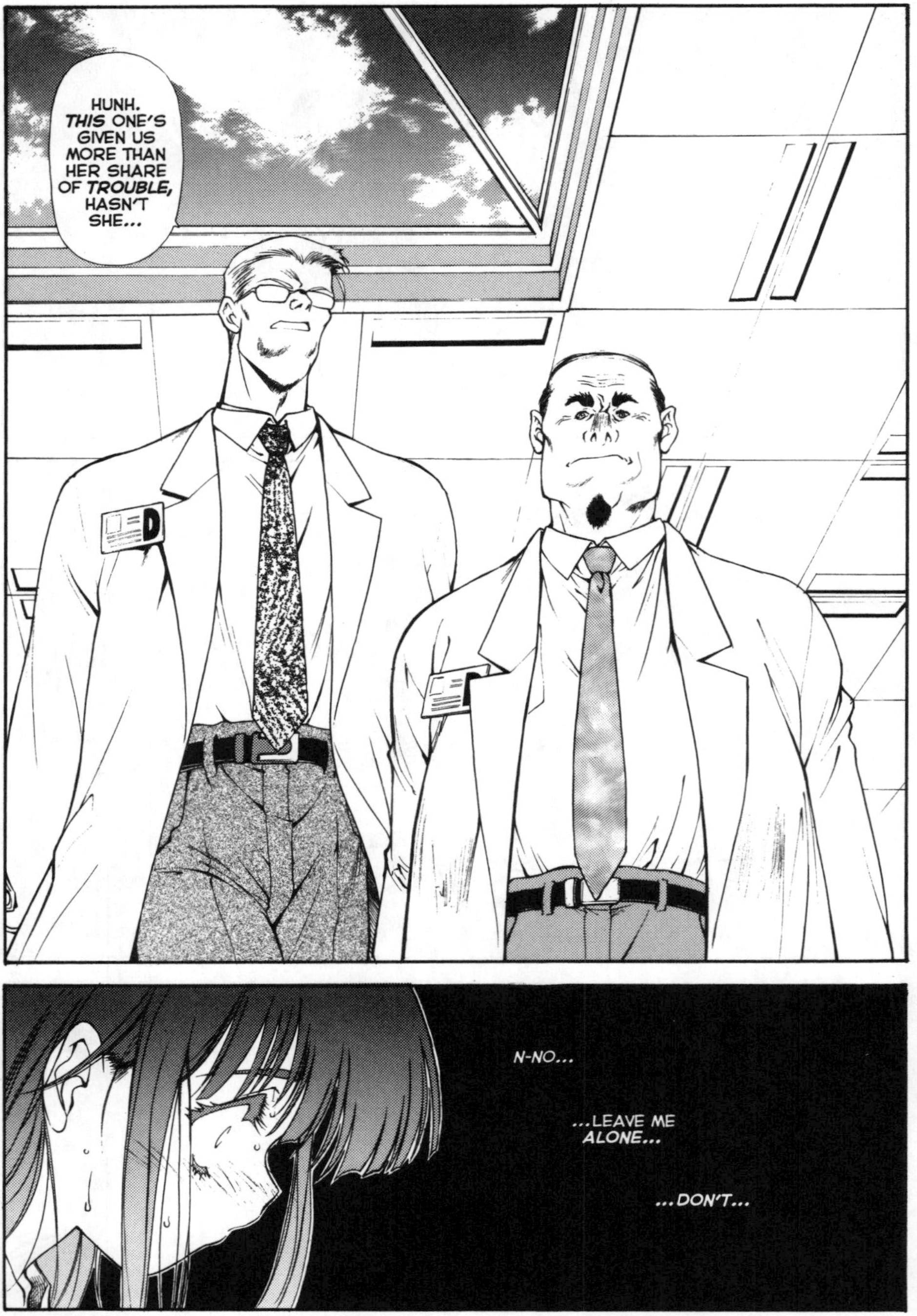
HUNH. *THIS* ONE'S GIVEN US MORE THAN HER SHARE OF *TROUBLE,* HASN'T SHE...
N-NO...
...LEAVE ME *ALONE*...
...DON'T...

THERE, NOW. BE A *GOOD* GIRL, WON'T YOU...

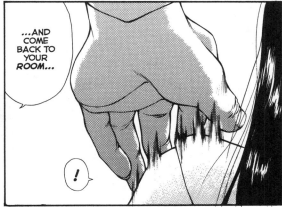

...AND COME BACK TO YOUR *ROOM*...

!

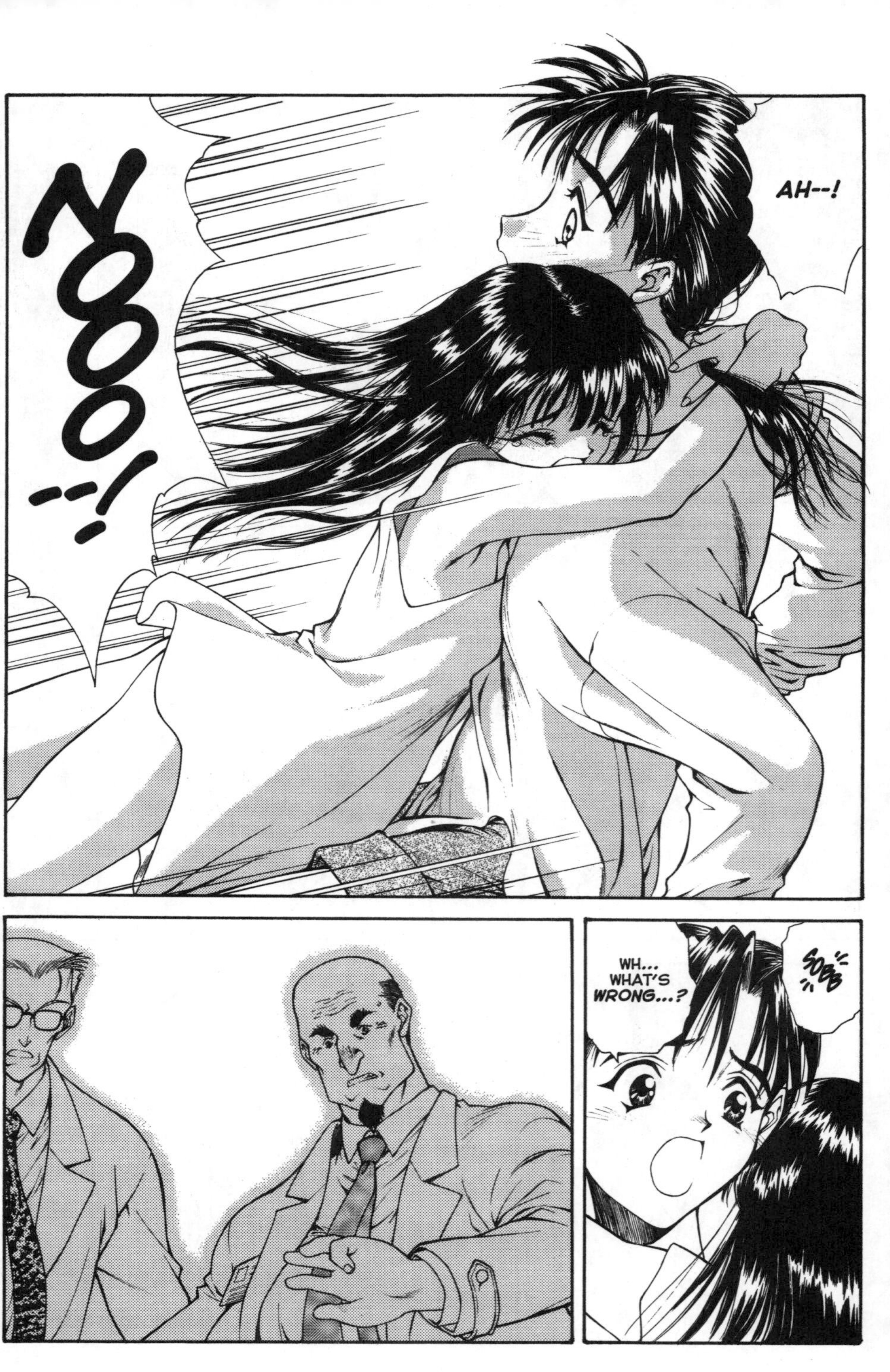
NOOO!--!
AH--!
WH... WHAT'S WRONG...?
SOBB

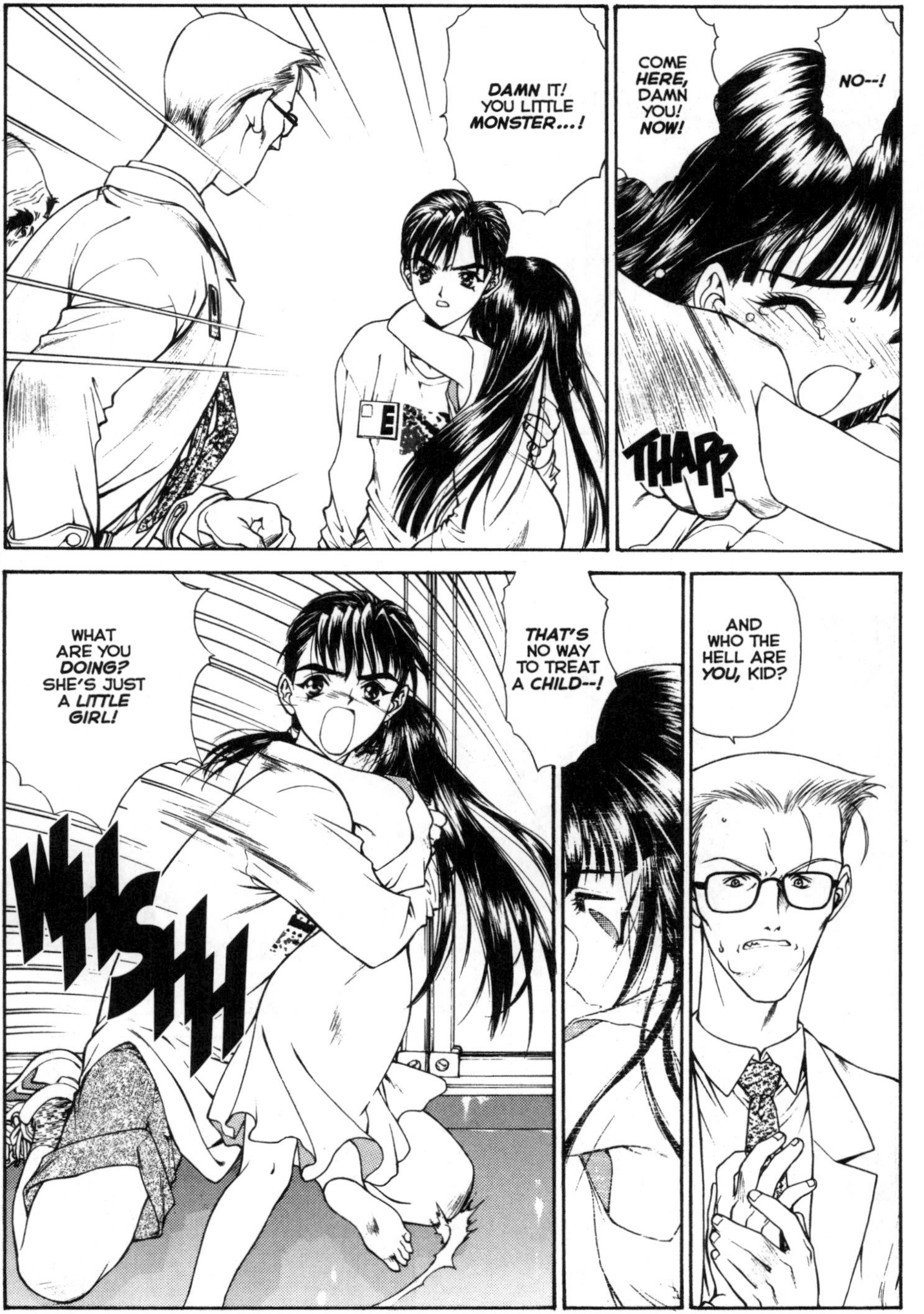
DAMN IT! YOU LITTLE MONSTER...!
COME HERE, DAMN YOU! NOW!
NO--!
THAPP
WHAT ARE YOU DOING? SHE'S JUST A LITTLE GIRL!
WHSHH
THAT'S NO WAY TO TREAT A CHILD--!
AND WHO THE HELL ARE YOU, KID?

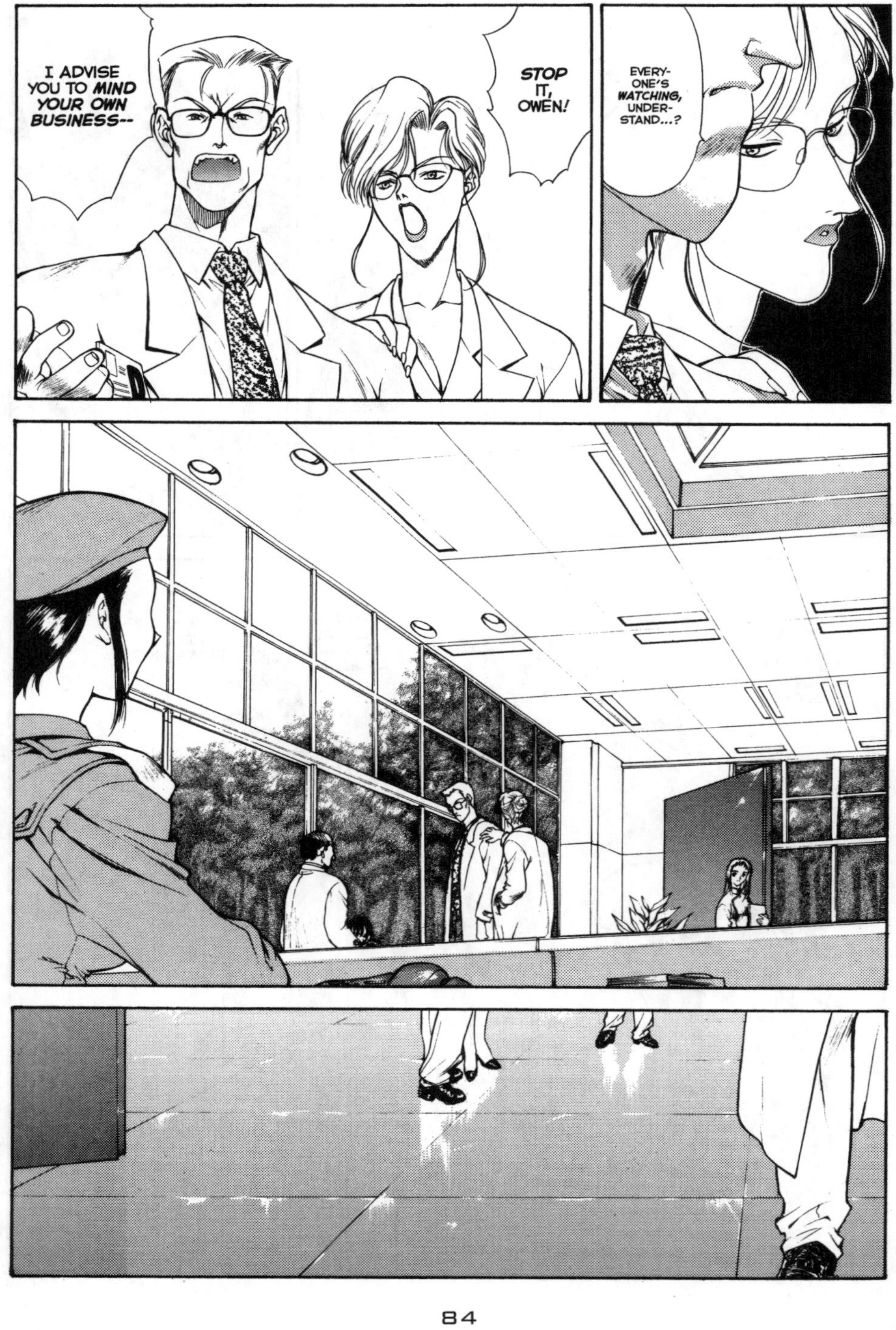

I ADVISE YOU TO MIND YOUR OWN BUSINESS--
STOP IT, OWEN!
EVERY-ONE'S WATCHING, UNDER-STAND...?

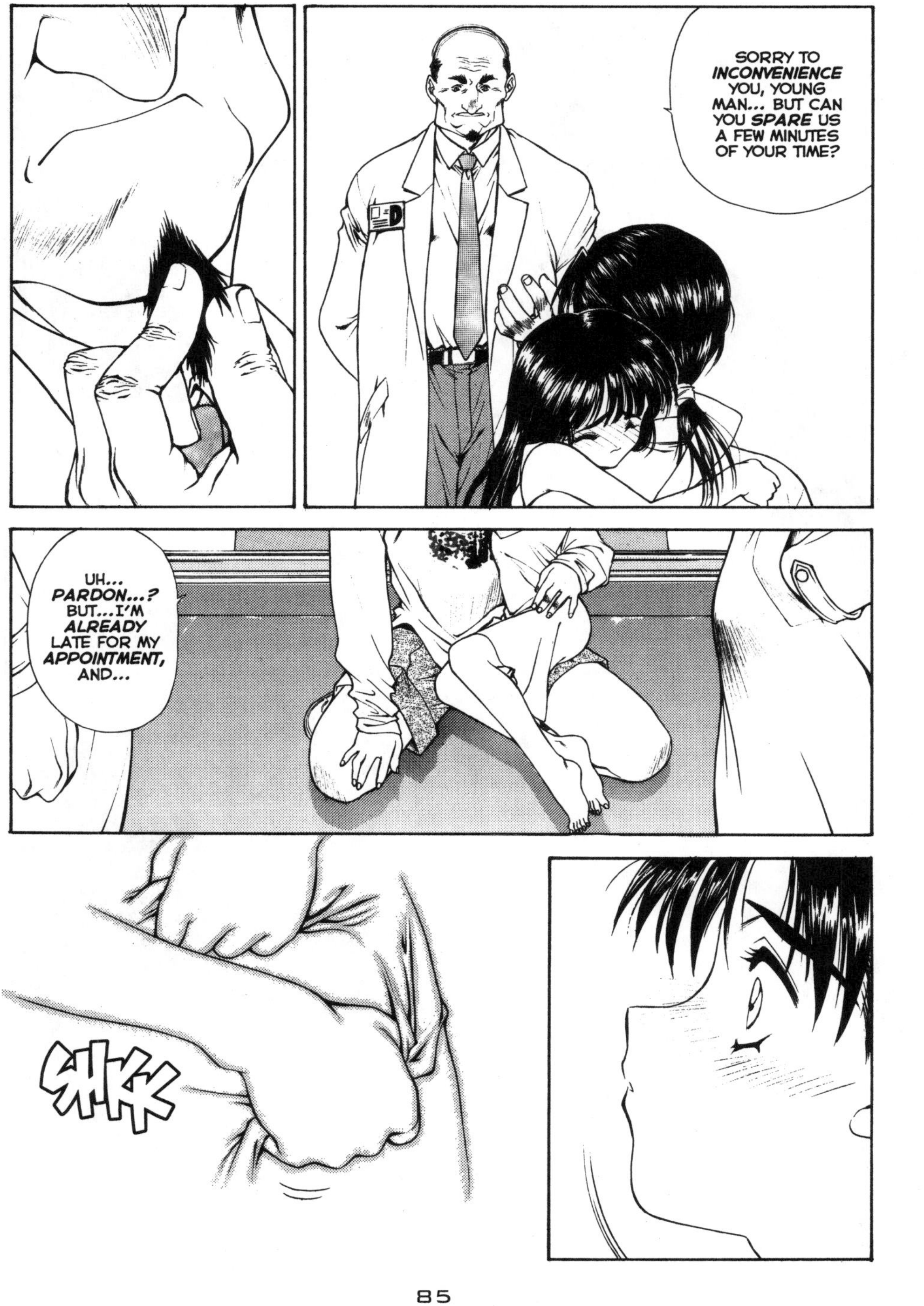
SORRY TO INCONVENIENCE YOU, YOUNG MAN... BUT CAN YOU SPARE US A FEW MINUTES OF YOUR TIME?
UH... PARDON...? BUT...I'M ALREADY LATE FOR MY APPOINTMENT, AND...
SHKK

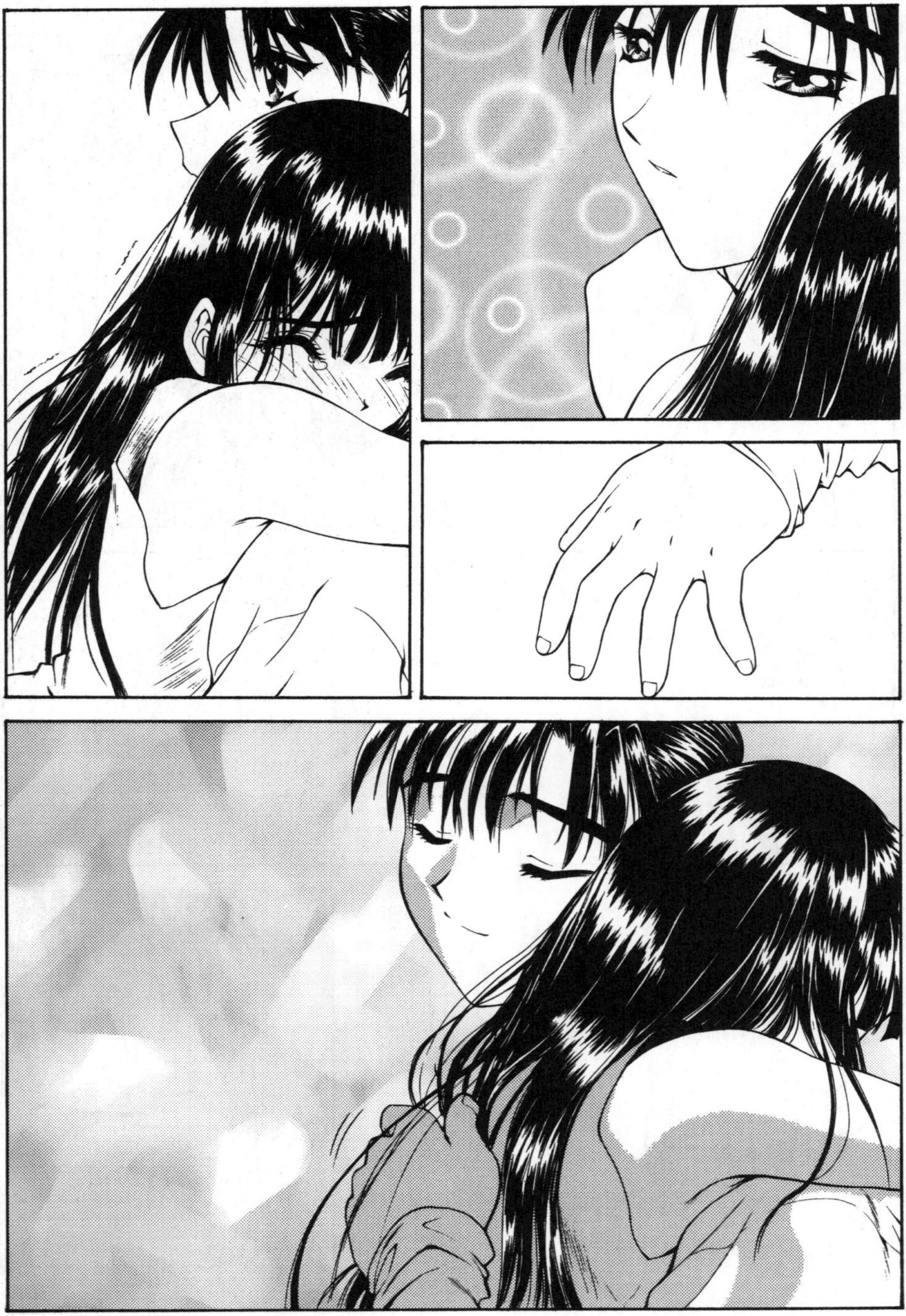

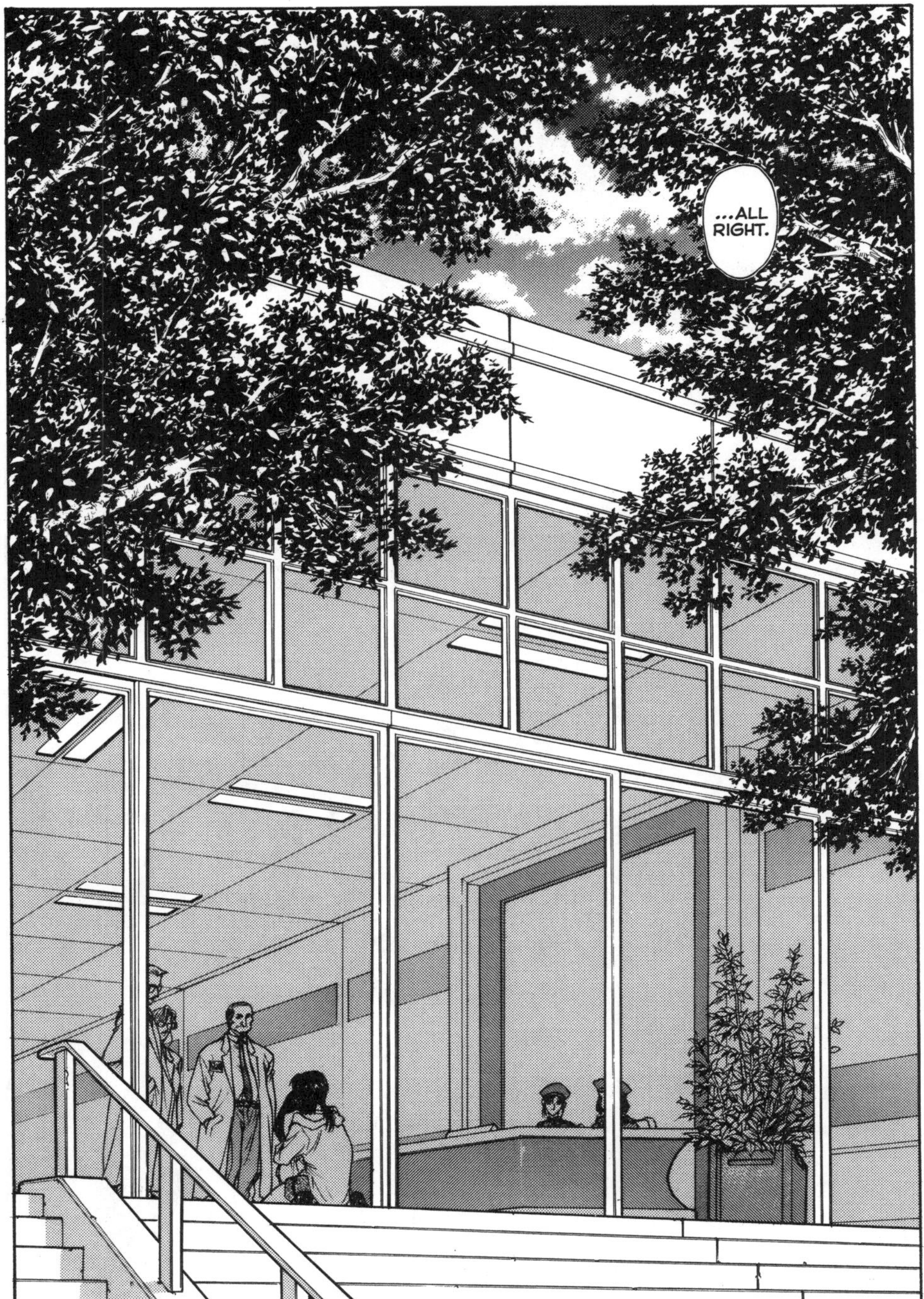
...ALL RIGHT.

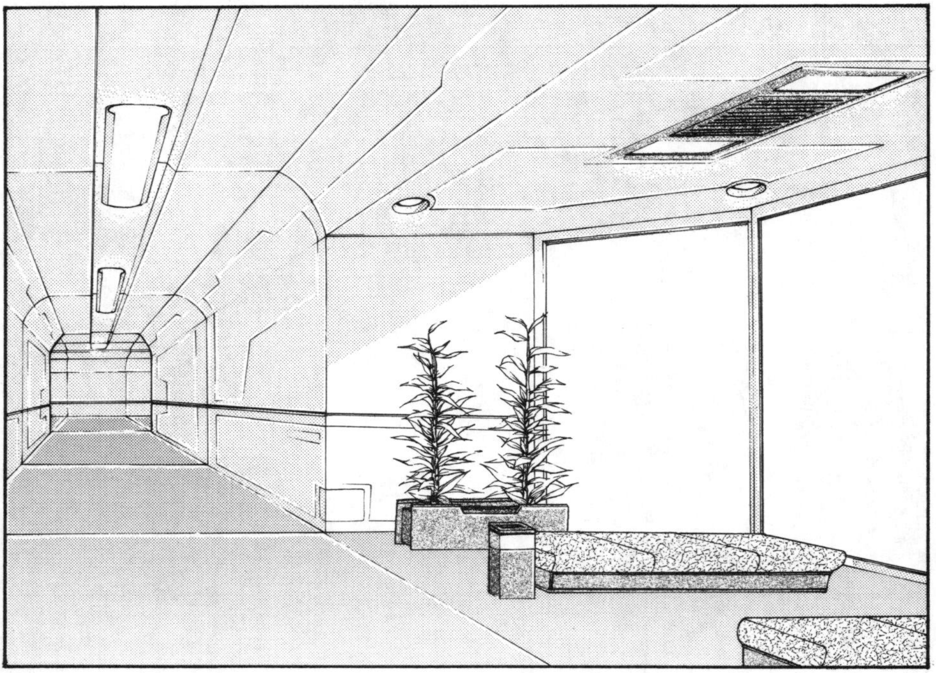

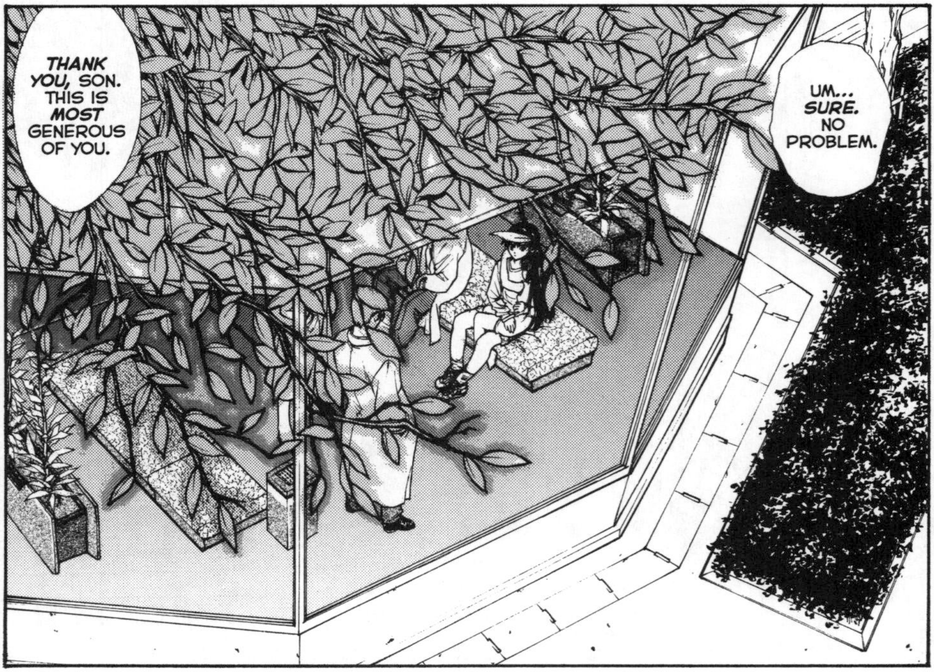

THANK YOU, SON. THIS IS MOST GENEROUS OF YOU.
UM... SURE. NO PROBLEM.

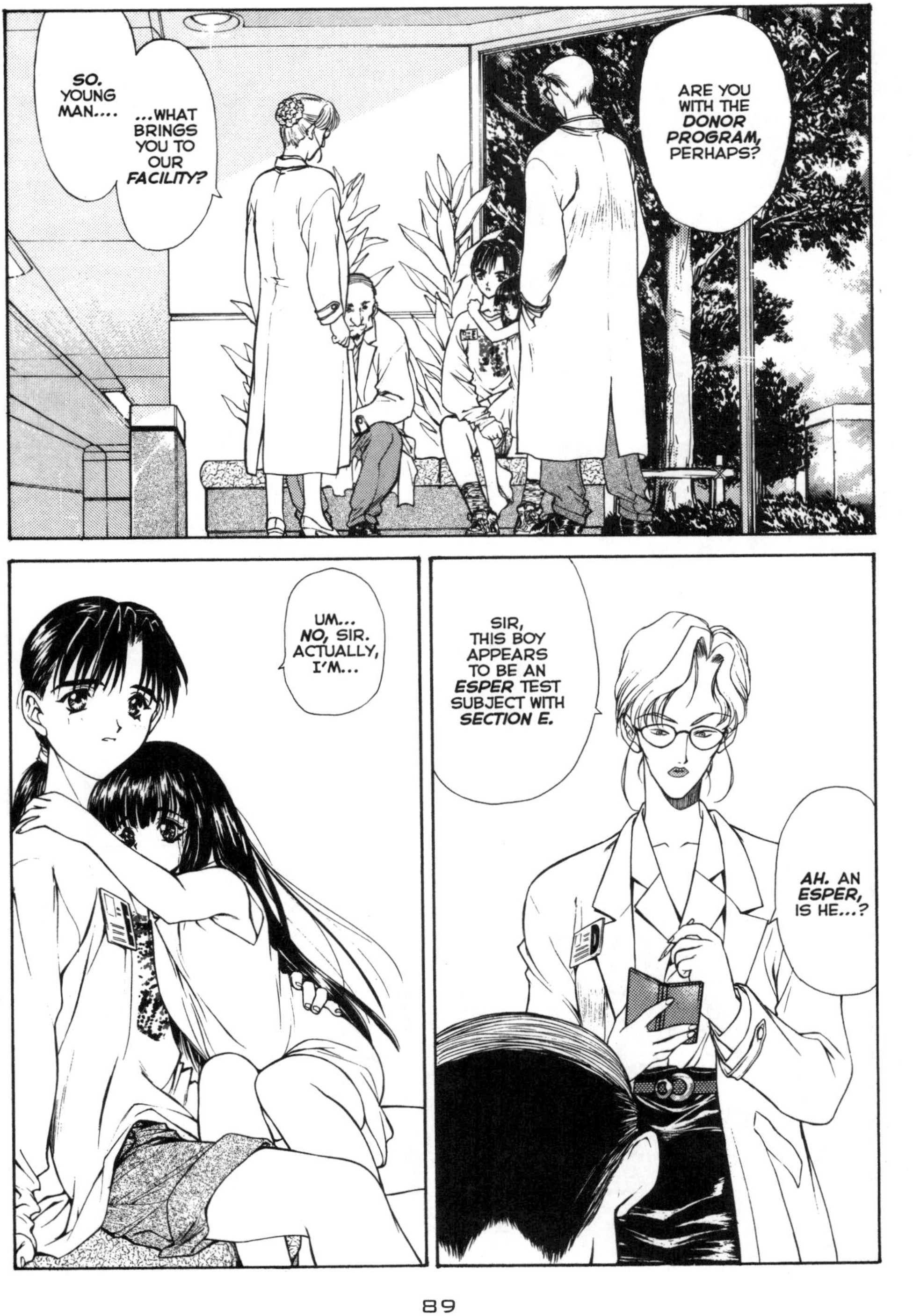
SO. YOUNG MAN....
...WHAT BRINGS YOU TO OUR FACILITY?
ARE YOU WITH THE DONOR PROGRAM, PERHAPS?
UM... NO, SIR. ACTUALLY, I'M...
SIR, THIS BOY APPEARS TO BE AN ESPER TEST SUBJECT WITH SECTION E.
AH. AN ESPER, IS HE...?

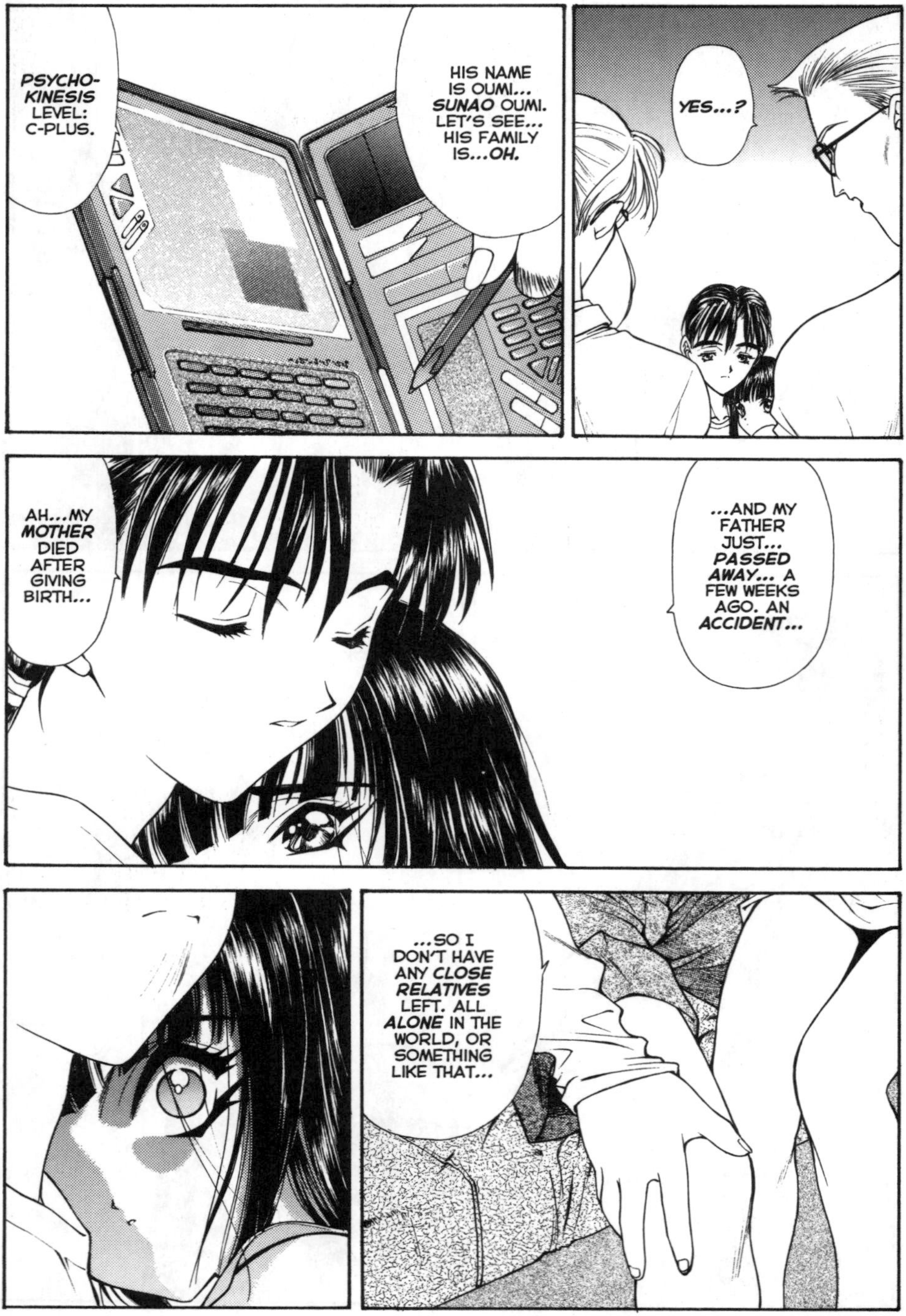
PSYCHO-KINESIS LEVEL: C-PLUS.
HIS NAME IS OUMI... SUNAO OUMI. LET'S SEE... HIS FAMILY IS...OH.
YES...?
AH...MY MOTHER DIED AFTER GIVING BIRTH...
...AND MY FATHER JUST... PASSED AWAY... A FEW WEEKS AGO. AN ACCIDENT...
...SO I DON'T HAVE ANY CLOSE RELATIVES LEFT. ALL ALONE IN THE WORLD, OR SOMETHING LIKE THAT...

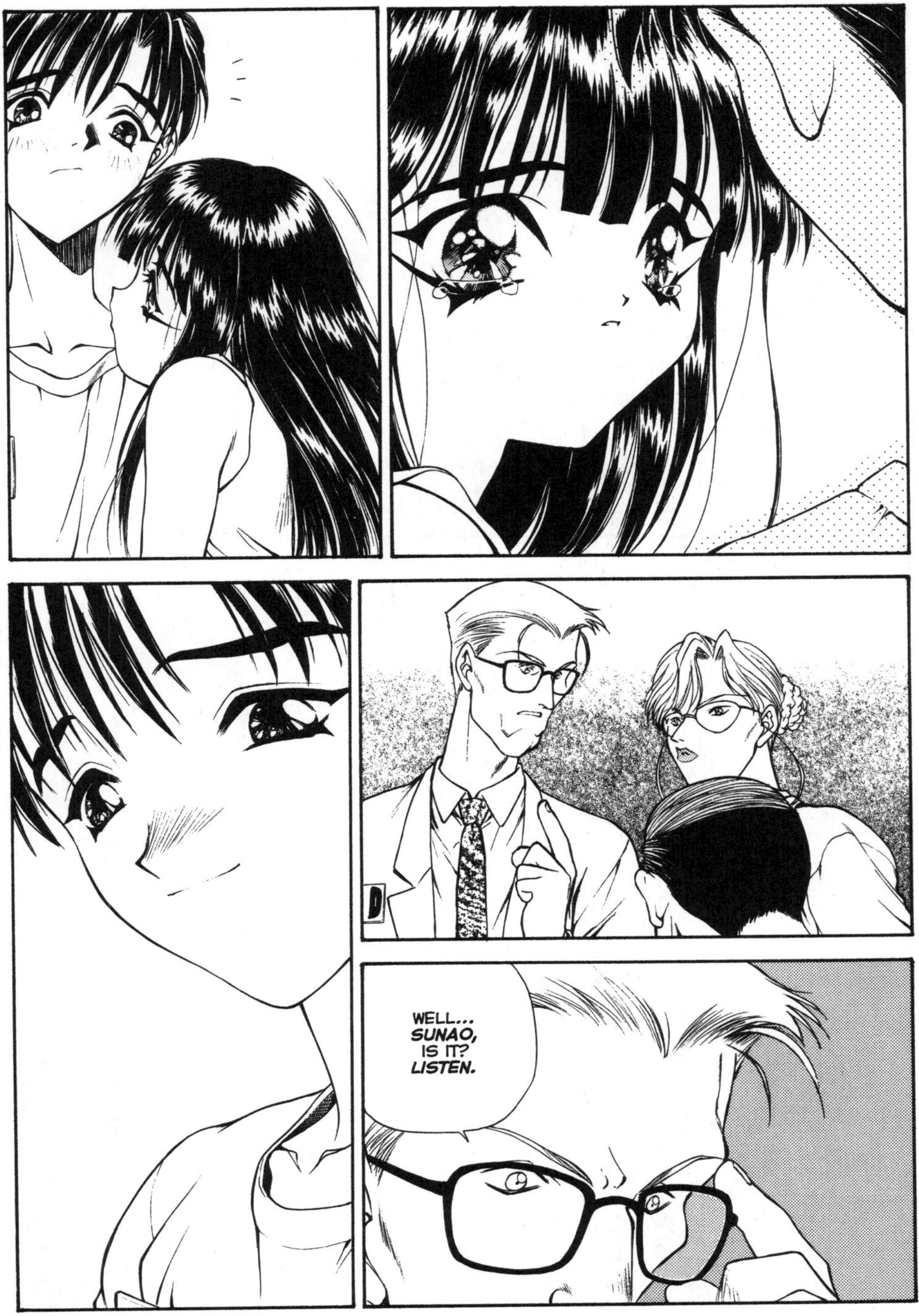
WELL... SUNAO, IS IT? LISTEN.

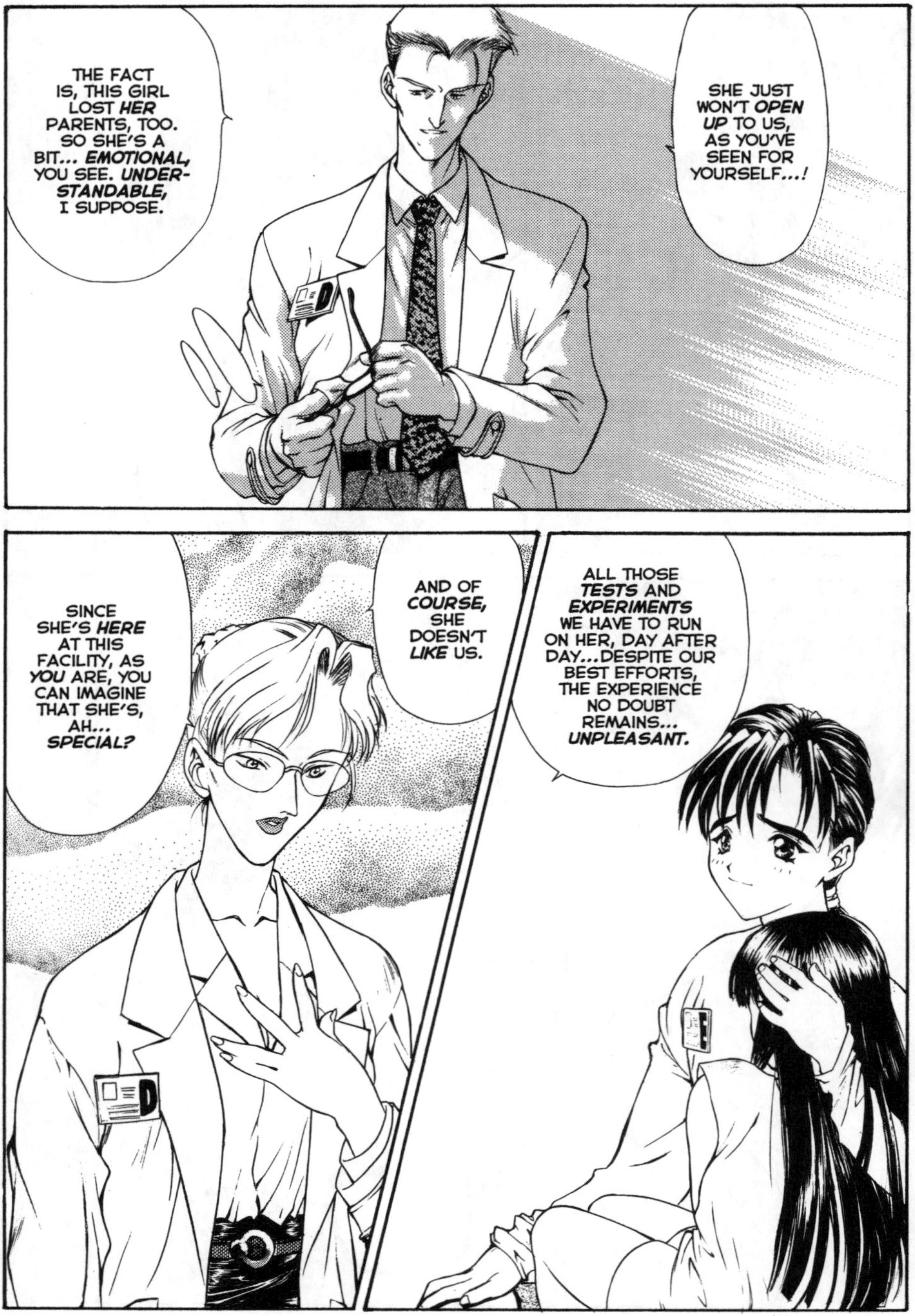
THE FACT IS, THIS GIRL LOST *HER* PARENTS, TOO. SO SHE'S A BIT... *EMOTIONAL,* YOU SEE. *UNDER-STANDABLE,* I SUPPOSE.
SHE JUST WON'T *OPEN UP* TO US, AS YOU'VE SEEN FOR YOURSELF...!
SINCE SHE'S *HERE* AT THIS FACILITY, AS *YOU* ARE, YOU CAN IMAGINE THAT SHE'S, AH... *SPECIAL?*
AND OF *COURSE,* SHE DOESN'T *LIKE* US.
ALL THOSE *TESTS* AND *EXPERIMENTS* WE HAVE TO RUN ON HER, DAY AFTER DAY...DESPITE OUR BEST EFFORTS, THE EXPERIENCE NO DOUBT REMAINS... *UNPLEASANT.*

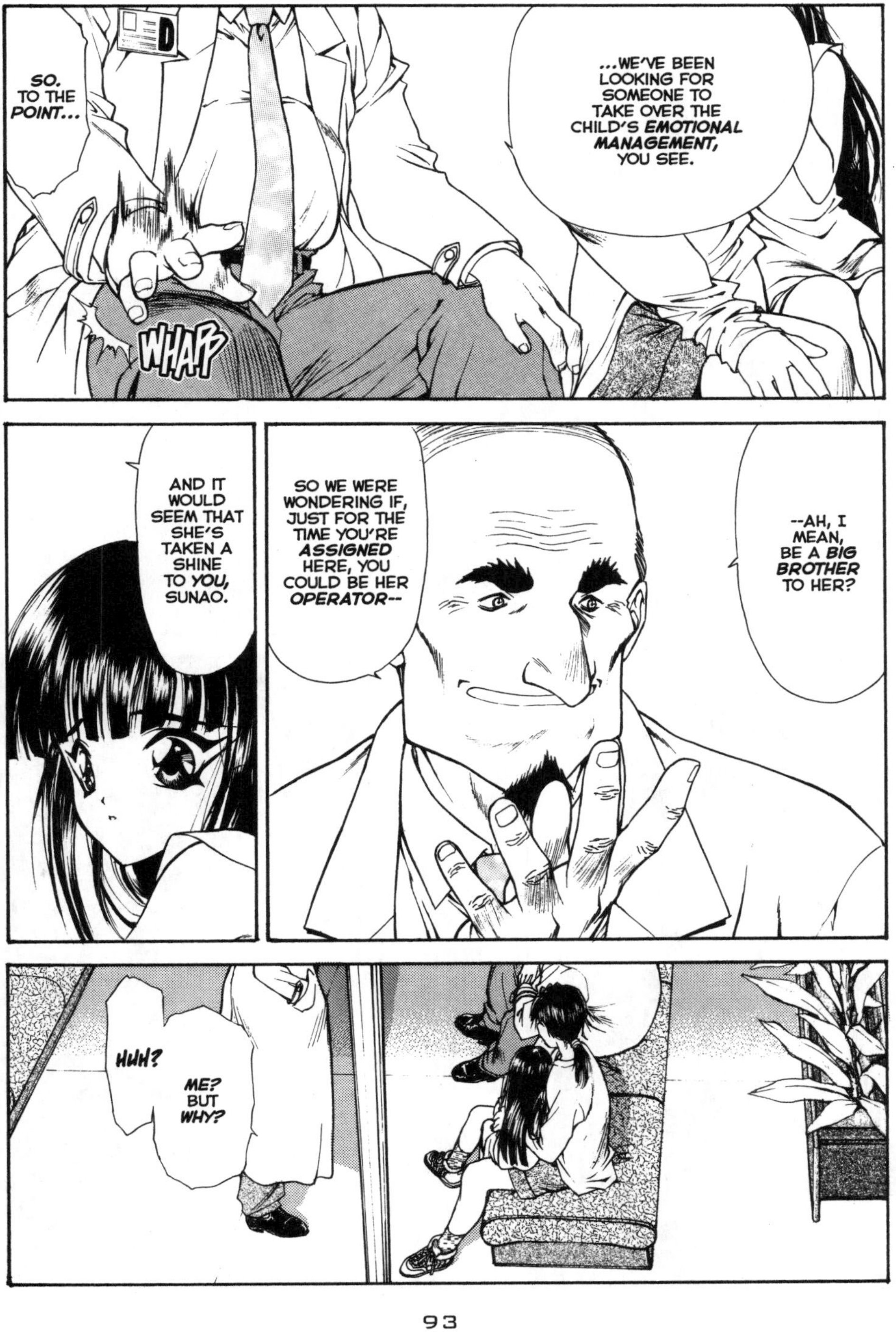
SO. TO THE *POINT...*
WHAP
...WE'VE BEEN LOOKING FOR SOMEONE TO TAKE OVER THE CHILD'S ***EMOTIONAL MANAGEMENT,*** YOU SEE.
AND IT WOULD SEEM THAT SHE'S TAKEN A SHINE TO *YOU,* SUNAO.
SO WE WERE WONDERING IF, JUST FOR THE TIME YOU'RE ***ASSIGNED*** HERE, YOU COULD BE HER ***OPERATOR--***
--AH, I MEAN, BE A ***BIG BROTHER*** TO HER?
HUH?
ME? BUT ***WHY?***

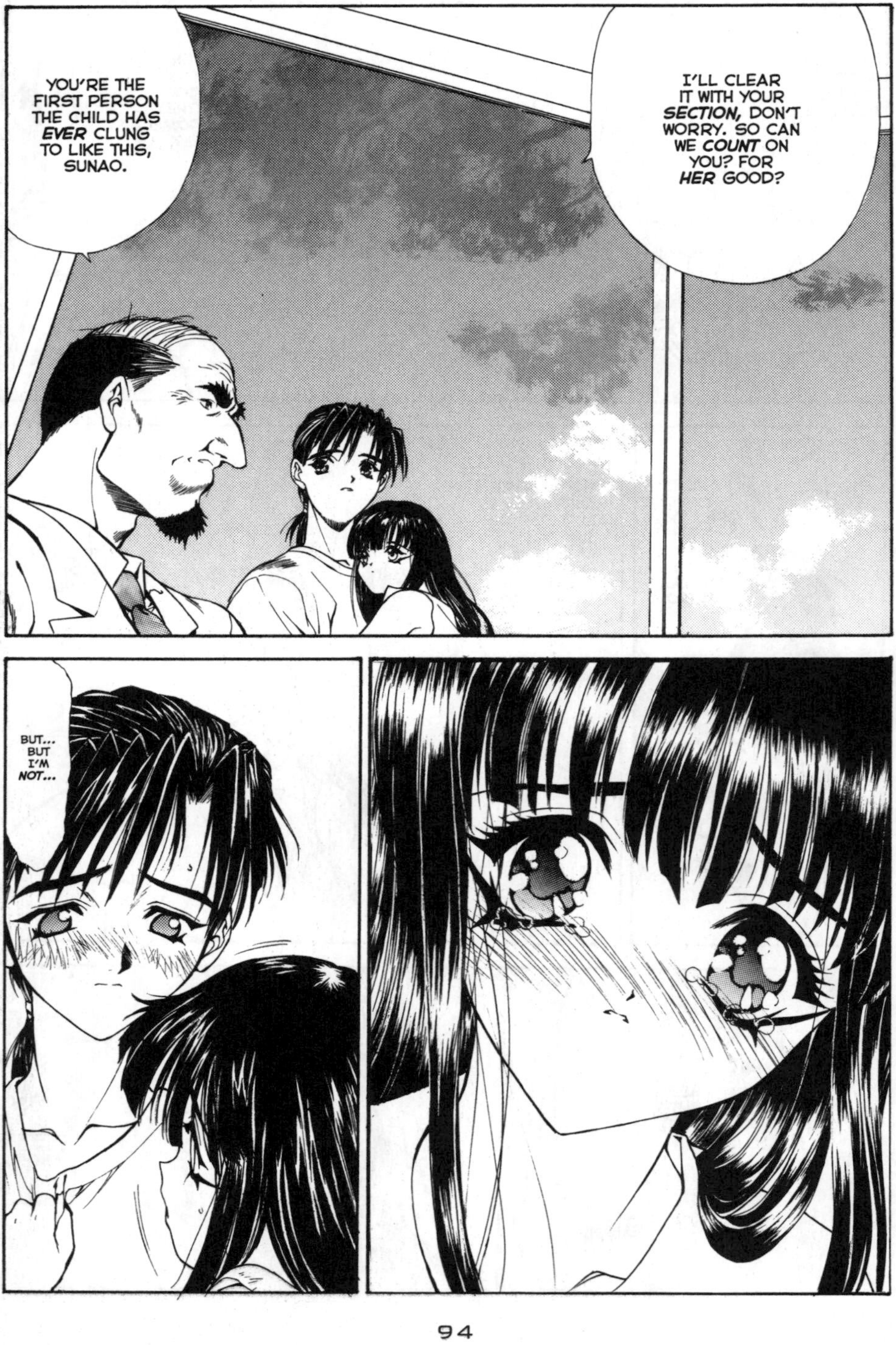
YOU'RE THE FIRST PERSON THE CHILD HAS EVER CLUNG TO LIKE THIS, SUNAO.
I'LL CLEAR IT WITH YOUR SECTION, DON'T WORRY. SO CAN WE COUNT ON YOU? FOR HER GOOD?
BUT... BUT I'M NOT...

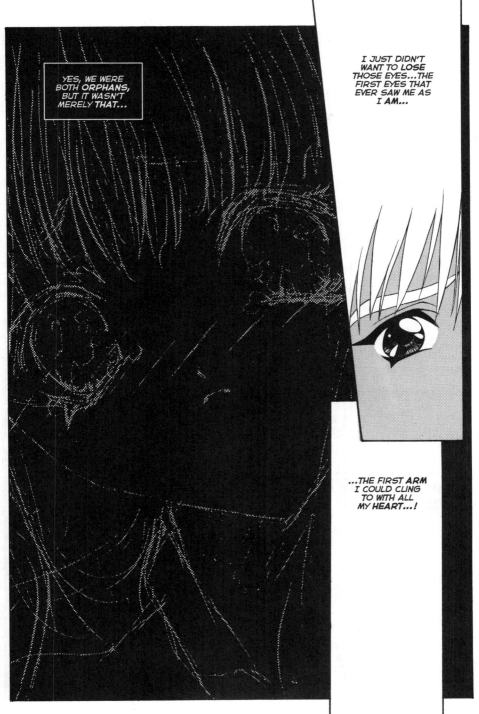

YES, WE WERE BOTH *ORPHANS,* BUT IT WASN'T MERELY *THAT...*

I JUST DIDN'T WANT TO LOSE THOSE EYES...THE FIRST EYES THAT EVER SAW ME AS I AM...

...THE FIRST *ARM* I COULD CLING TO WITH ALL MY *HEART...!*

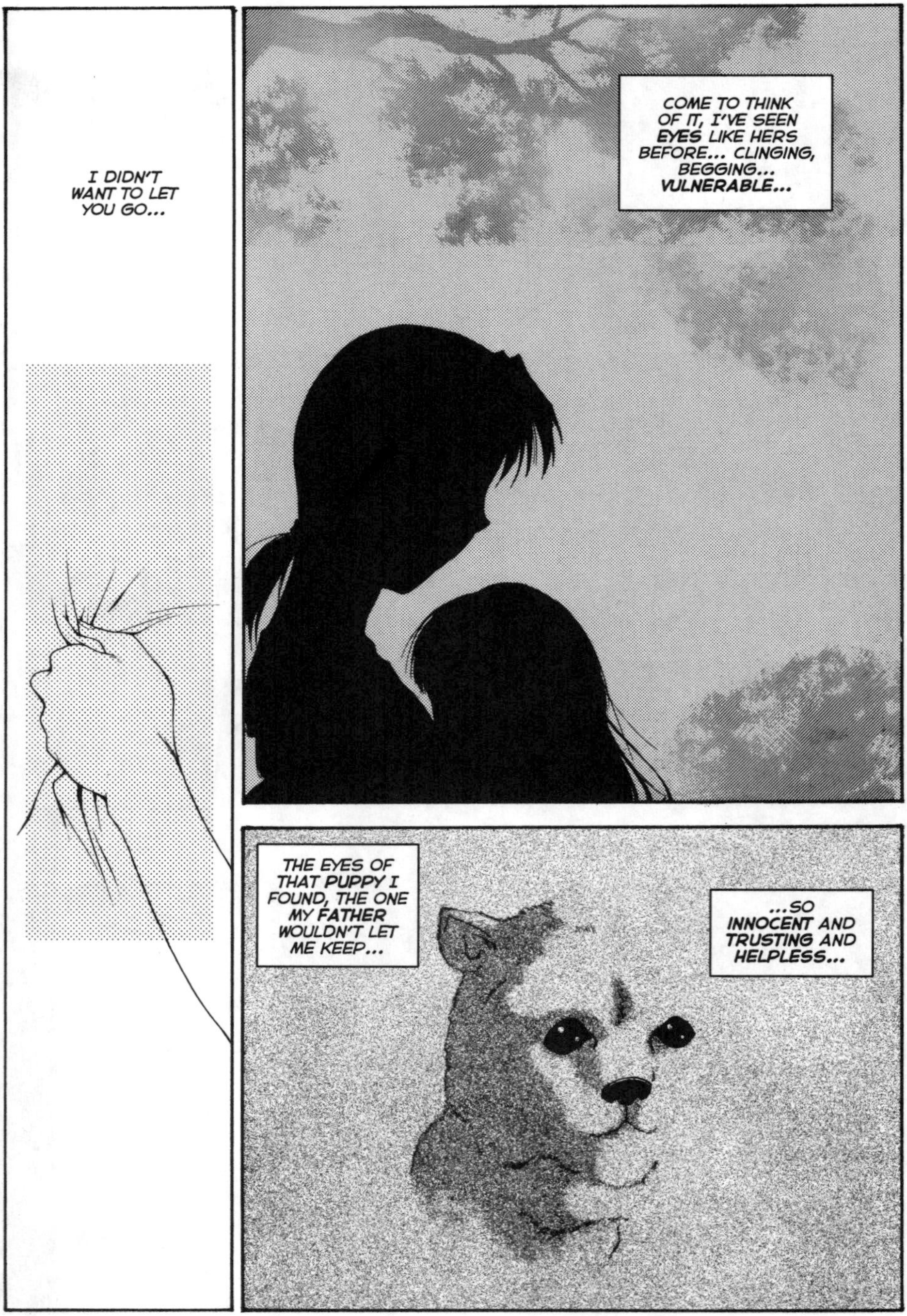
I DIDN'T WANT TO LET YOU GO...
COME TO THINK OF IT, I'VE SEEN EYES LIKE HERS BEFORE... CLINGING, BEGGING... VULNERABLE...
THE EYES OF THAT PUPPY I FOUND, THE ONE MY FATHER WOULDN'T LET ME KEEP...
...SO INNOCENT AND TRUSTING AND HELPLESS...

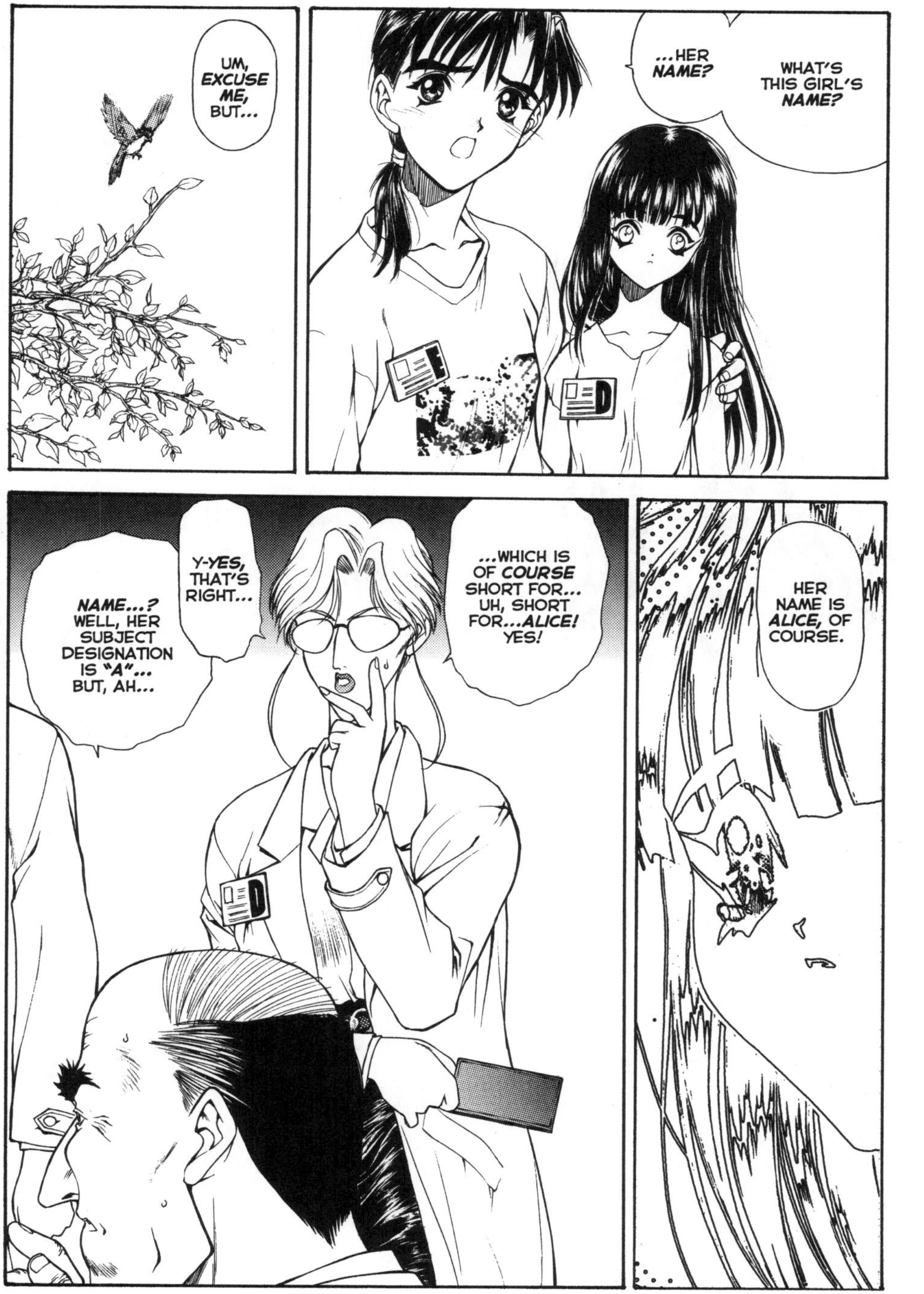
UM, EXCUSE ME, BUT...
...HER NAME?
WHAT'S THIS GIRL'S NAME?
NAME...? WELL, HER SUBJECT DESIGNATION IS "A"... BUT, AH...
Y-YES, THAT'S RIGHT...
...WHICH IS OF COURSE SHORT FOR... UH, SHORT FOR...ALICE! YES!
HER NAME IS ALICE, OF COURSE.

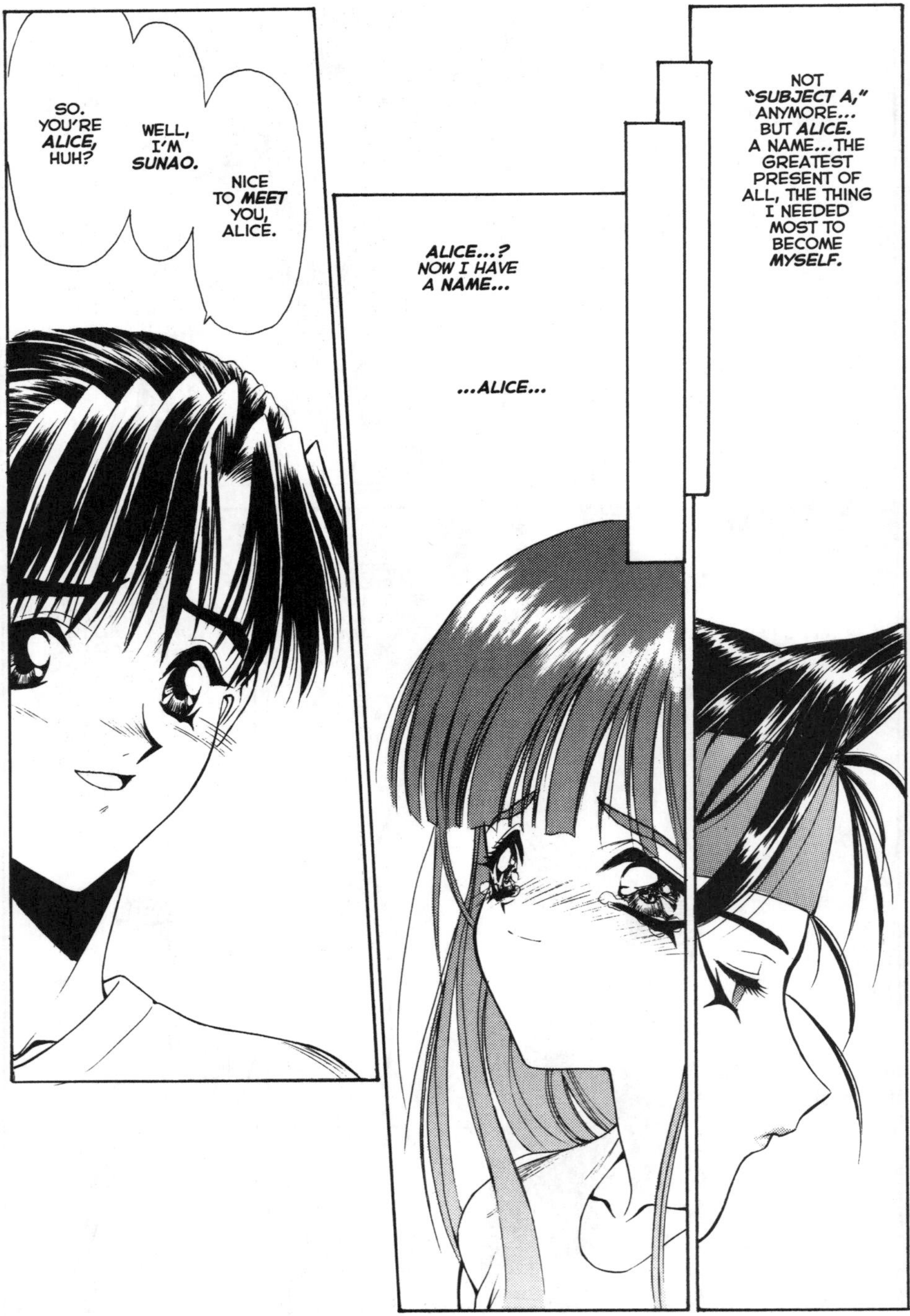
SO. YOU'RE *ALICE,* HUH?
WELL, I'M *SUNAO.*
NICE TO *MEET* YOU, ALICE.
ALICE...? NOW I HAVE A NAME...
...ALICE...
NOT *"SUBJECT A,"* ANYMORE... BUT *ALICE.* A NAME...THE GREATEST PRESENT OF ALL, THE THING I NEEDED MOST TO BECOME *MYSELF.*

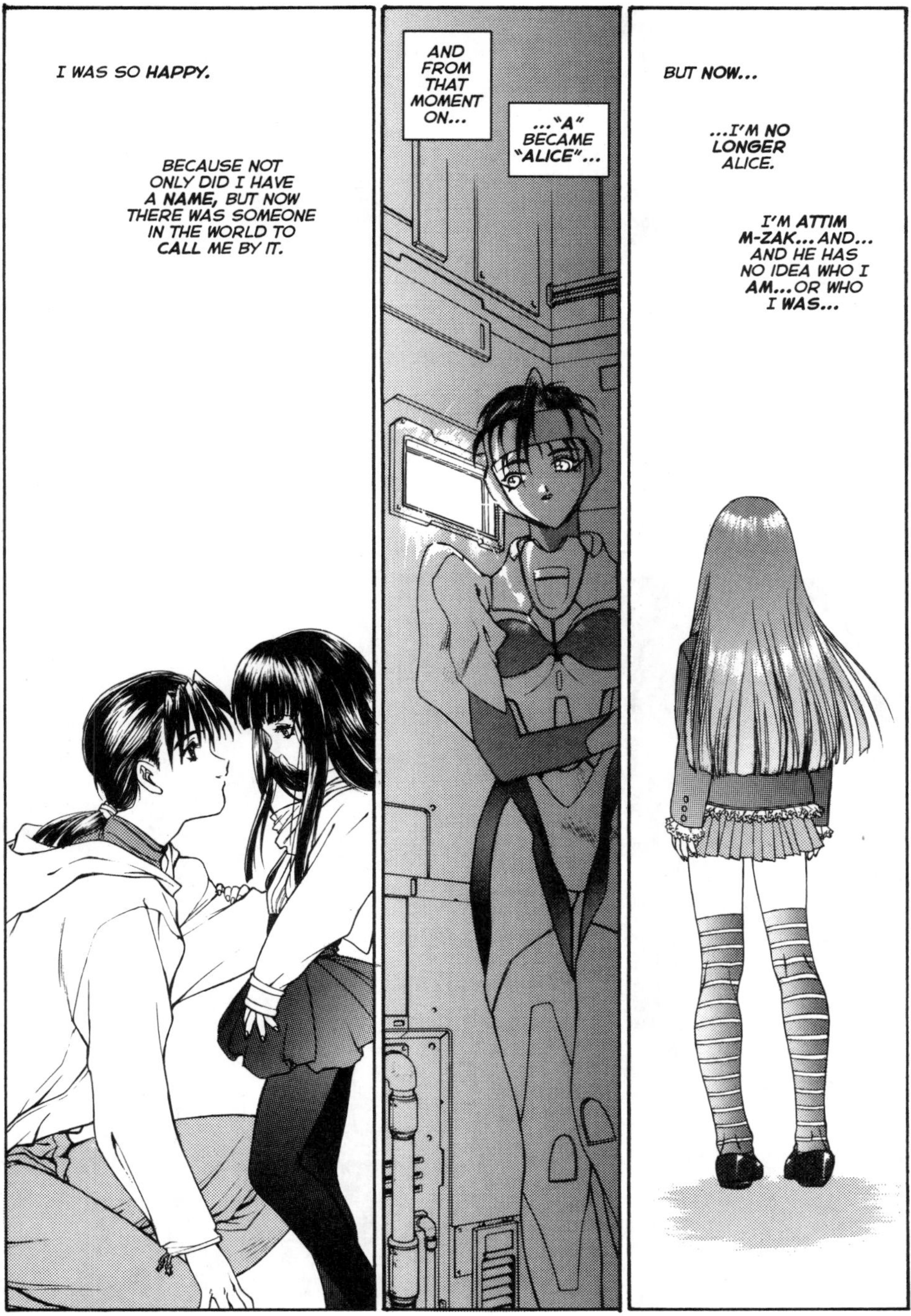
I WAS SO HAPPY.
BECAUSE NOT ONLY DID I HAVE A NAME, BUT NOW THERE WAS SOMEONE IN THE WORLD TO CALL ME BY IT.
AND FROM THAT MOMENT ON...
..."A" BECAME "ALICE"...
BUT NOW...
...I'M NO LONGER ALICE.
I'M ATTIM M-ZAK...AND... AND HE HAS NO IDEA WHO I AM...OR WHO I WAS...

WHY...?

WHY AM I
THINKING
ABOUT THIS
NOW...NOW,
OF ALL
TIMES...?

S-SUNAO...

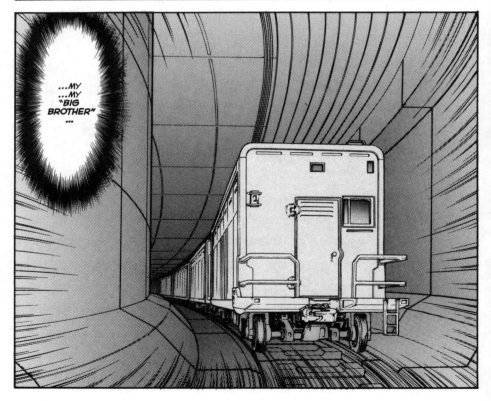

...MY
...MY
"BIG
BROTHER"
...

ACT 22

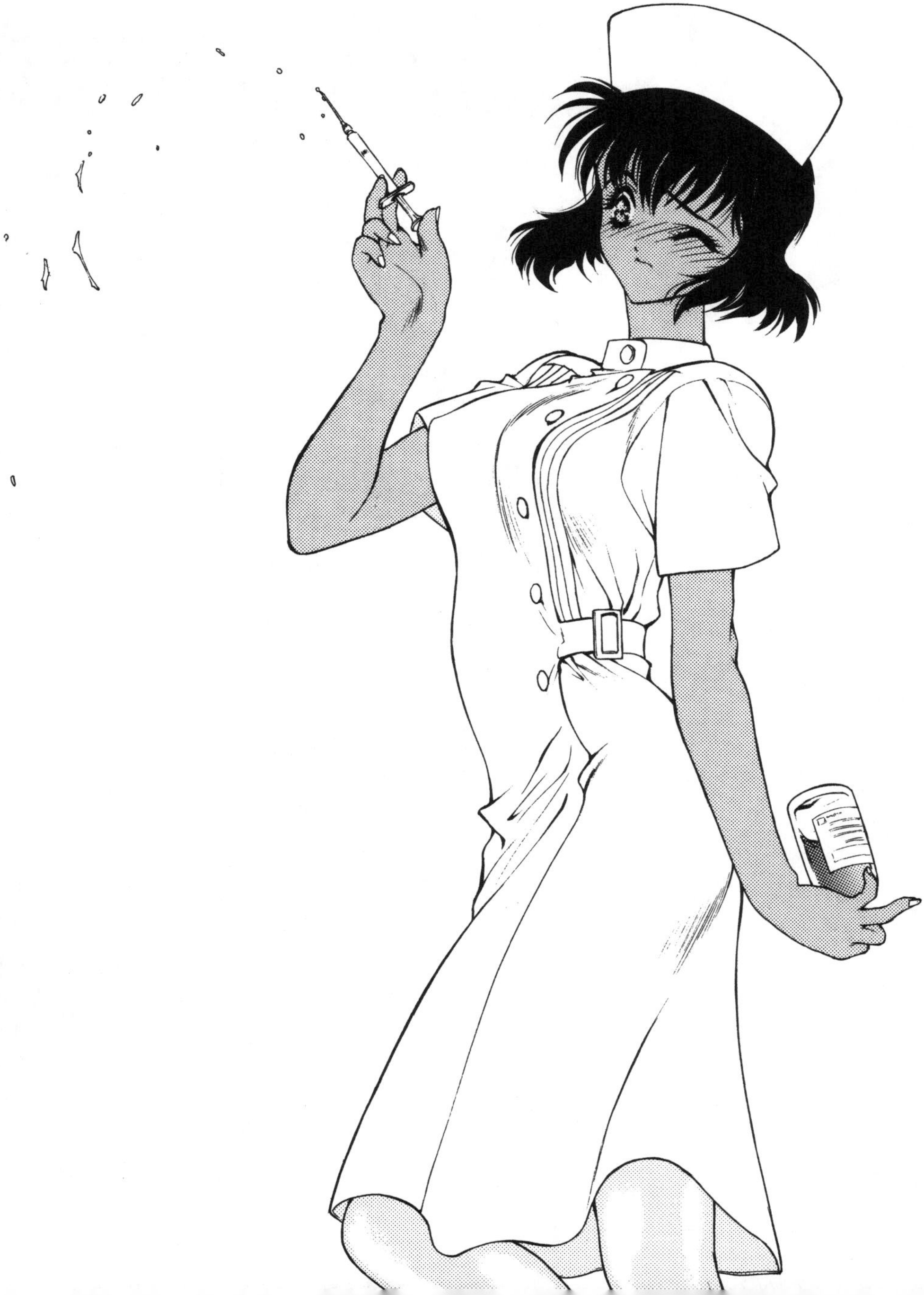

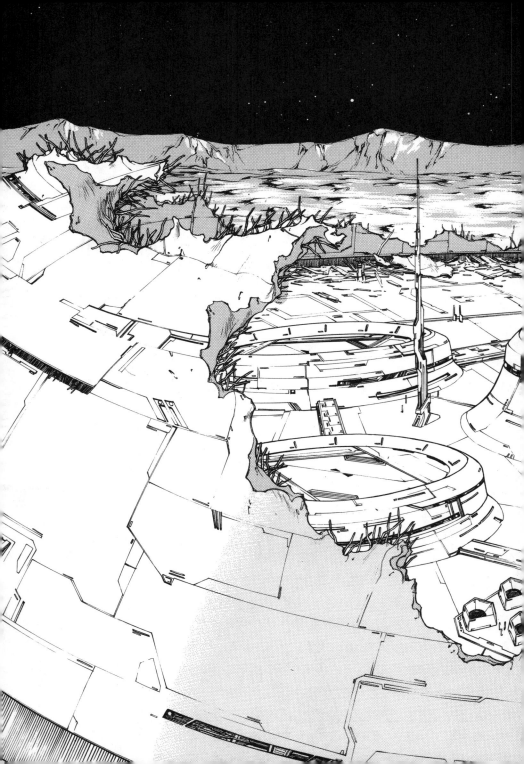

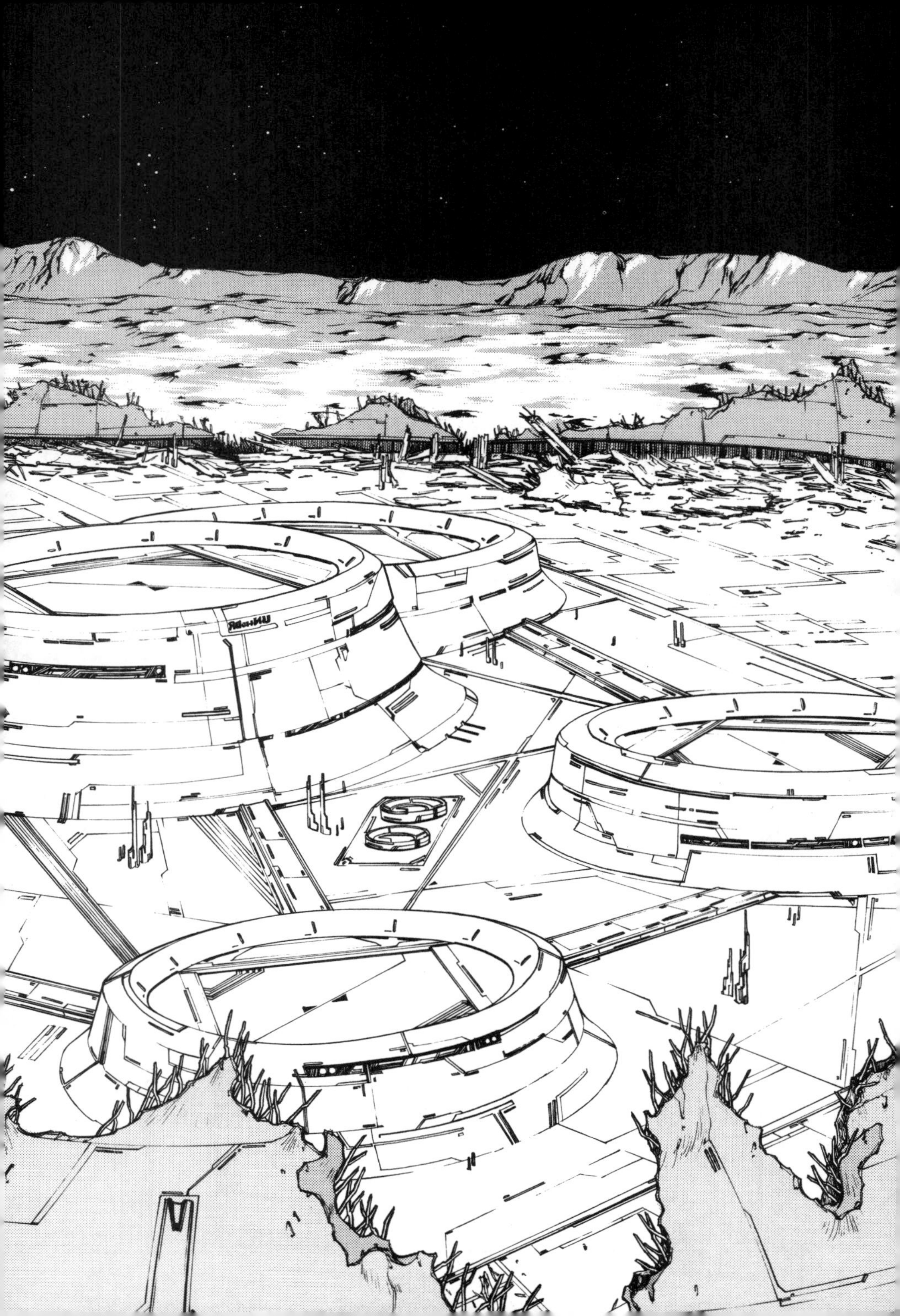

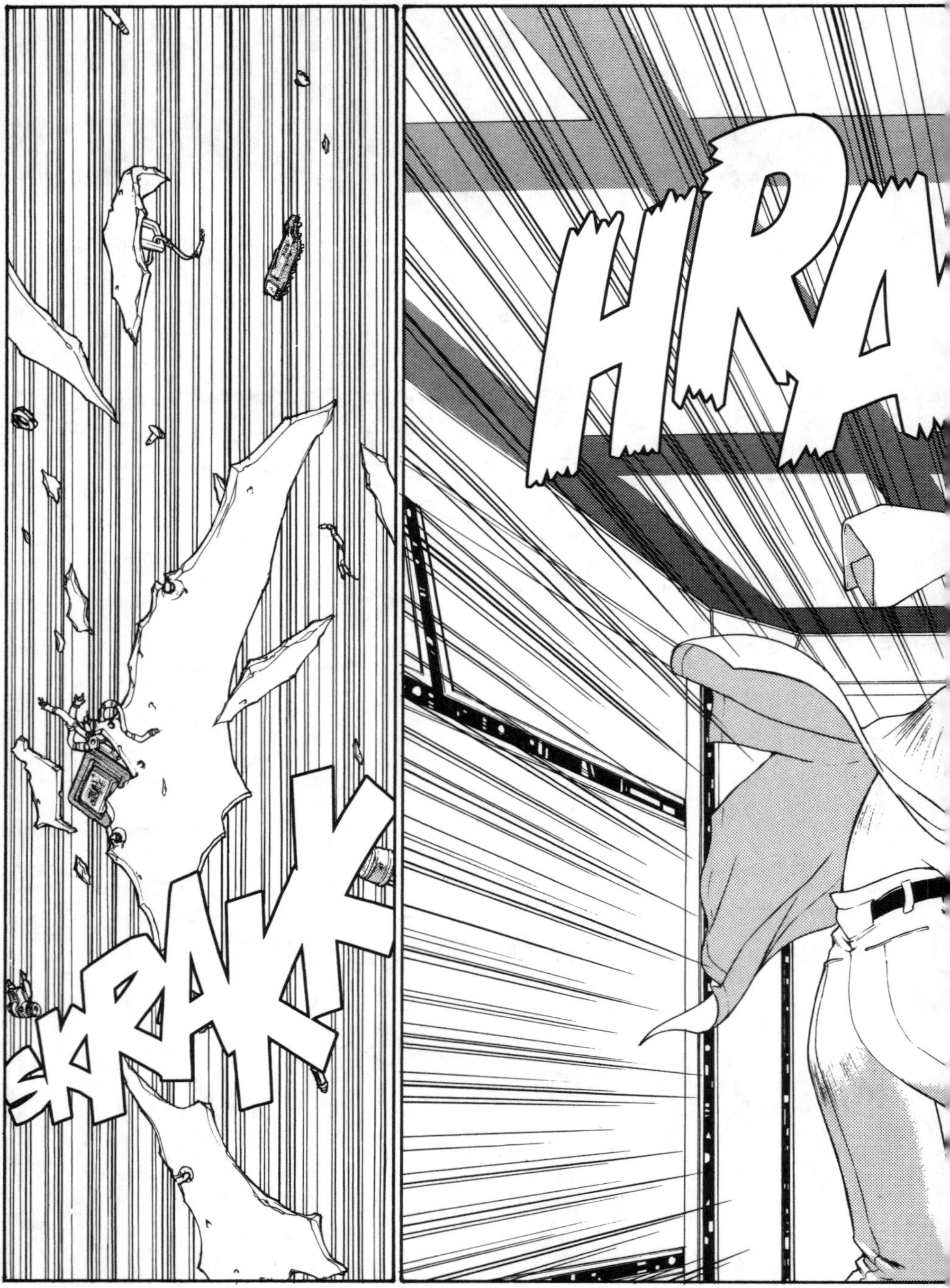
SKRAKK
HRA

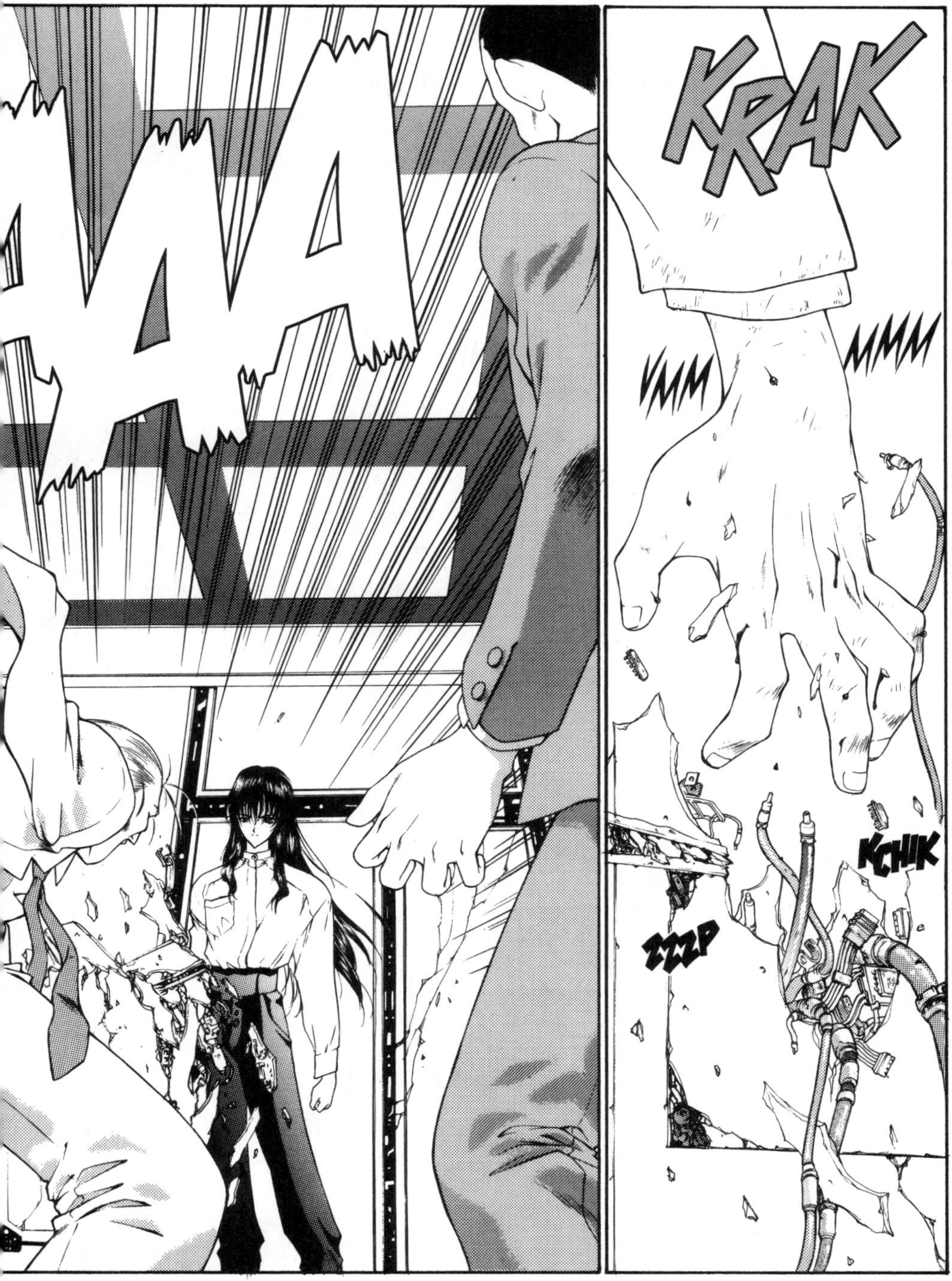
AA
KRAK
VMMM
MMMM
KCHIK
ZZZP

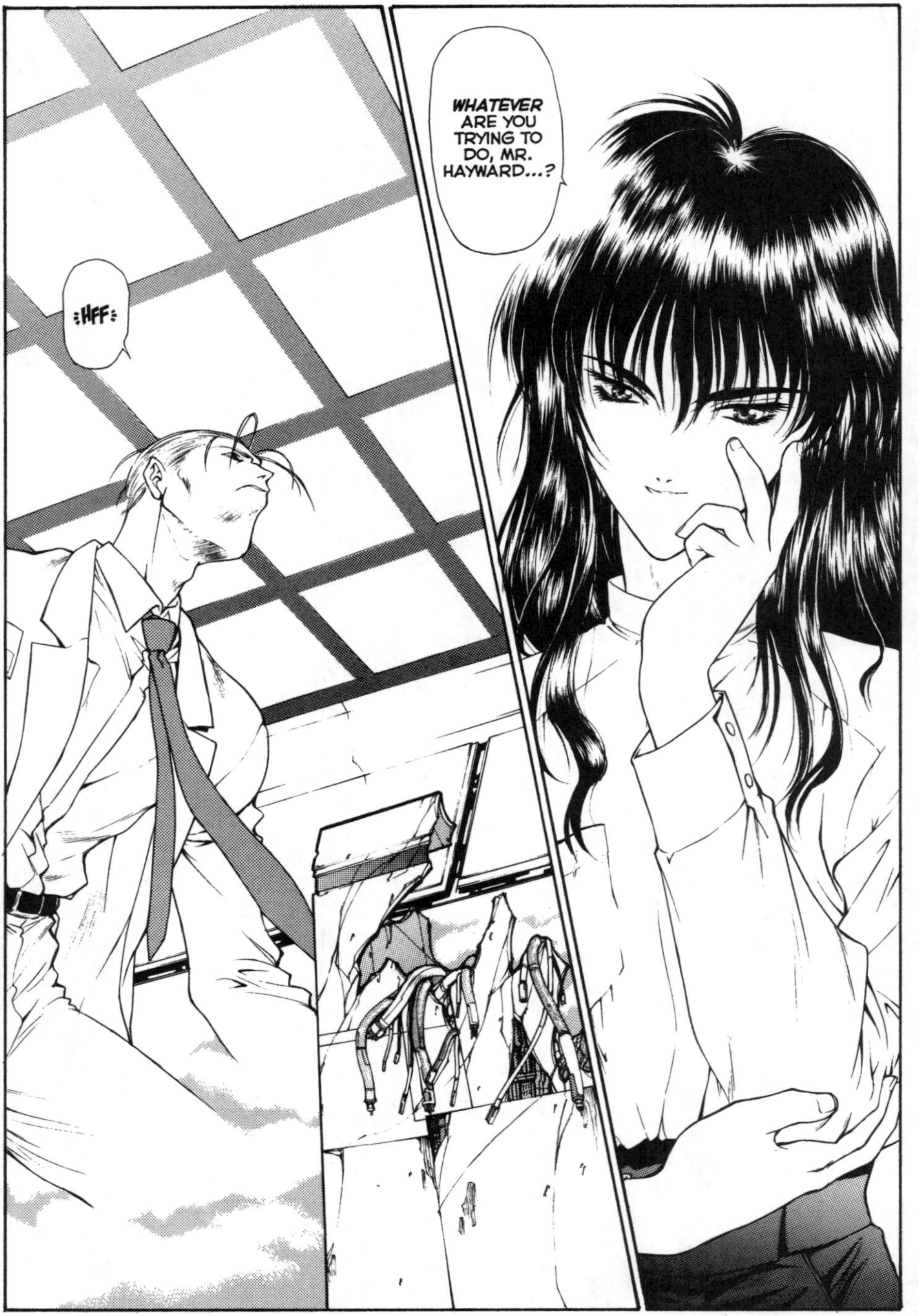
HFF
WHATEVER ARE YOU TRYING TO DO, MR. HAYWARD...?

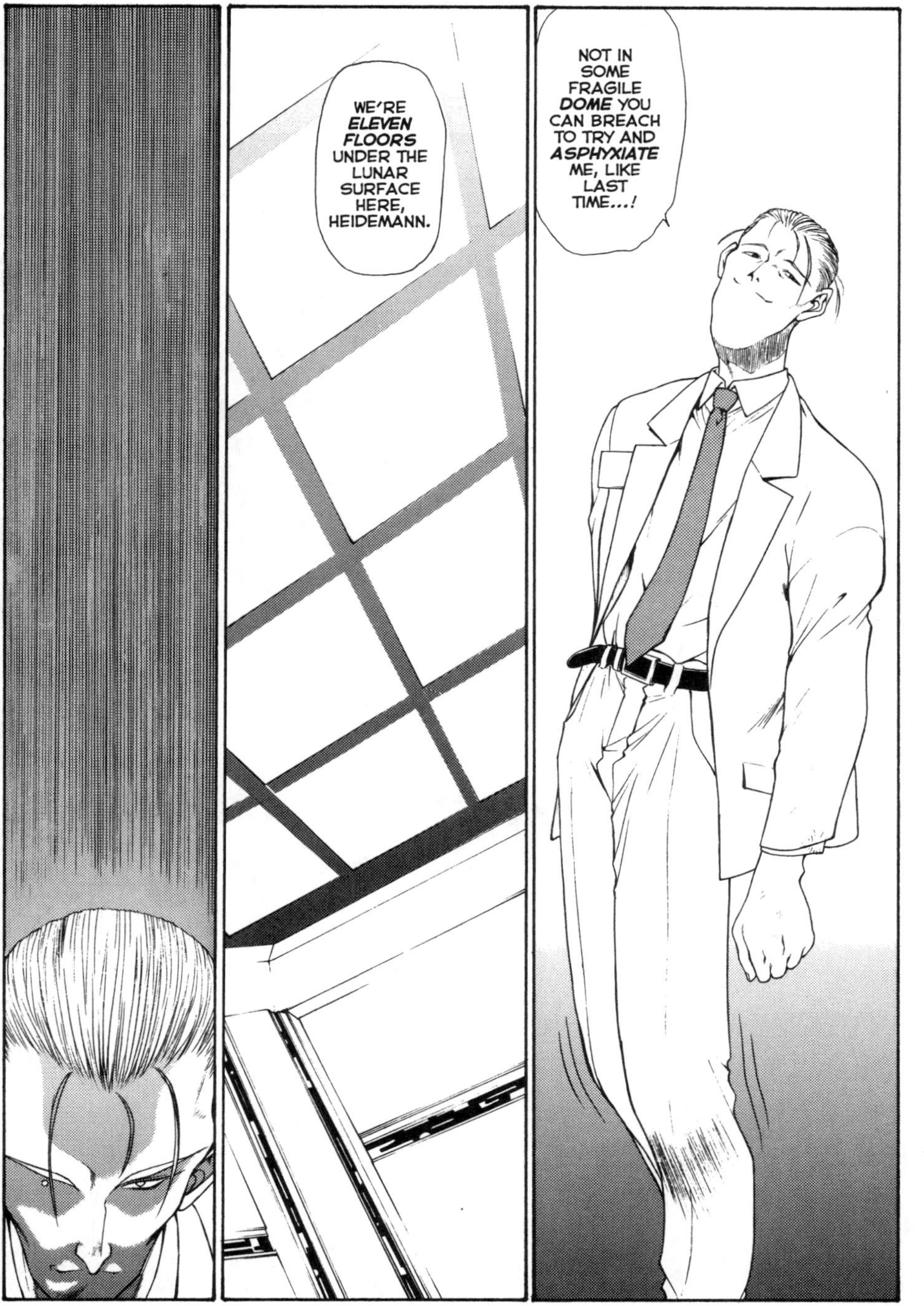
WE'RE **ELEVEN FLOORS** UNDER THE LUNAR SURFACE HERE, HEIDEMANN.
NOT IN SOME FRAGILE **DOME** YOU CAN BREACH TO TRY AND **ASPHYXIATE** ME, LIKE LAST TIME...!

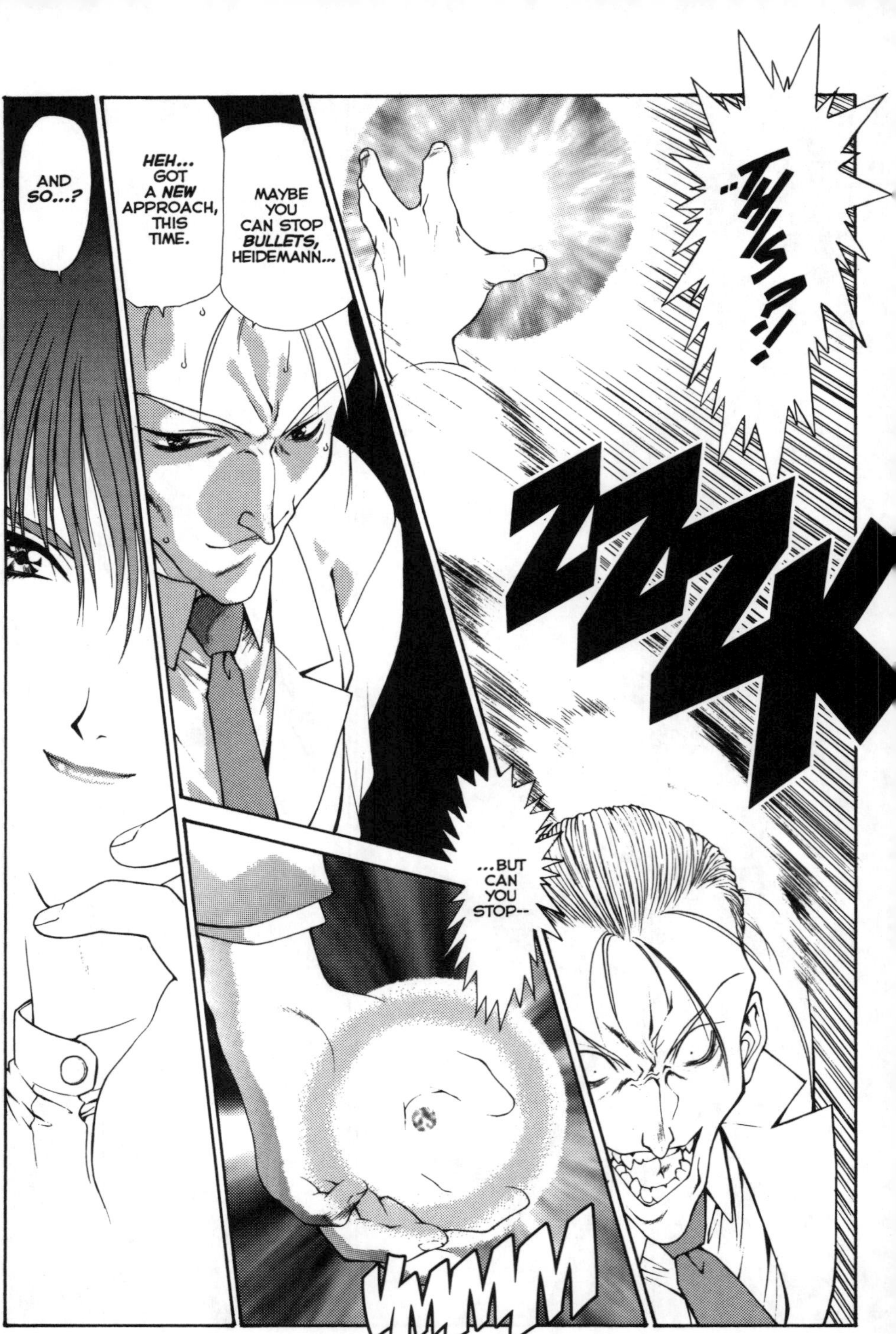
AND SO...?
HEH... GOT A *NEW* APPROACH, THIS TIME.
MAYBE YOU CAN STOP *BULLETS,* HEIDEMANN...
...THIS?!!
ZZZK
...BUT CAN YOU STOP--
VMMM

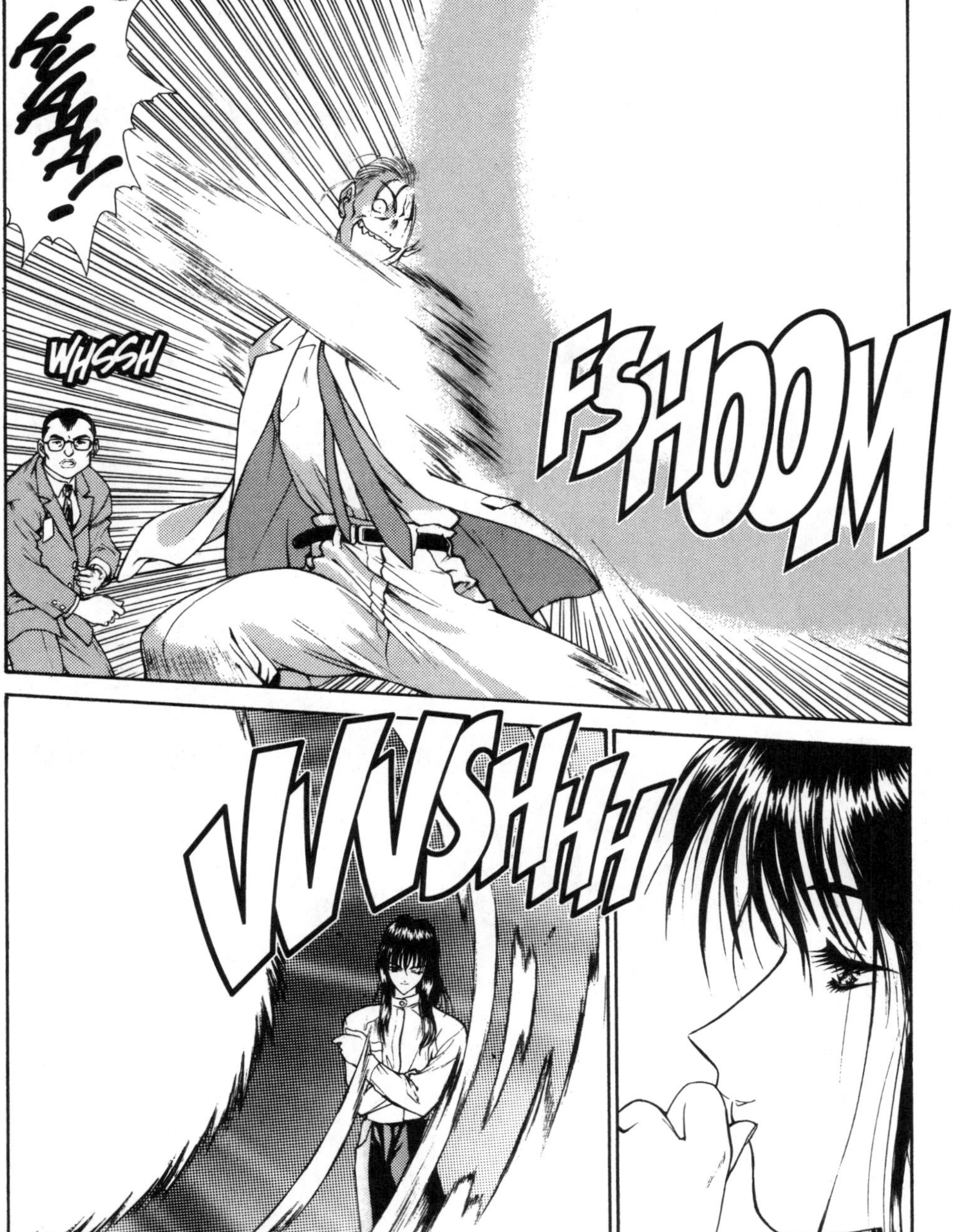
HUAAA!
WHSSH
FSHOOM
JJJSHHH

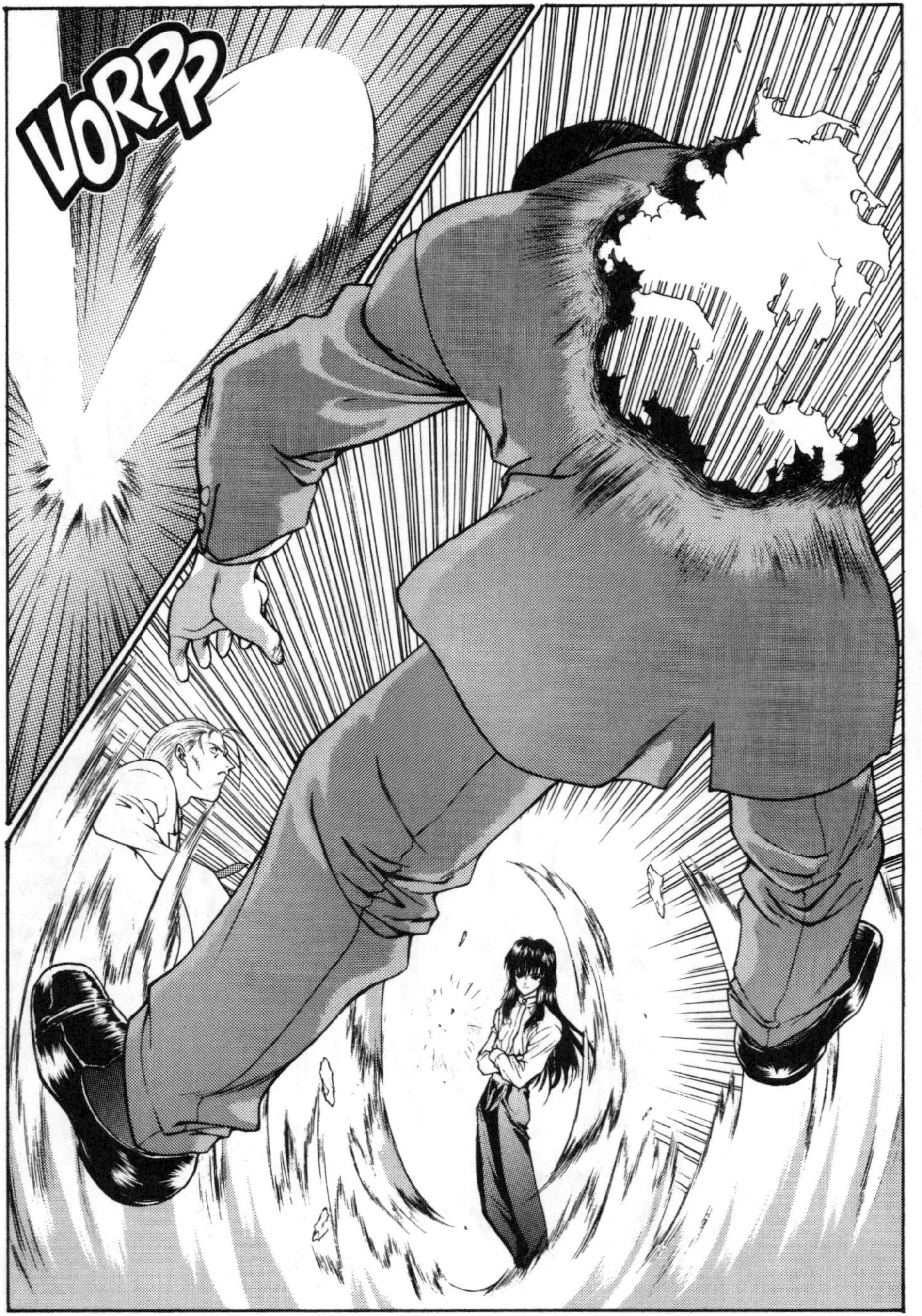
VORPP

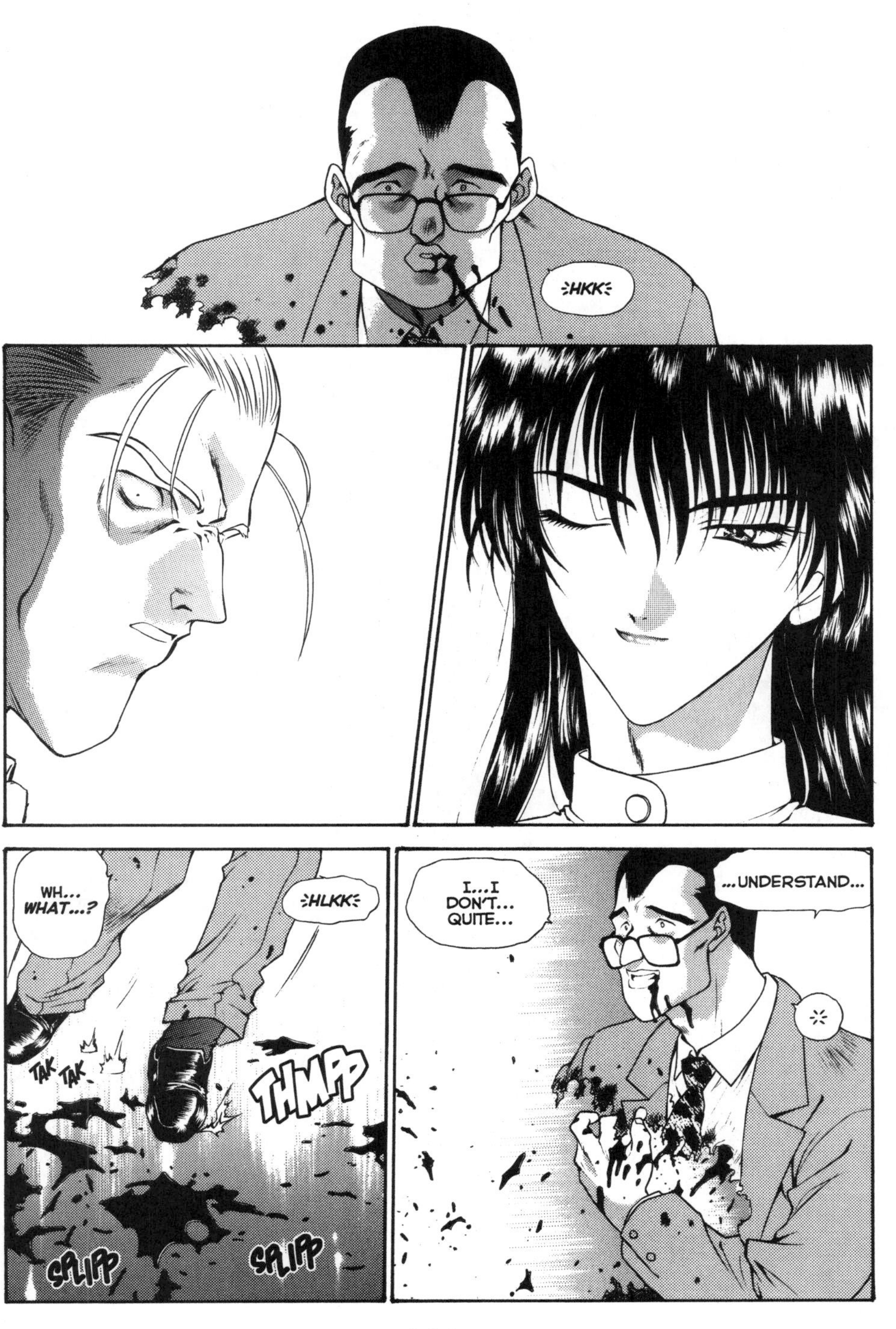
HKK
WH... WHAT...?
HLKK
TAK TAK
THMPP
SPLIPP
SPLIPP
I...I DON'T... QUITE...
...UNDERSTAND...

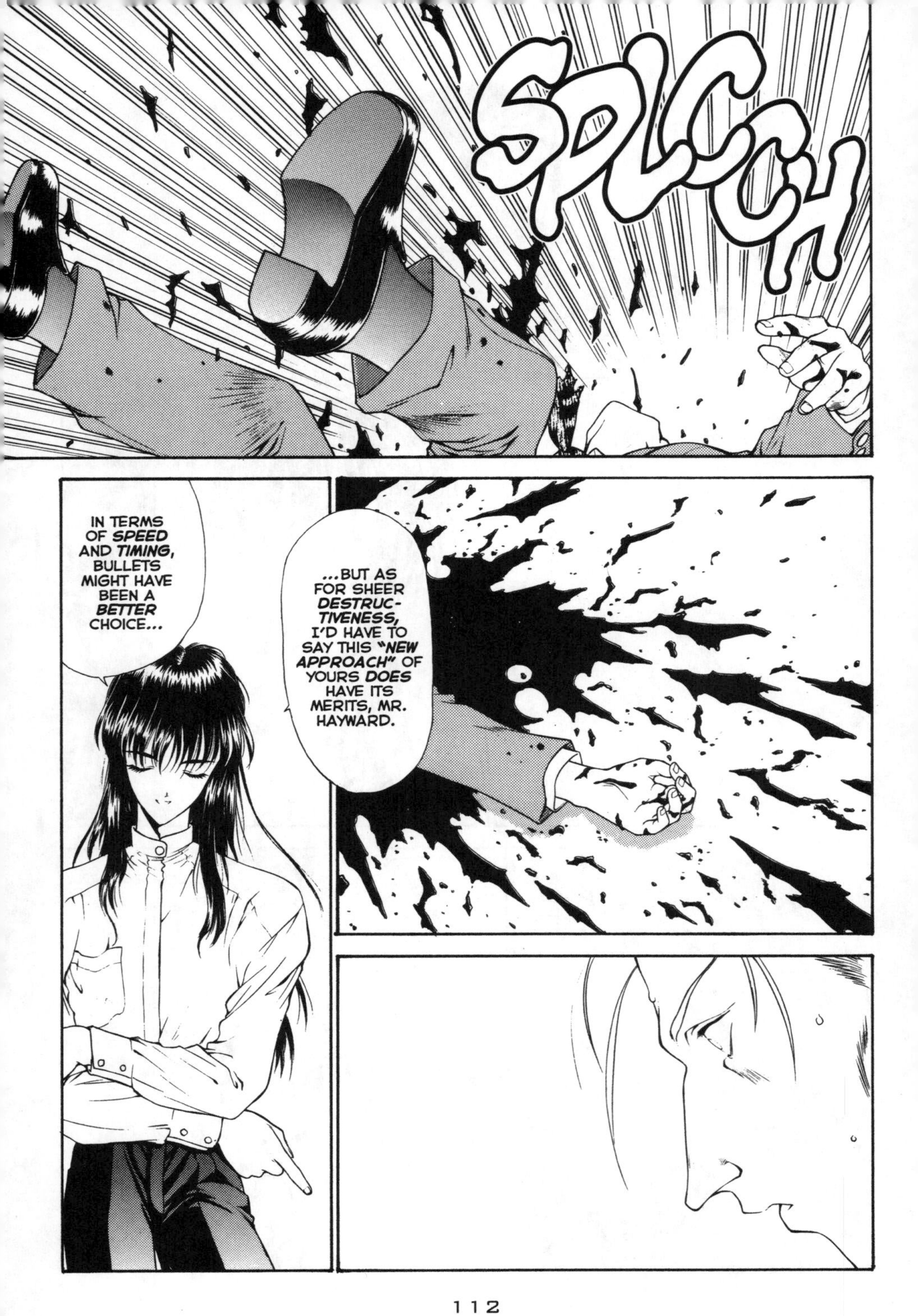
SPLCCH
IN TERMS OF *SPEED* AND *TIMING*, BULLETS MIGHT HAVE BEEN A *BETTER* CHOICE...
...BUT AS FOR SHEER *DESTRUCTIVENESS*, I'D HAVE TO SAY THIS *"NEW APPROACH"* OF YOURS *DOES* HAVE ITS MERITS, MR. HAYWARD.

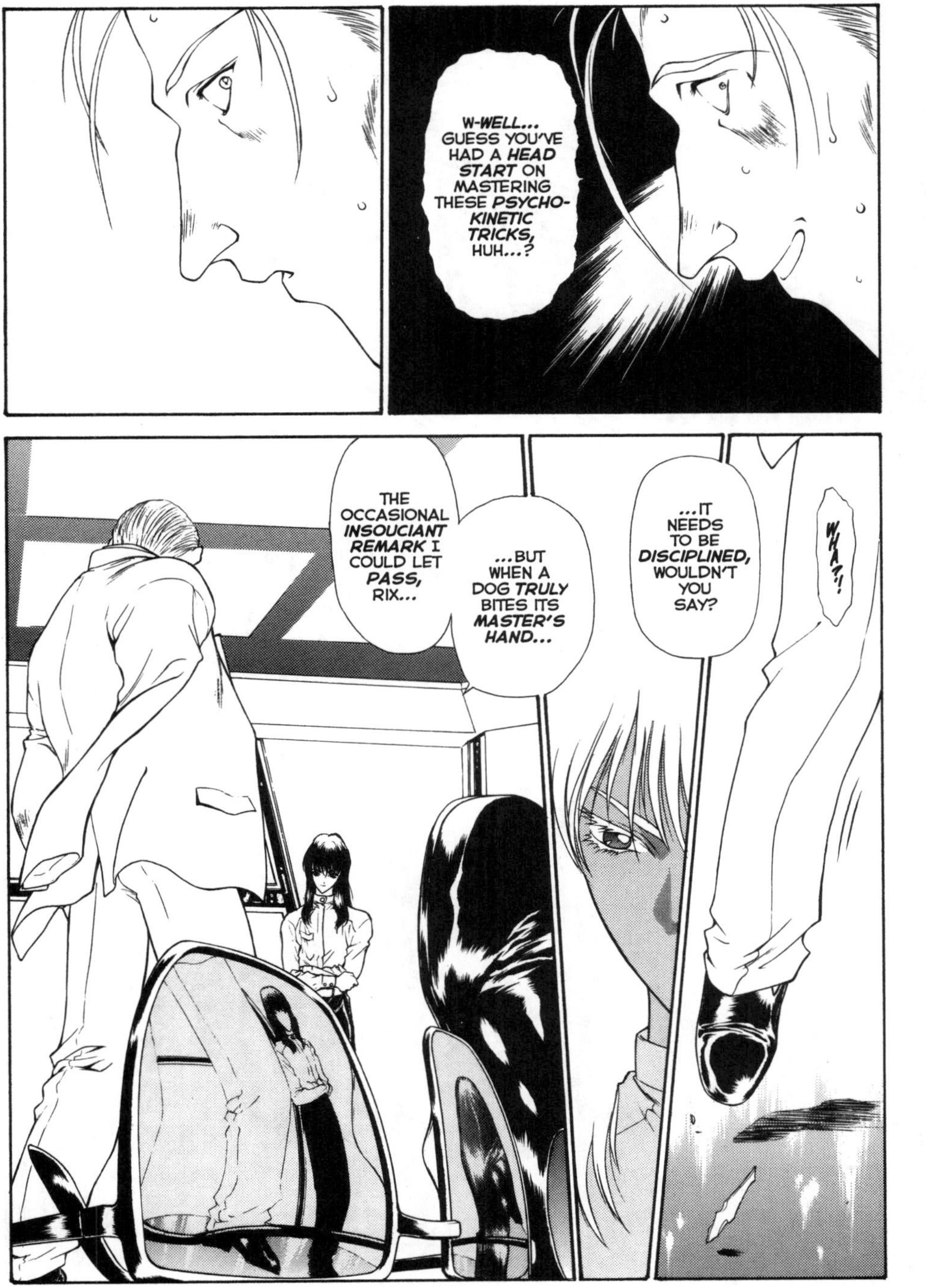
W-WELL... GUESS YOU'VE HAD A HEAD START ON MASTERING THESE PSYCHO-KINETIC TRICKS, HUH...?
THE OCCASIONAL INSOUCIANT REMARK I COULD LET PASS, RIX...
...BUT WHEN A DOG TRULY BITES ITS MASTER'S HAND...
...IT NEEDS TO BE DISCIPLINED, WOULDN'T YOU SAY?
WHA?!

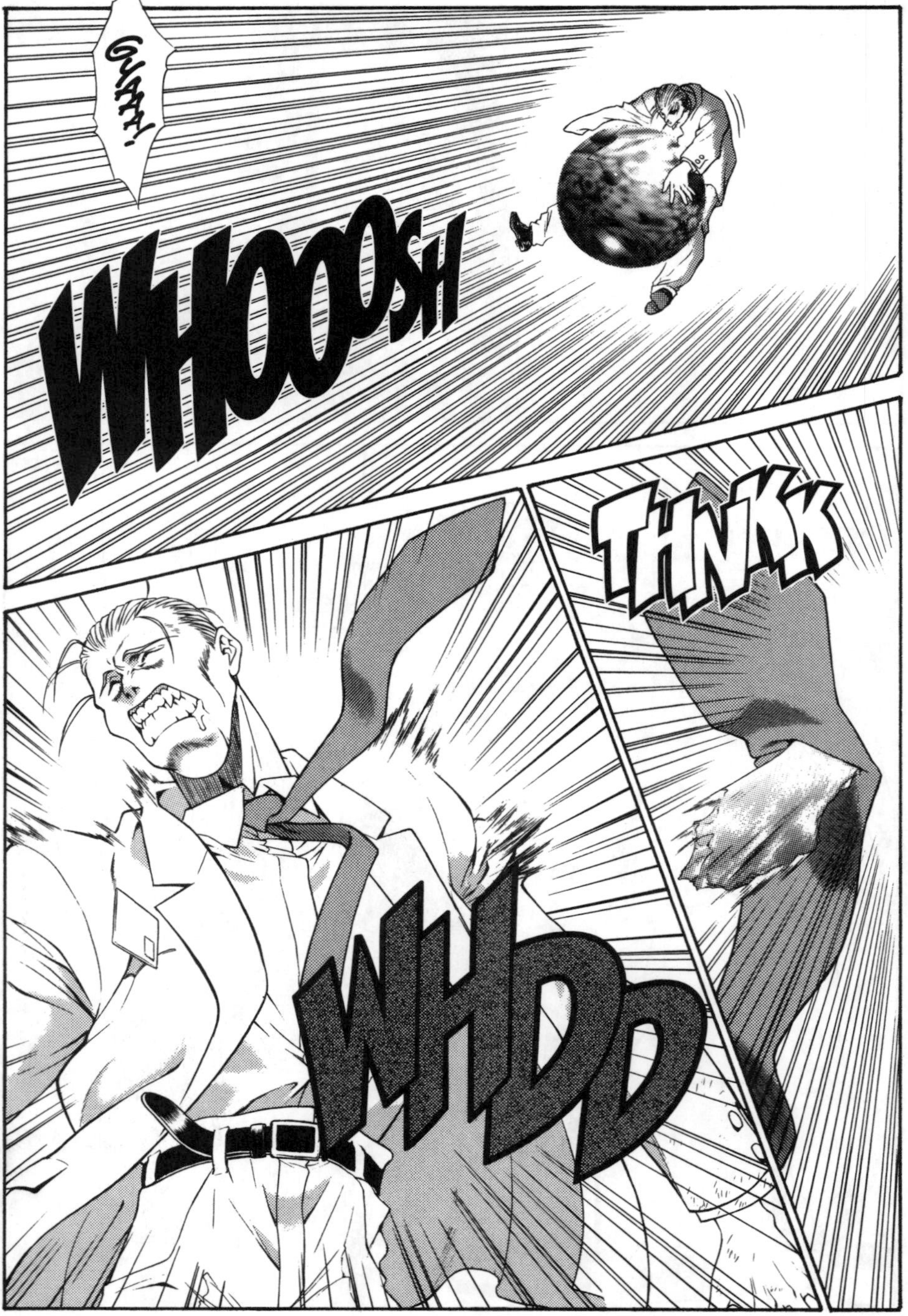
GUAAA!
WHOOOSH
WHDD
THNKK

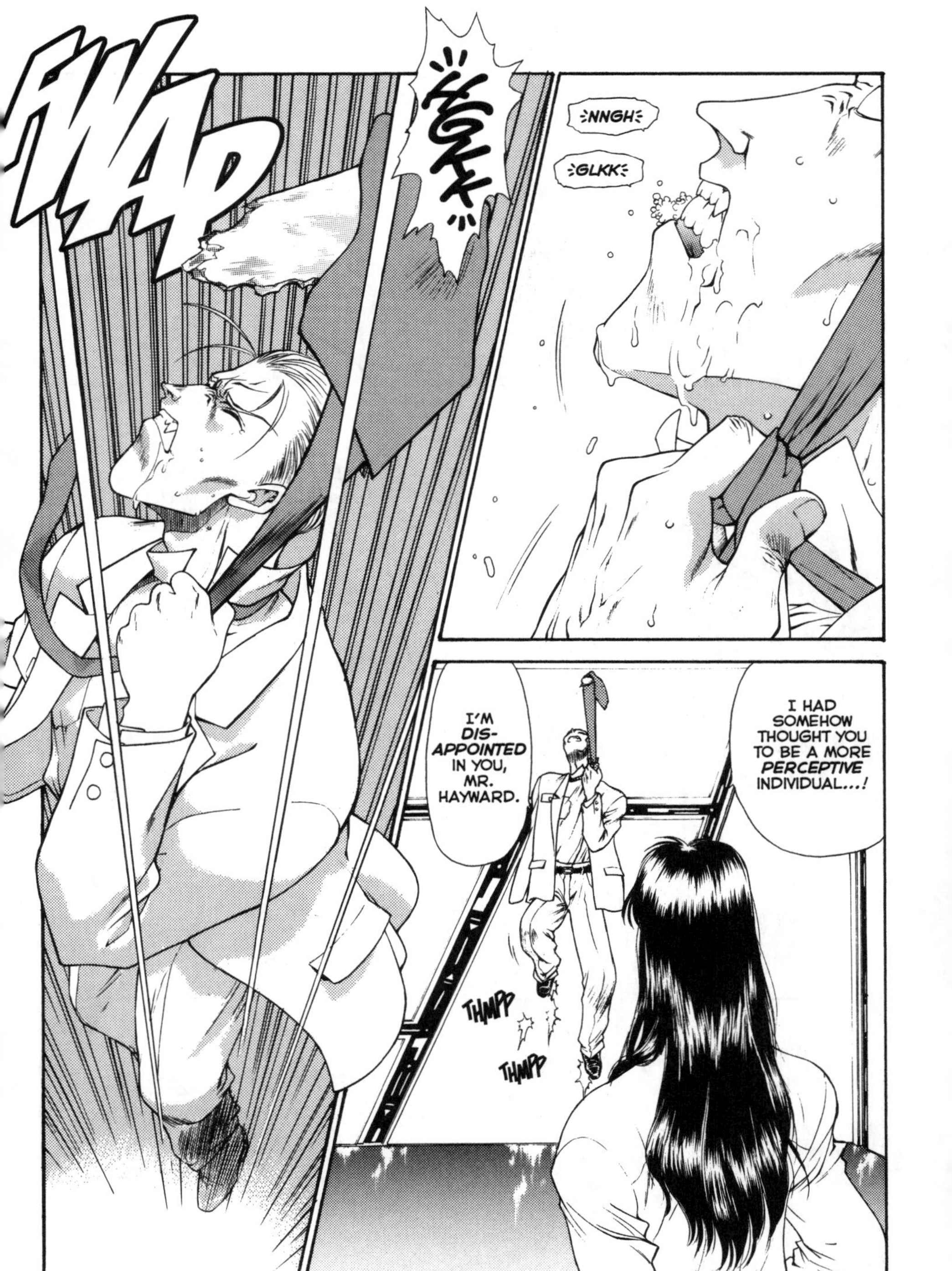
FWAP
KGKK
NNGH
GLKK
I'M DIS-APPOINTED IN YOU, MR. HAYWARD.
I HAD SOMEHOW THOUGHT YOU TO BE A MORE PERCEPTIVE INDIVIDUAL...!
THMPP
THMPP

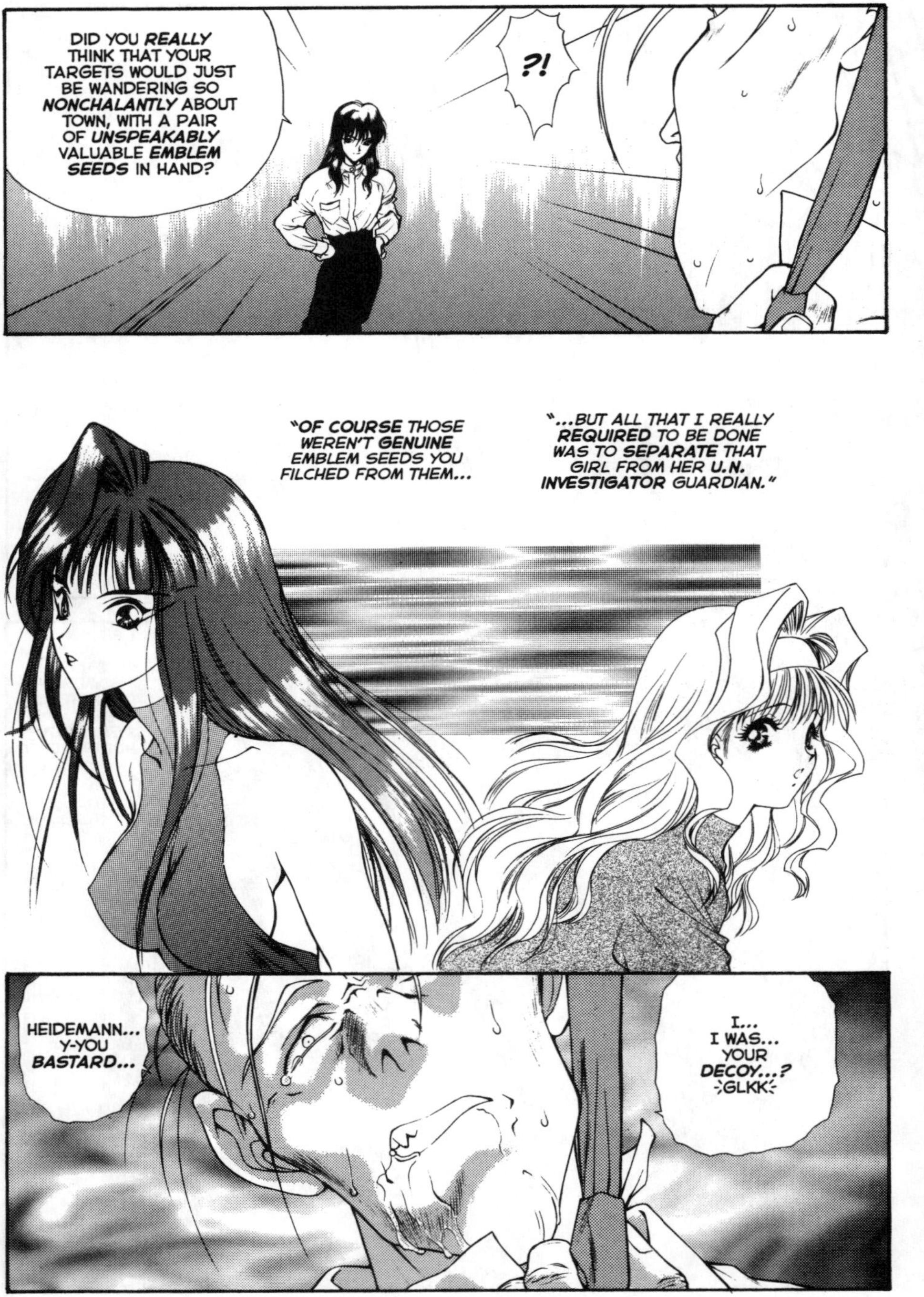
DID YOU REALLY THINK THAT YOUR TARGETS WOULD JUST BE WANDERING SO NONCHALANTLY ABOUT TOWN, WITH A PAIR OF UNSPEAKABLY VALUABLE EMBLEM SEEDS IN HAND?
?!
"OF COURSE THOSE WEREN'T GENUINE EMBLEM SEEDS YOU FILCHED FROM THEM...
"...BUT ALL THAT I REALLY REQUIRED TO BE DONE WAS TO SEPARATE THAT GIRL FROM HER U.N. INVESTIGATOR GUARDIAN."
HEIDEMANN... Y-YOU BASTARD...
I... I WAS... YOUR DECOY...? -GLKK-

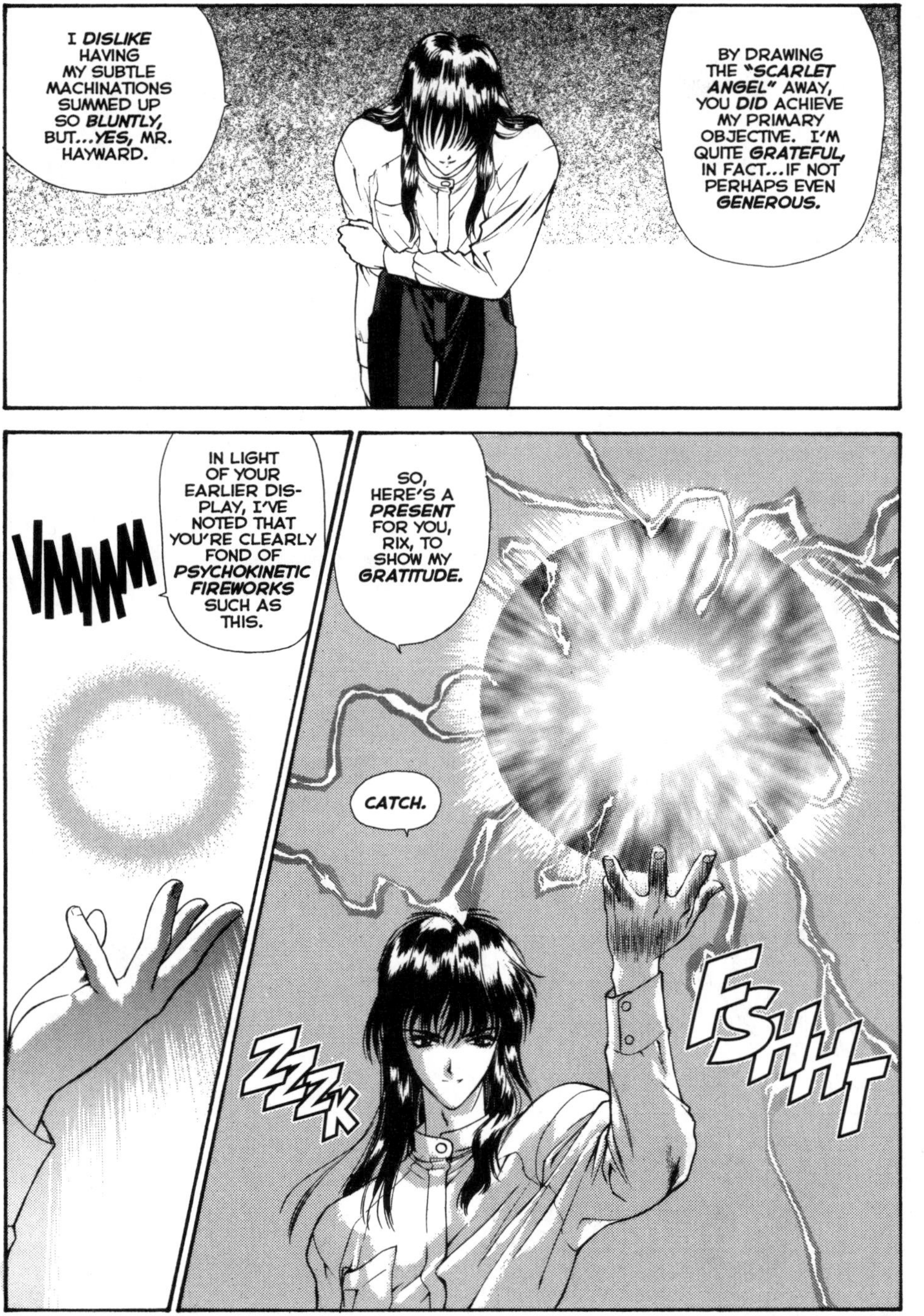
I DISLIKE HAVING MY SUBTLE MACHINATIONS SUMMED UP SO BLUNTLY, BUT...YES, MR. HAYWARD.
BY DRAWING THE "SCARLET ANGEL" AWAY, YOU DID ACHIEVE MY PRIMARY OBJECTIVE. I'M QUITE GRATEFUL, IN FACT...IF NOT PERHAPS EVEN GENEROUS.
VMMMM
IN LIGHT OF YOUR EARLIER DIS-PLAY, I'VE NOTED THAT YOU'RE CLEARLY FOND OF PSYCHOKINETIC FIREWORKS SUCH AS THIS.
SO, HERE'S A PRESENT FOR YOU, RIX, TO SHOW MY GRATITUDE.
CATCH.
ZZZK
FSHHT

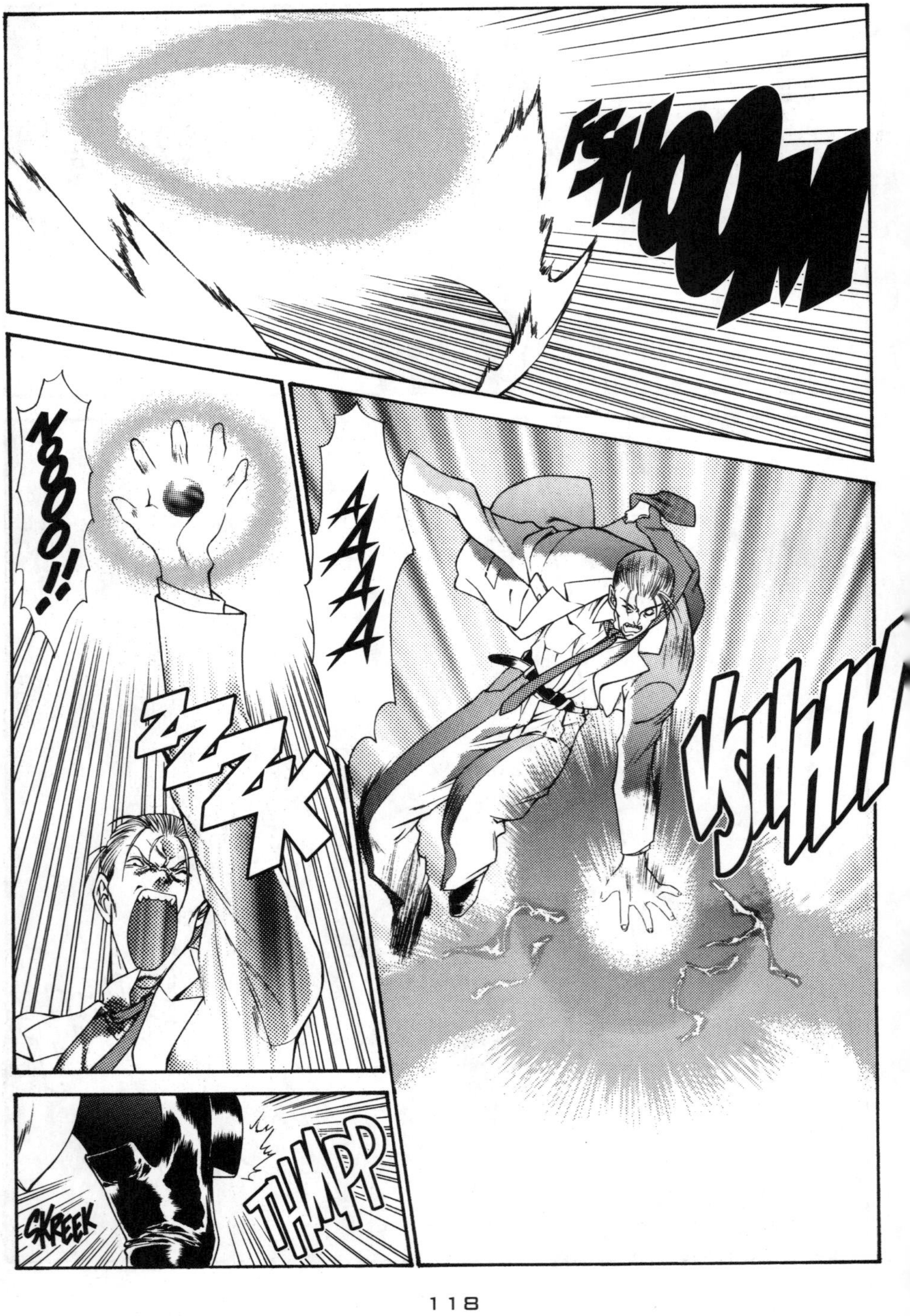
FSHOOM
NOOOOO!!
ZZZK
SKREEK
THMPP
AAAA
VSHHH

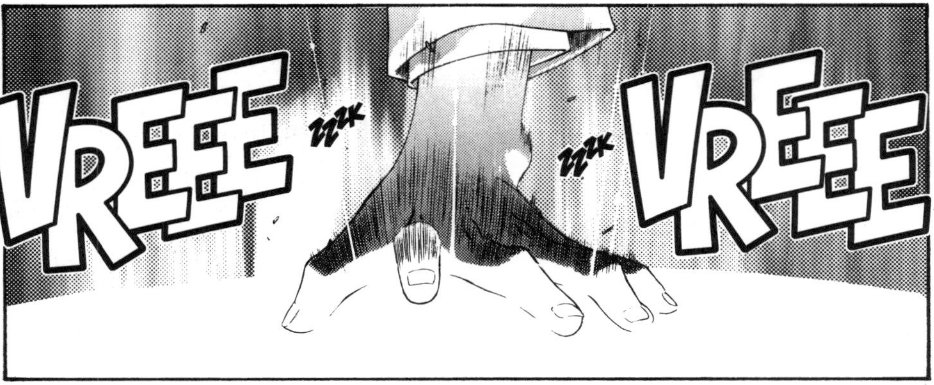
VREEE
ZZZK
ZZZK
VREEE
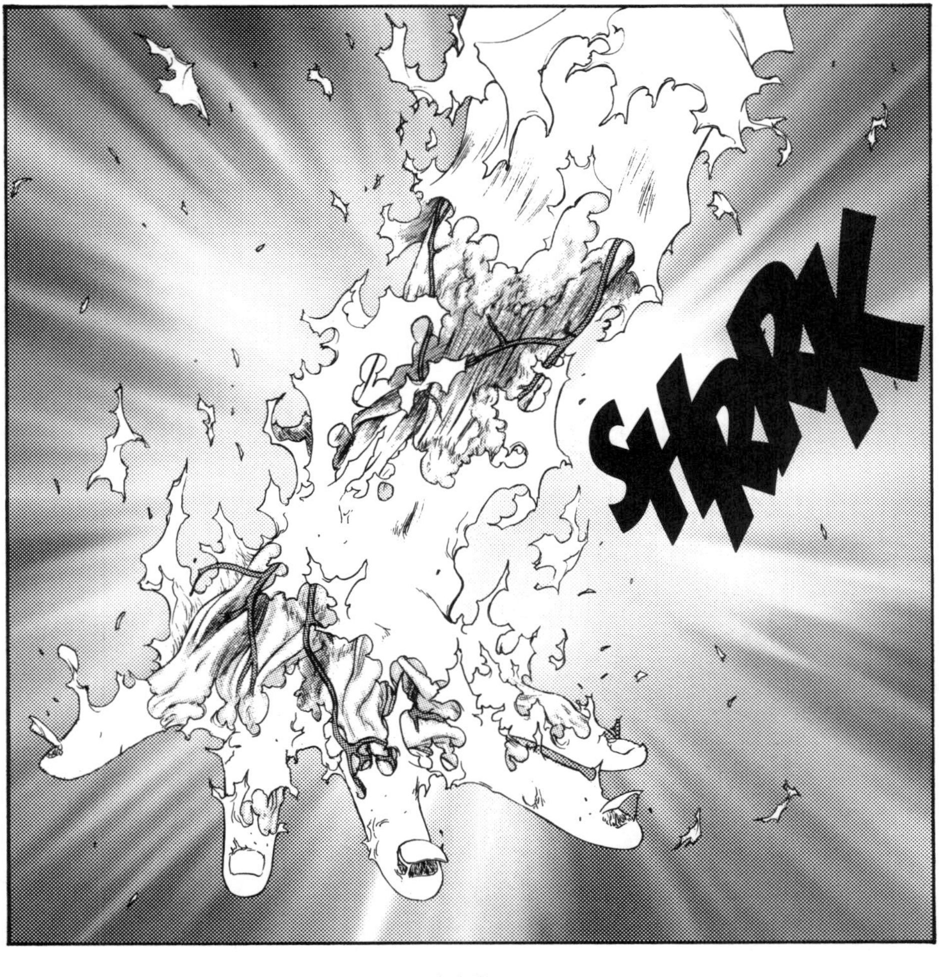
SHRRK

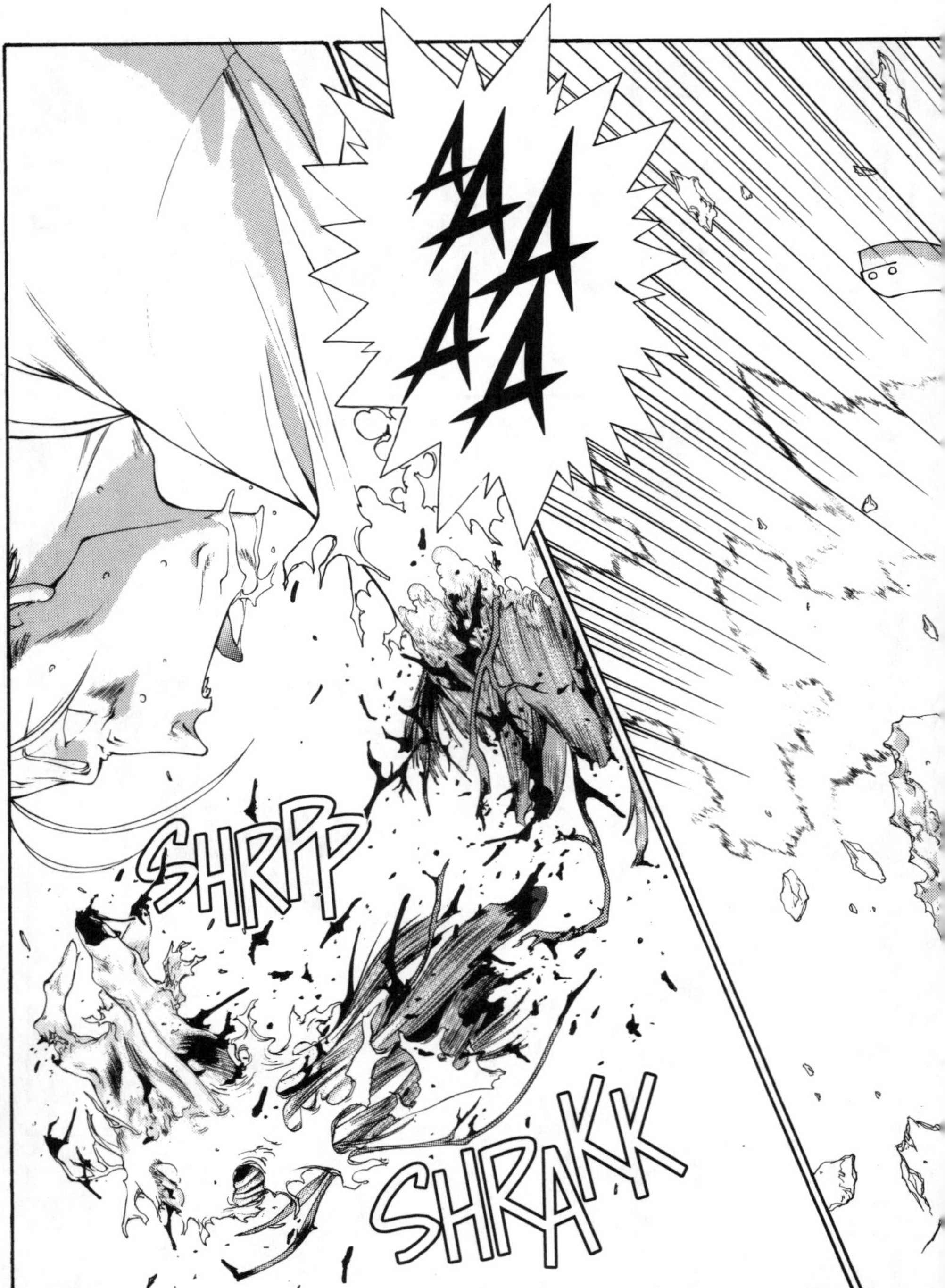
AAAAAAA
SHRPP
SHRAKK

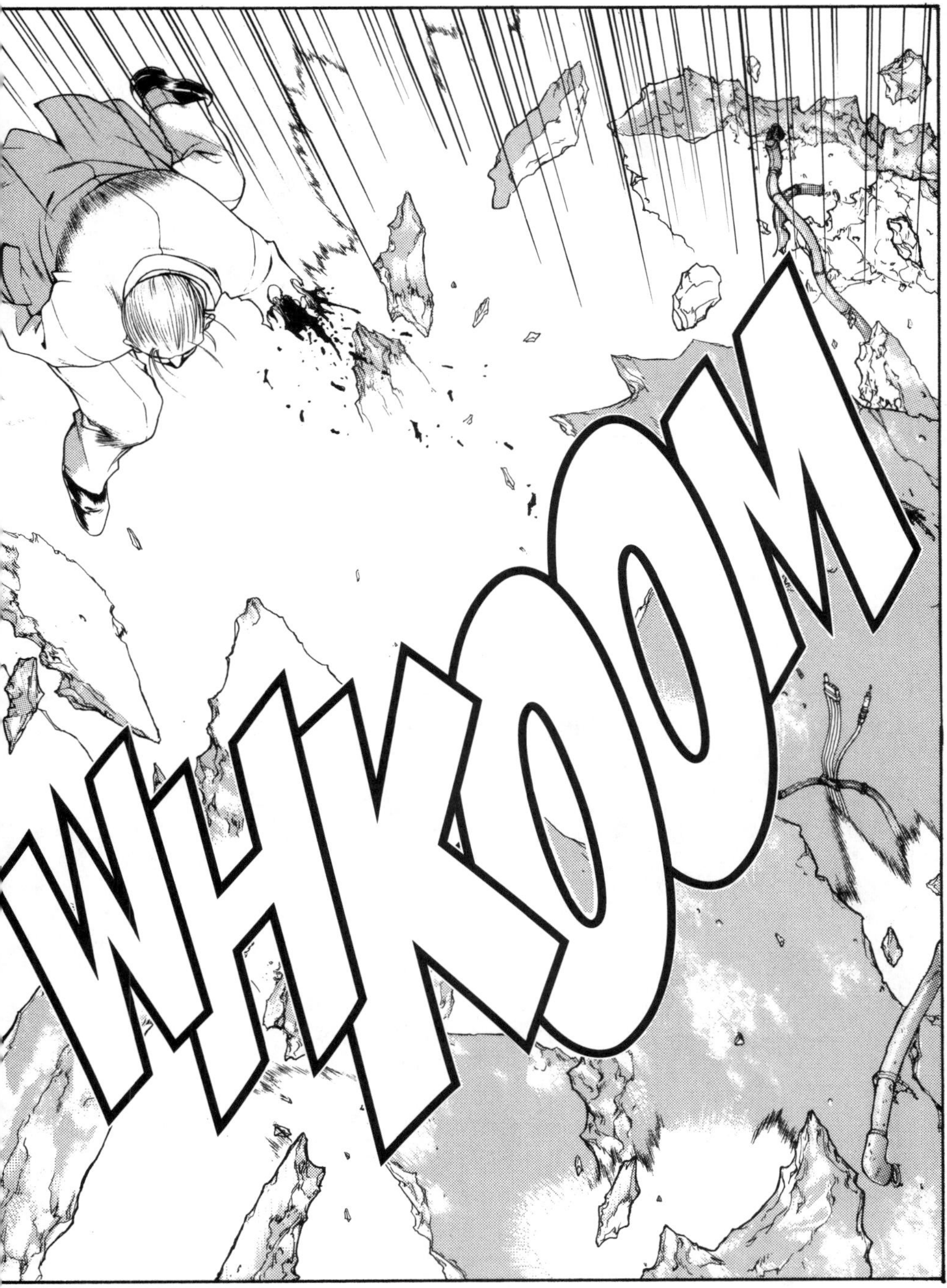
WHKOOM

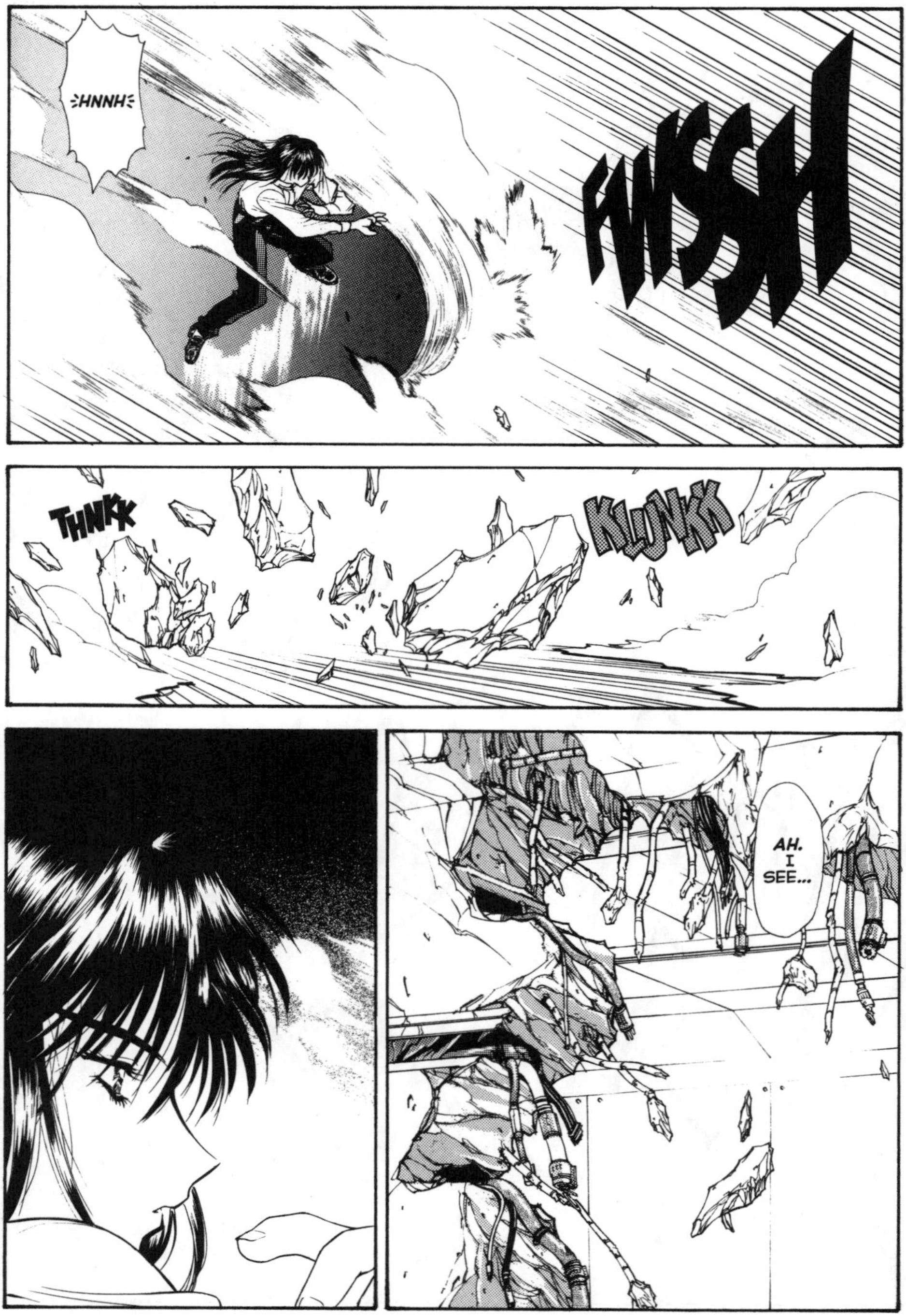
HNNH
FWSSH
THNKK
KLUNKK
AH. I SEE...

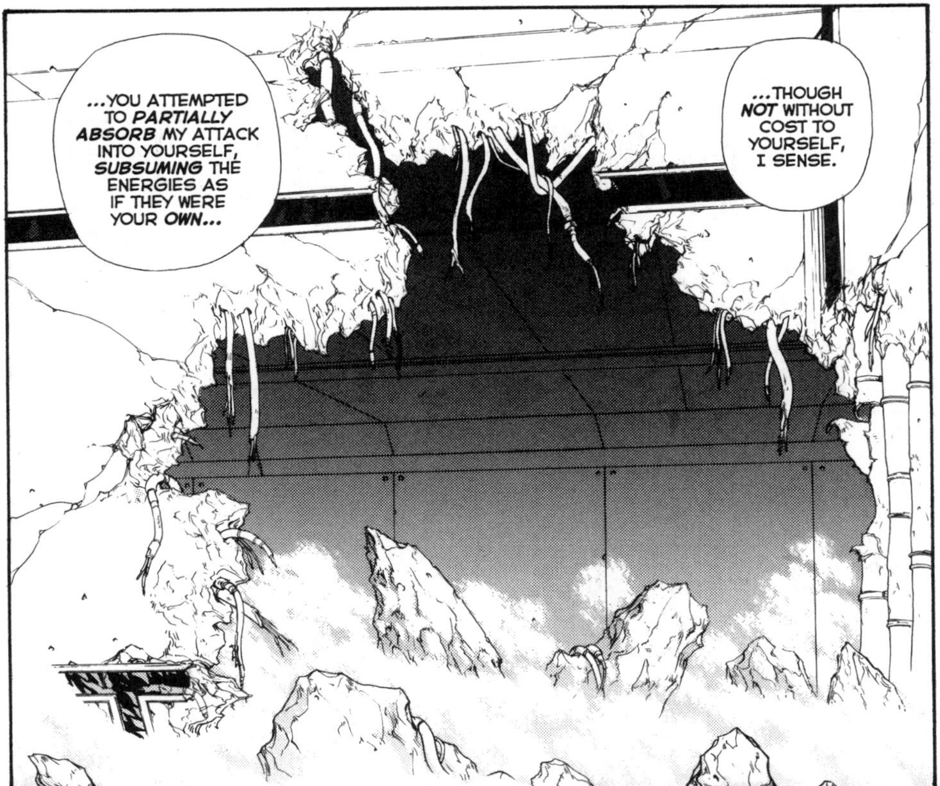
...YOU ATTEMPTED TO PARTIALLY ABSORB MY ATTACK INTO YOURSELF, SUBSUMING THE ENERGIES AS IF THEY WERE YOUR OWN...
...THOUGH NOT WITHOUT COST TO YOURSELF, I SENSE.

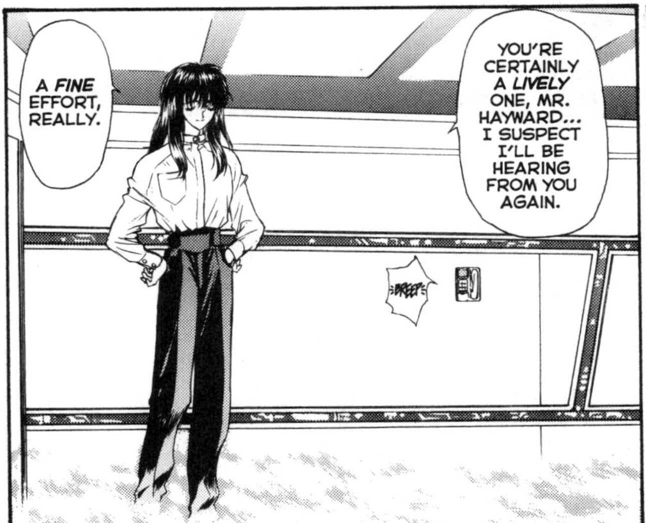
A FINE EFFORT, REALLY.
YOU'RE CERTAINLY A LIVELY ONE, MR. HAYWARD... I SUSPECT I'LL BE HEARING FROM YOU AGAIN.
BREEP

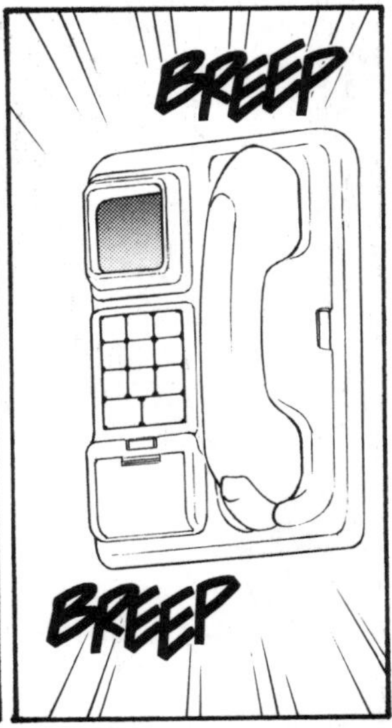
BREEP
BREEP

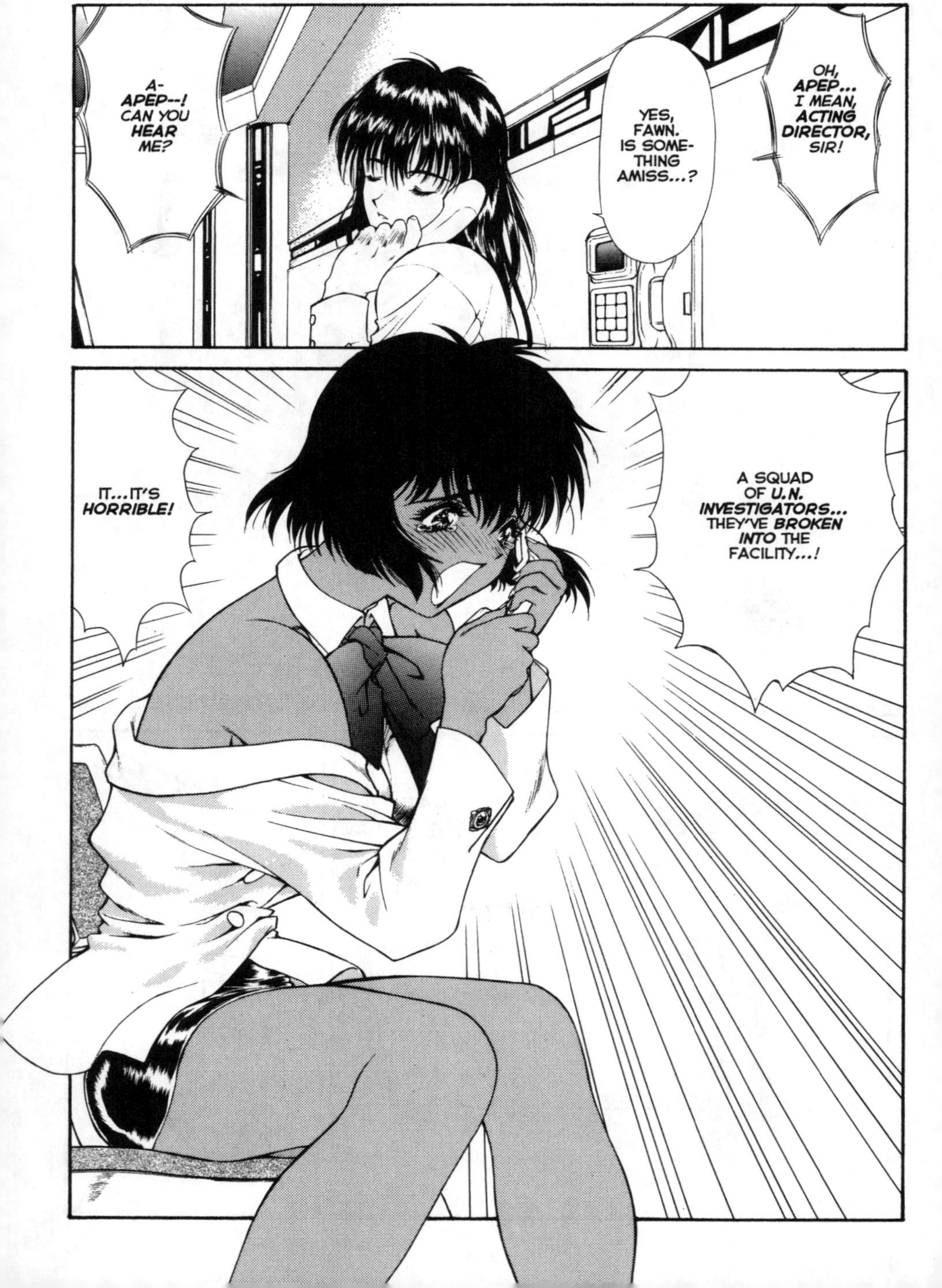
A- APEP--! CAN YOU HEAR ME?
YES, FAWN. IS SOME-THING AMISS...?
OH, APEP... I MEAN, ACTING DIRECTOR, SIR!
IT...IT'S HORRIBLE!
A SQUAD OF U.N. INVESTIGATORS... THEY'VE BROKEN INTO THE FACILITY...!

ACT 23

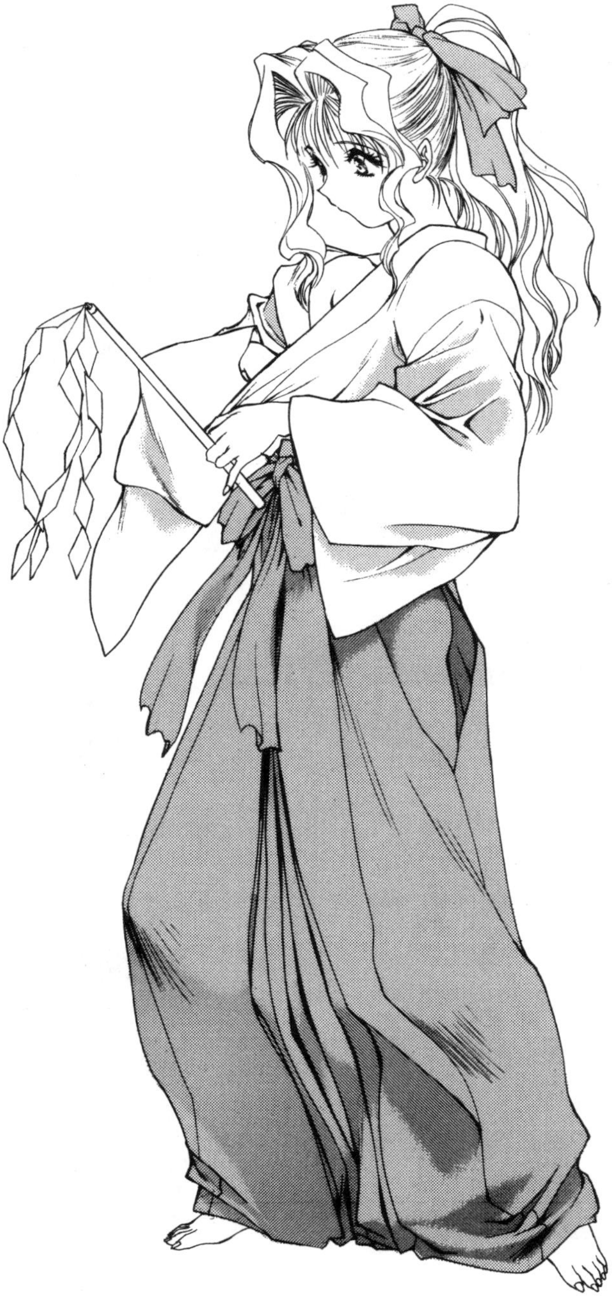

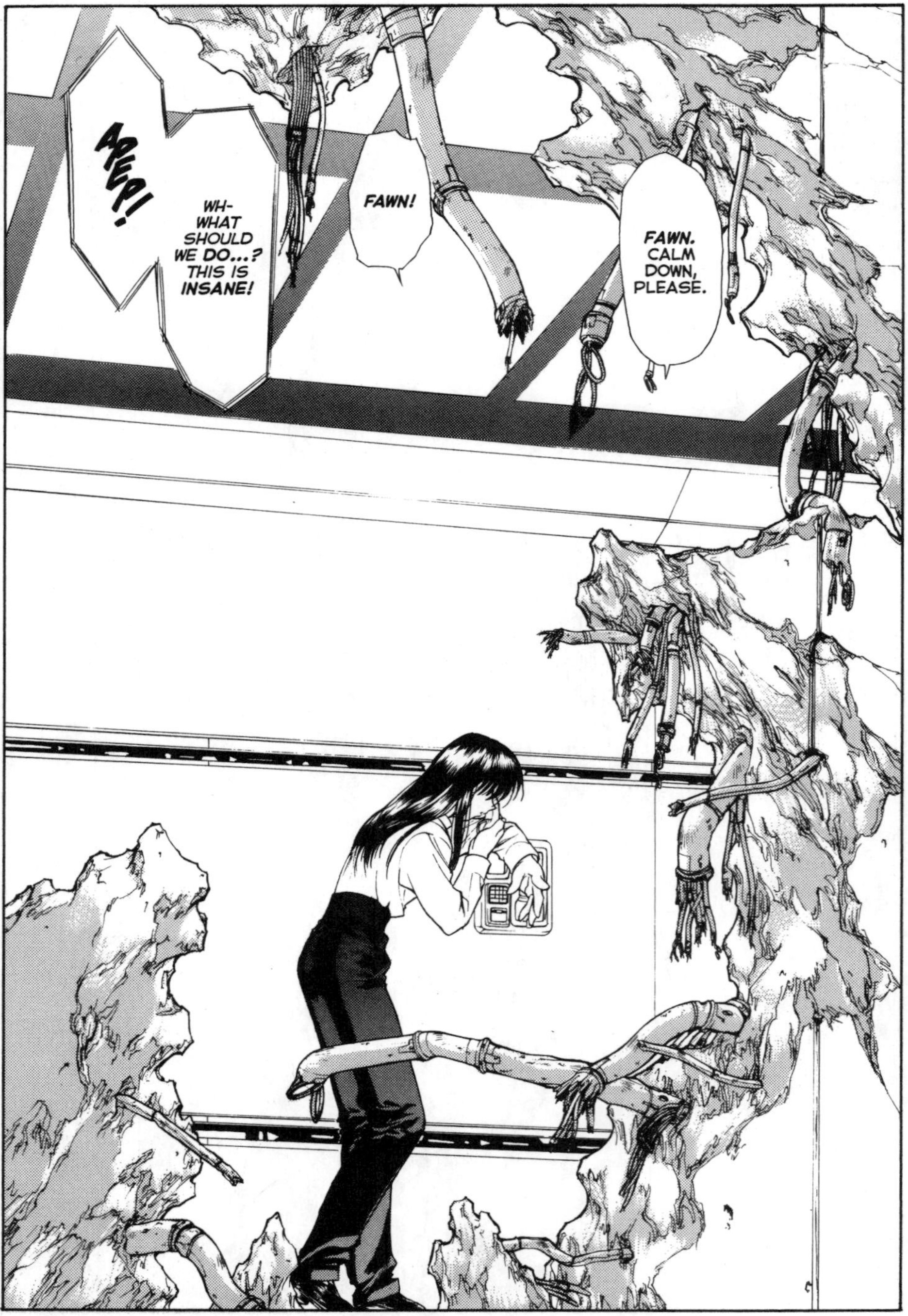
AEEP!
WH- WHAT SHOULD WE DO...? THIS IS INSANE!
FAWN!
FAWN. CALM DOWN, PLEASE.

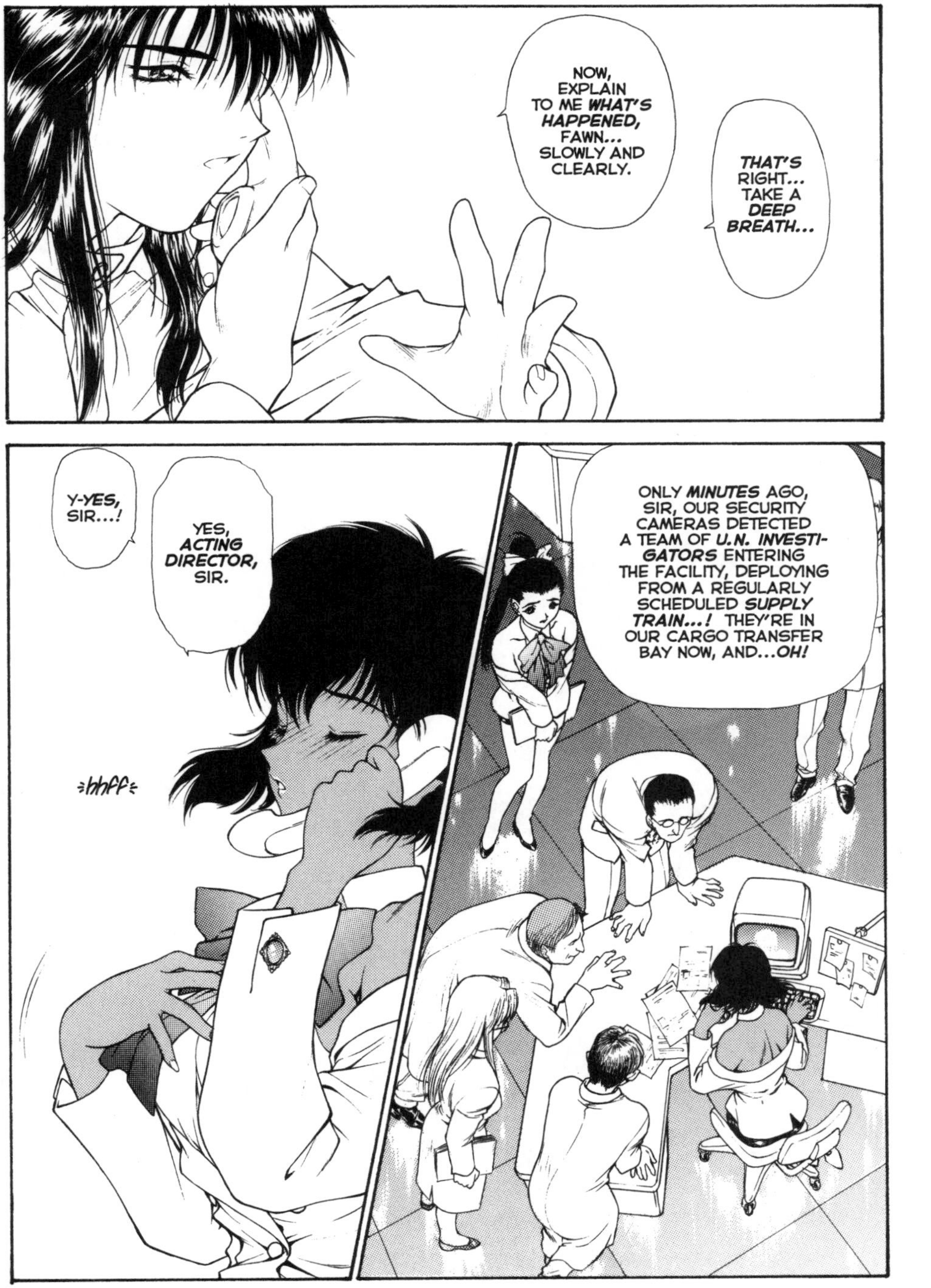
NOW, EXPLAIN TO ME WHAT'S HAPPENED, FAWN... SLOWLY AND CLEARLY.
THAT'S RIGHT... TAKE A DEEP BREATH...
Y-YES, SIR...!
YES, ACTING DIRECTOR, SIR.
hhff
ONLY MINUTES AGO, SIR, OUR SECURITY CAMERAS DETECTED A TEAM OF U.N. INVESTI-GATORS ENTERING THE FACILITY, DEPLOYING FROM A REGULARLY SCHEDULED SUPPLY TRAIN...! THEY'RE IN OUR CARGO TRANSFER BAY NOW, AND...OH!

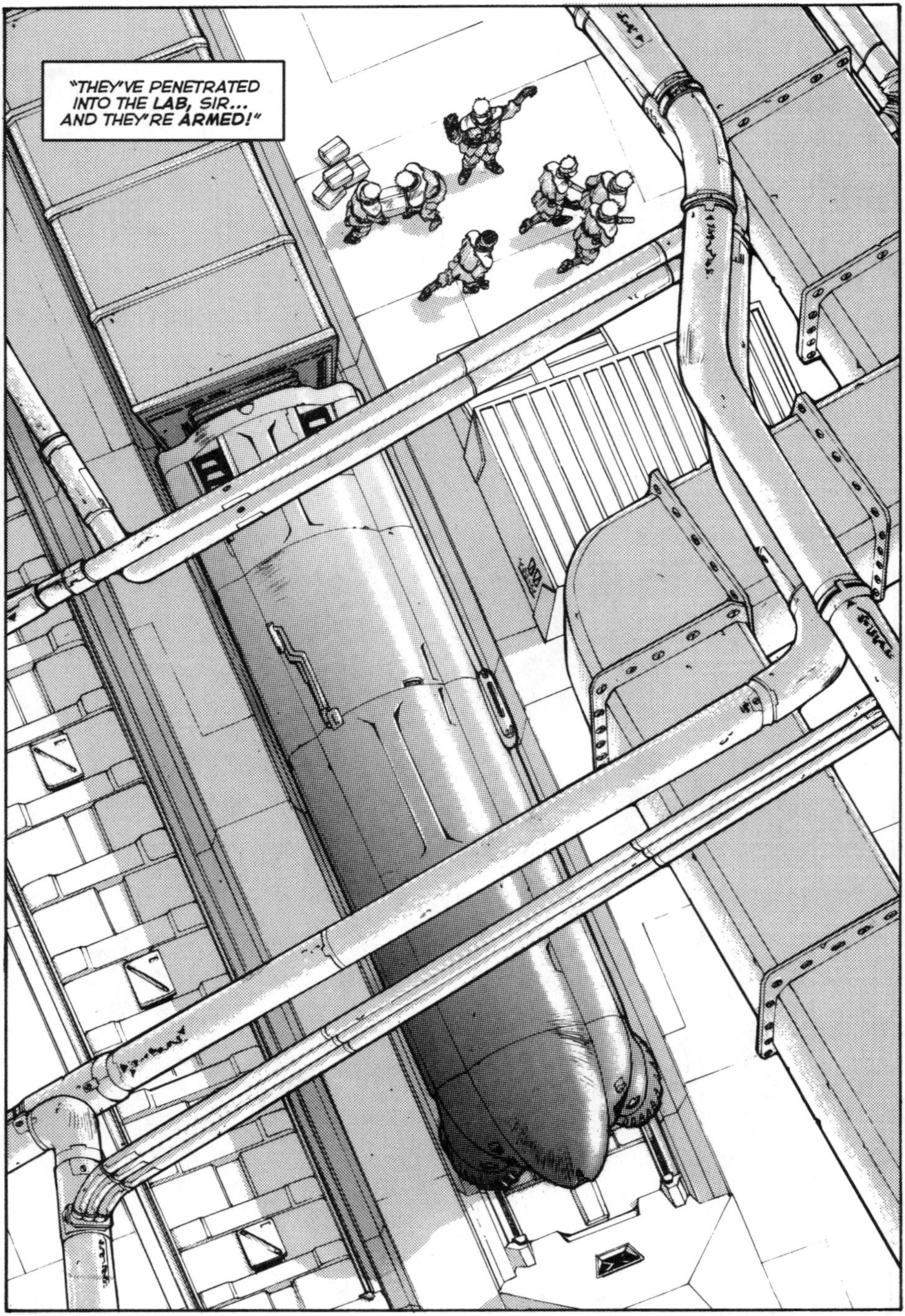
"THEY'VE PENETRATED INTO THE LAB, SIR... AND THEY'RE ARMED!"

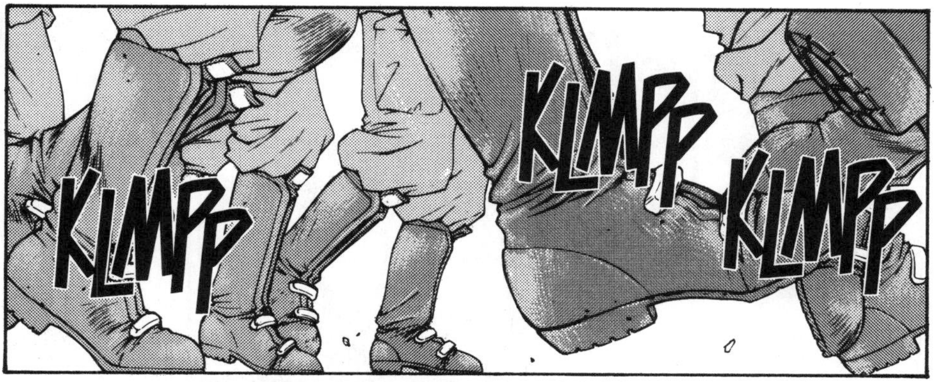
KLMPP
KLMPP
KLMPP
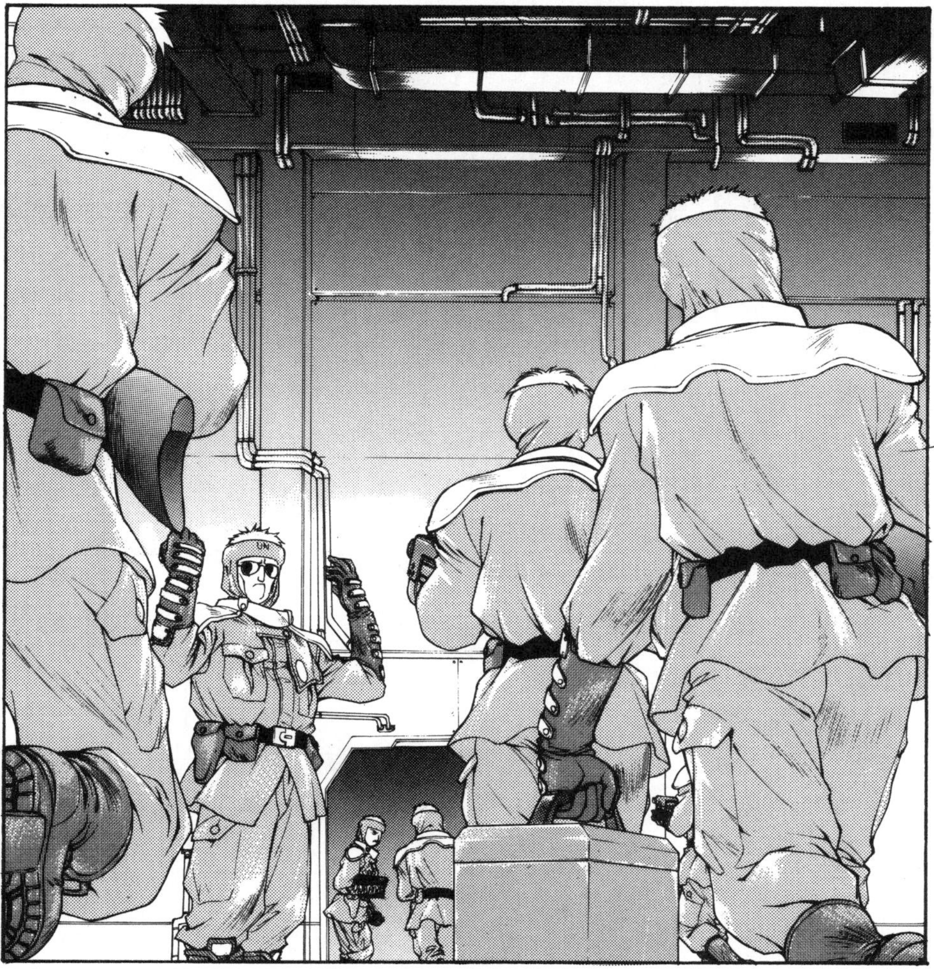

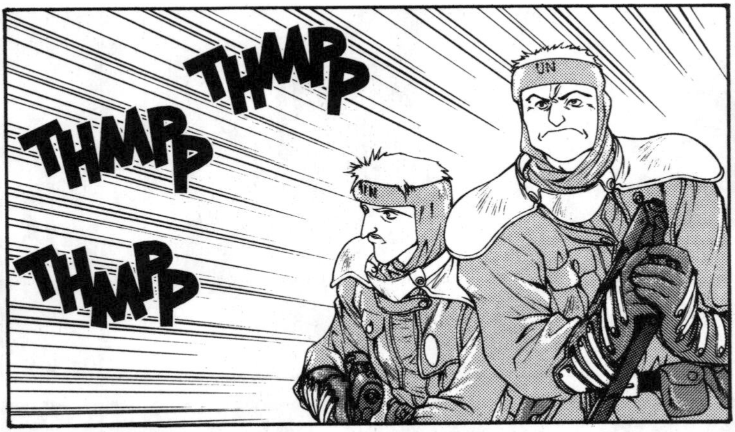
THMPP
THMPP
THMPP
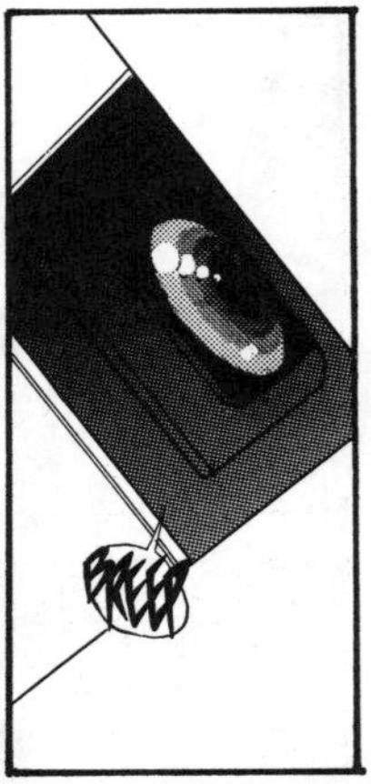
BREEP
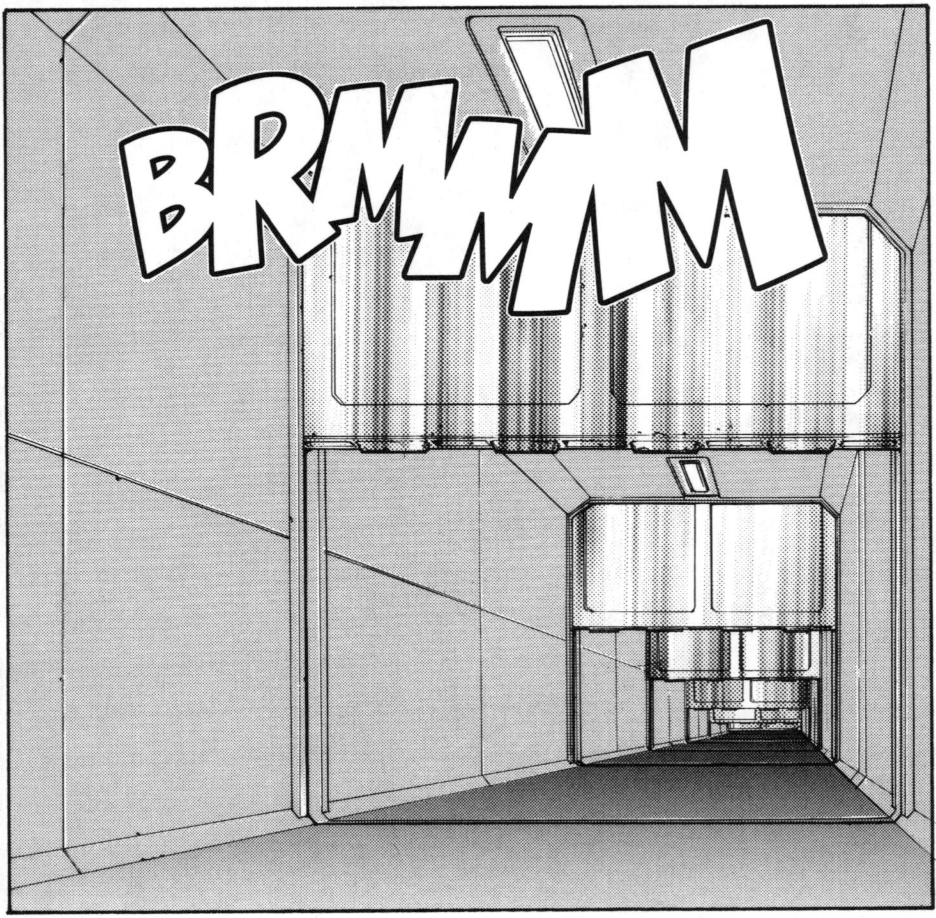
BRMMM

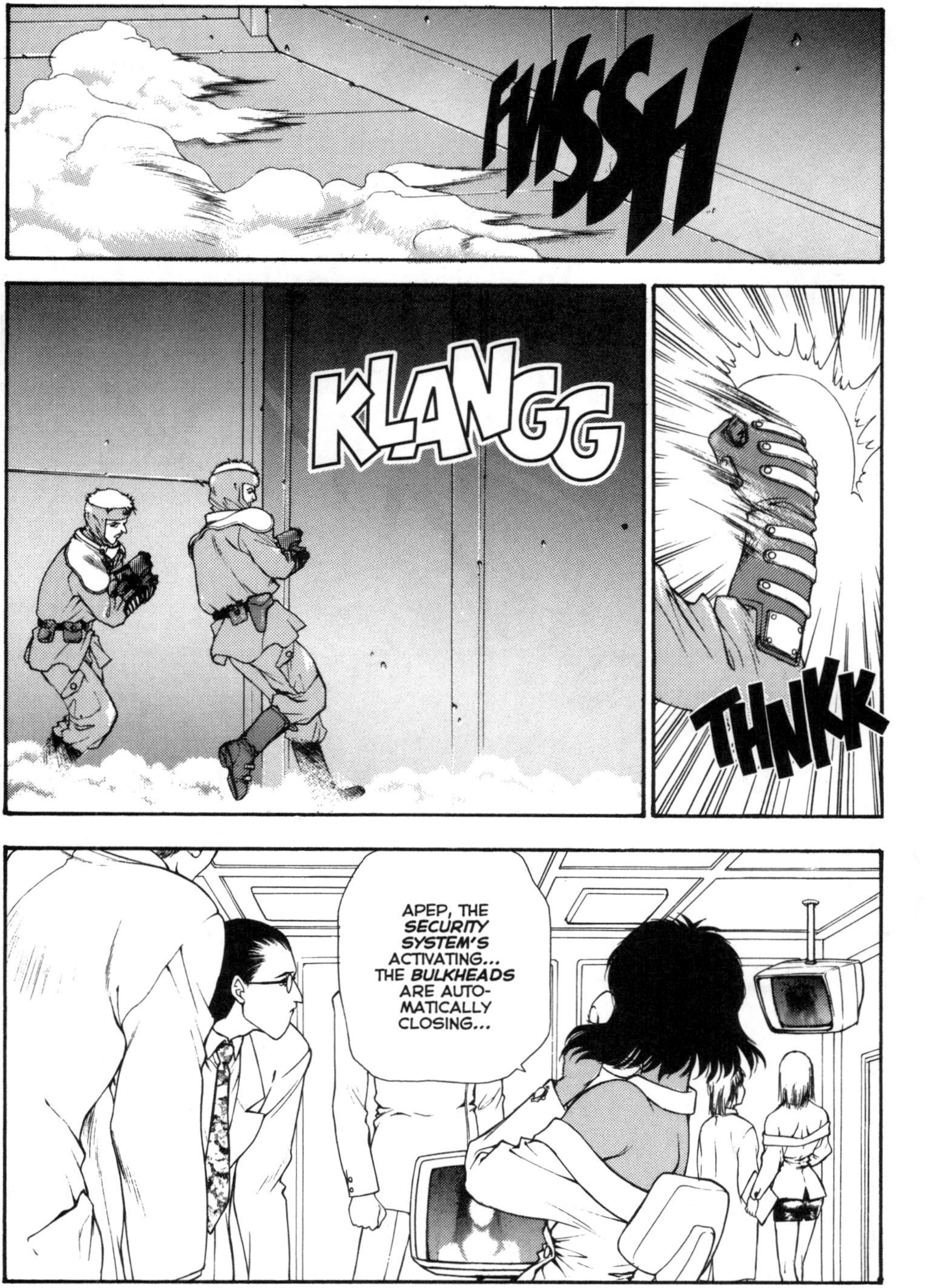
FWSSH
KLANGG
THNKK
APEP, THE *SECURITY SYSTEM'S* ACTIVATING... THE *BULKHEADS* ARE AUTO-MATICALLY CLOSING...

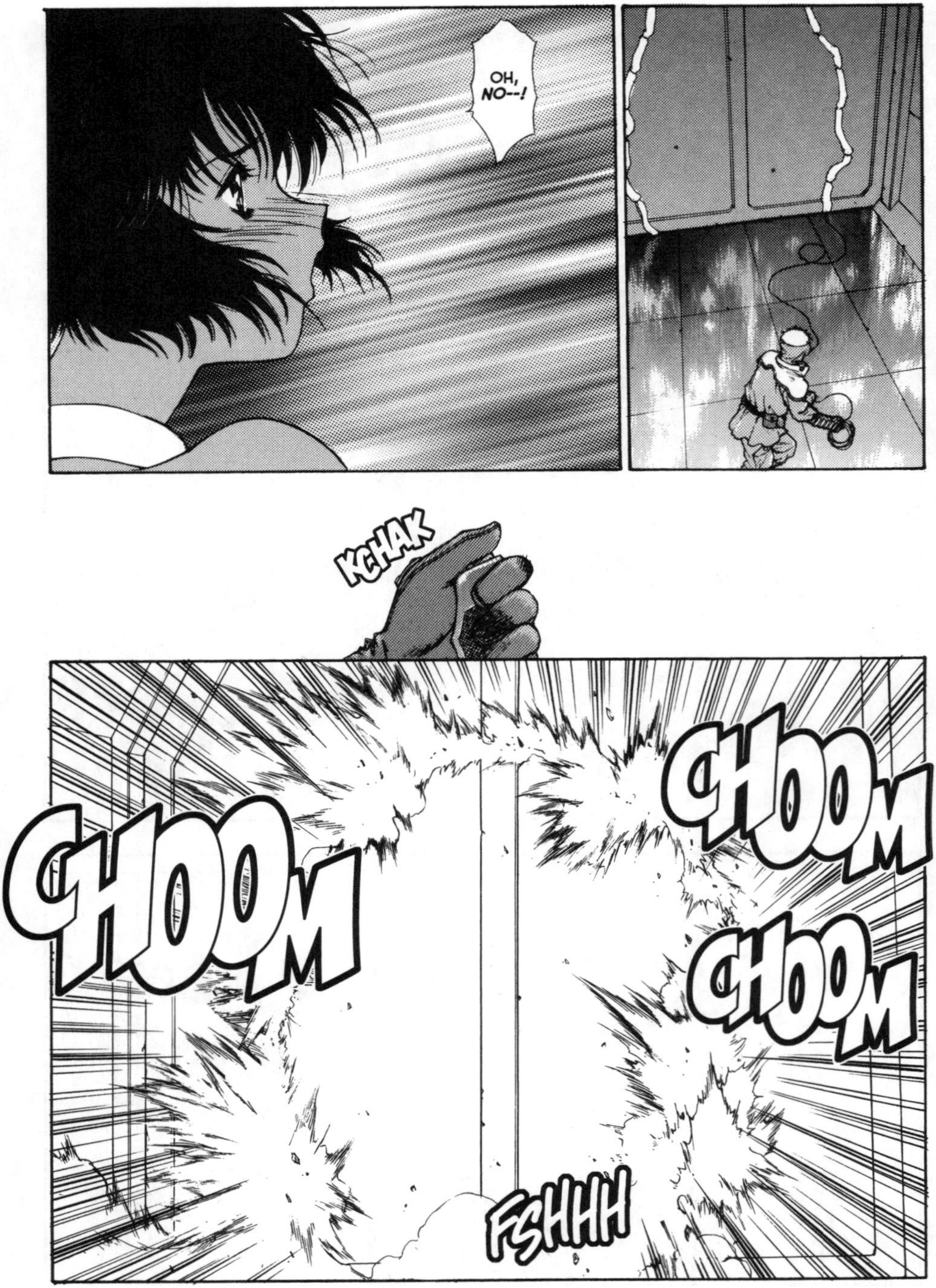
OH, NO--!
KCHAK
CHOOM
CHOOM
CHOOM
FSHHH

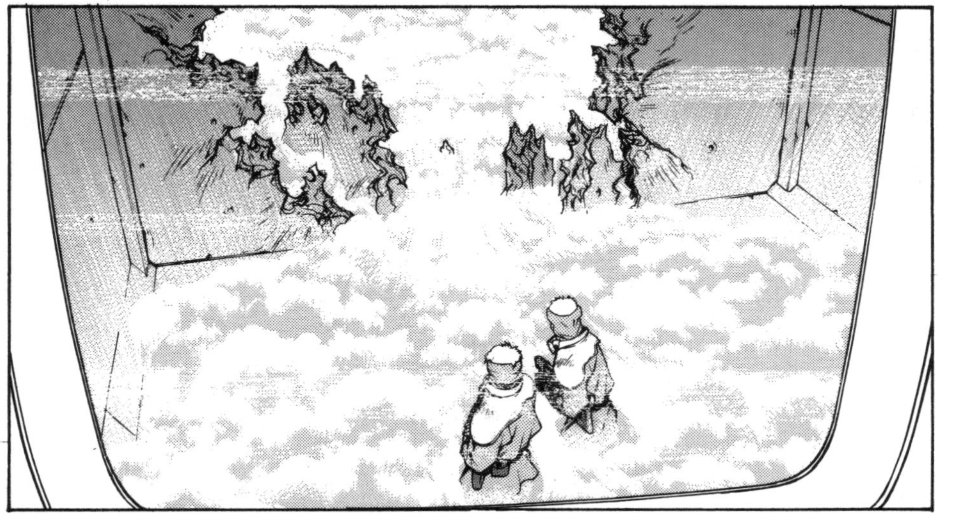

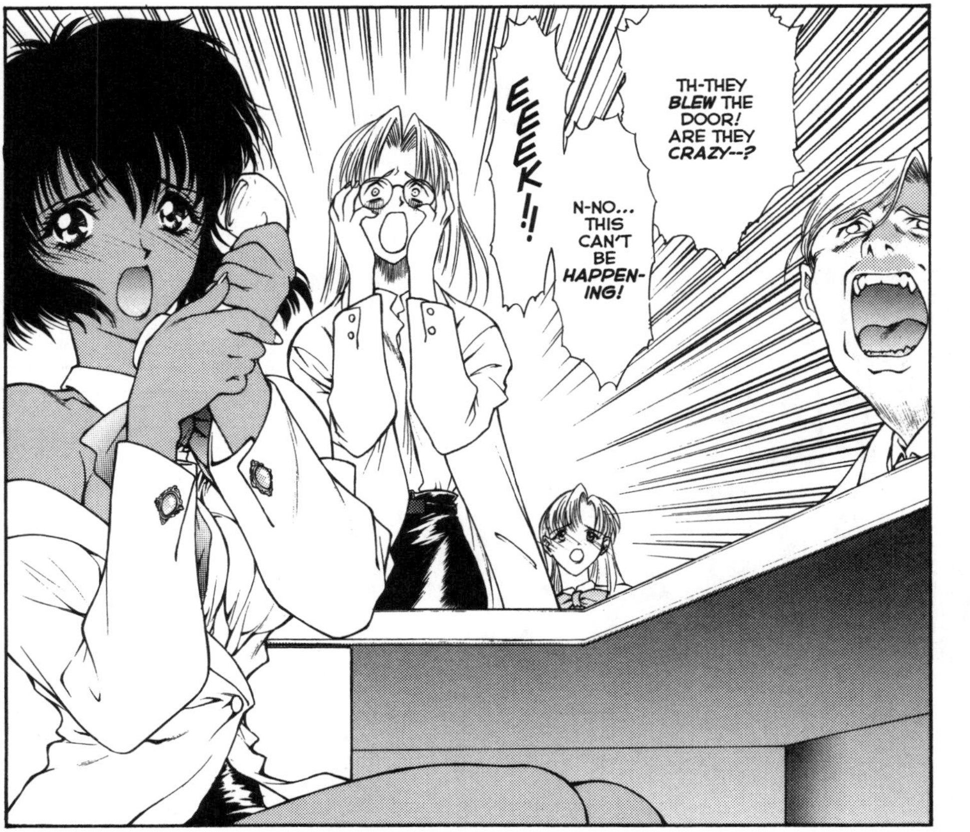
EEEEK!!!
TH-THEY BLEW THE DOOR! ARE THEY CRAZY--?
N-NO... THIS CAN'T BE HAPPENING!

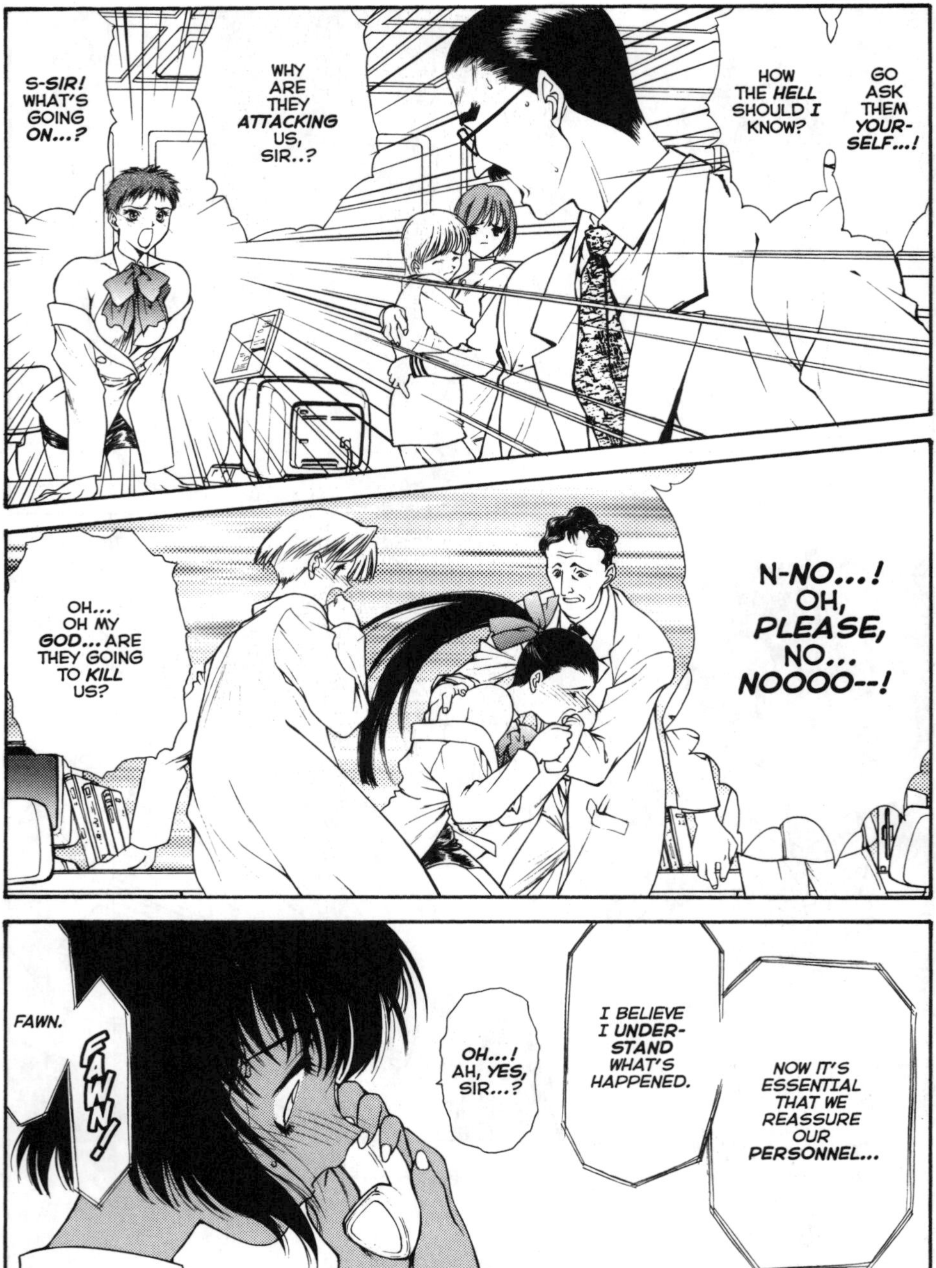
S-SIR! WHAT'S GOING ON...?
WHY ARE THEY ATTACKING US, SIR..?
HOW THE HELL SHOULD I KNOW?
GO ASK THEM YOURSELF...!
OH... OH MY GOD... ARE THEY GOING TO KILL US?
N-NO...! OH, PLEASE, NO... NOOOO--!
FAWN.
FAWN!
OH...! AH, YES, SIR...?
I BELIEVE I UNDERSTAND WHAT'S HAPPENED.
NOW IT'S ESSENTIAL THAT WE REASSURE OUR PERSONNEL...

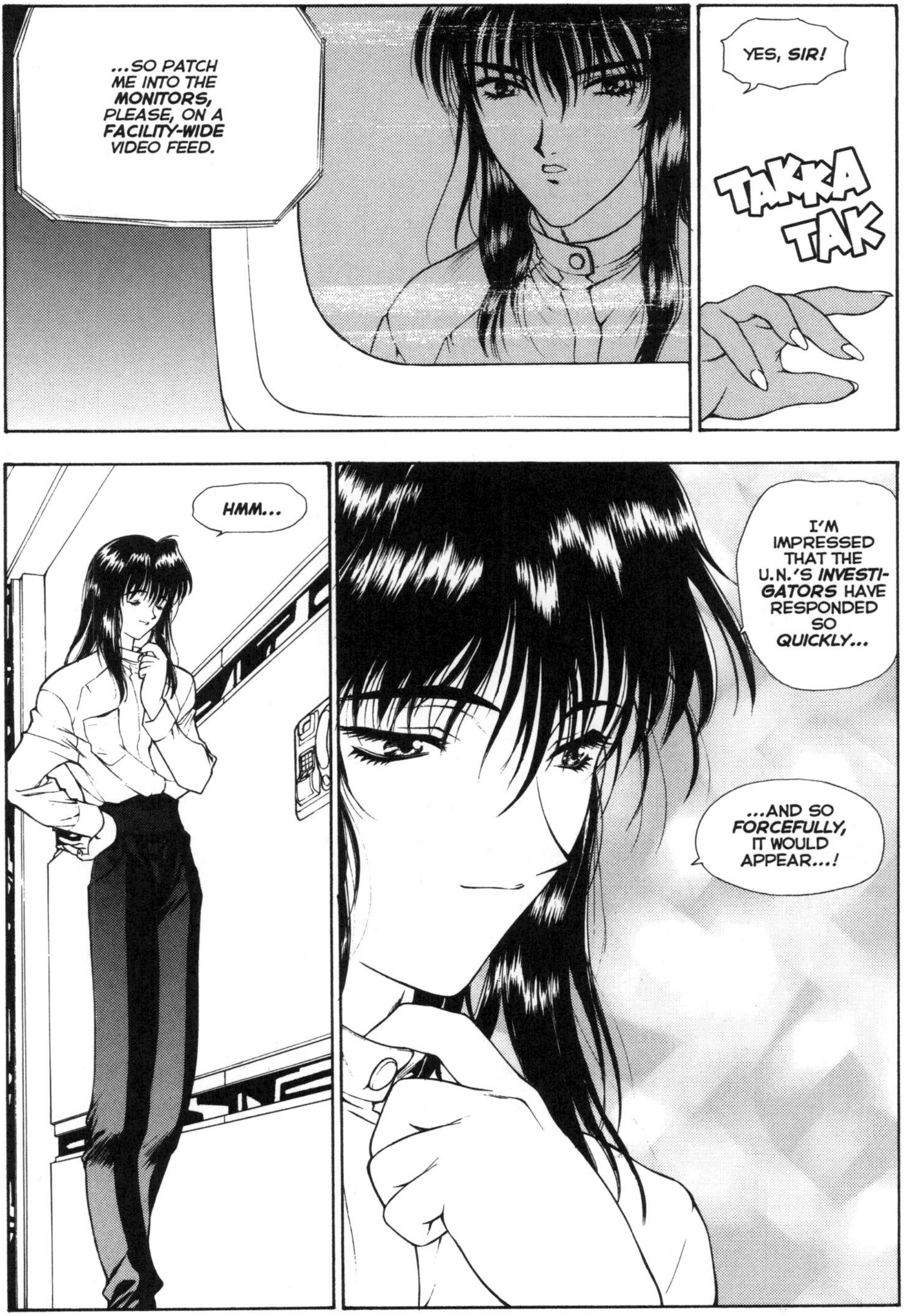
...SO PATCH ME INTO THE MONITORS, PLEASE, ON A FACILITY-WIDE VIDEO FEED.
YES, SIR!
TAKKA TAK
HMM...
I'M IMPRESSED THAT THE U.N.'S INVESTIGATORS HAVE RESPONDED SO QUICKLY...
...AND SO FORCEFULLY, IT WOULD APPEAR...!

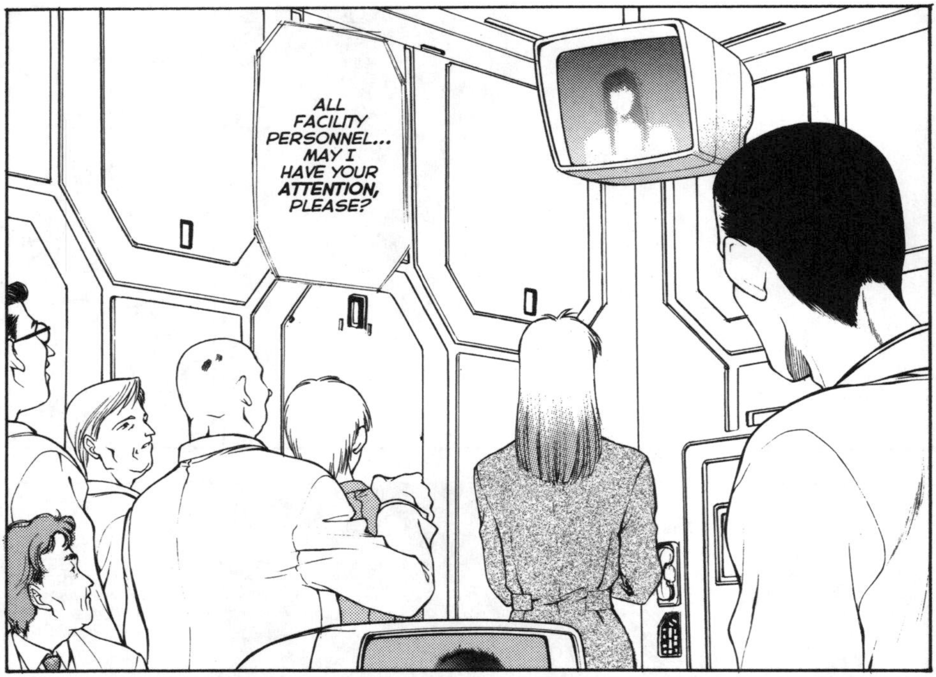
ALL FACILITY PERSONNEL... MAY I HAVE YOUR ATTENTION, PLEASE?

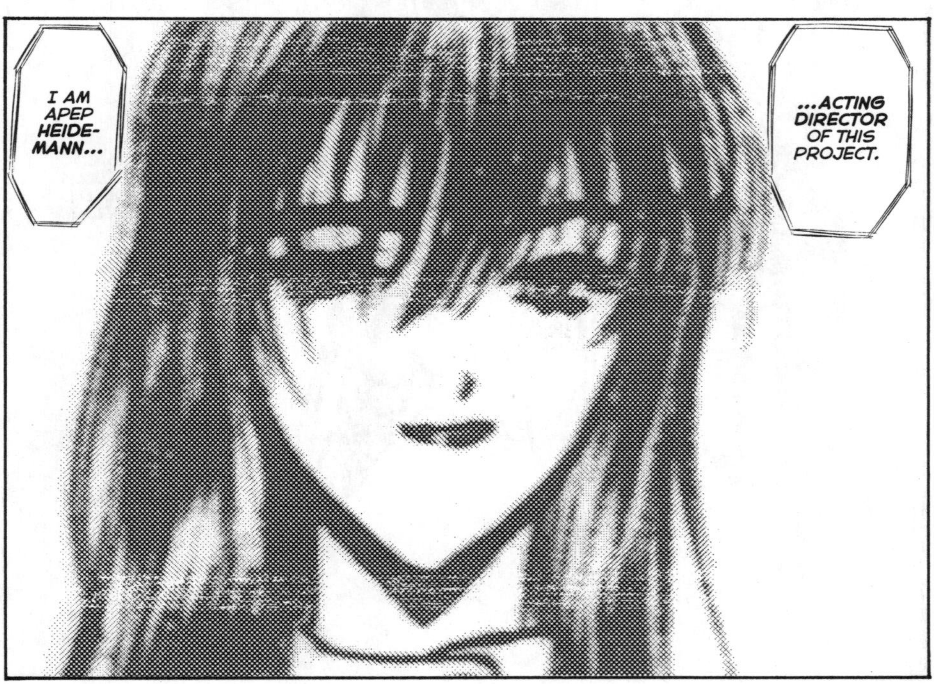
I AM APEP HEIDE-MANN...
...ACTING DIRECTOR OF THIS PROJECT.

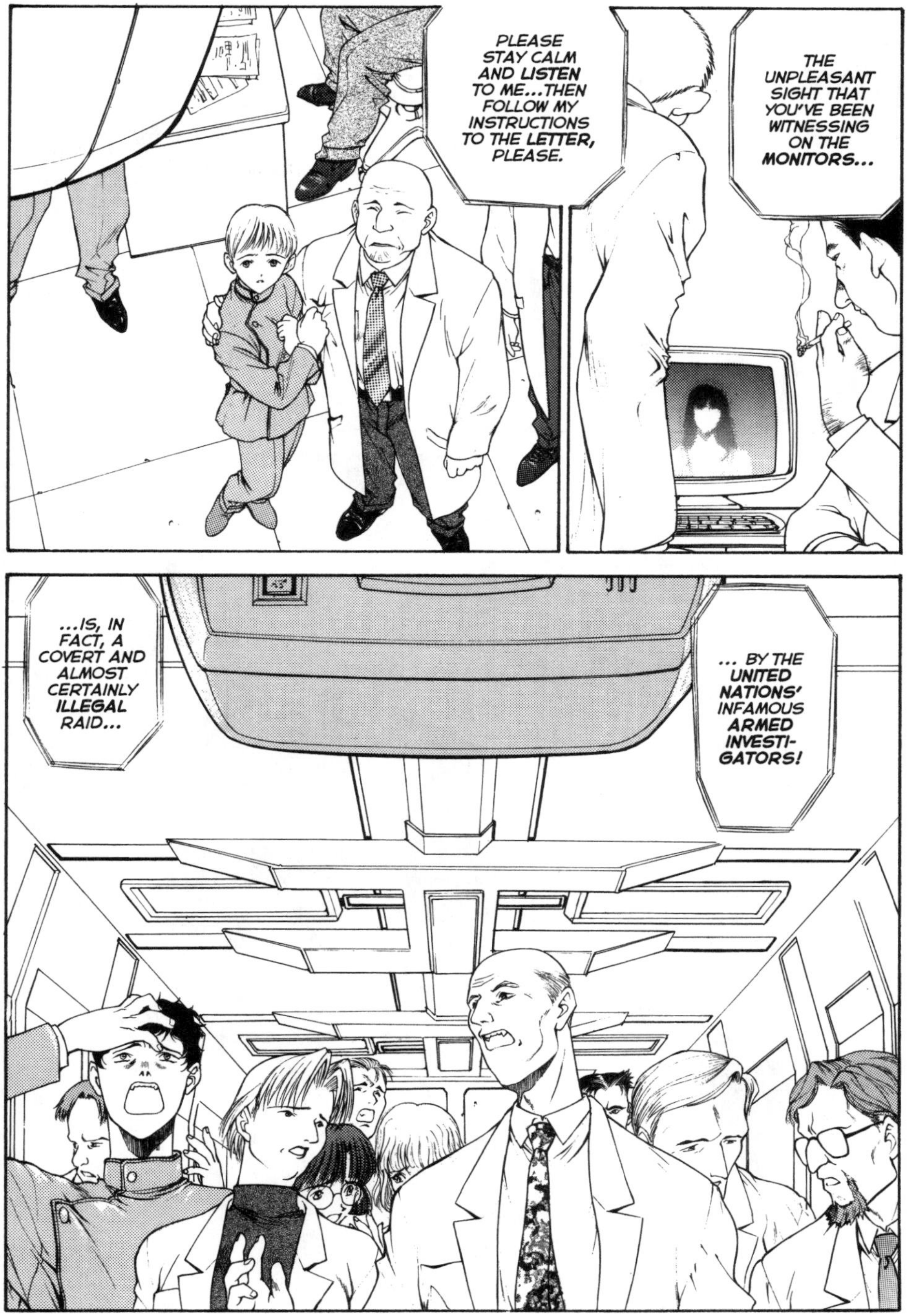
PLEASE STAY CALM AND LISTEN TO ME...THEN FOLLOW MY INSTRUCTIONS TO THE LETTER, PLEASE.
THE UNPLEASANT SIGHT THAT YOU'VE BEEN WITNESSING ON THE MONITORS...
...IS, IN FACT, A COVERT AND ALMOST CERTAINLY ILLEGAL RAID...
... BY THE UNITED NATIONS' INFAMOUS ARMED INVESTI-GATORS!

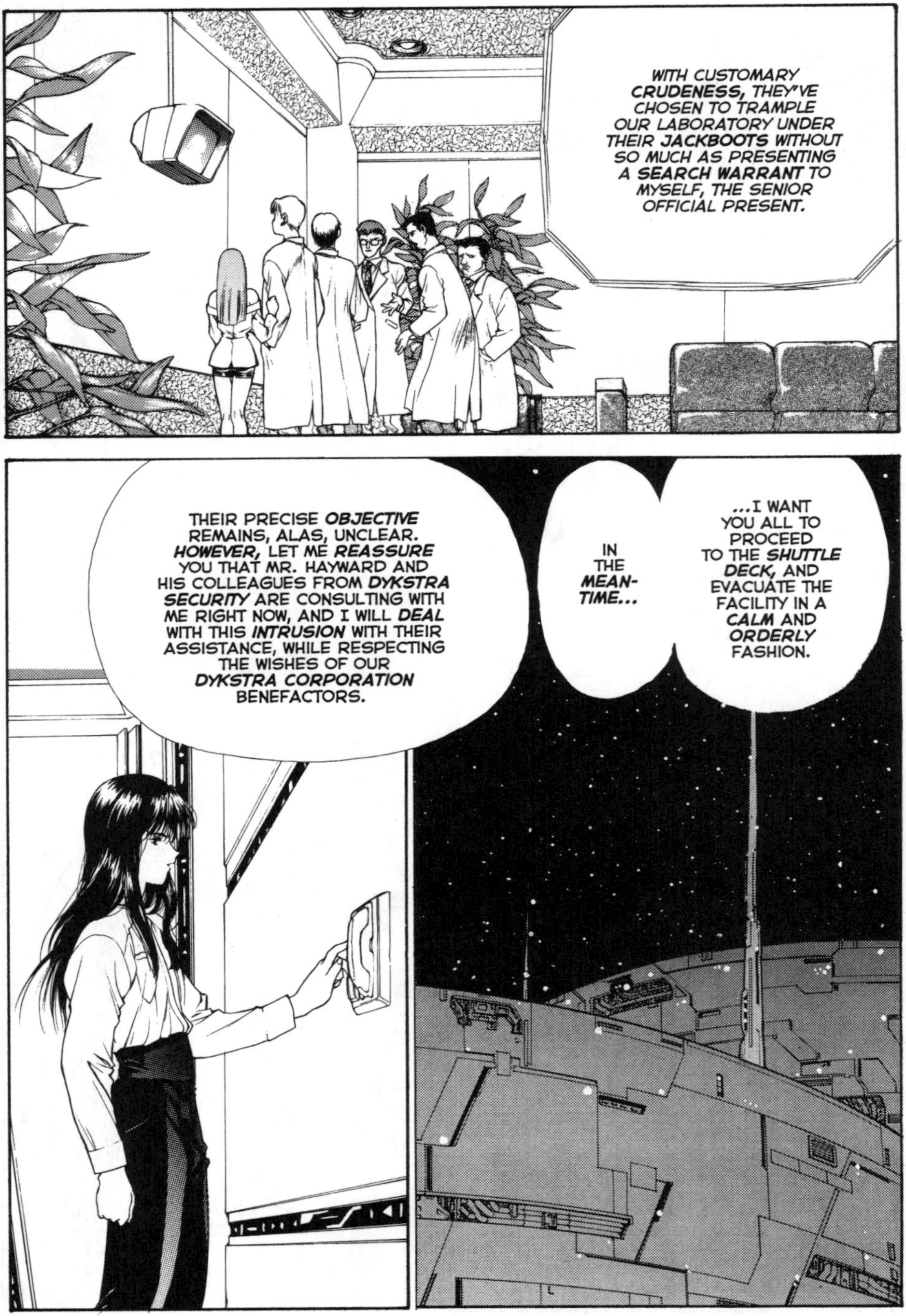
WITH CUSTOMARY CRUDENESS, THEY'VE CHOSEN TO TRAMPLE OUR LABORATORY UNDER THEIR JACKBOOTS WITHOUT SO MUCH AS PRESENTING A SEARCH WARRANT TO MYSELF, THE SENIOR OFFICIAL PRESENT.
THEIR PRECISE OBJECTIVE REMAINS, ALAS, UNCLEAR. HOWEVER, LET ME REASSURE YOU THAT MR. HAYWARD AND HIS COLLEAGUES FROM DYKSTRA SECURITY ARE CONSULTING WITH ME RIGHT NOW, AND I WILL DEAL WITH THIS INTRUSION WITH THEIR ASSISTANCE, WHILE RESPECTING THE WISHES OF OUR DYKSTRA CORPORATION BENEFACTORS.
IN THE MEAN-TIME...
...I WANT YOU ALL TO PROCEED TO THE SHUTTLE DECK, AND EVACUATE THE FACILITY IN A CALM AND ORDERLY FASHION.

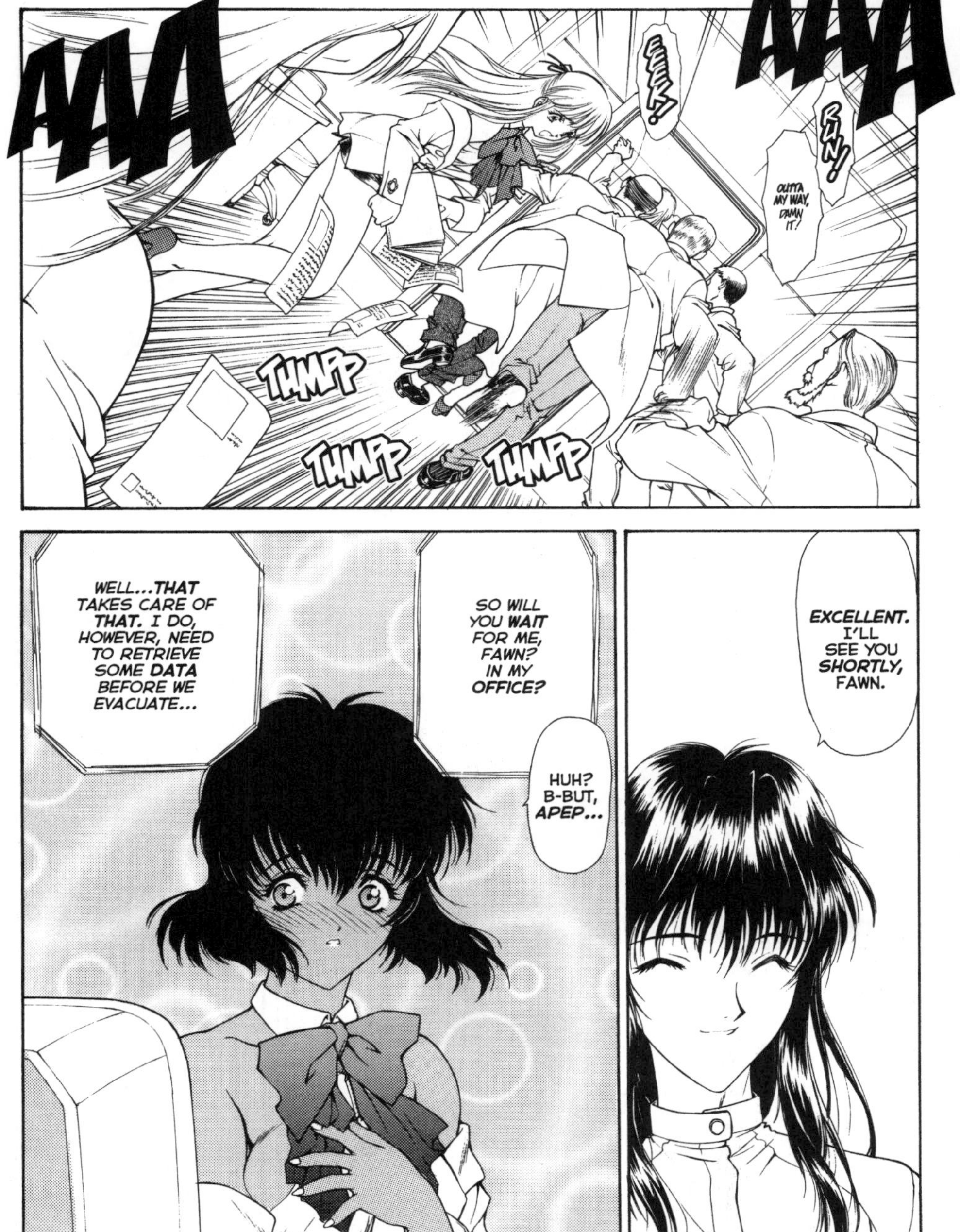
AAAA
EEEK!
AAAA
RUN!
OUTTA MY WAY, DAMN IT!
THMPP
THMPP
THMPP
WELL...THAT TAKES CARE OF THAT. I DO, HOWEVER, NEED TO RETRIEVE SOME DATA BEFORE WE EVACUATE...
SO WILL YOU WAIT FOR ME, FAWN? IN MY OFFICE?
HUH? B-BUT, APEP...
EXCELLENT. I'LL SEE YOU SHORTLY, FAWN.

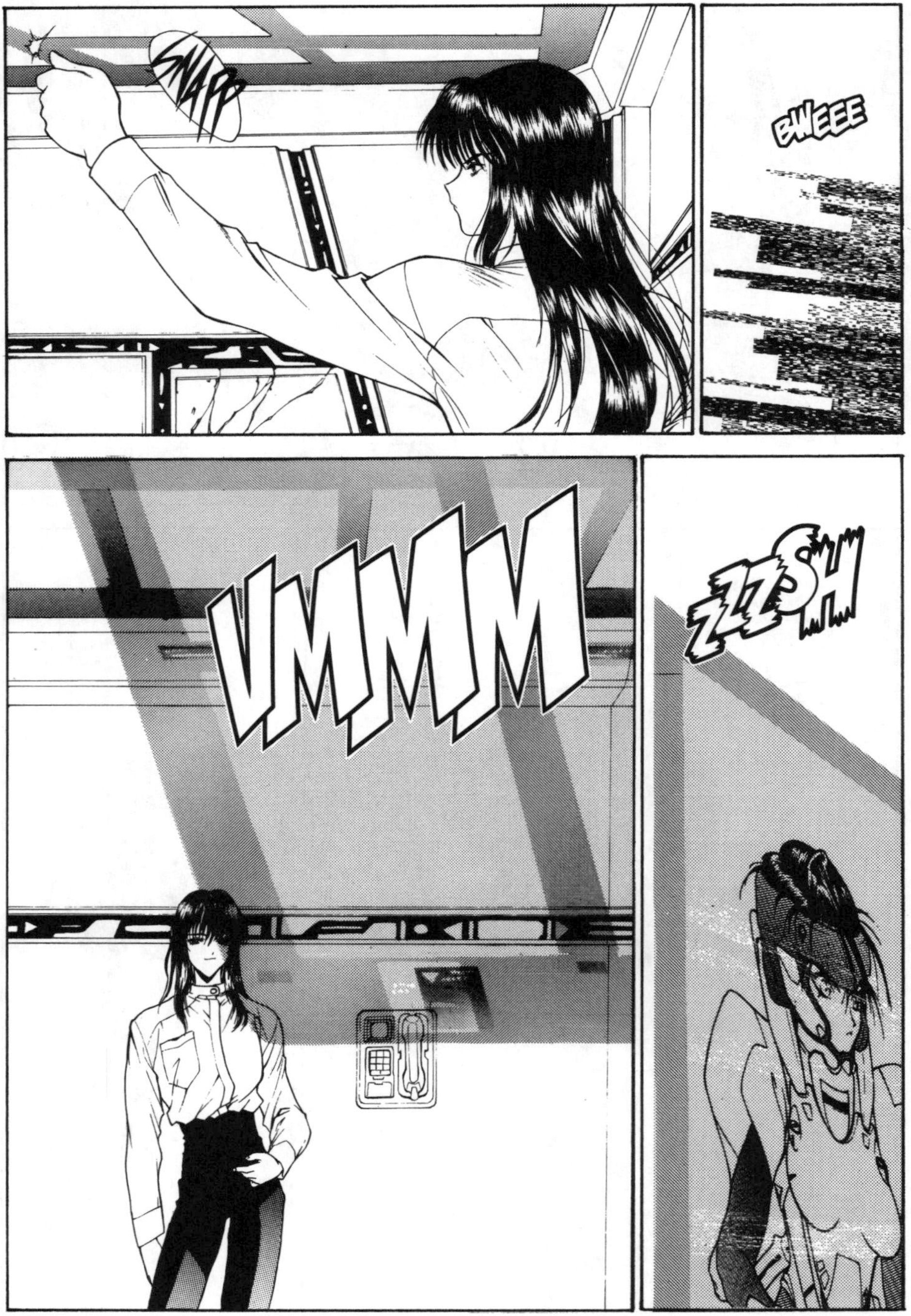
SNAP
BWEEE
VMMM
ZZZSH

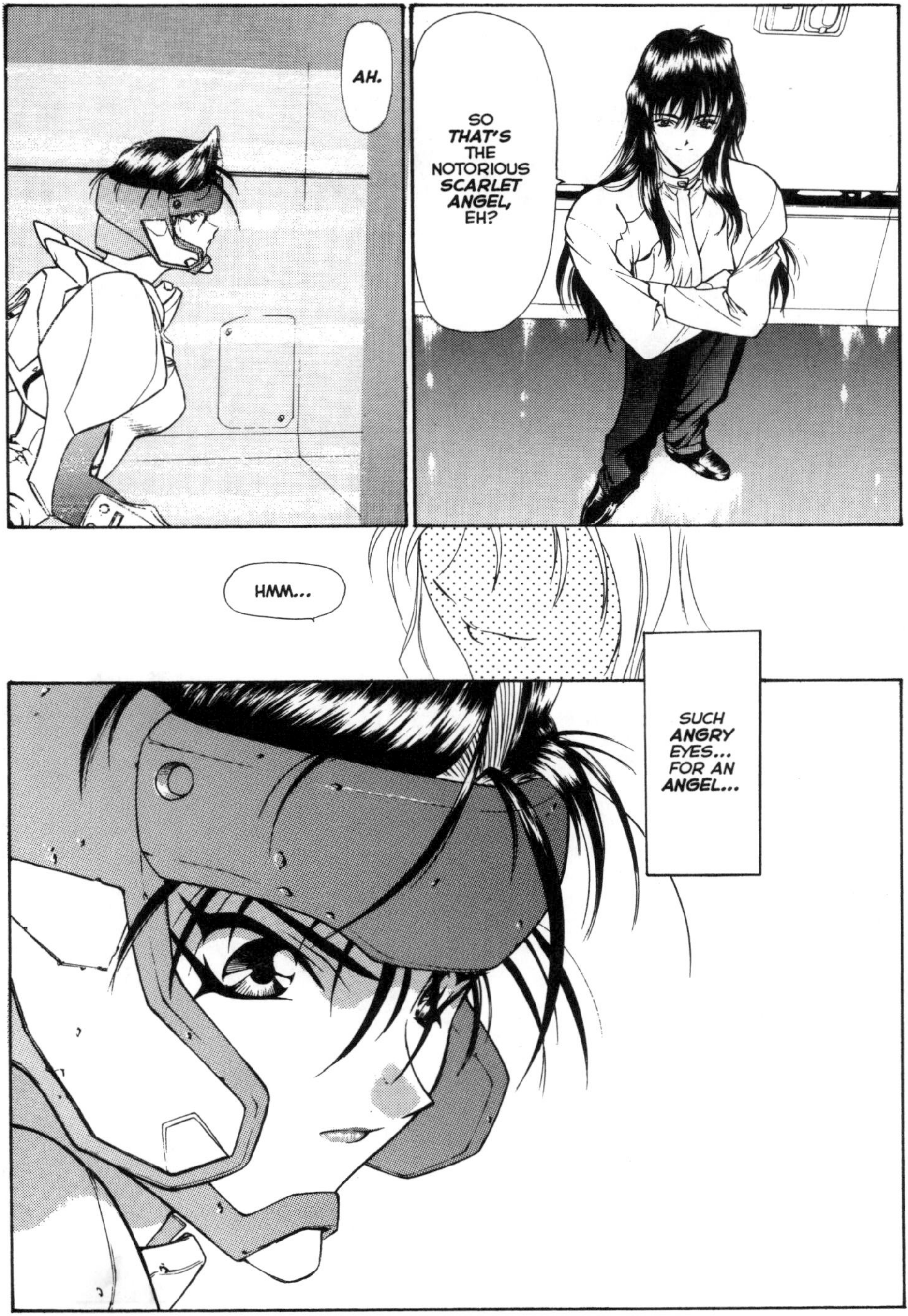
AH.
SO *THAT'S* THE NOTORIOUS *SCARLET ANGEL,* EH?
HMM...
SUCH ANGRY EYES... FOR AN ANGEL...

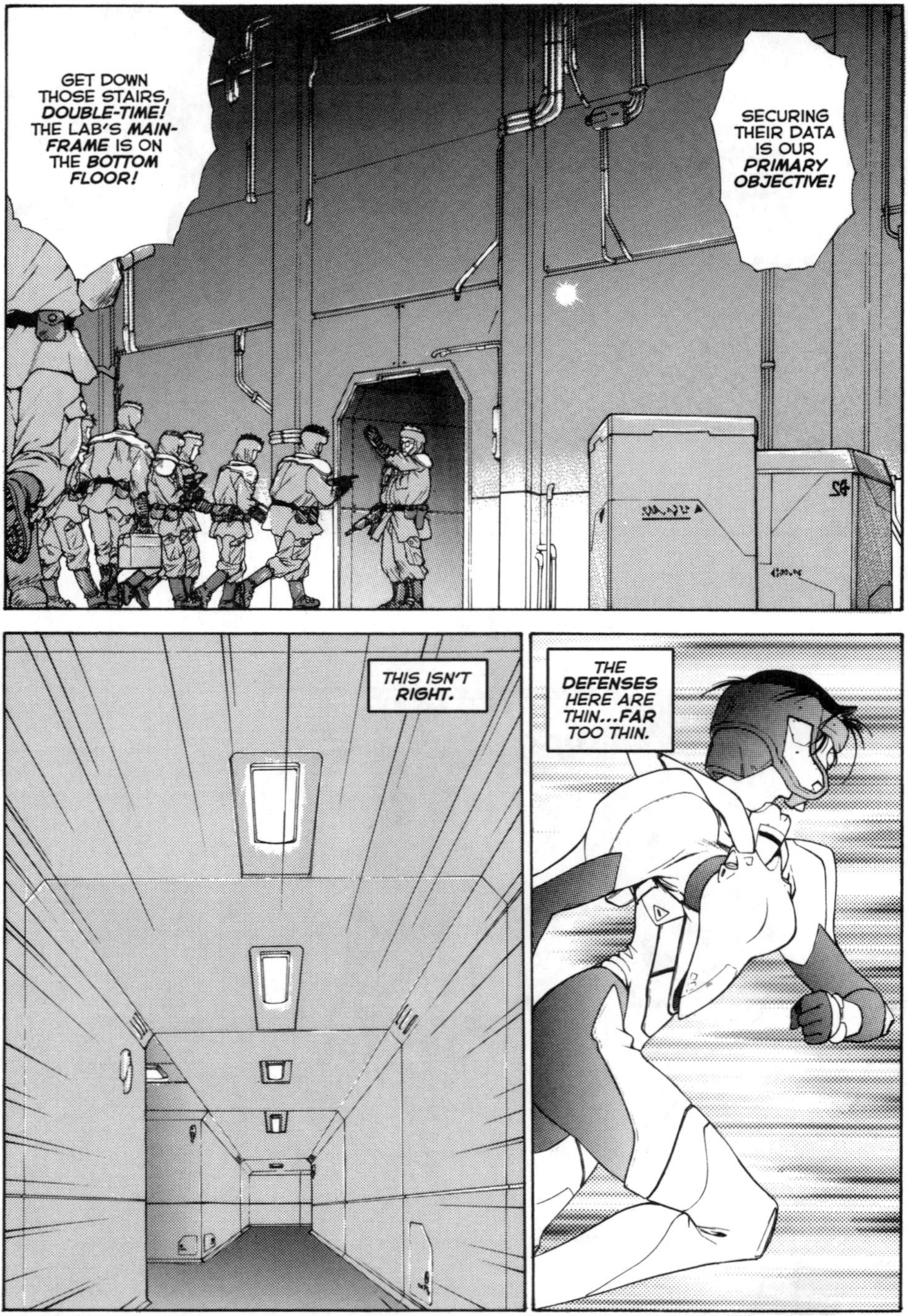
GET DOWN THOSE STAIRS, DOUBLE-TIME! THE LAB'S MAIN-FRAME IS ON THE BOTTOM FLOOR!
SECURING THEIR DATA IS OUR PRIMARY OBJECTIVE!
THIS ISN'T RIGHT.
THE DEFENSES HERE ARE THIN...FAR TOO THIN.

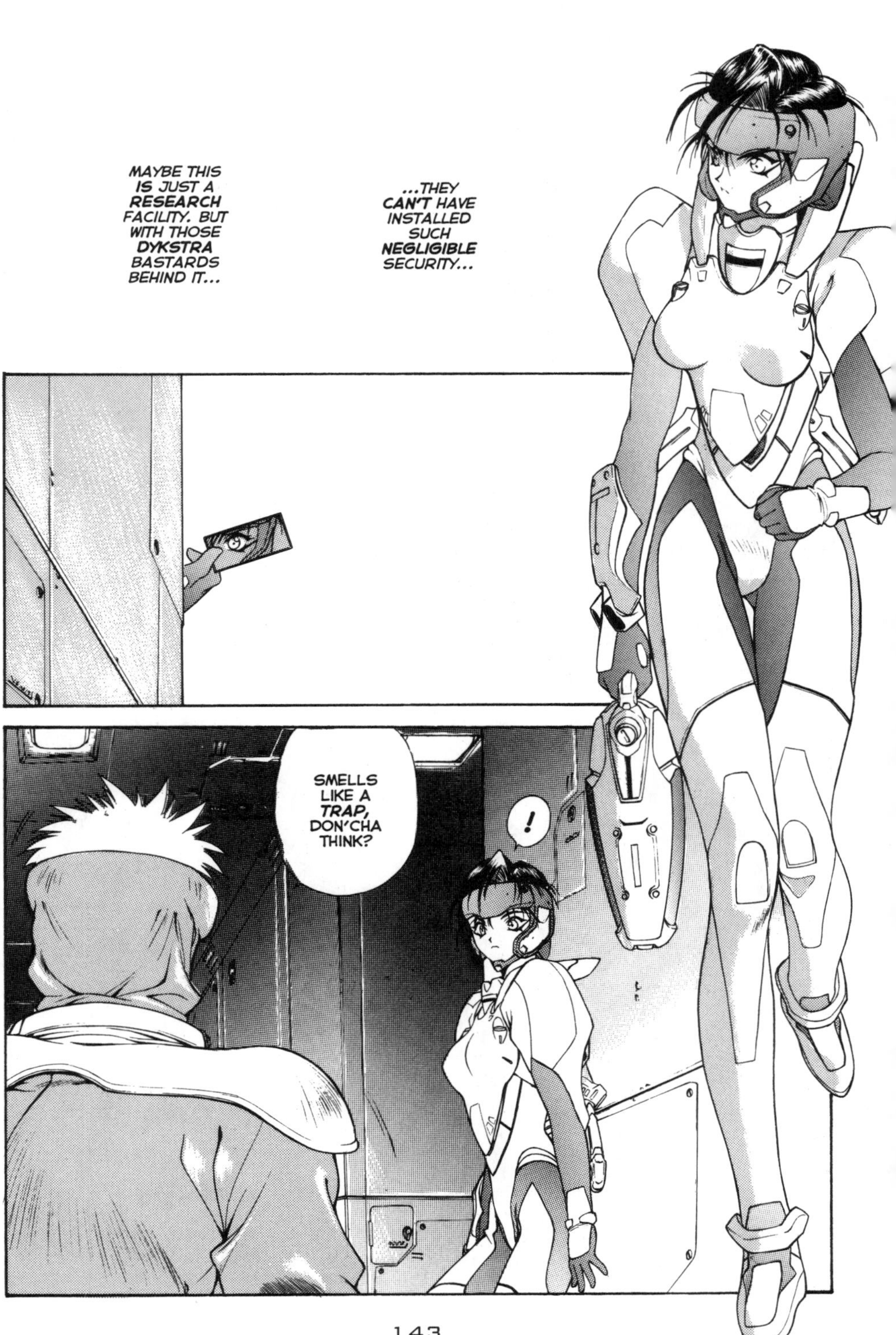
MAYBE THIS IS JUST A RESEARCH FACILITY. BUT WITH THOSE DYKSTRA BASTARDS BEHIND IT...
...THEY CAN'T HAVE INSTALLED SUCH NEGLIGIBLE SECURITY...
SMELLS LIKE A TRAP, DON'CHA THINK?
!

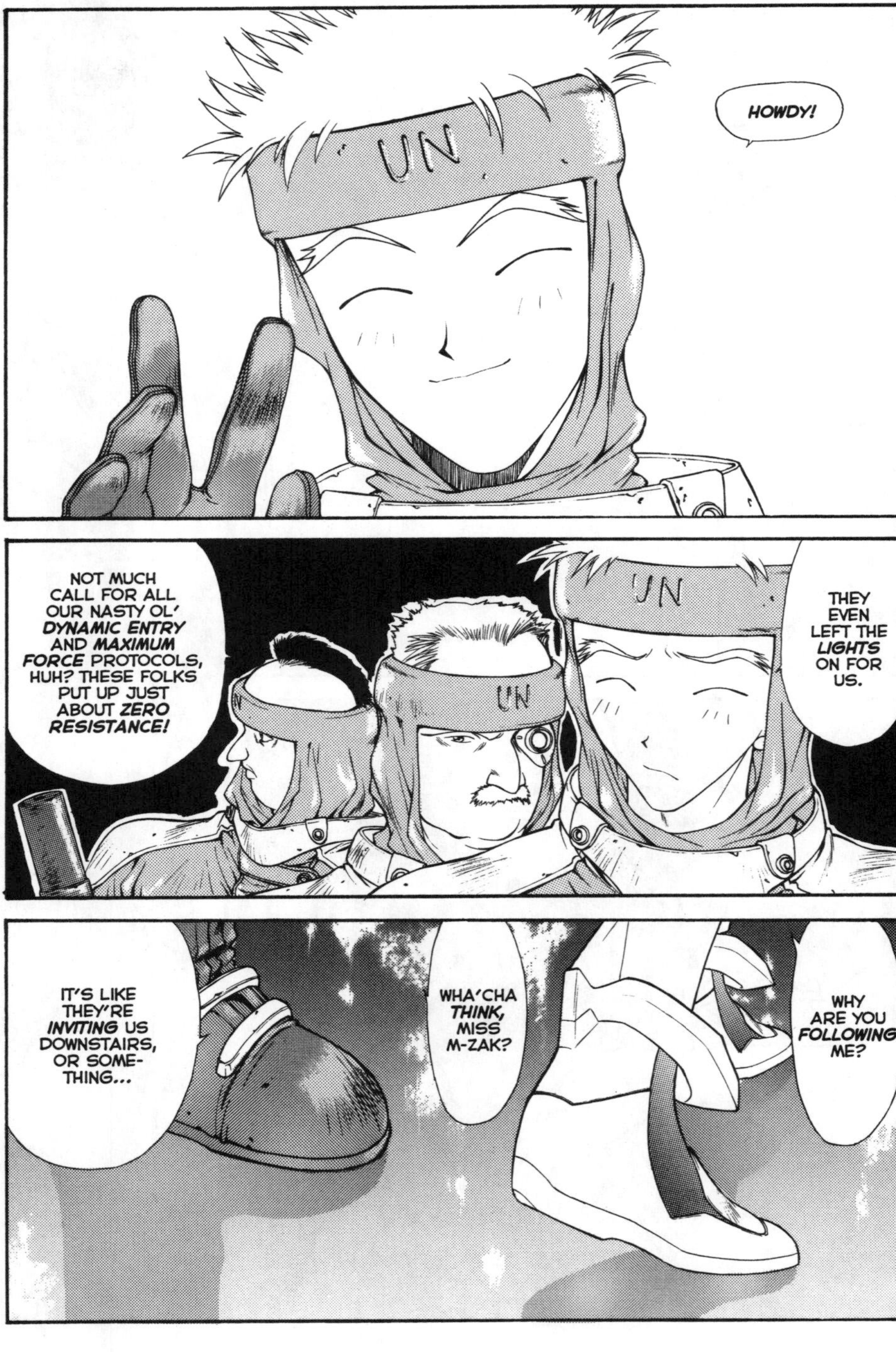
HOWDY!
NOT MUCH CALL FOR ALL OUR NASTY OL' DYNAMIC ENTRY AND MAXIMUM FORCE PROTOCOLS, HUH? THESE FOLKS PUT UP JUST ABOUT ZERO RESISTANCE!
THEY EVEN LEFT THE LIGHTS ON FOR US.
IT'S LIKE THEY'RE INVITING US DOWNSTAIRS, OR SOME-THING...
WHA'CHA THINK, MISS M-ZAK?
WHY ARE YOU FOLLOWING ME?

I SAID, WHY ARE YOU *FOLLOWING* ME...?

HUH?

WHY?

'CAUSE OL' *LEN* FEELS *SAFER* WITH THE TOUGHEST KID ON THE BLOCK, *THAT'S* WHY! AN' *BESIDES*...

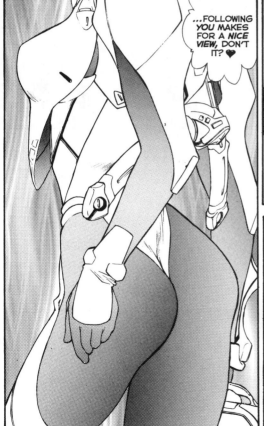

...FOLLOWING *YOU* MAKES FOR A *NICE VIEW*, DON'T IT? ♥

KRAK

OW!

YEE-OW...!

GEEZ!

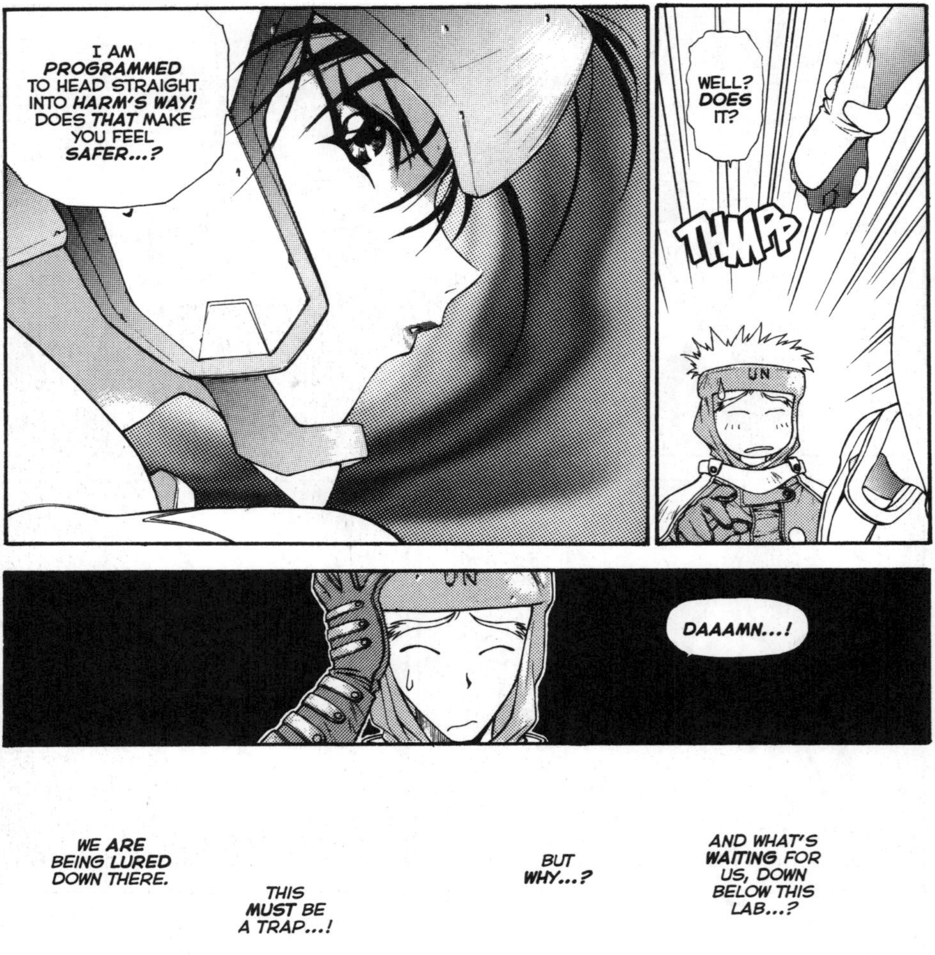
I AM PROGRAMMED TO HEAD STRAIGHT INTO HARM'S WAY! DOES THAT MAKE YOU FEEL SAFER...?
WELL? DOES IT?
THMPP
DAAAMN...!
WE ARE BEING LURED DOWN THERE.
THIS MUST BE A TRAP...!
BUT WHY...?
AND WHAT'S WAITING FOR US, DOWN BELOW THIS LAB...?

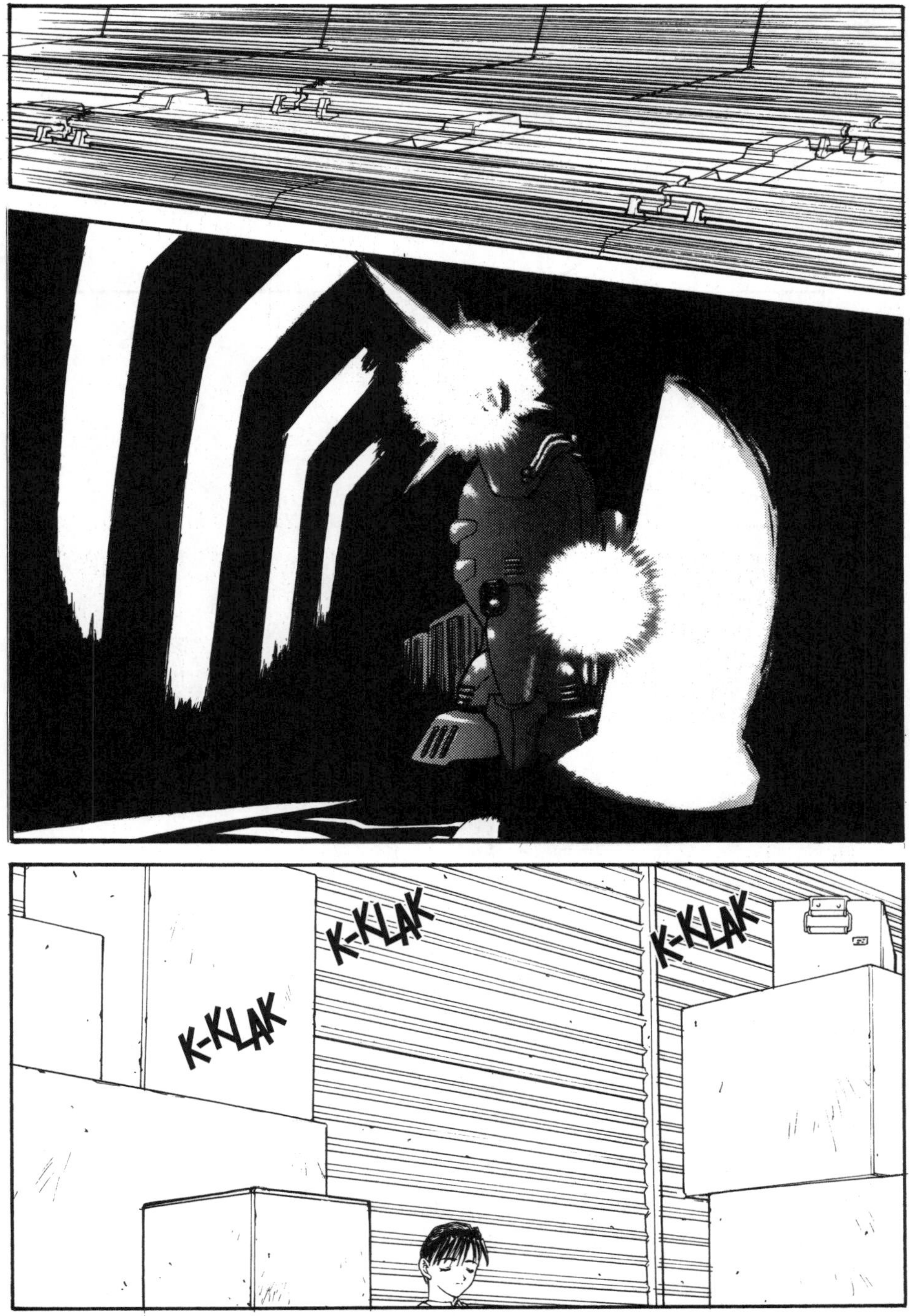
K-KLAK
K-KLAK
K-KLAK

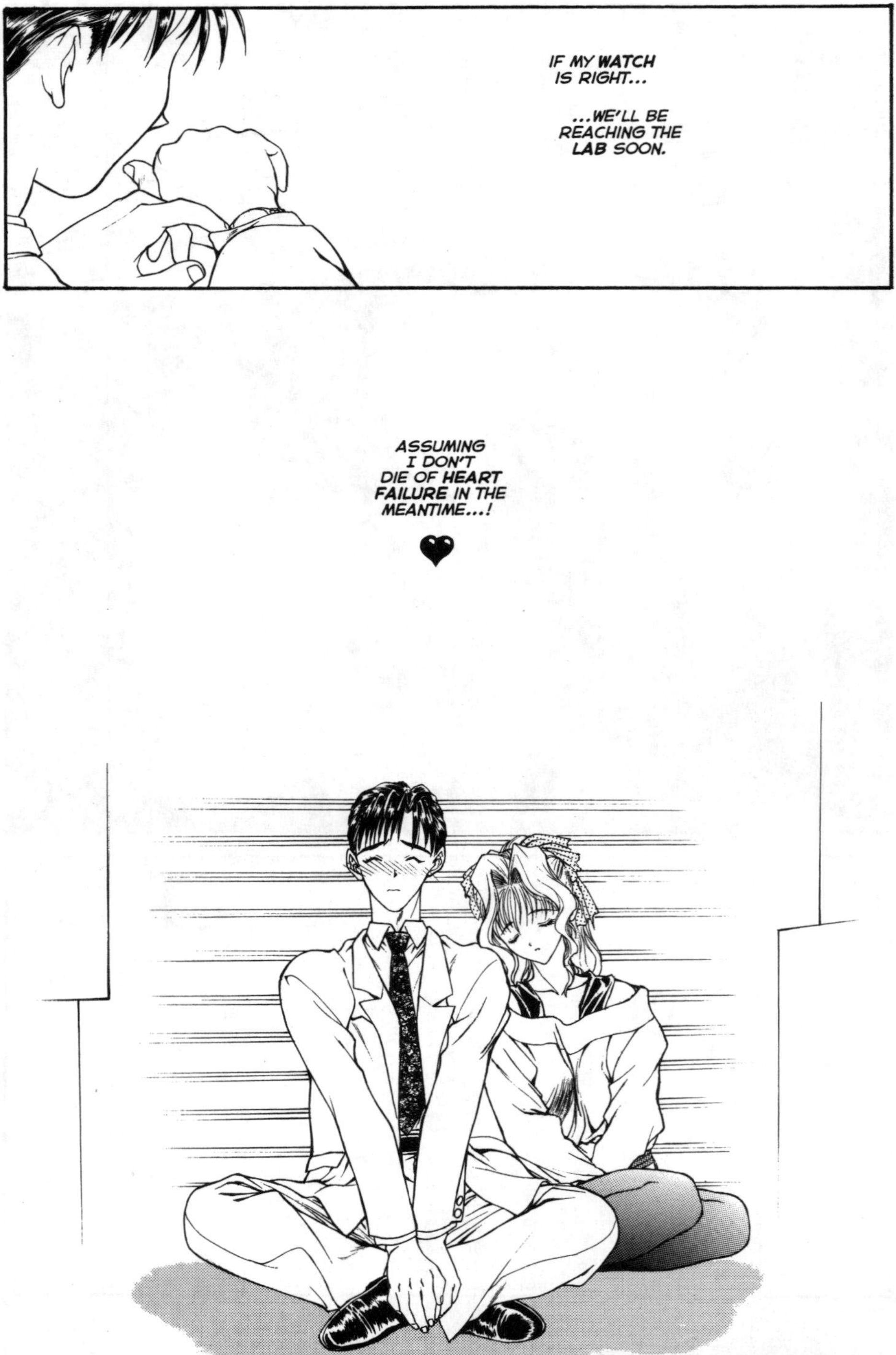
IF MY WATCH IS RIGHT...
...WE'LL BE REACHING THE LAB SOON.
ASSUMING I DON'T DIE OF HEART FAILURE IN THE MEANTIME...!

ACT 24

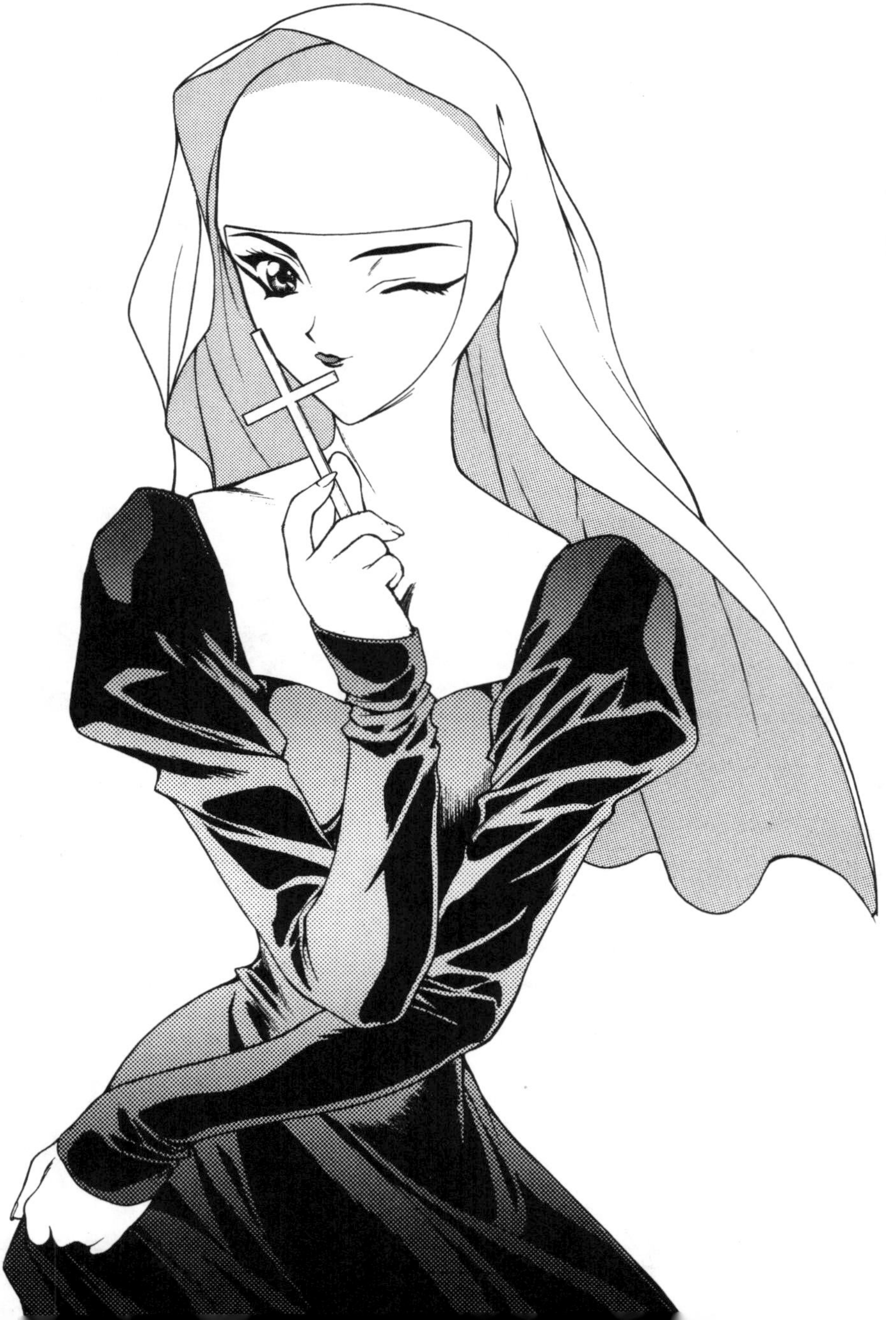

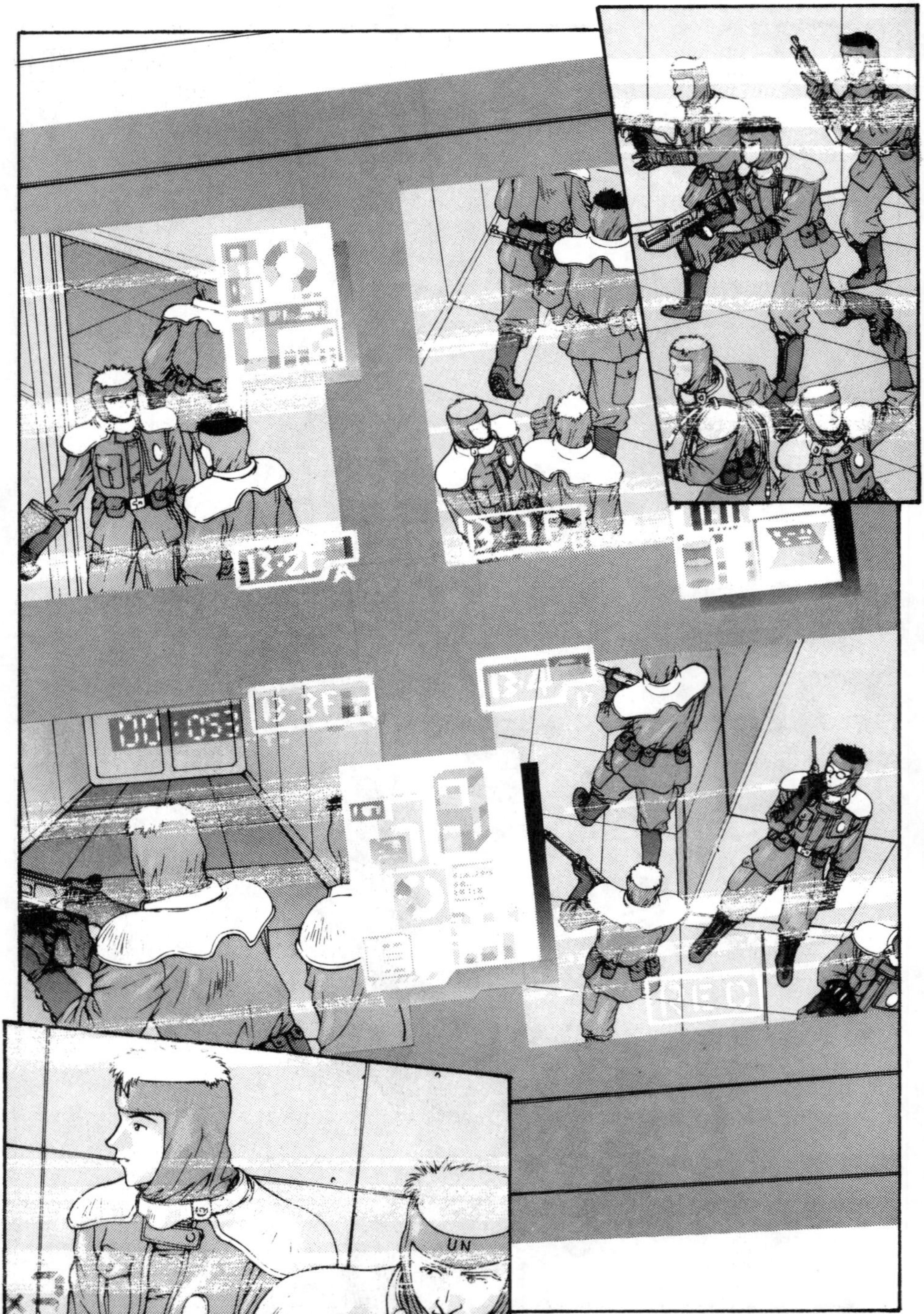
13·2F
13·3F
REC
UN

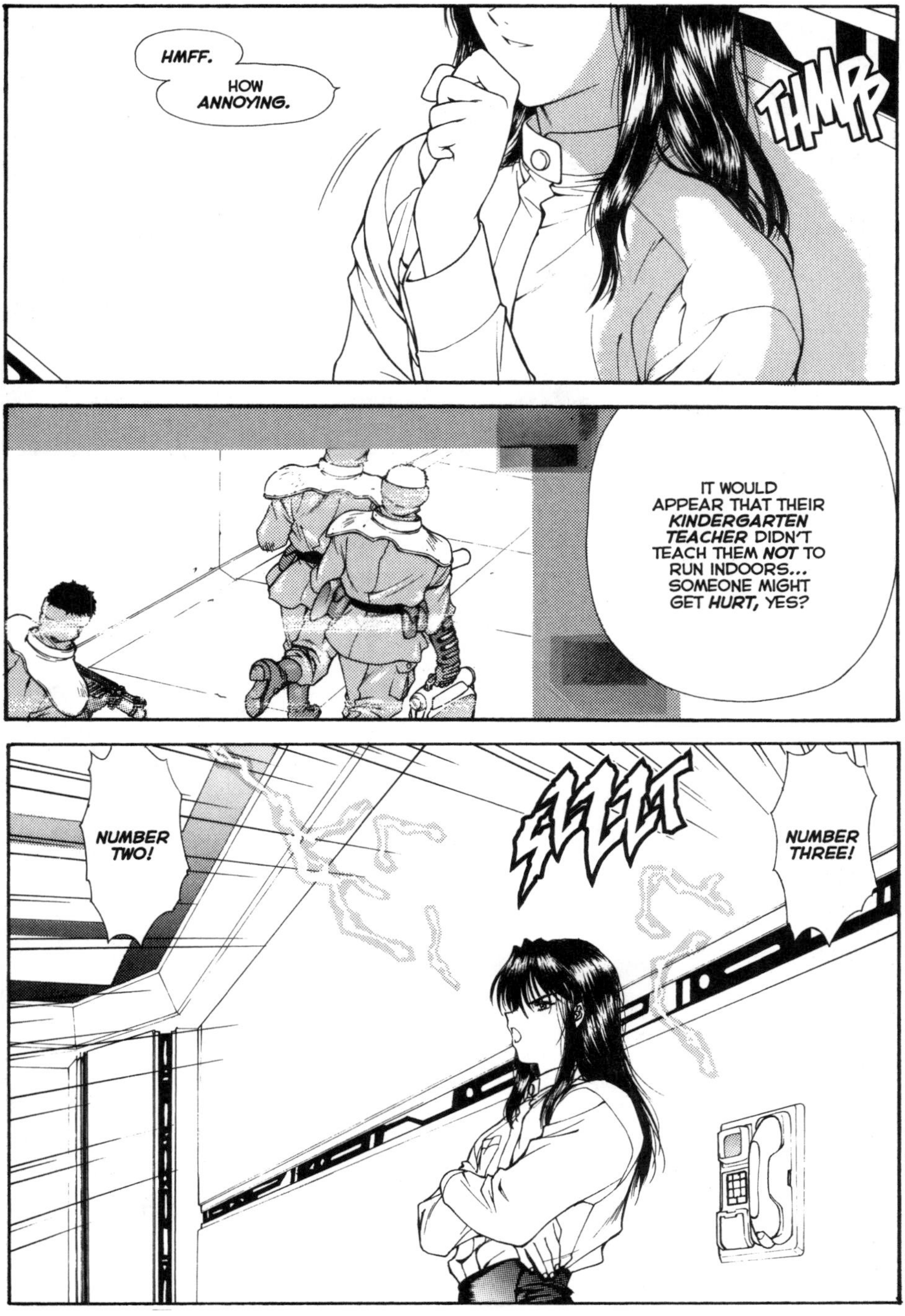
HMFF.
HOW ANNOYING.
THMP
IT WOULD APPEAR THAT THEIR KINDERGARTEN TEACHER DIDN'T TEACH THEM NOT TO RUN INDOORS... SOMEONE MIGHT GET HURT, YES?
NUMBER TWO!
SZZZT
NUMBER THREE!

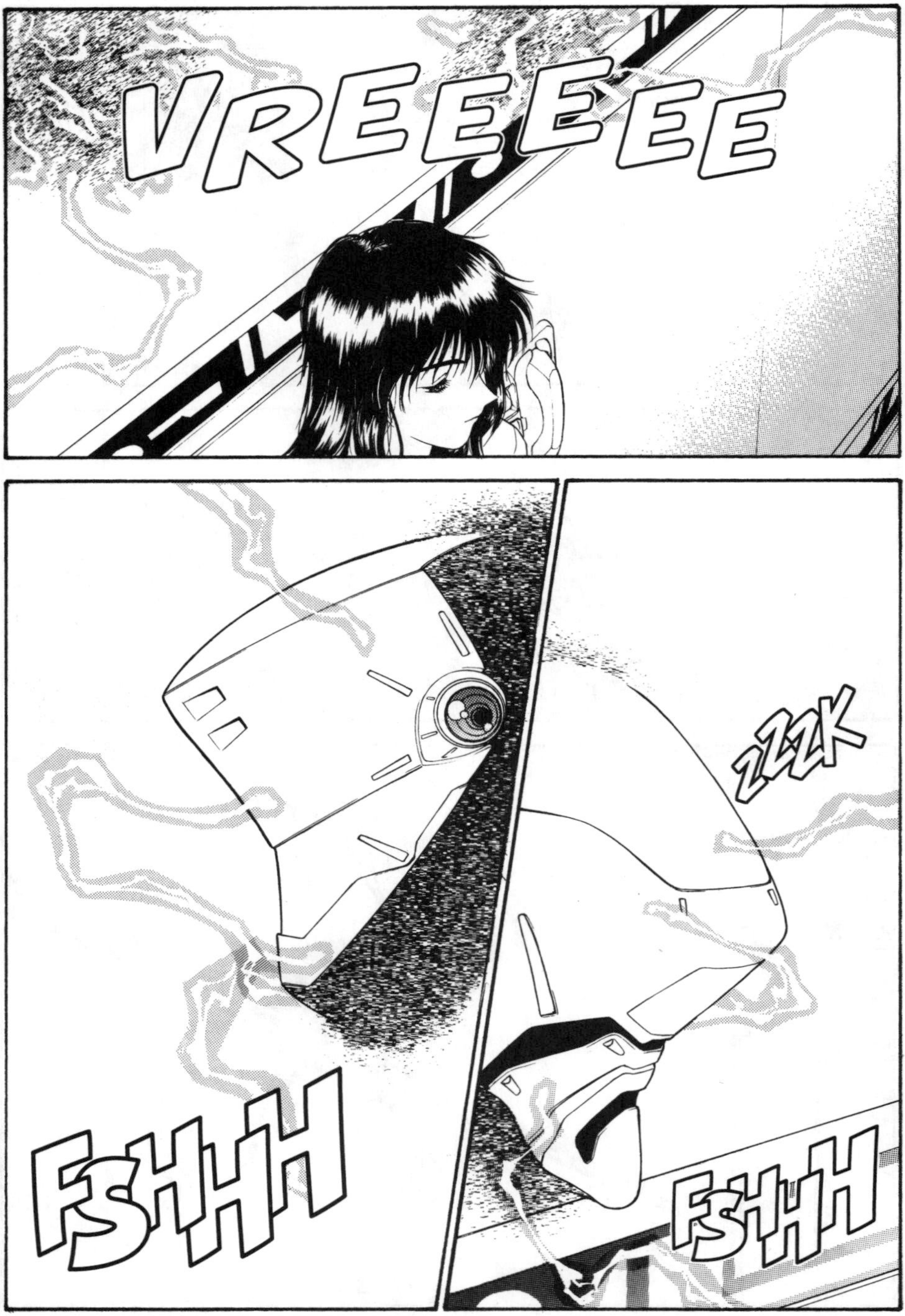
VREEEEEE
FSHHH
zZZK
FSHHH

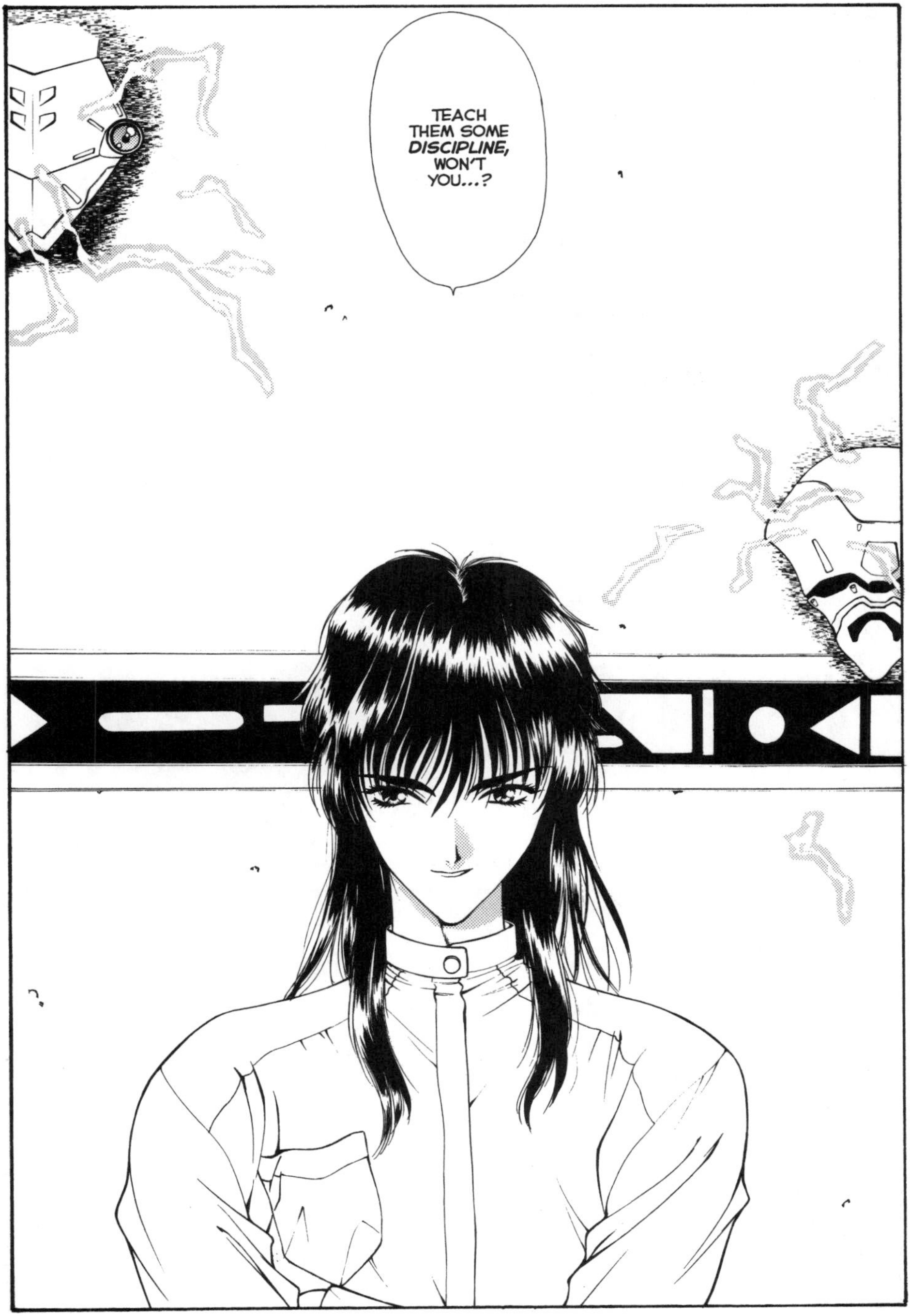
TEACH THEM SOME ***DISCIPLINE,*** WON'T YOU...?

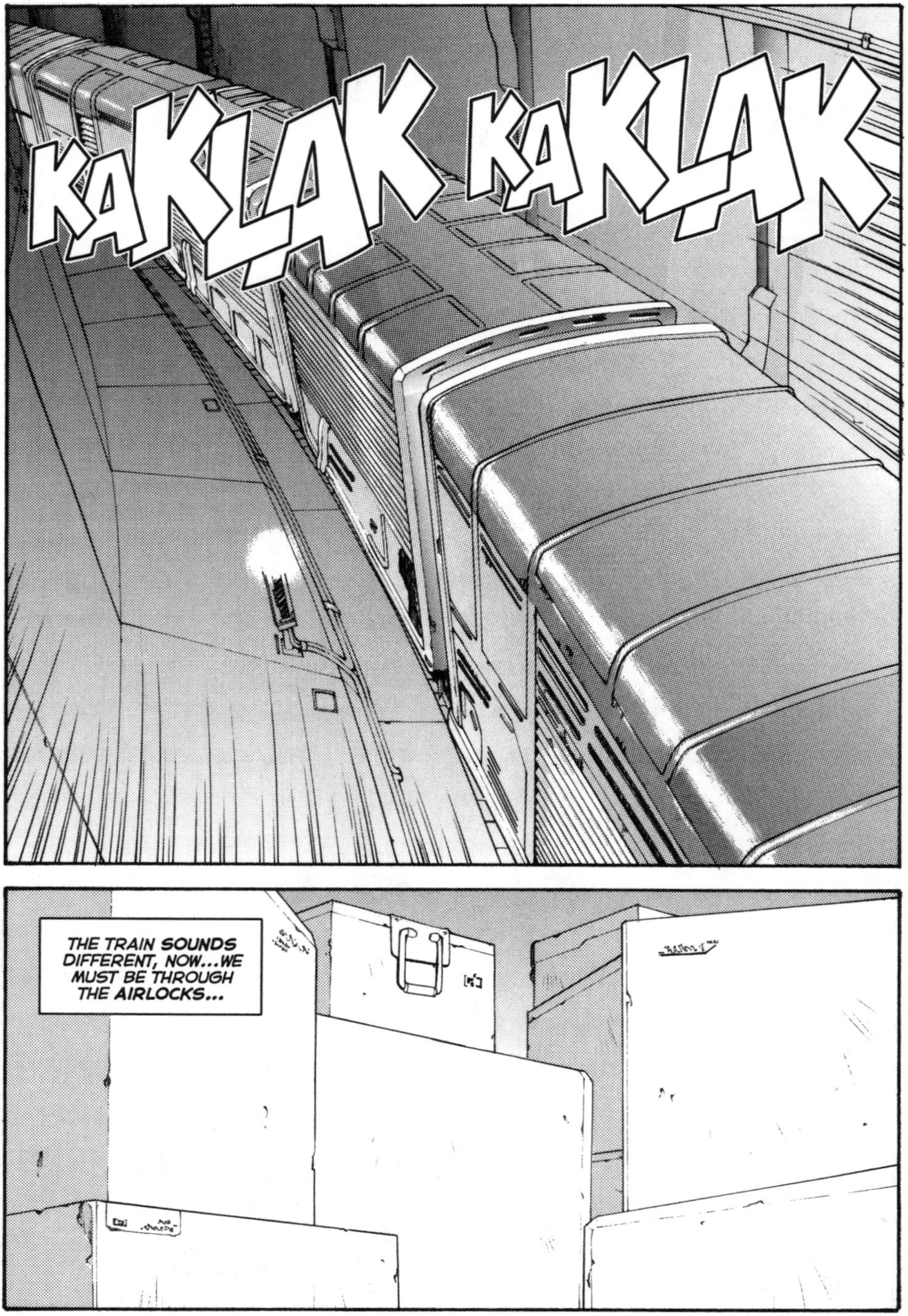
KAKLAK KAKLAK
THE TRAIN SOUNDS DIFFERENT, NOW...WE MUST BE THROUGH THE AIRLOCKS...

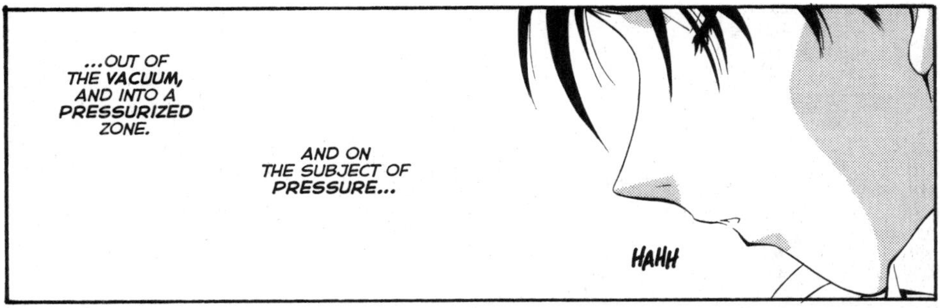
...OUT OF THE VACUUM, AND INTO A PRESSURIZED ZONE.
AND ON THE SUBJECT OF PRESSURE...
HAHH

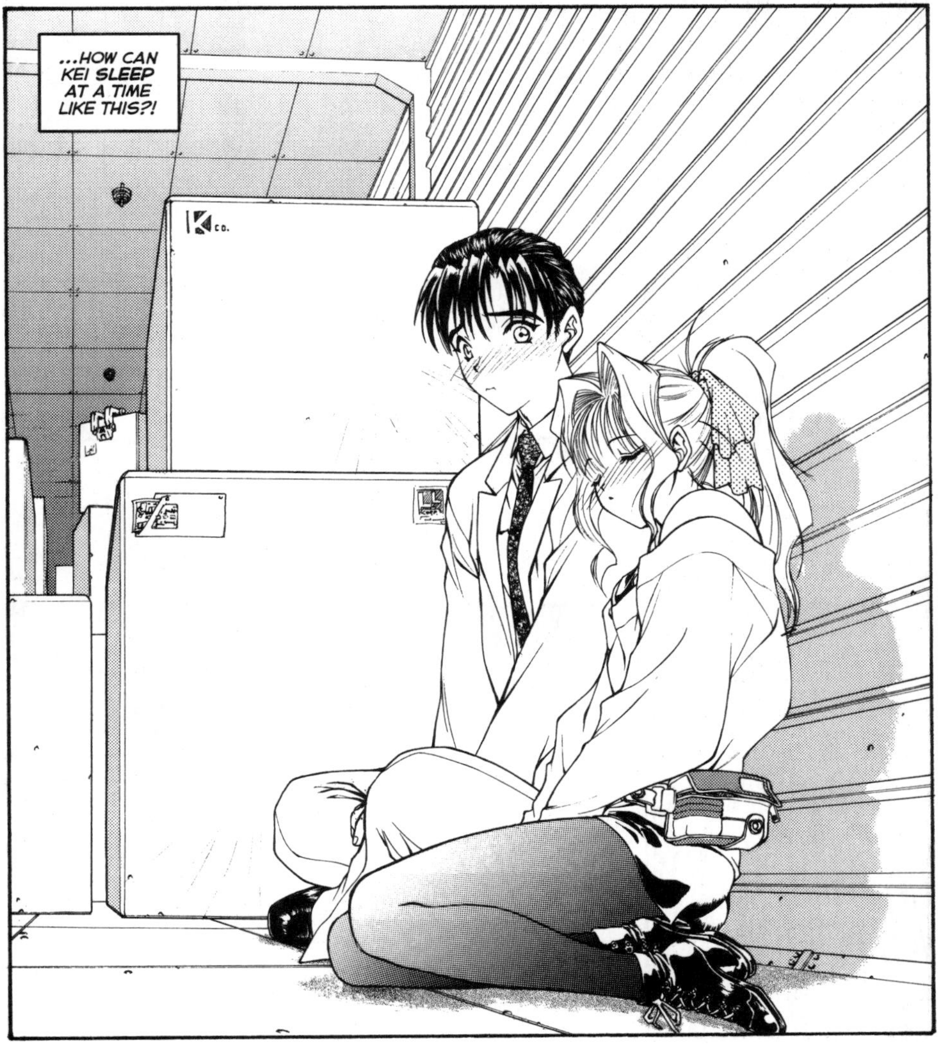
...HOW CAN KEI SLEEP AT A TIME LIKE THIS?!

THE TWO OF US, ALONE, IN A CLOSED ROOM...!

IF I JUST PUT ONE HAND ON HER SHOULDER... I COULD HOLD HER TIGHT...

MY HEART'S SWOLLEN TO BURSTING!

NOT TO MENTION... OTHER THINGS.

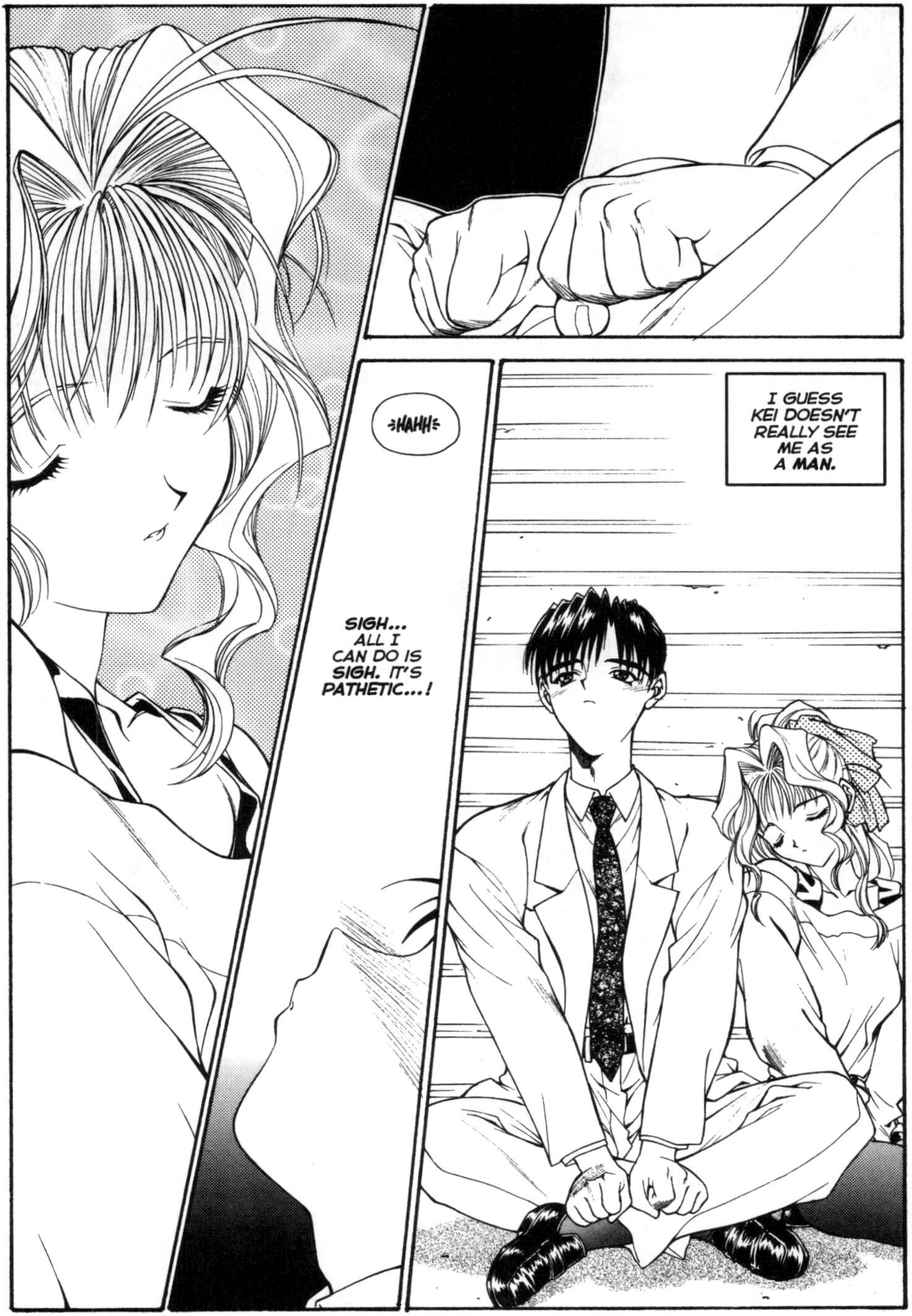
HAHH
SIGH... ALL I CAN DO IS SIGH. IT'S PATHETIC...!
I GUESS KEI DOESN'T REALLY SEE ME AS A MAN.

THAT'S UNDERSTANDABLE, I GUESS...WE HAVEN'T SEEN EACH OTHER SINCE WAY BACK WHEN, YEARS AGO...

IN HER MIND'S EYE, I'M *STILL* A LITTLE BOY.

A LITTLE BOY...

WAIT A MINUTE, THOUGH... SHE'S OLDER THAN I AM... ISN'T SHE...?

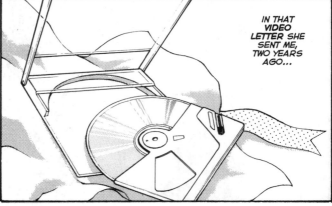

IN THAT VIDEO LETTER SHE SENT ME, TWO YEARS AGO...

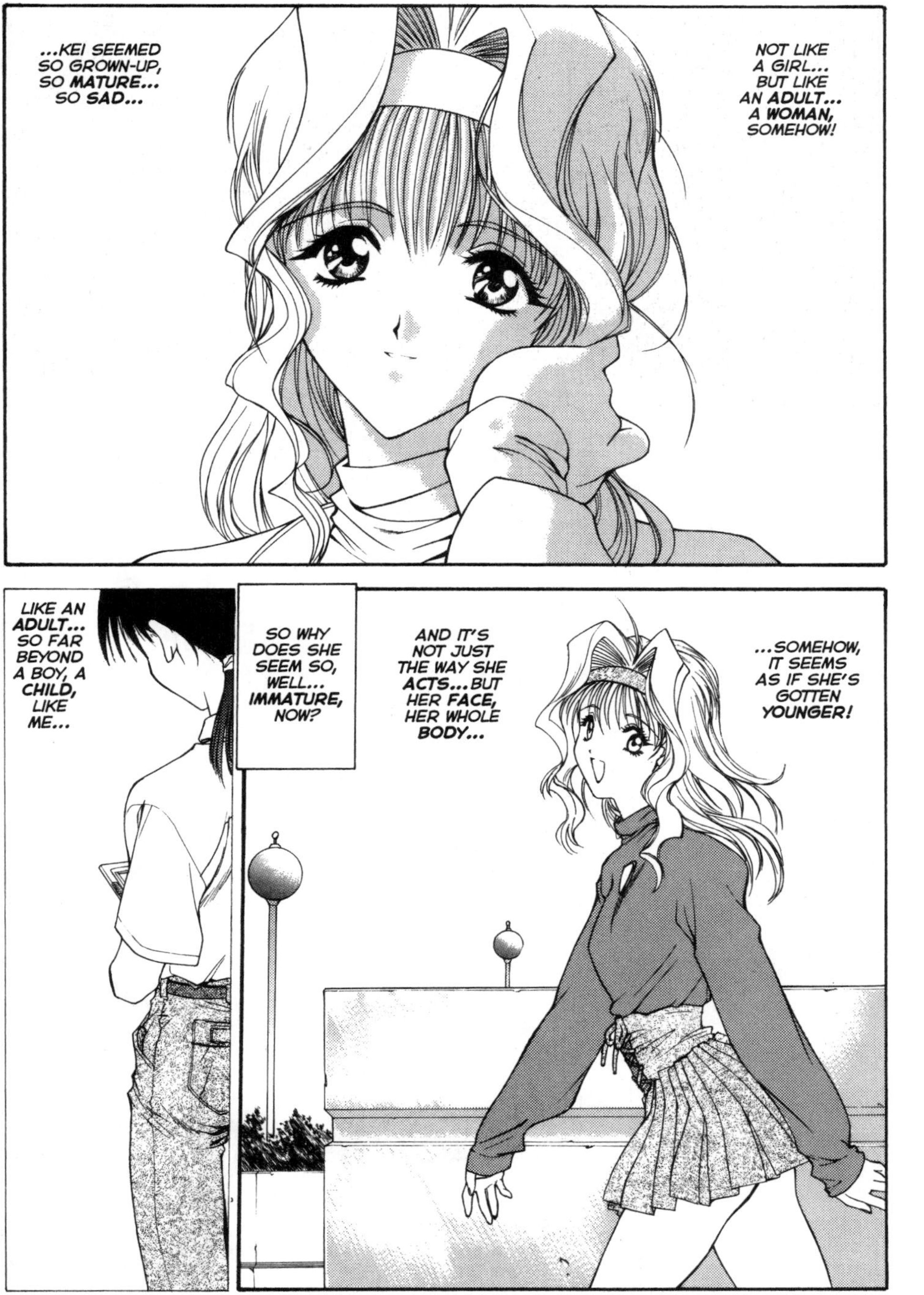
...KEI SEEMED SO GROWN-UP, SO MATURE... SO SAD...
NOT LIKE A GIRL... BUT LIKE AN ADULT... A WOMAN, SOMEHOW!
LIKE AN ADULT... SO FAR BEYOND A BOY, A CHILD, LIKE ME...
SO WHY DOES SHE SEEM SO, WELL... IMMATURE, NOW?
AND IT'S NOT JUST THE WAY SHE ACTS... BUT HER FACE, HER WHOLE BODY...
...SOMEHOW, IT SEEMS AS IF SHE'S GOTTEN YOUNGER!

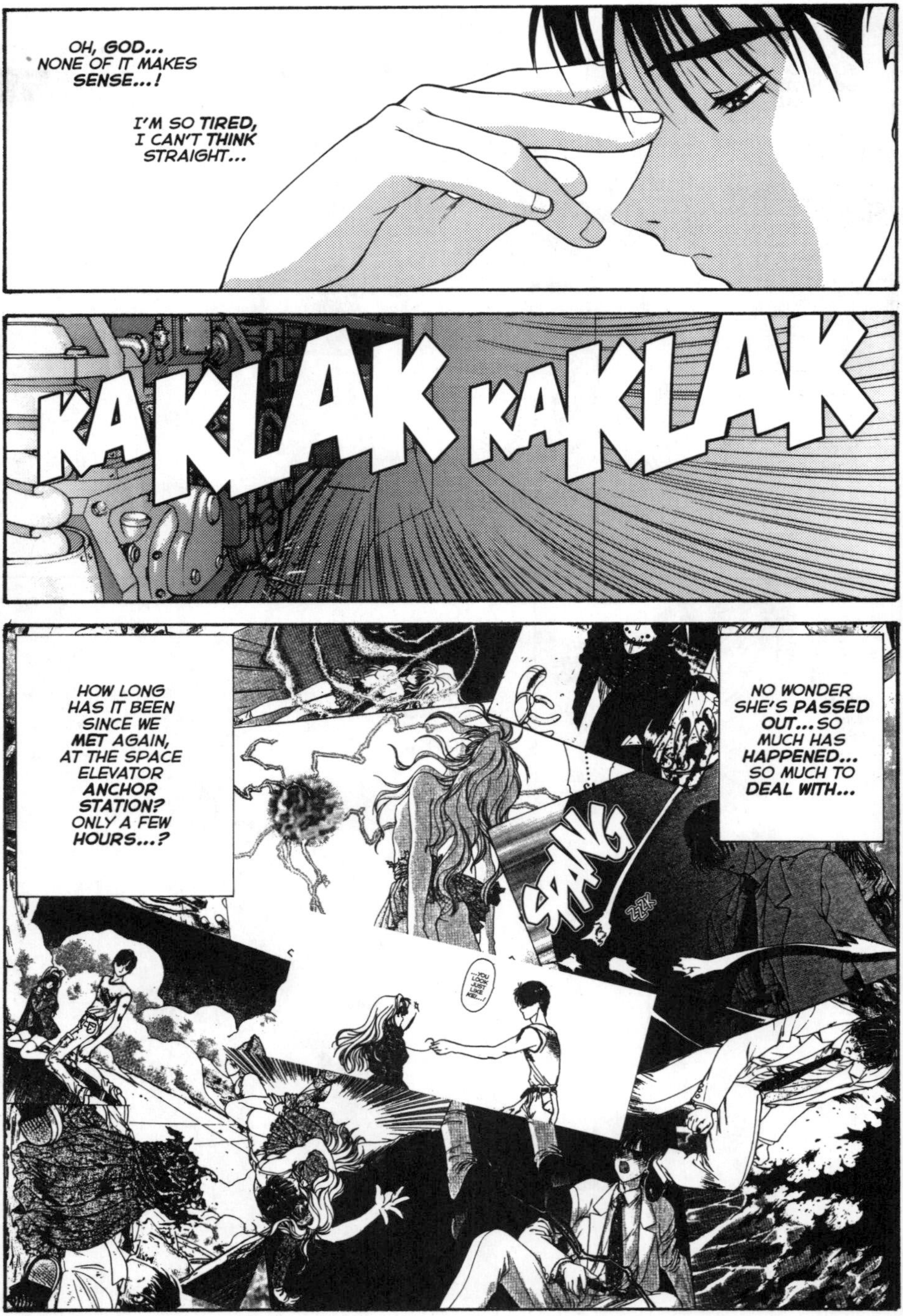
OH, GOD... NONE OF IT MAKES SENSE...!
I'M SO TIRED, I CAN'T THINK STRAIGHT...
KAKLAK KAKLAK
HOW LONG HAS IT BEEN SINCE WE MET AGAIN, AT THE SPACE ELEVATOR ANCHOR STATION? ONLY A FEW HOURS...?
NO WONDER SHE'S PASSED OUT... SO MUCH HAS HAPPENED... SO MUCH TO DEAL WITH...
SPANG
...YOU LOOK JUST LIKE KEI...!

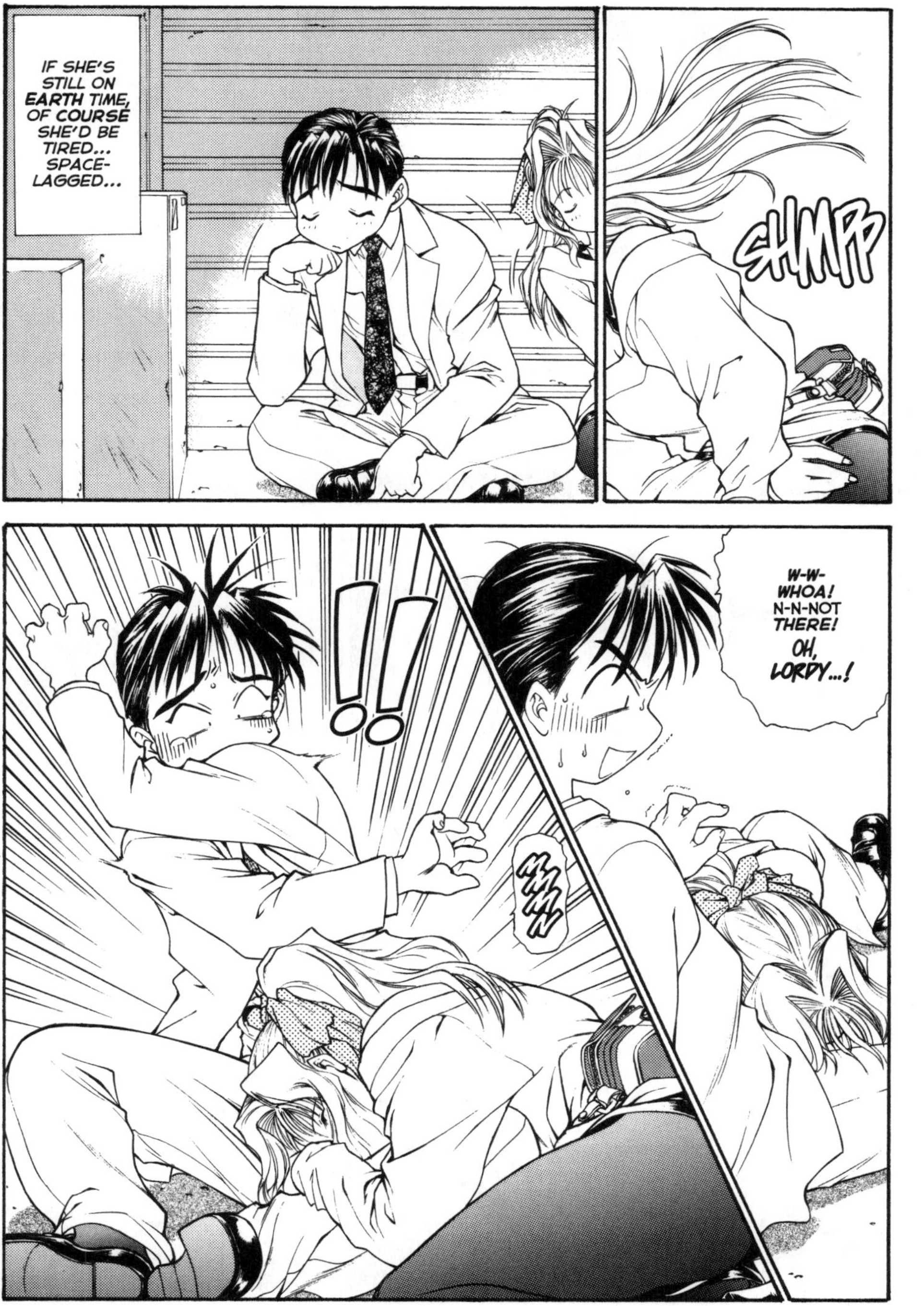
IF SHE'S STILL ON EARTH TIME, OF COURSE SHE'D BE TIRED... SPACE-LAGGED...
SHMPP
!!
W-W-WHOA! N-N-NOT THERE! OH, LORDY...!
MMMN

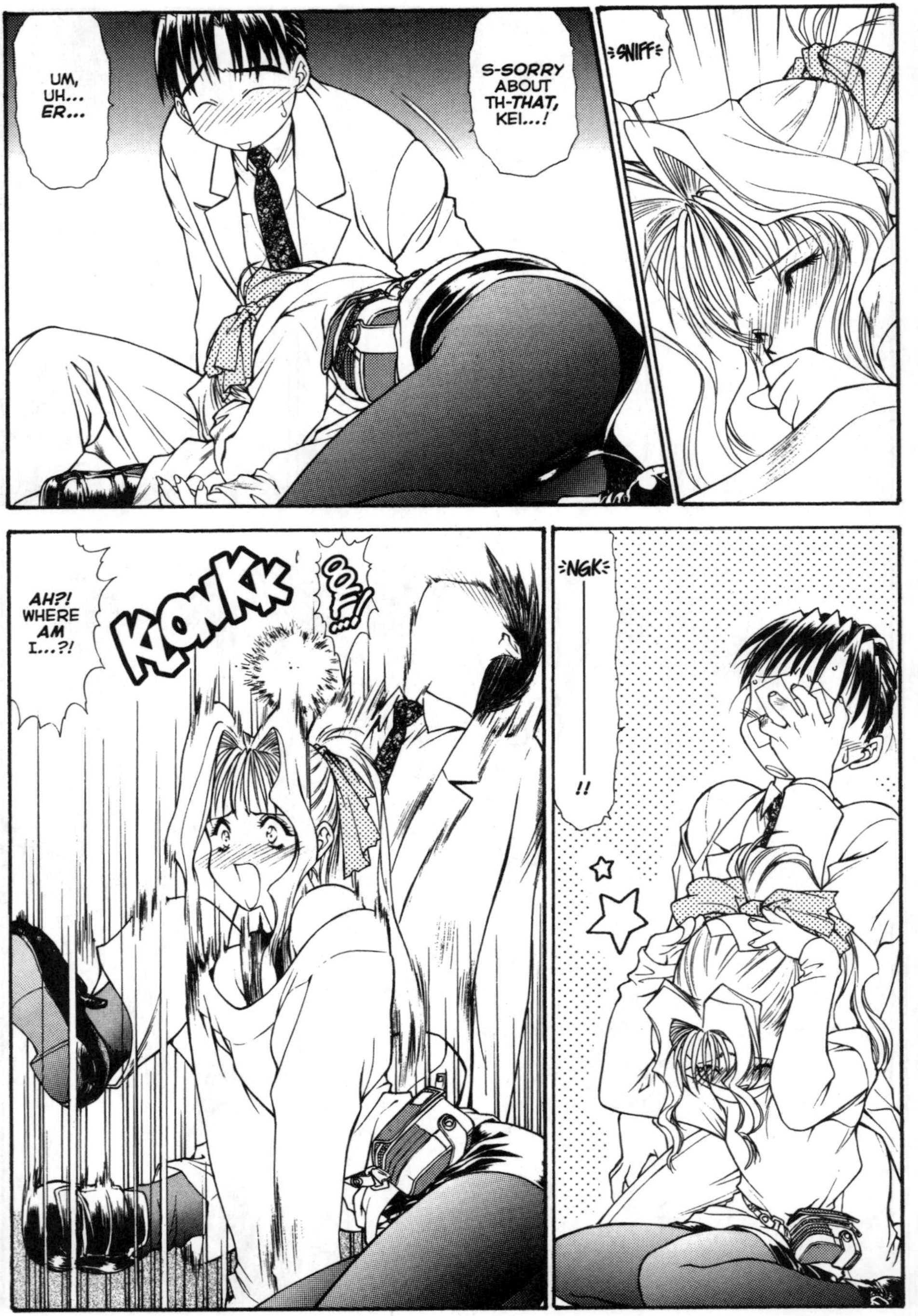
UM, UH... ER...
S-SORRY ABOUT TH-THAT, KEI...!
SNIFF
AH?! WHERE AM I...?!
KLONKK
OOF!...
NGK——!!

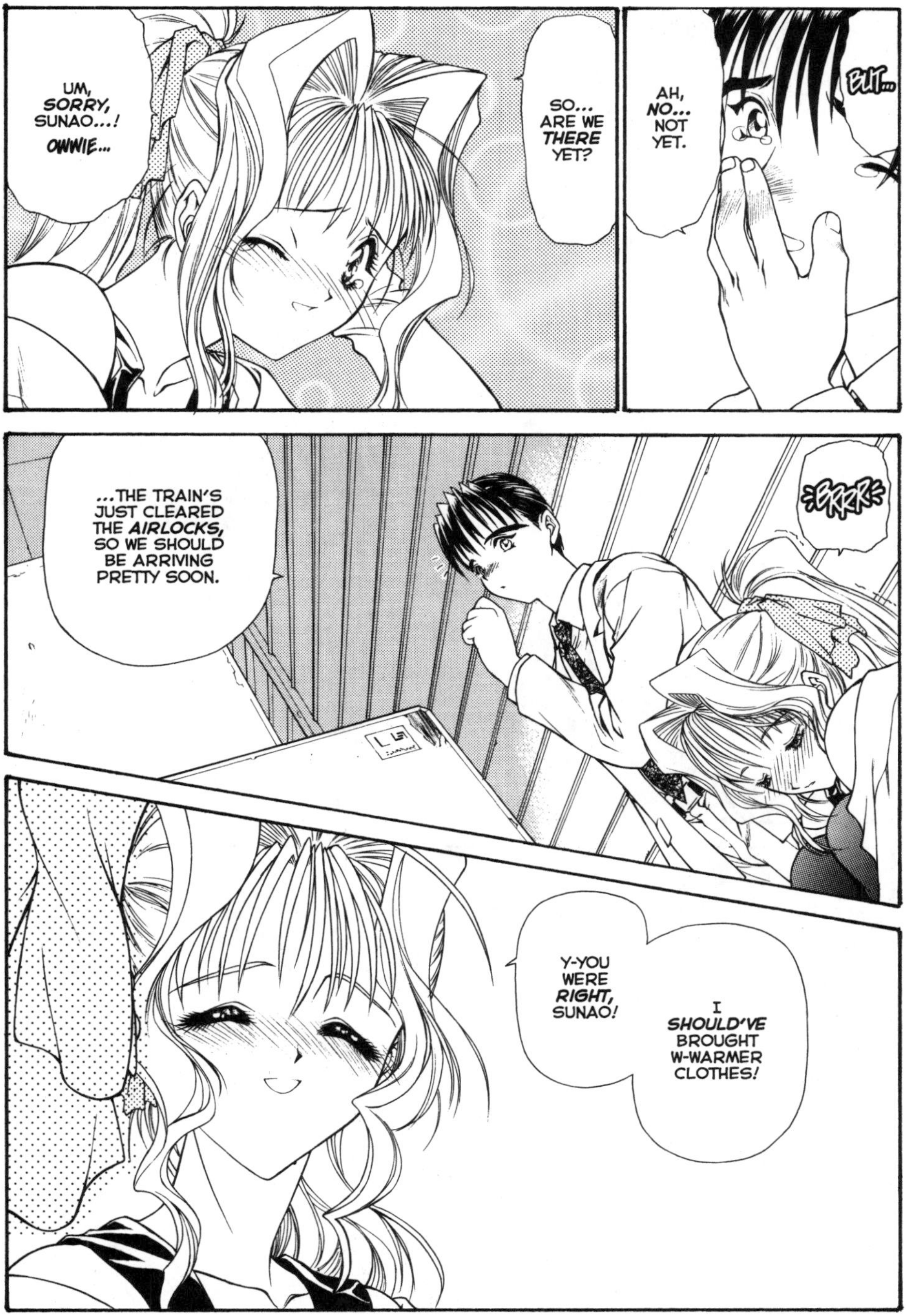
UM, SORRY, SUNAO...! OWWIE...
SO... ARE WE THERE YET?
AH, NO... NOT YET.
BUT...
...THE TRAIN'S JUST CLEARED THE AIRLOCKS, SO WE SHOULD BE ARRIVING PRETTY SOON.
BRRR
Y-YOU WERE RIGHT, SUNAO!
I SHOULD'VE BROUGHT W-WARMER CLOTHES!

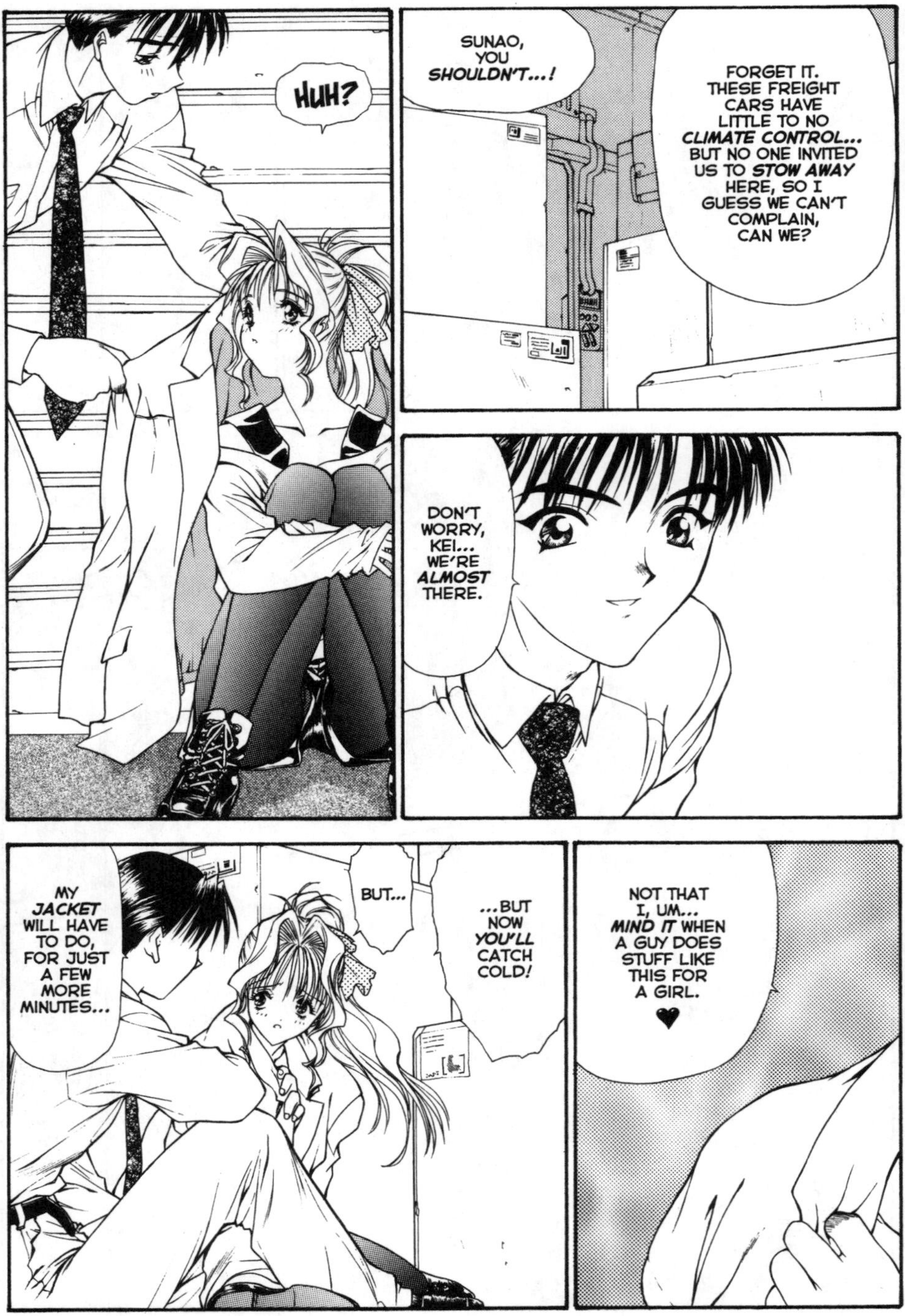
HUH?
SUNAO, YOU SHOULDN'T...!
FORGET IT. THESE FREIGHT CARS HAVE LITTLE TO NO CLIMATE CONTROL... BUT NO ONE INVITED US TO STOW AWAY HERE, SO I GUESS WE CAN'T COMPLAIN, CAN WE?
DON'T WORRY, KEI... WE'RE ALMOST THERE.
MY JACKET WILL HAVE TO DO, FOR JUST A FEW MORE MINUTES...
BUT...
...BUT NOW YOU'LL CATCH COLD!
NOT THAT I, UM... MIND IT WHEN A GUY DOES STUFF LIKE THIS FOR A GIRL. ♥

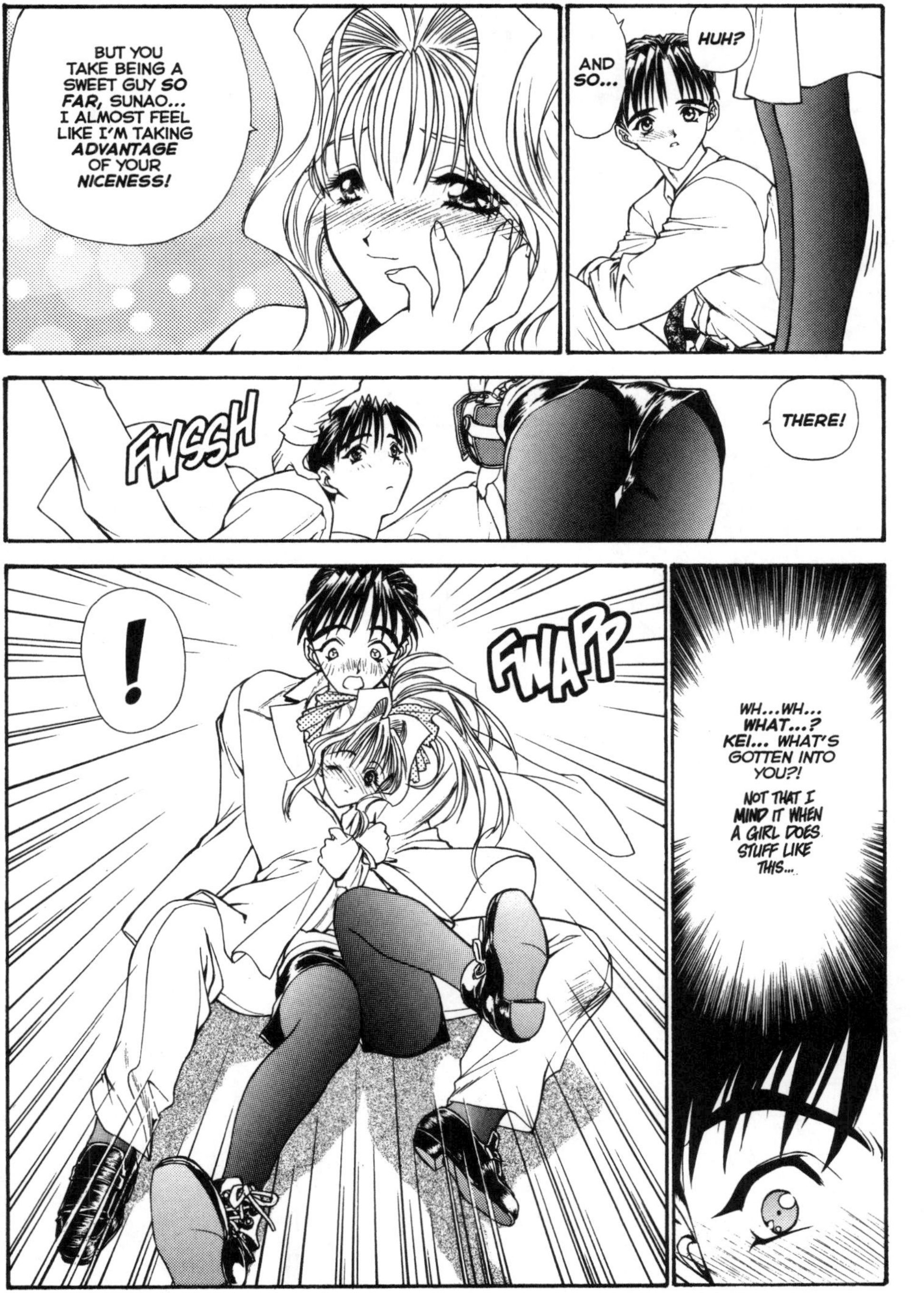
BUT YOU TAKE BEING A SWEET GUY SO FAR, SUNAO... I ALMOST FEEL LIKE I'M TAKING ADVANTAGE OF YOUR NICENESS!
AND SO...
HUH?
FWSSH
THERE!
!
FWAPP
WH...WH... WHAT...? KEI... WHAT'S GOTTEN INTO YOU?!
NOT THAT I MIND IT WHEN A GIRL DOES STUFF LIKE THIS...

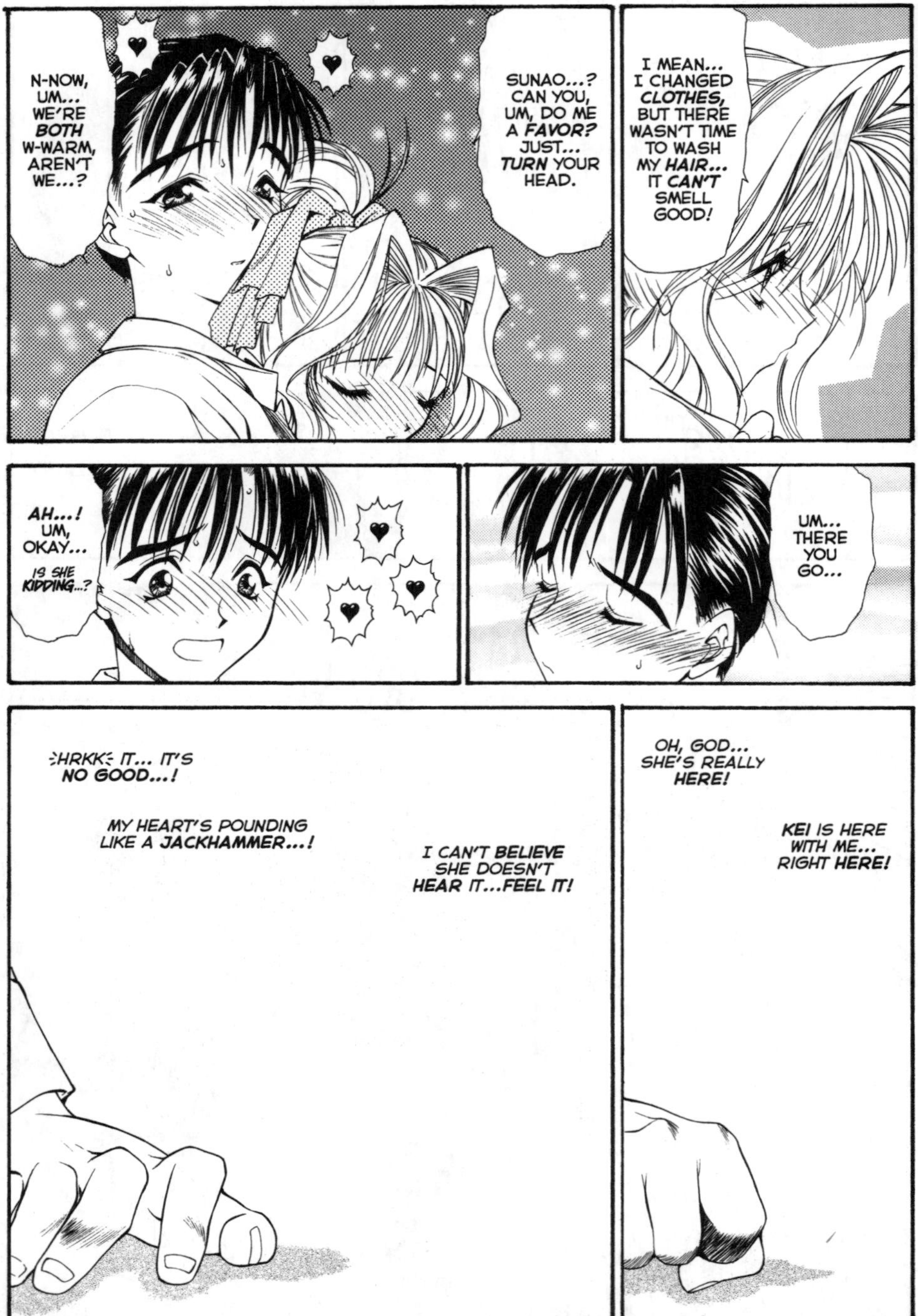

N-NOW, UM... WE'RE **BOTH** W-WARM, AREN'T WE...?
SUNAO...? CAN YOU, UM, DO ME A **FAVOR?** JUST... **TURN** YOUR HEAD.
I MEAN... I CHANGED **CLOTHES,** BUT THERE WASN'T TIME TO WASH MY **HAIR...** IT **CAN'T** SMELL GOOD!
AH...! UM, OKAY...
IS SHE KIDDING...?
UM... THERE YOU GO...
HRKK IT... IT'S **NO GOOD...!**
MY HEART'S POUNDING LIKE A **JACKHAMMER...!**
I CAN'T **BELIEVE** SHE DOESN'T **HEAR** IT...**FEEL IT!**
OH, GOD... SHE'S REALLY **HERE!**
KEI IS HERE WITH ME... RIGHT **HERE!**

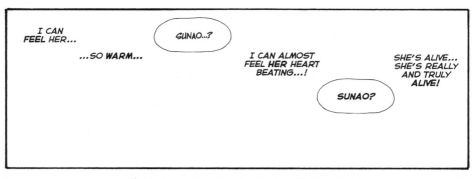

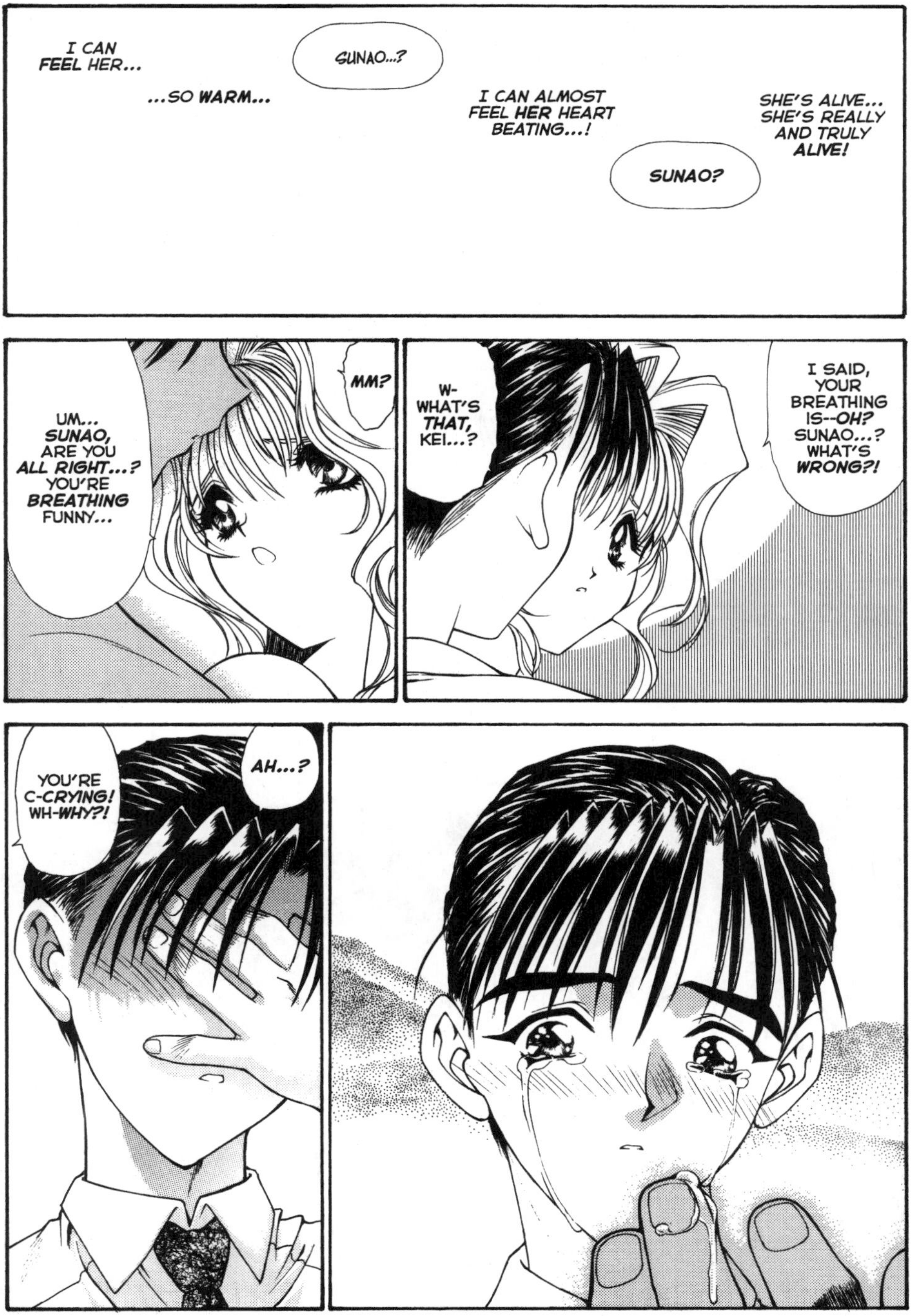
I CAN FEEL HER...
SUNAO...?
...SO WARM...
I CAN ALMOST FEEL HER HEART BEATING...!
SHE'S ALIVE... SHE'S REALLY AND TRULY ALIVE!
SUNAO?
UM... SUNAO, ARE YOU ALL RIGHT...? YOU'RE BREATHING FUNNY...
MM?
W-WHAT'S THAT, KEI...?
I SAID, YOUR BREATHING IS--OH? SUNAO...? WHAT'S WRONG?!
AH...?
YOU'RE C-CRYING! WH-WHY?!

OH... UH, I'M *FINE!*

IT'S JUST BEEN S-SO LONG... SINCE I'VE *SEEN* YOU, KEI...

OH, SUNAO... F-*FORGIVE* ME....! AT THE *ANCHOR STATION*... WHEN WE FIRST *MET*...

...AND I...I DIDN'T EVEN REALIZE IT WAS YOU...IT MUST HAVE HURT... OH, *SUNAO!* I'M SO, *SO* SORRY!

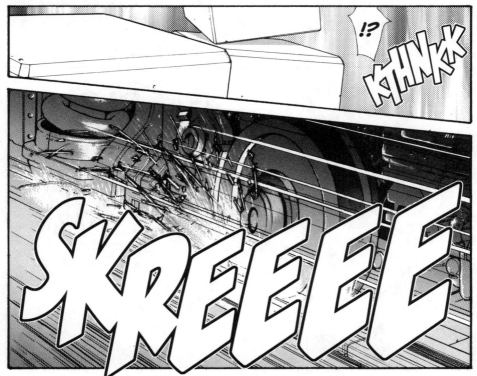

!?

KTHNKK

SKREEEE

ACT 25

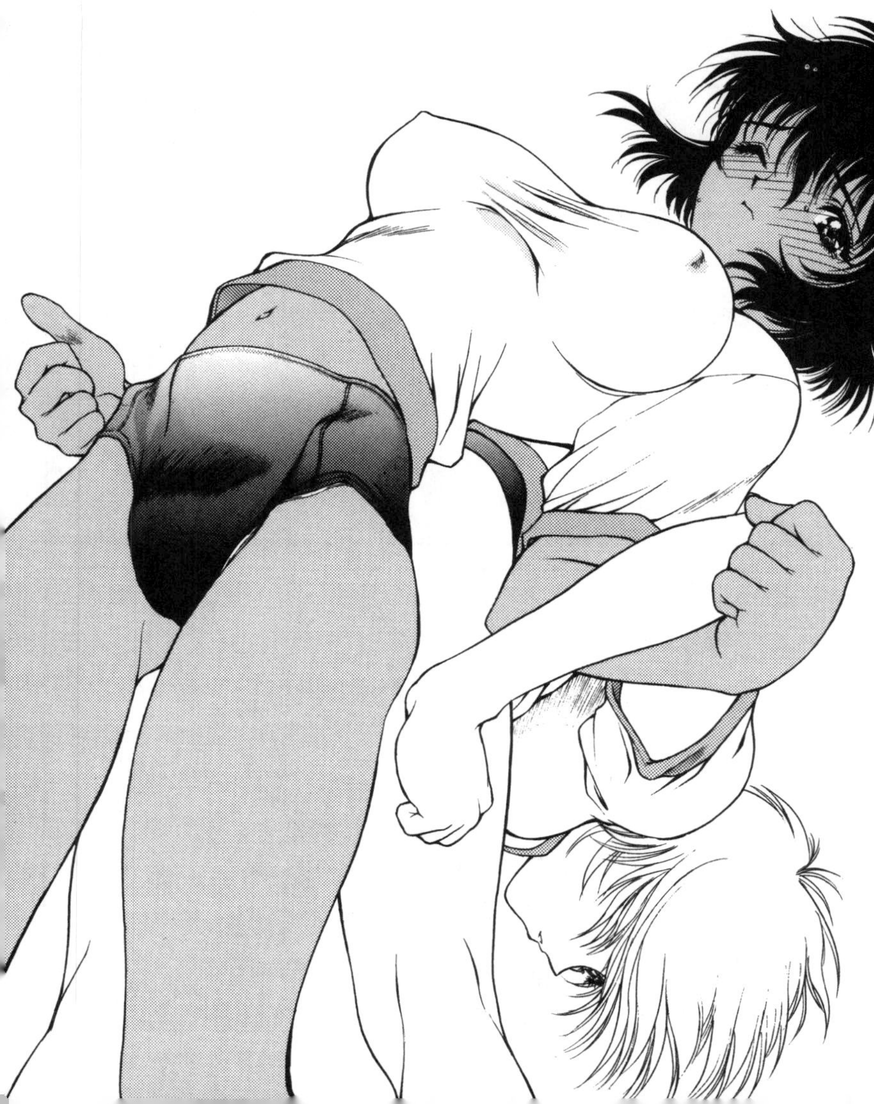

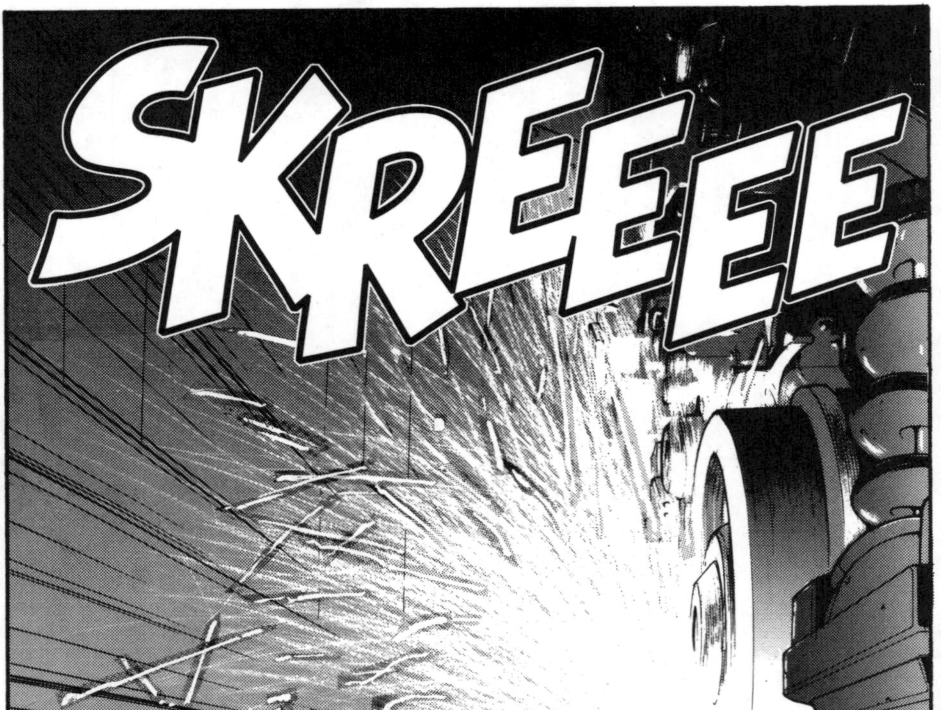
SKREEEE

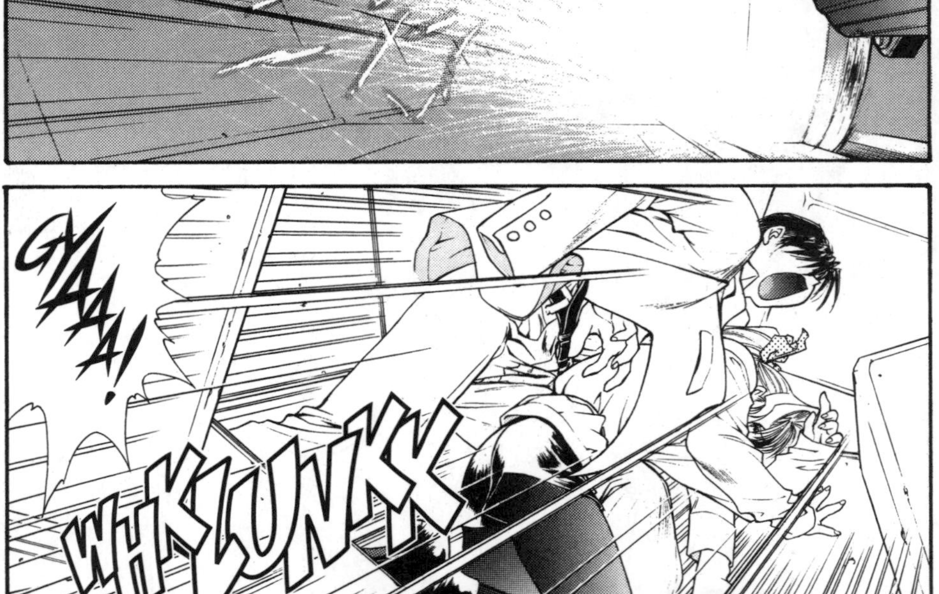
GYAAAA!
WHKLUNK

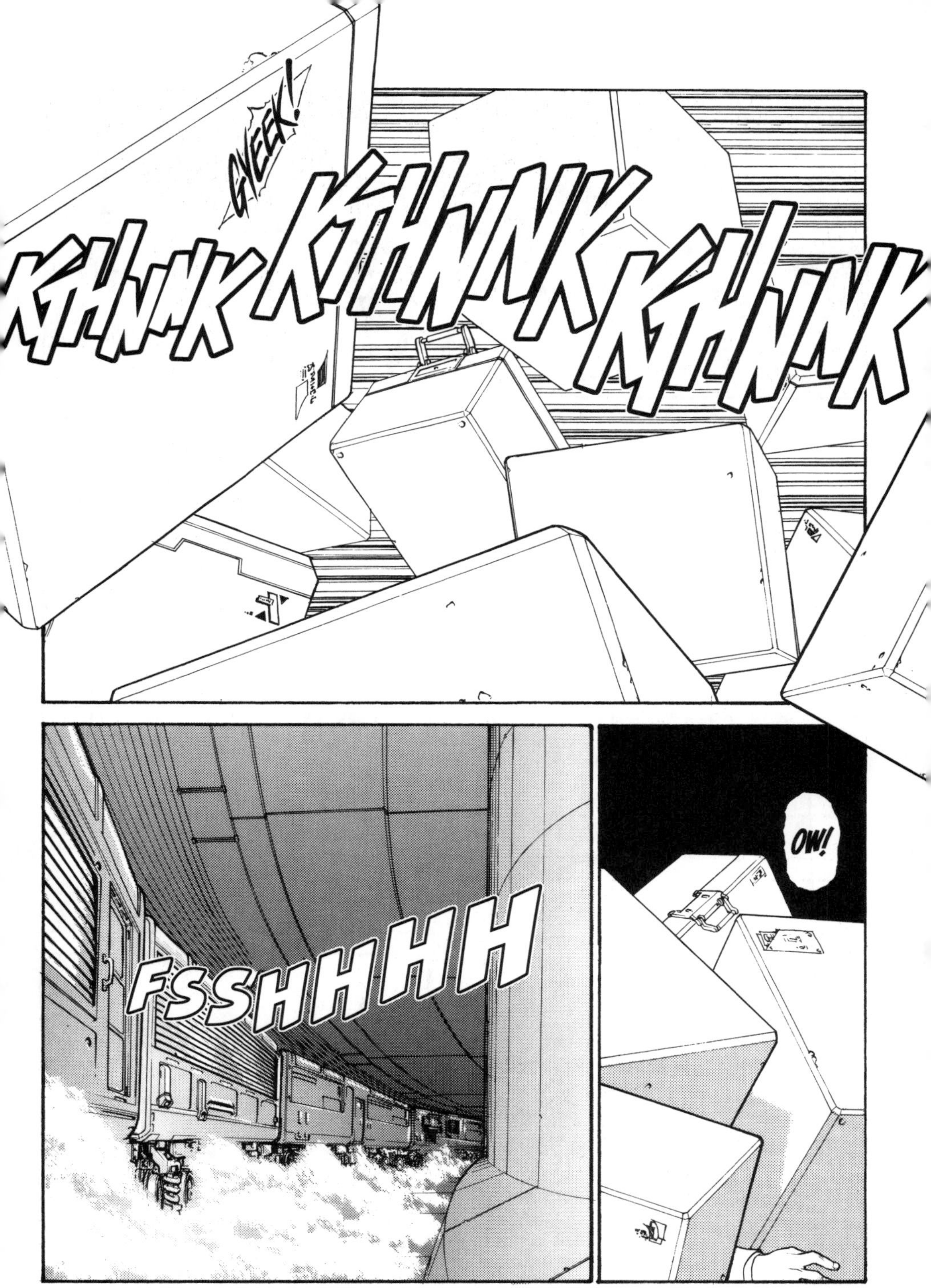
GYEEK!
KTHUNK KTHUNK KTHUNK
FSSHHHHH
OW!

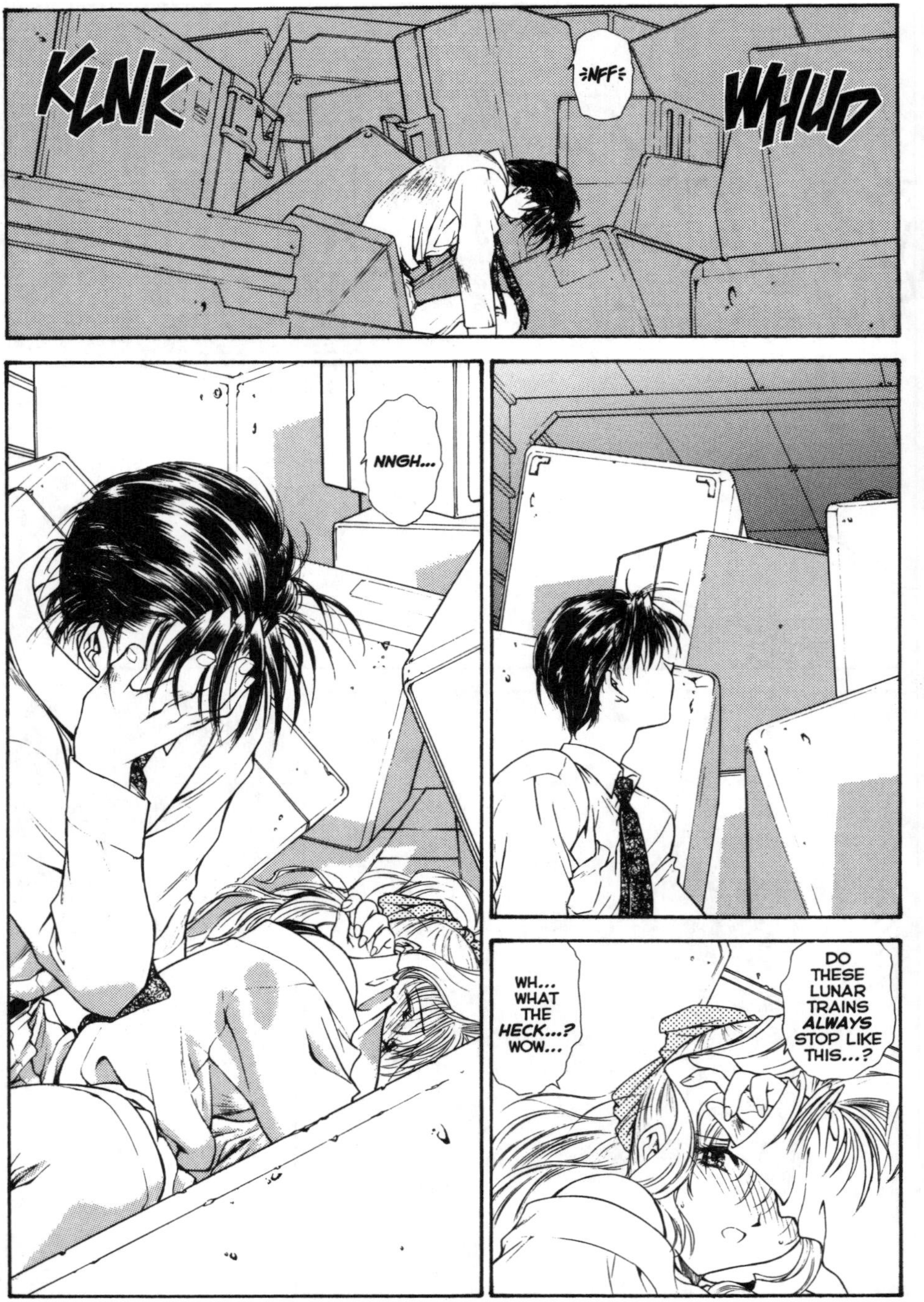
KLNK
NFF
WHUD
NNGH...
WH... WHAT THE HECK...? WOW...
DO THESE LUNAR TRAINS ALWAYS STOP LIKE THIS...?

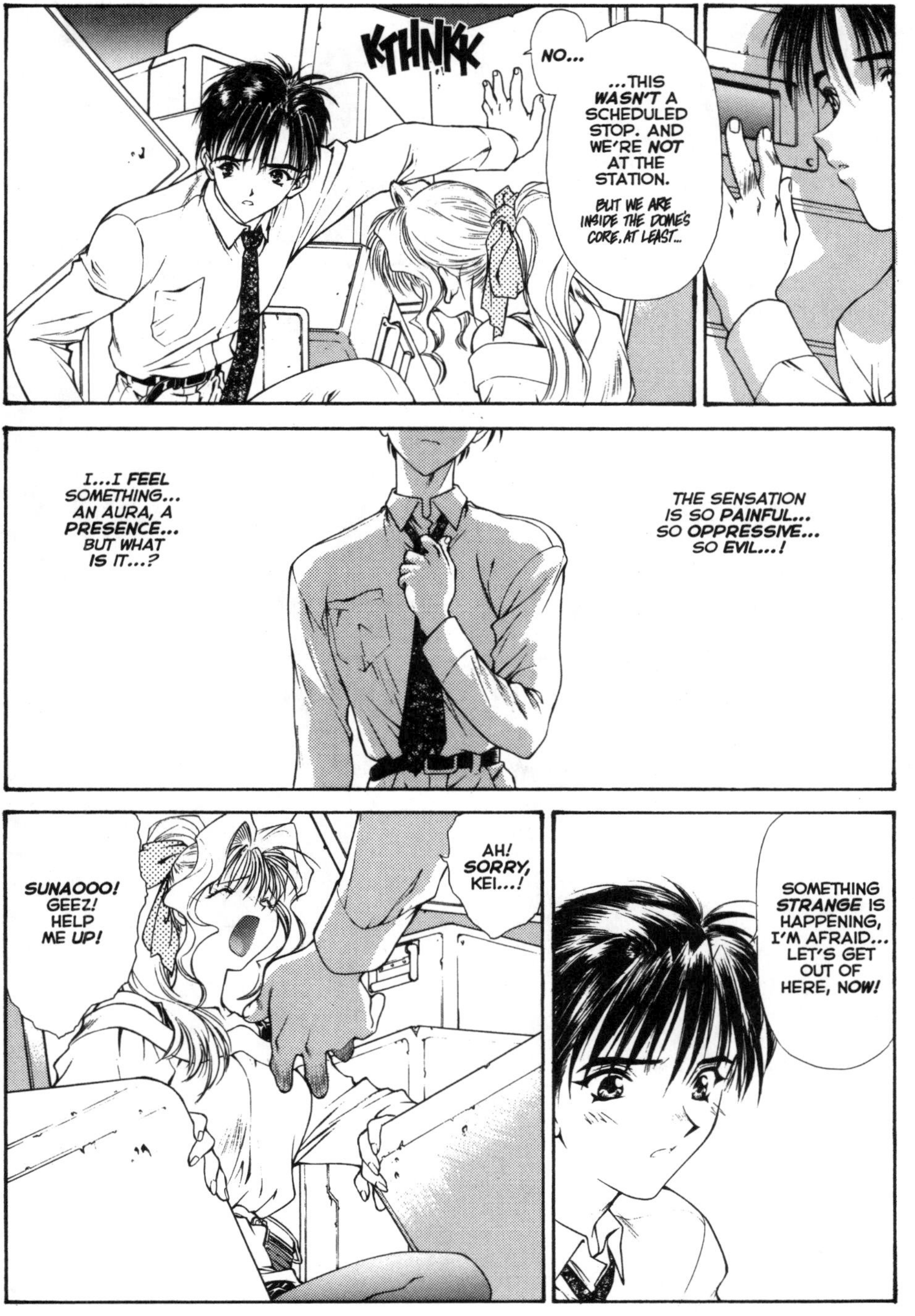
KTHNKK
NO...
...THIS WASN'T A SCHEDULED STOP. AND WE'RE NOT AT THE STATION.
BUT WE ARE INSIDE THE DOME'S CORE, AT LEAST...
I...I FEEL SOMETHING... AN AURA, A PRESENCE... BUT WHAT IS IT...?
THE SENSATION IS SO PAINFUL... SO OPPRESSIVE... SO EVIL...!
SUNAOOO! GEEZ! HELP ME UP!
AH! SORRY, KEI...!
SOMETHING STRANGE IS HAPPENING, I'M AFRAID... LET'S GET OUT OF HERE, NOW!

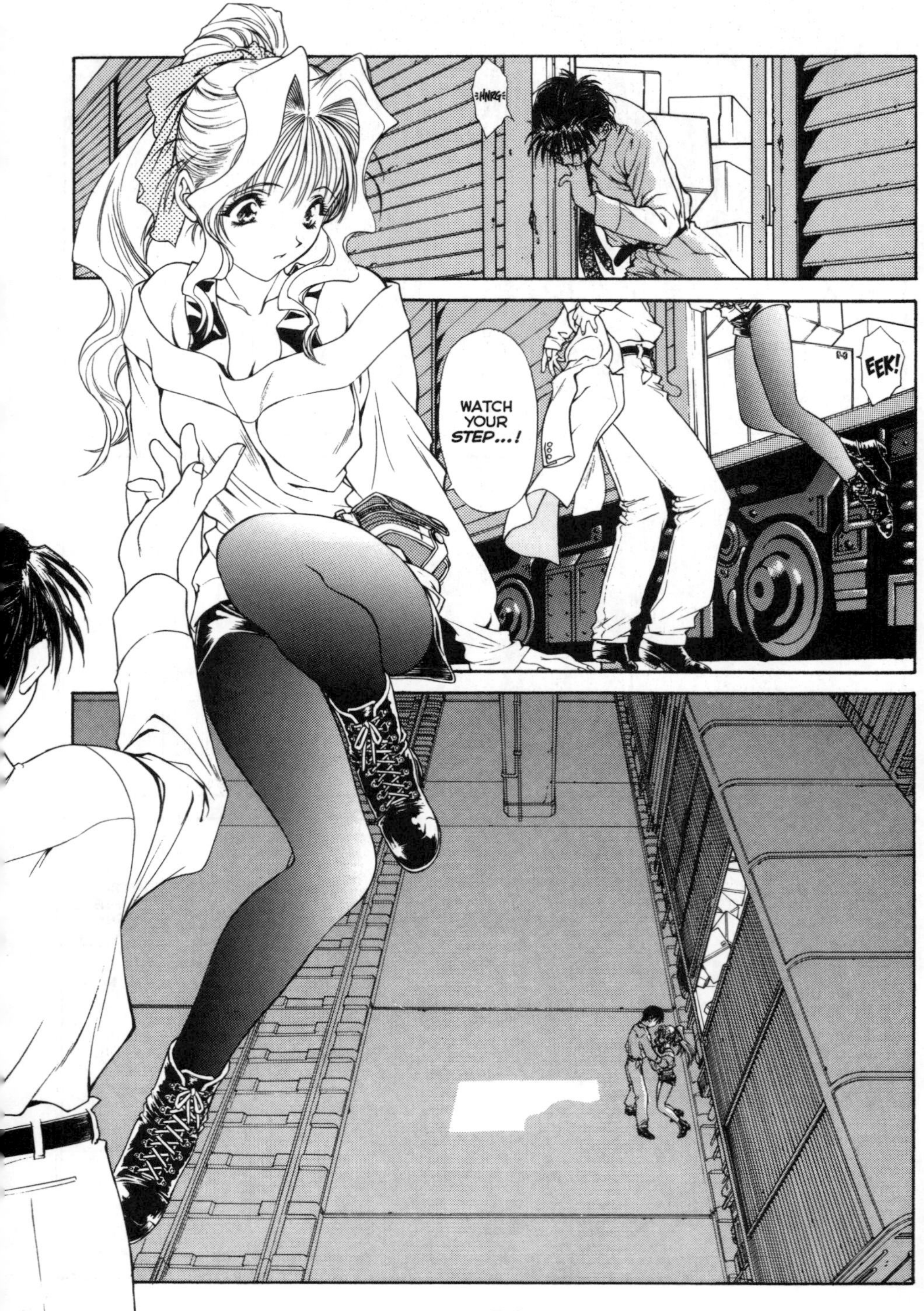
HNRG
WATCH YOUR STEP...!
EEK!

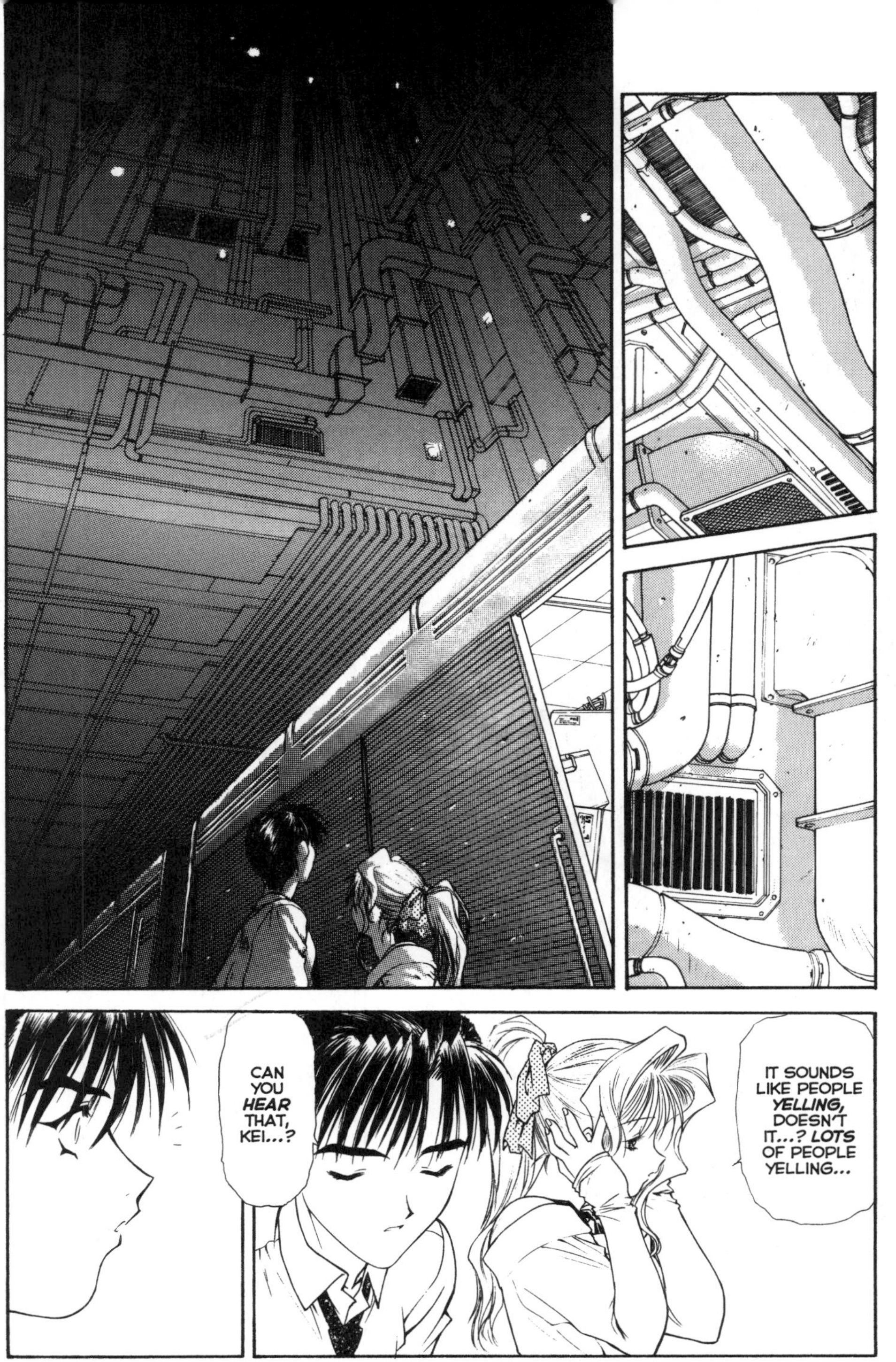
CAN YOU *HEAR* THAT, KEI...?
IT SOUNDS LIKE PEOPLE *YELLING,* DOESN'T IT...? *LOTS* OF PEOPLE YELLING...

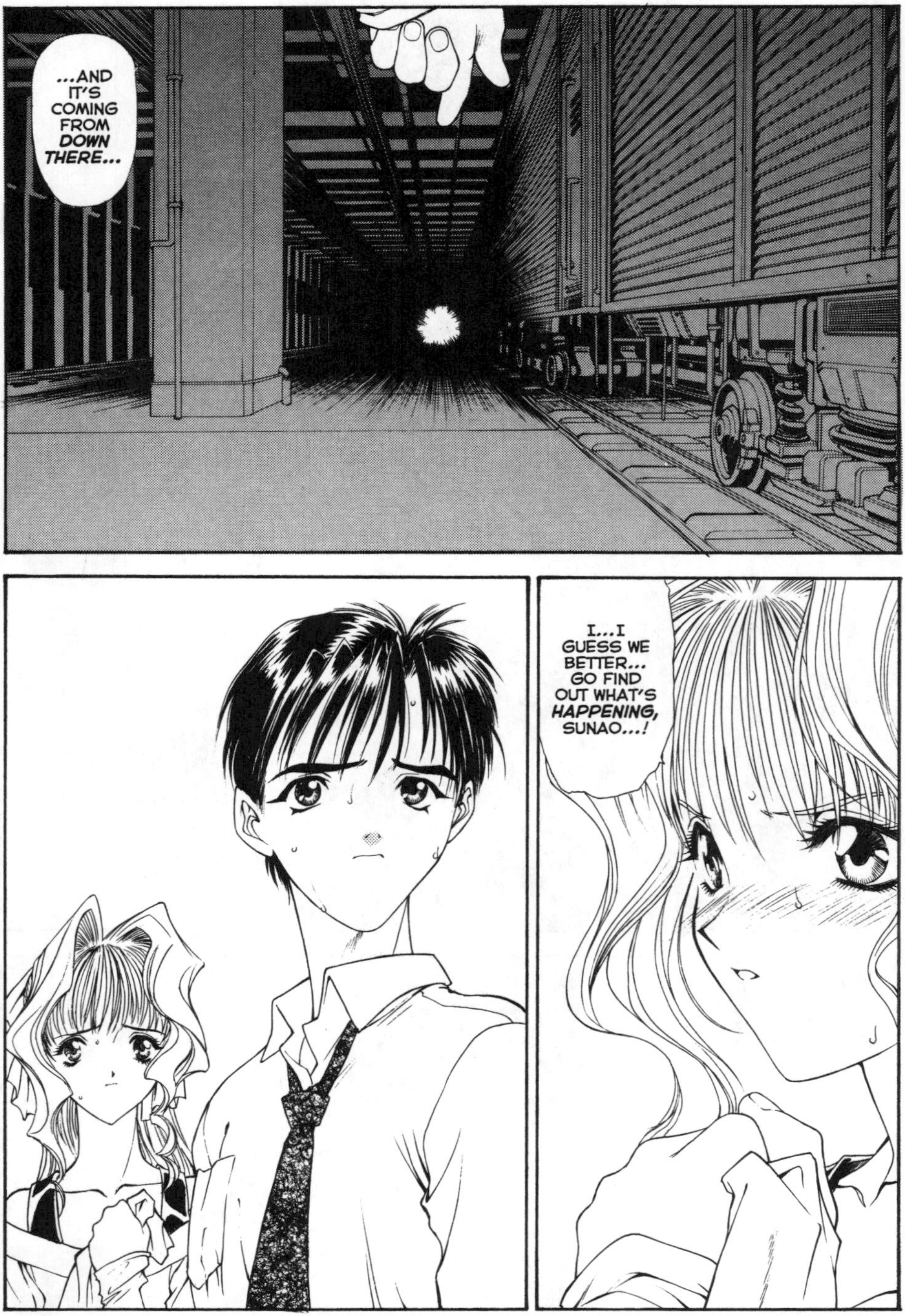
...AND IT'S COMING FROM DOWN THERE...
I...I GUESS WE BETTER... GO FIND OUT WHAT'S HAPPENING, SUNAO...!

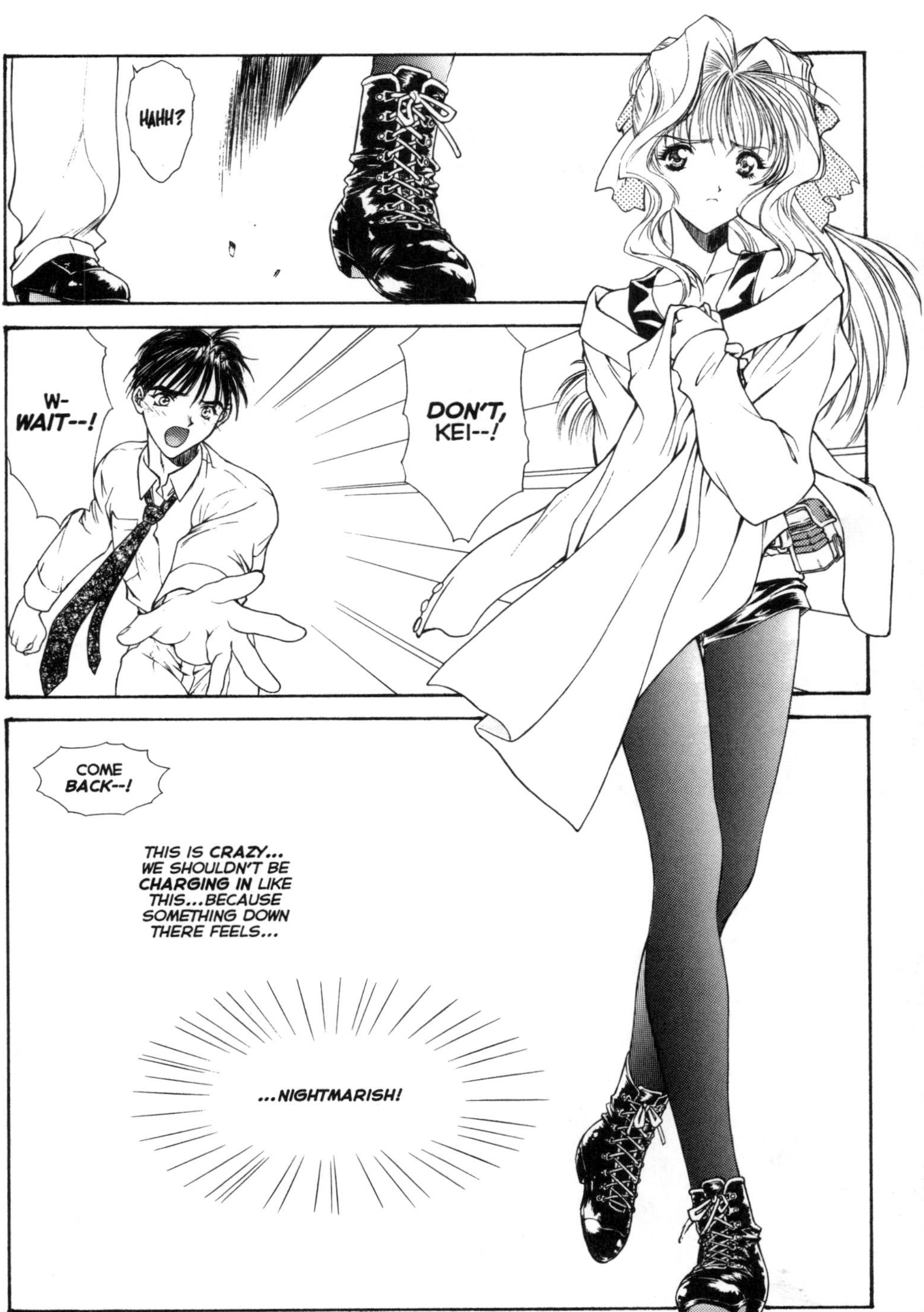
HAHH?
W-
WAIT--!
DON'T, KEI--!
COME BACK--!
THIS IS CRAZY... WE SHOULDN'T BE CHARGING IN LIKE THIS...BECAUSE SOMETHING DOWN THERE FEELS...
...NIGHTMARISH!

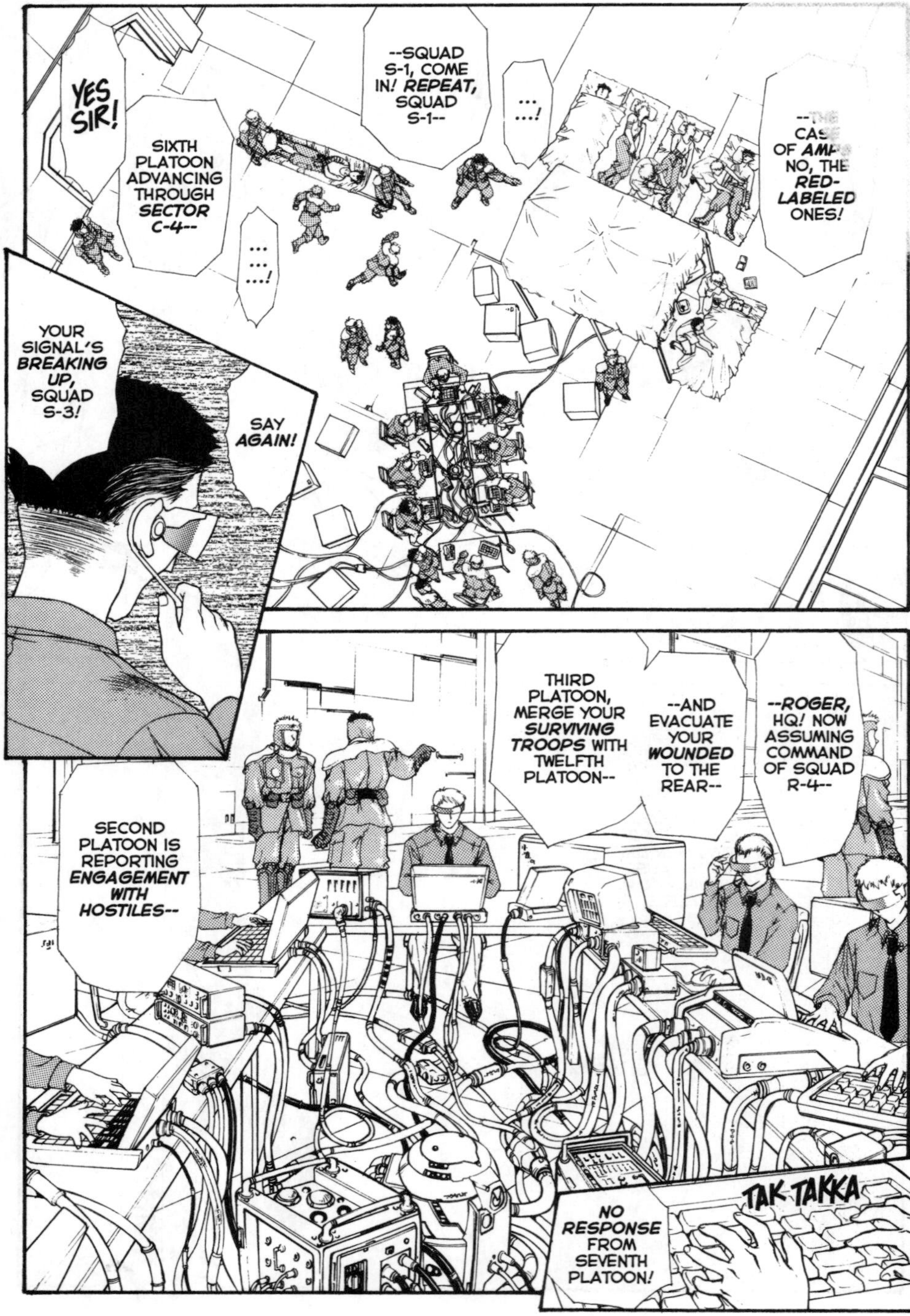
--THE CASE OF AMPS NO, THE RED-LABELED ONES!
...
...!
--SQUAD S-1, COME IN! REPEAT, SQUAD S-1--
...
...
...!
SIXTH PLATOON ADVANCING THROUGH SECTOR C-4--
YES SIR!
SAY AGAIN!
YOUR SIGNAL'S BREAKING UP, SQUAD S-3!
--ROGER, HQ! NOW ASSUMING COMMAND OF SQUAD R-4--
--AND EVACUATE YOUR WOUNDED TO THE REAR--
THIRD PLATOON, MERGE YOUR SURVIVING TROOPS WITH TWELFTH PLATOON--
SECOND PLATOON IS REPORTING ENGAGEMENT WITH HOSTILES--
TAK TAKKA
NO RESPONSE FROM SEVENTH PLATOON!

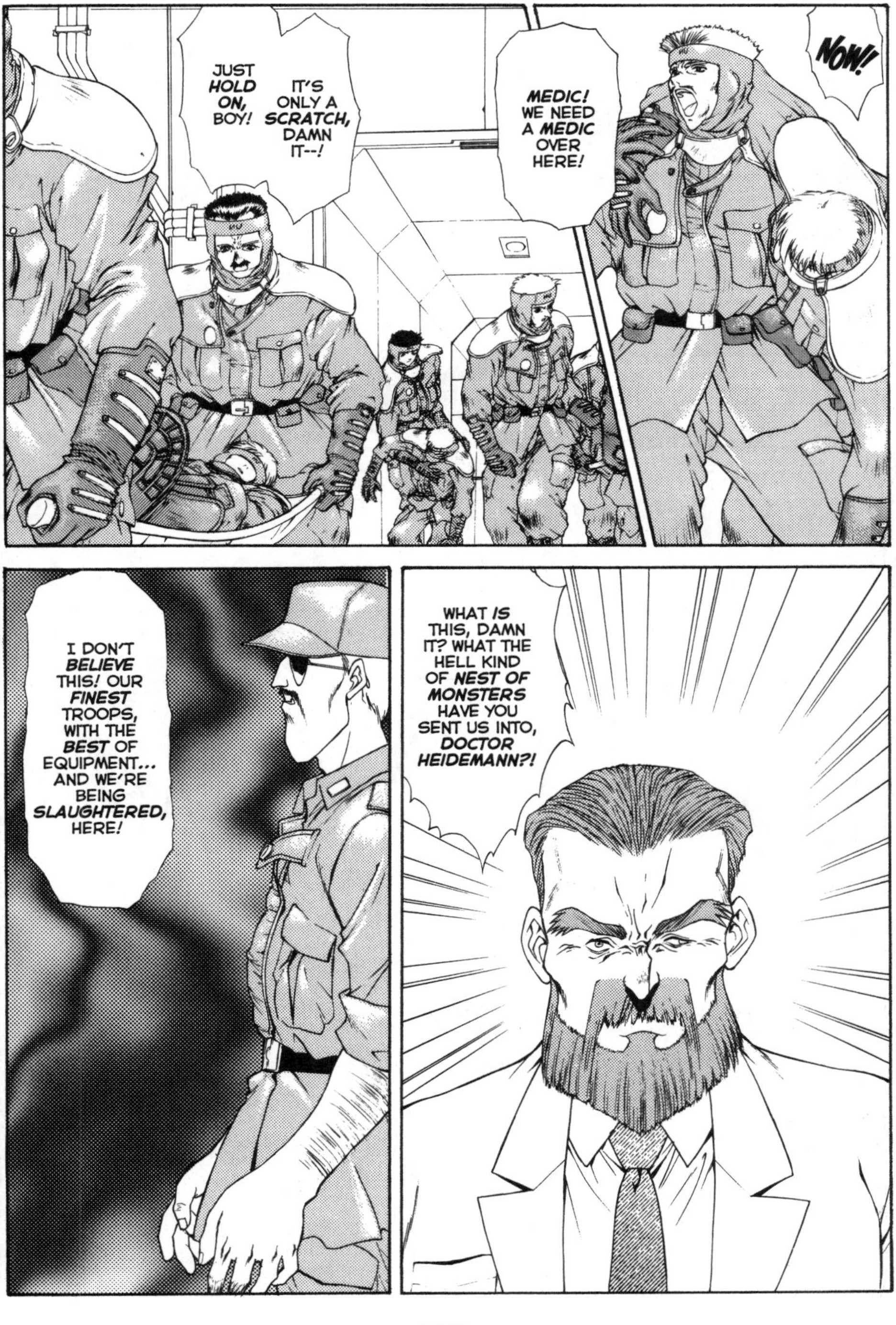
JUST HOLD ON, BOY!
IT'S ONLY A SCRATCH, DAMN IT--!
MEDIC! WE NEED A MEDIC OVER HERE!
NOW!
I DON'T BELIEVE THIS! OUR FINEST TROOPS, WITH THE BEST OF EQUIPMENT... AND WE'RE BEING SLAUGHTERED, HERE!
WHAT IS THIS, DAMN IT? WHAT THE HELL KIND OF NEST OF MONSTERS HAVE YOU SENT US INTO, DOCTOR HEIDEMANN?!

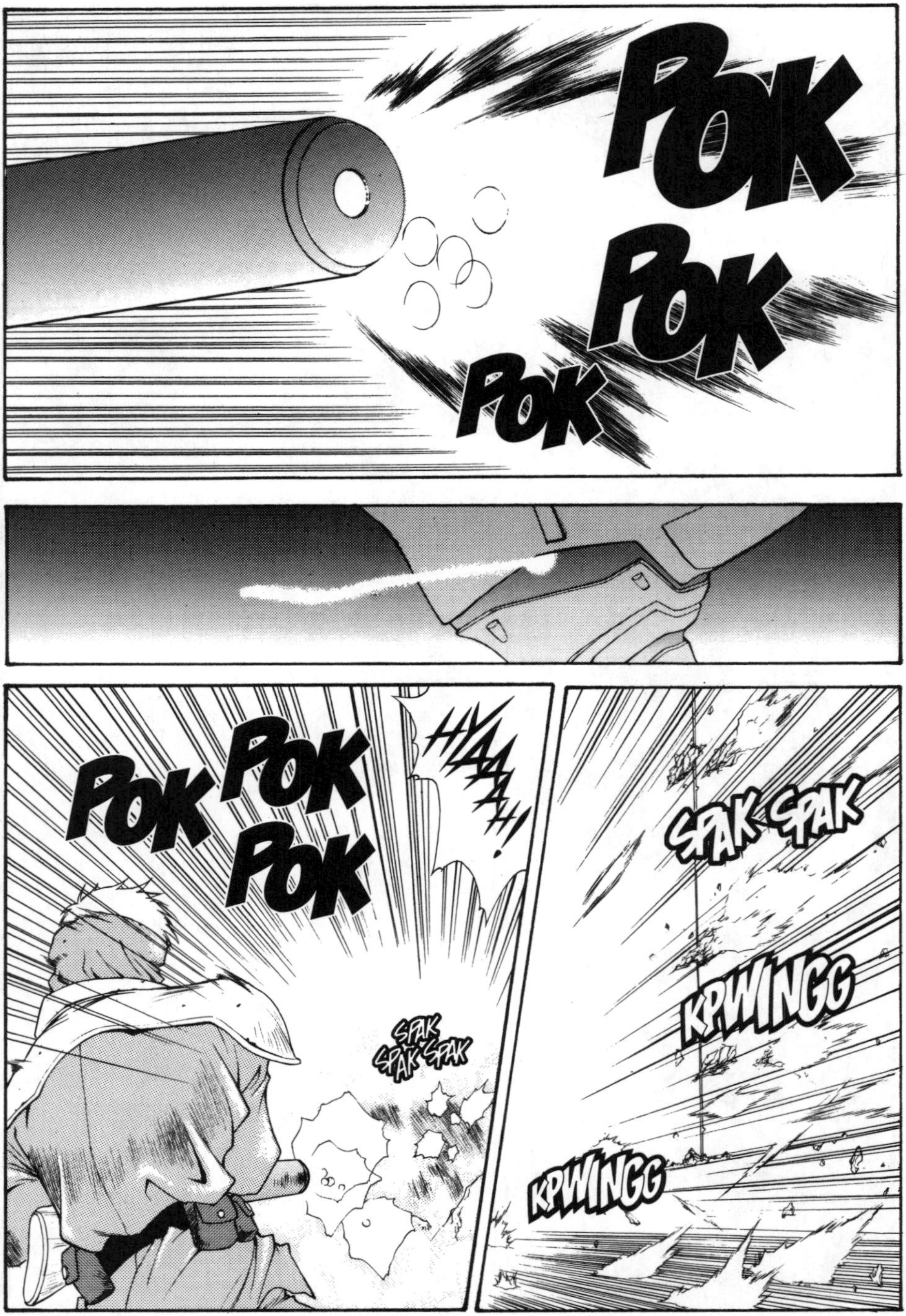
POK
POK
POK
POK POK
POK
HYAAAH!
SPAK
SPAK SPAK
SPAK SPAK
KPWINGG
KPWINGG

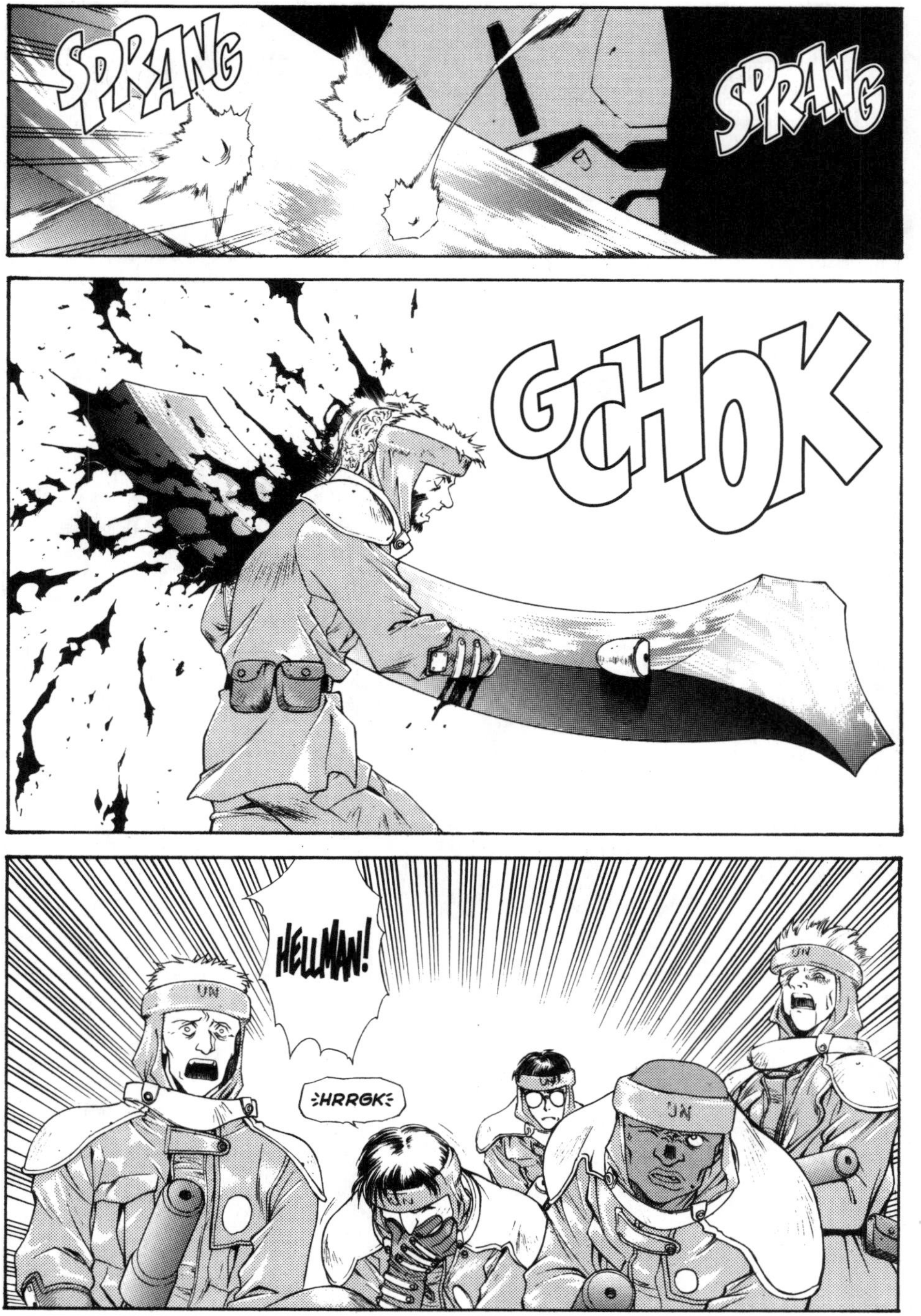
SPRANG
SPRANG
GCHOK
HELLMAN!
HRRGK

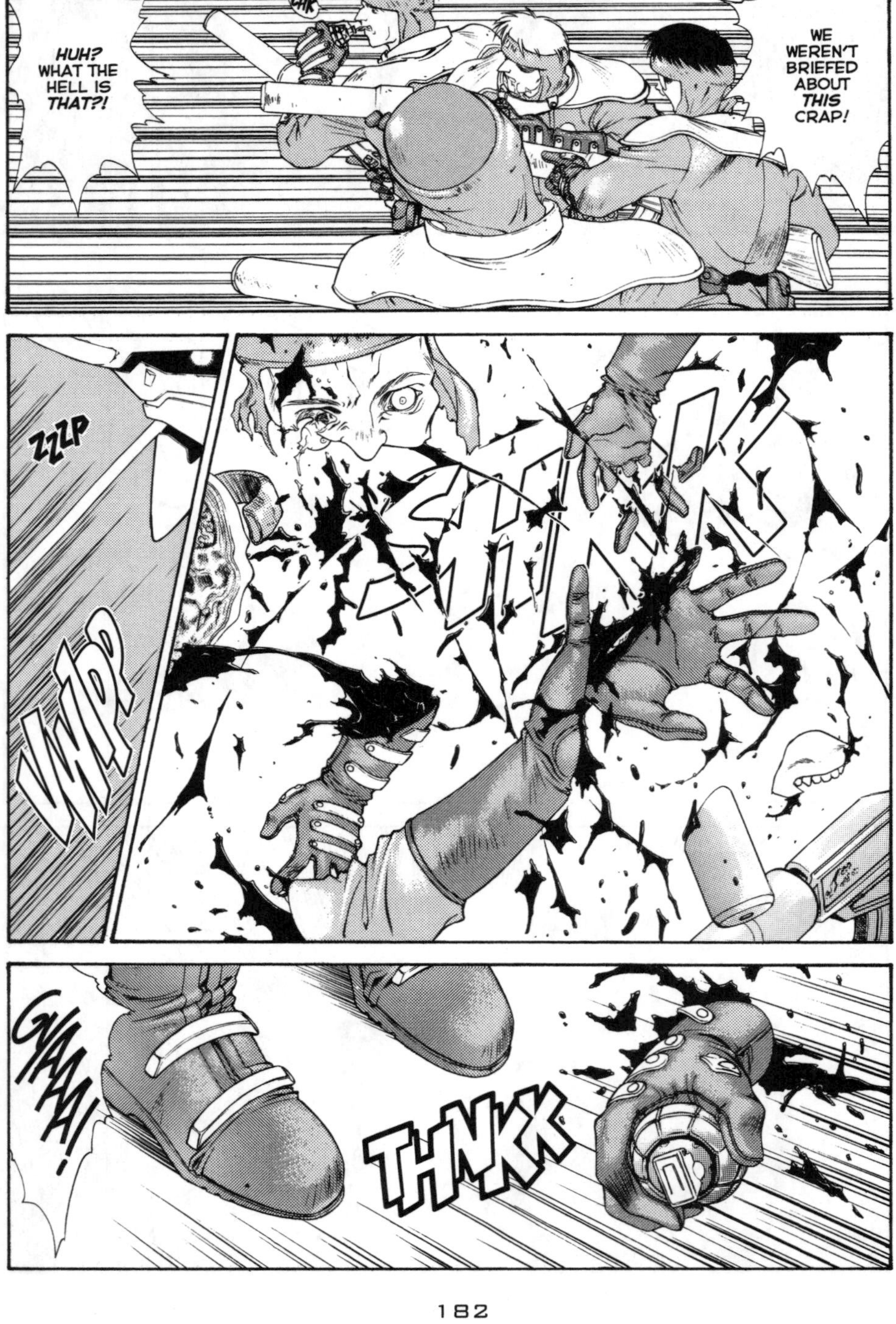
CHK
HUH? WHAT THE HELL IS THAT?!
WE WEREN'T BRIEFED ABOUT THIS CRAP!
ZZZP
WHIPP
GYAAAA!
THNKK

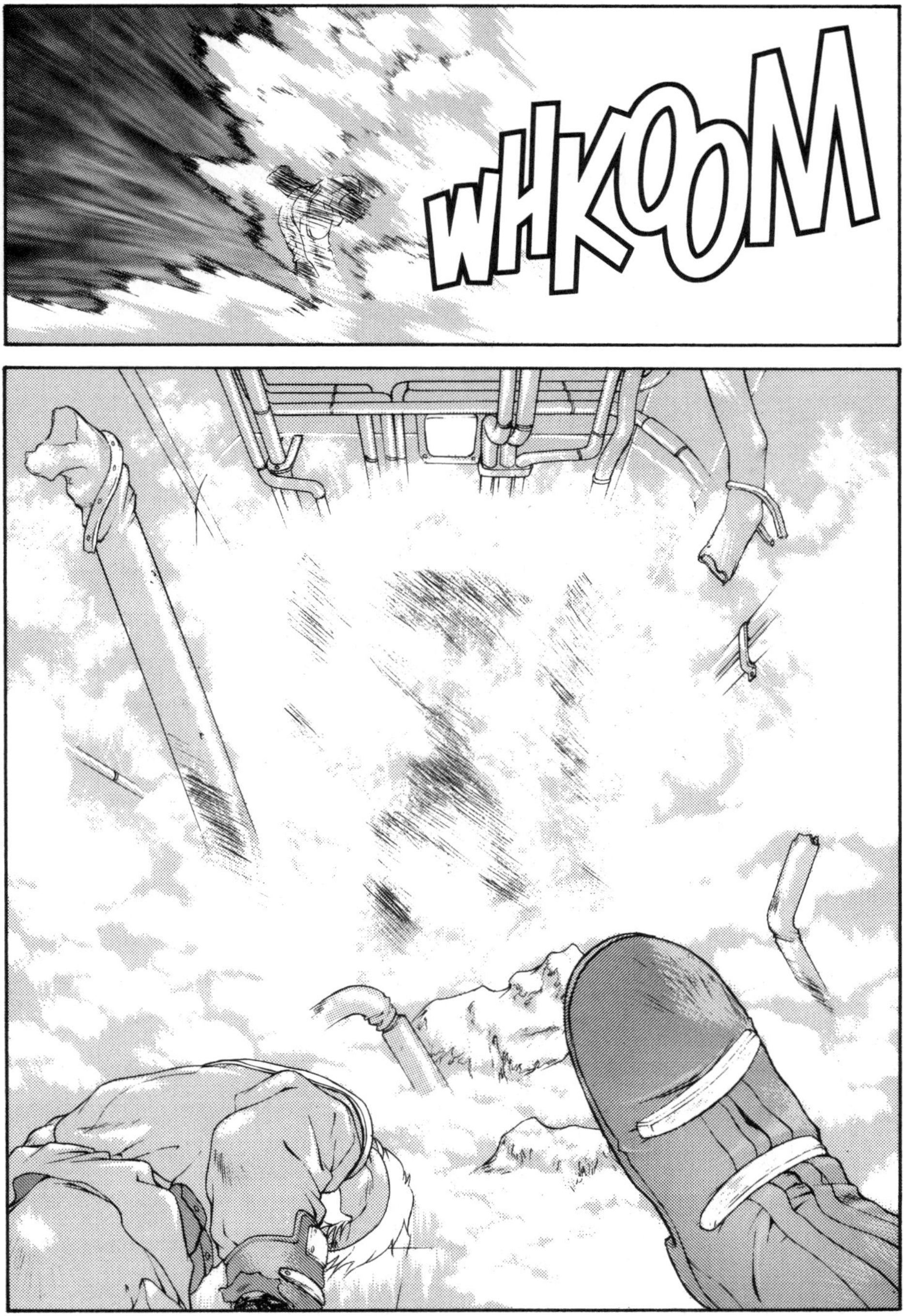
WHKOOM

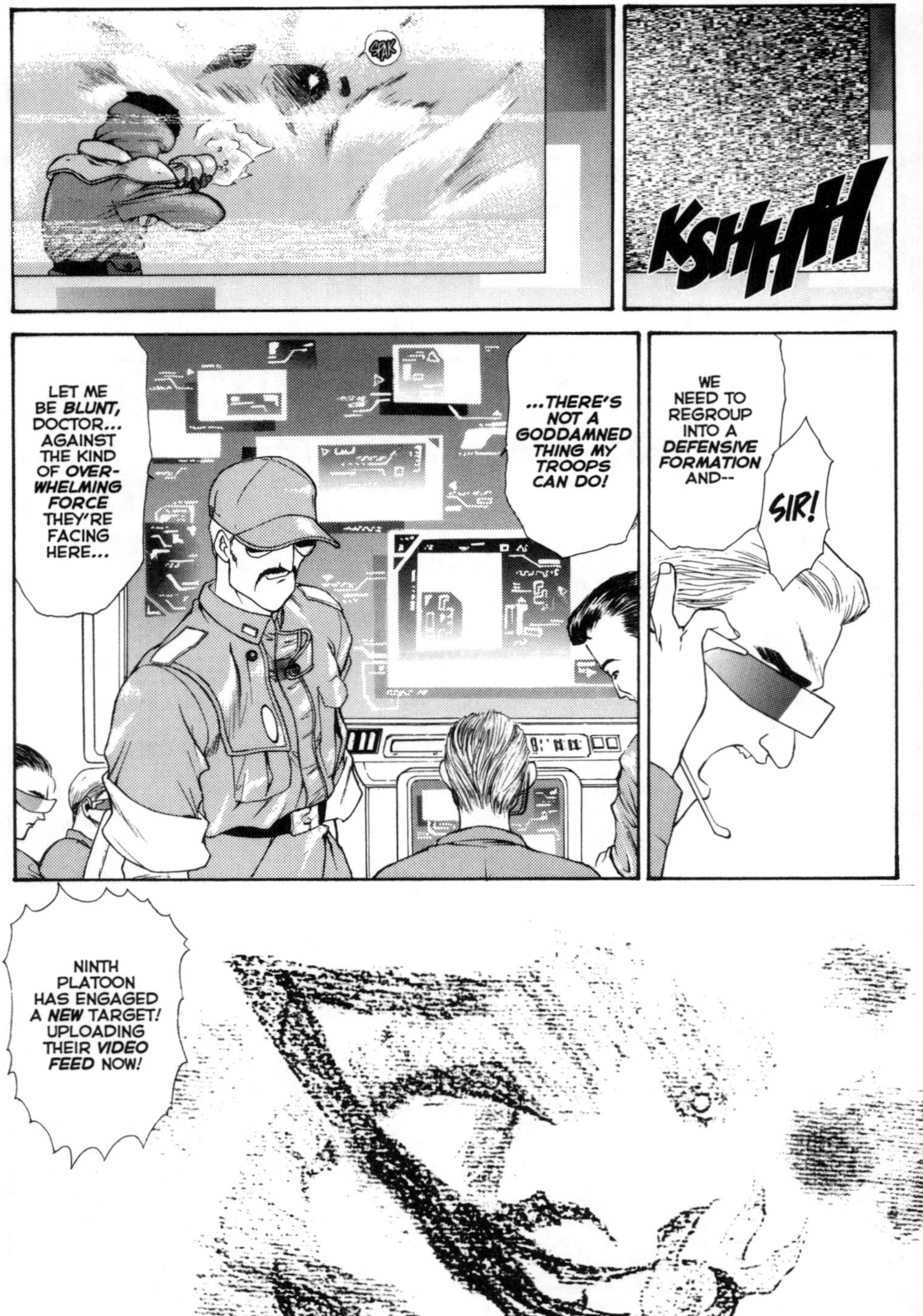
SPAK
KSHHHH
LET ME BE BLUNT, DOCTOR... AGAINST THE KIND OF OVER-WHELMING FORCE THEY'RE FACING HERE...
...THERE'S NOT A GODDAMNED THING MY TROOPS CAN DO!
WE NEED TO REGROUP INTO A DEFENSIVE FORMATION AND--
SIR!
NINTH PLATOON HAS ENGAGED A NEW TARGET! UPLOADING THEIR VIDEO FEED NOW!

ACT 26

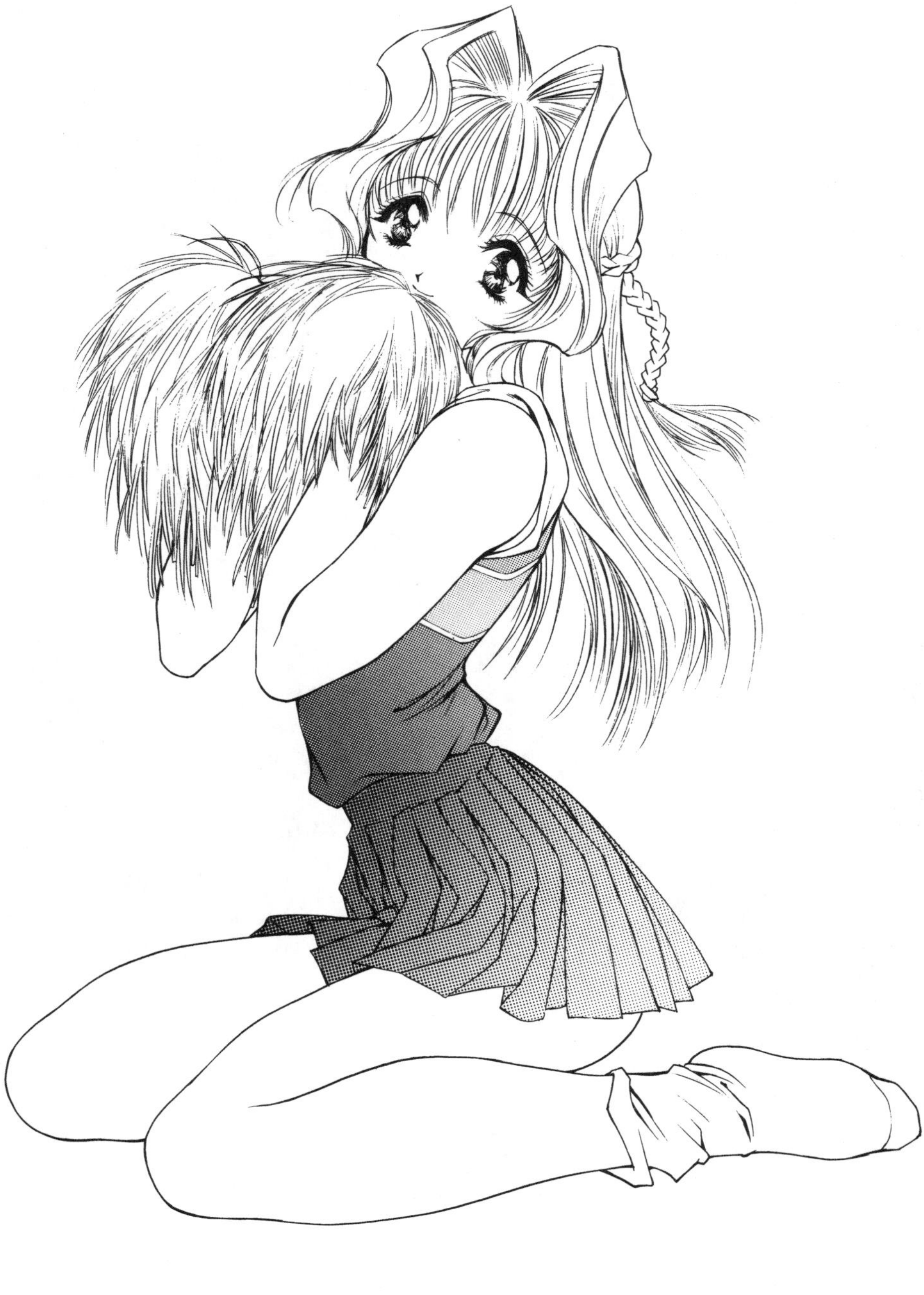

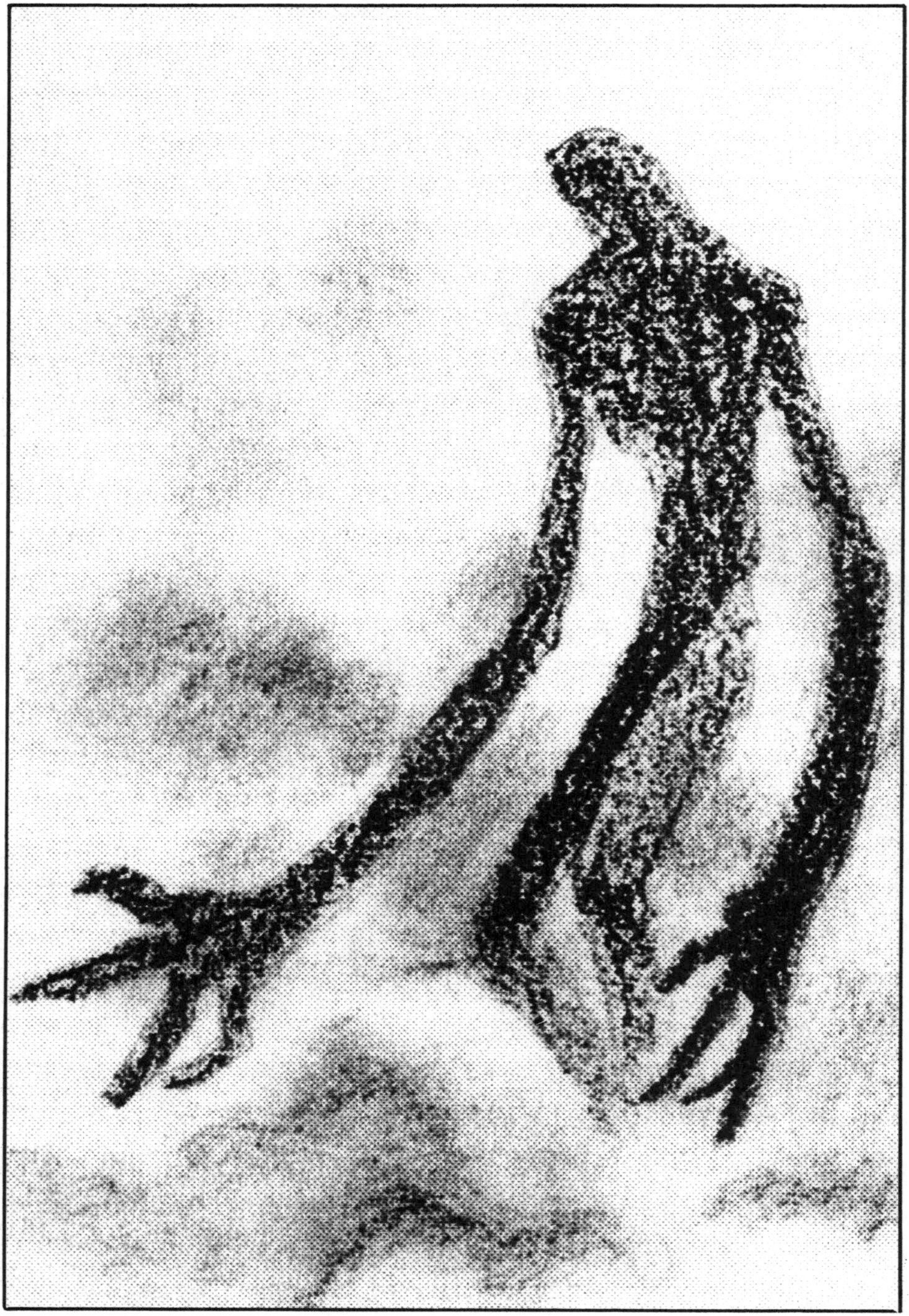

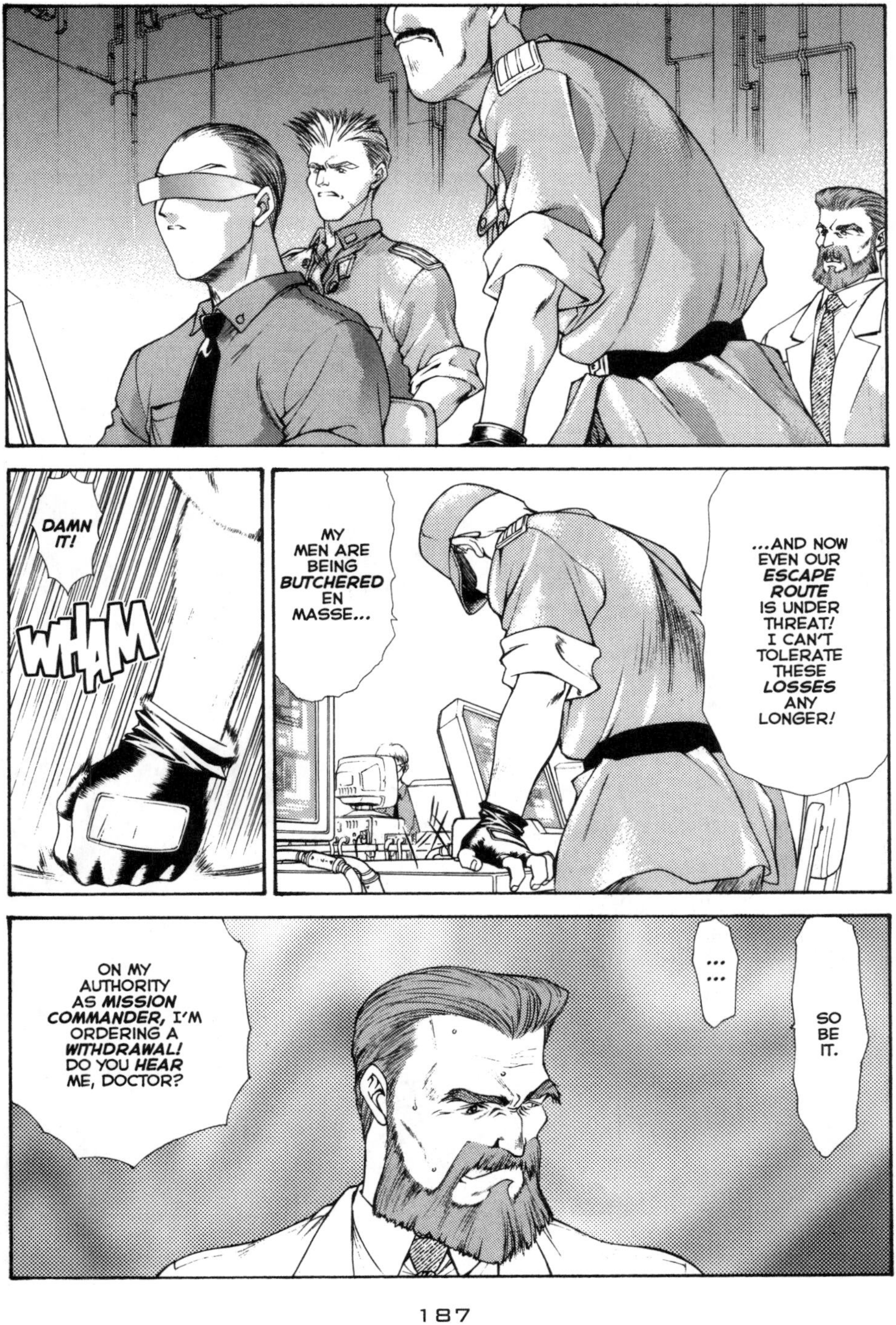
DAMN IT!
WHAM
MY MEN ARE BEING BUTCHERED EN MASSE...
...AND NOW EVEN OUR ESCAPE ROUTE IS UNDER THREAT! I CAN'T TOLERATE THESE LOSSES ANY LONGER!
ON MY AUTHORITY AS MISSION COMMANDER, I'M ORDERING A WITHDRAWAL! DO YOU HEAR ME, DOCTOR?
... ...
SO BE IT.

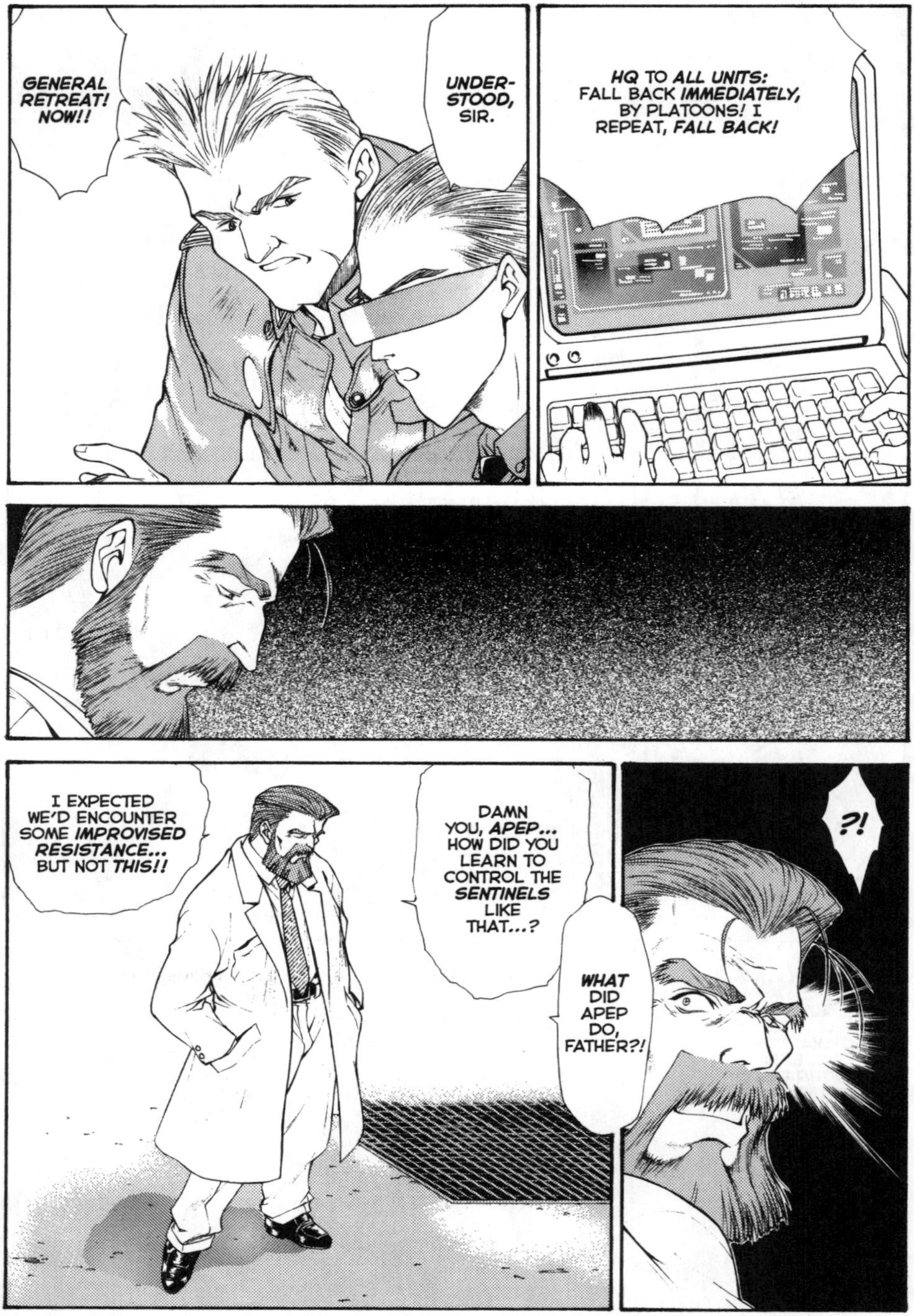
GENERAL RETREAT! NOW!!
UNDER-STOOD, SIR.
HQ TO ALL UNITS: FALL BACK IMMEDIATELY, BY PLATOONS! I REPEAT, FALL BACK!
I EXPECTED WE'D ENCOUNTER SOME IMPROVISED RESISTANCE... BUT NOT THIS!!
DAMN YOU, APEP... HOW DID YOU LEARN TO CONTROL THE SENTINELS LIKE THAT...?
WHAT DID APEP DO, FATHER?!
?!

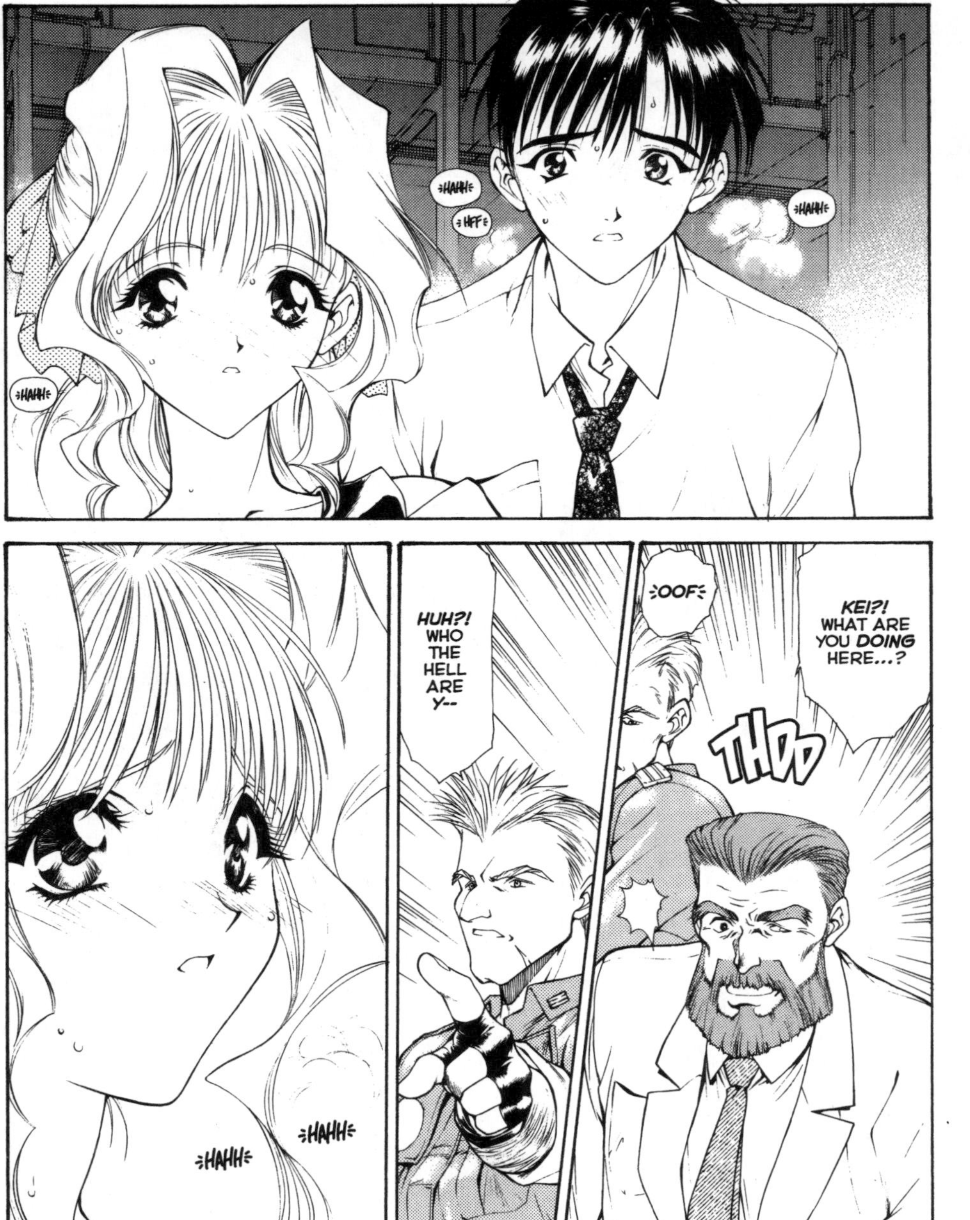
HAHH
HFF
HAHH
HAHH
HAHH
HAHH
HUH?! WHO THE HELL ARE Y--
OOF
KEI?! WHAT ARE YOU DOING HERE...?
THDD

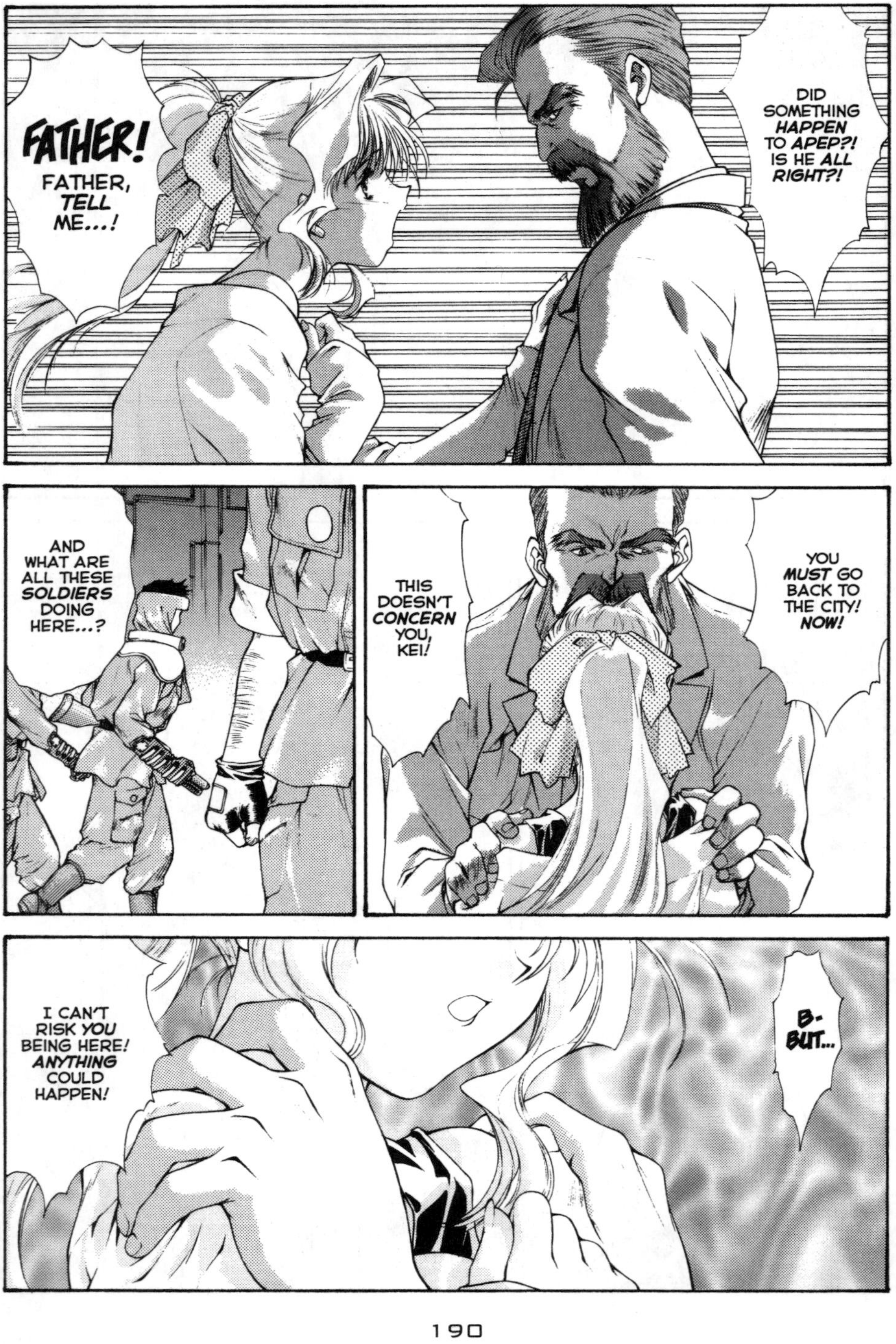
FATHER!
FATHER, TELL ME...!
DID SOMETHING HAPPEN TO APEP?! IS HE ALL RIGHT?!
AND WHAT ARE ALL THESE SOLDIERS DOING HERE...?
THIS DOESN'T CONCERN YOU, KEI!
YOU MUST GO BACK TO THE CITY! NOW!
I CAN'T RISK YOU BEING HERE! ANYTHING COULD HAPPEN!
B-BUT...

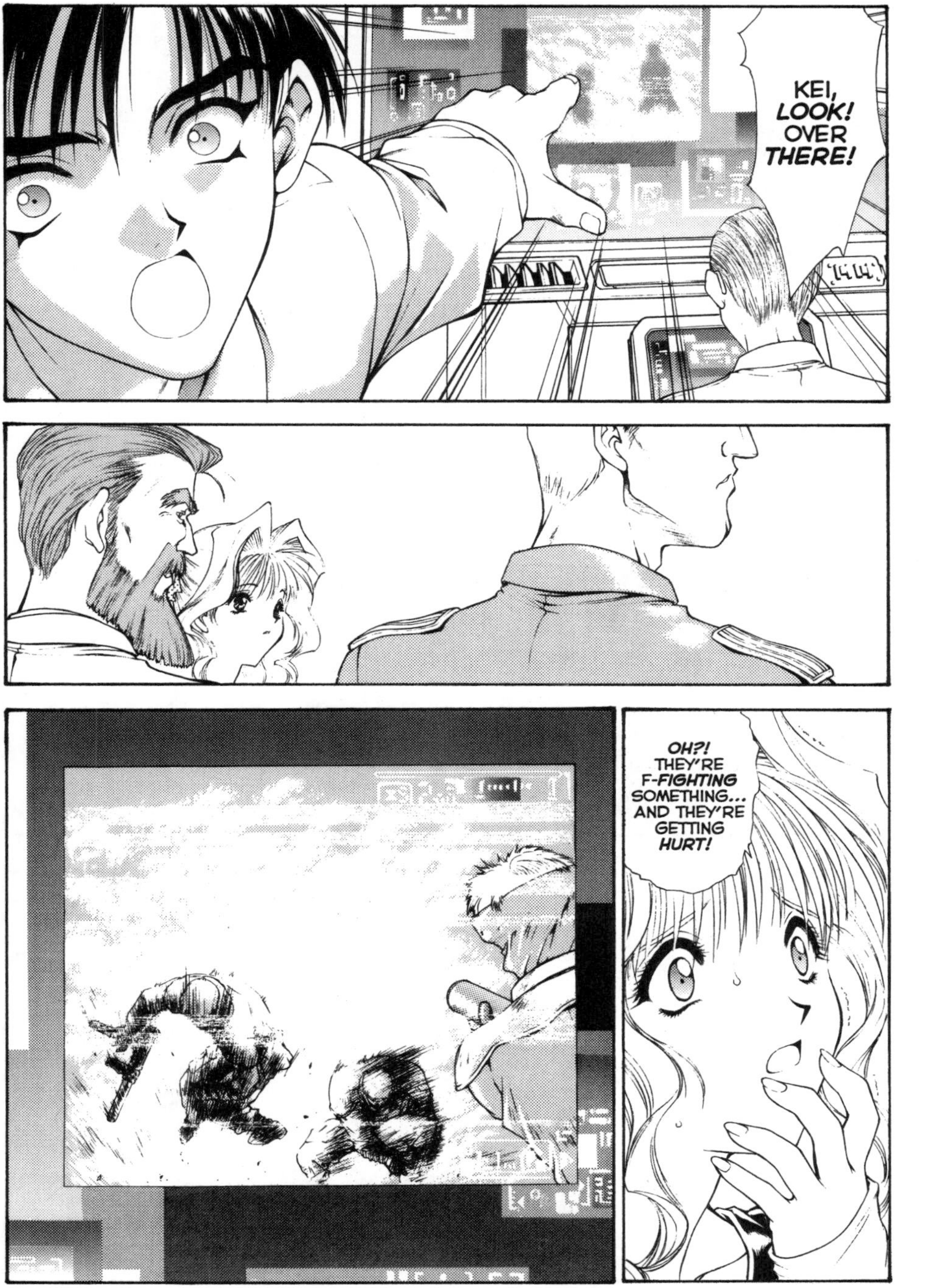
KEI, LOOK! OVER THERE!
OH?! THEY'RE F-FIGHTING SOMETHING... AND THEY'RE GETTING HURT!

SUNAO... WHAT'S GOING ON...?

NO!

NOT THAT ONE..!

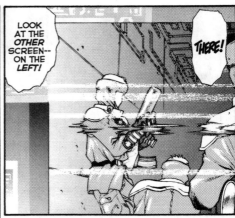

LOOK AT THE *OTHER* SCREEN-- ON THE *LEFT!*

THERE!

SEE ...?

!

KEI... ISN'T THAT MISS M-ZAK...?

OH, *GOD*... YES, THAT'S *HER*...!

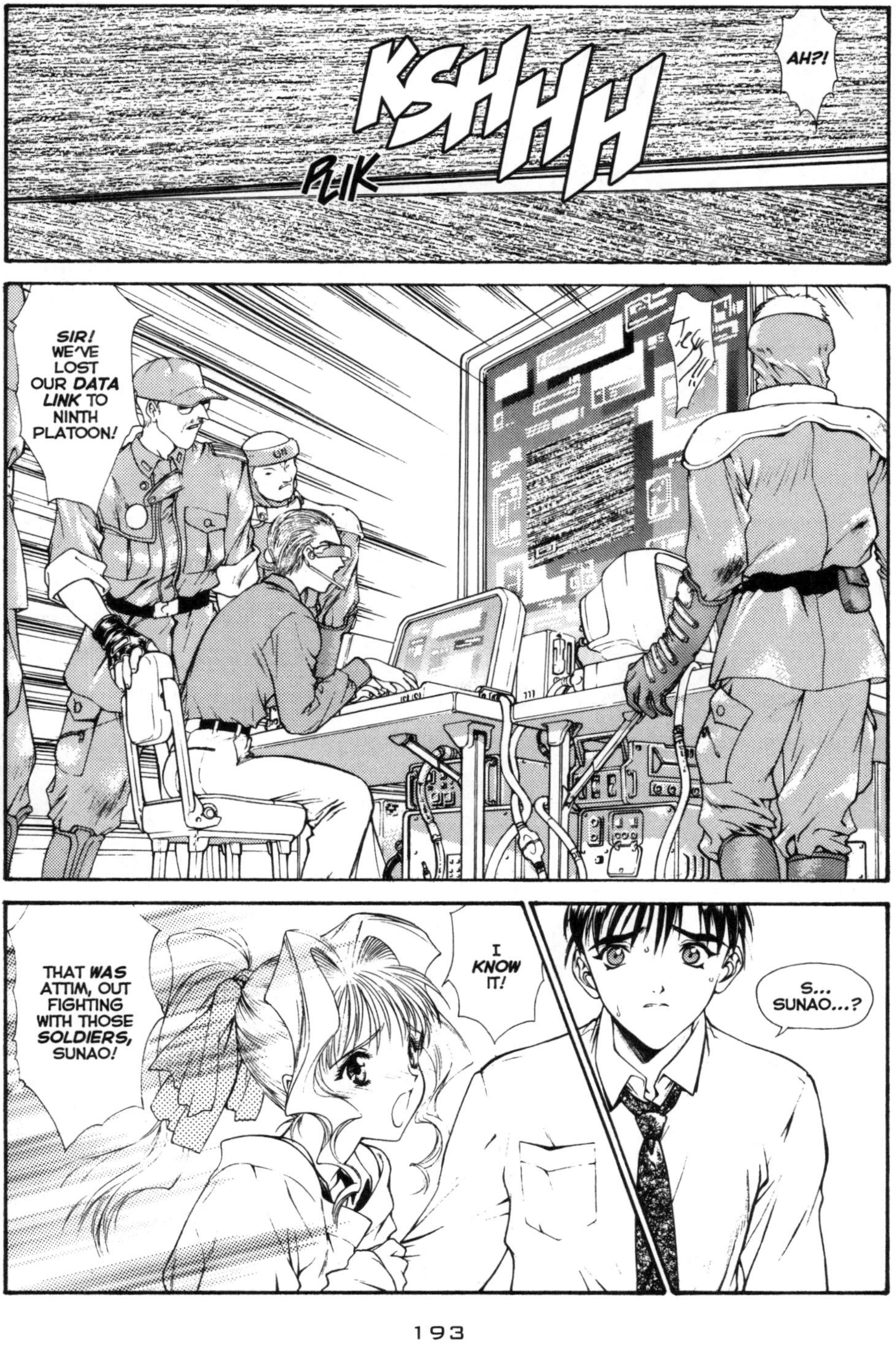
KSHHHH
PLIK
AH?!
SIR! WE'VE LOST OUR **DATA LINK** TO NINTH PLATOON!
THAT **WAS** ATTIM, OUT FIGHTING WITH THOSE **SOLDIERS,** SUNAO!
I **KNOW** IT!
S... SUNAO...?

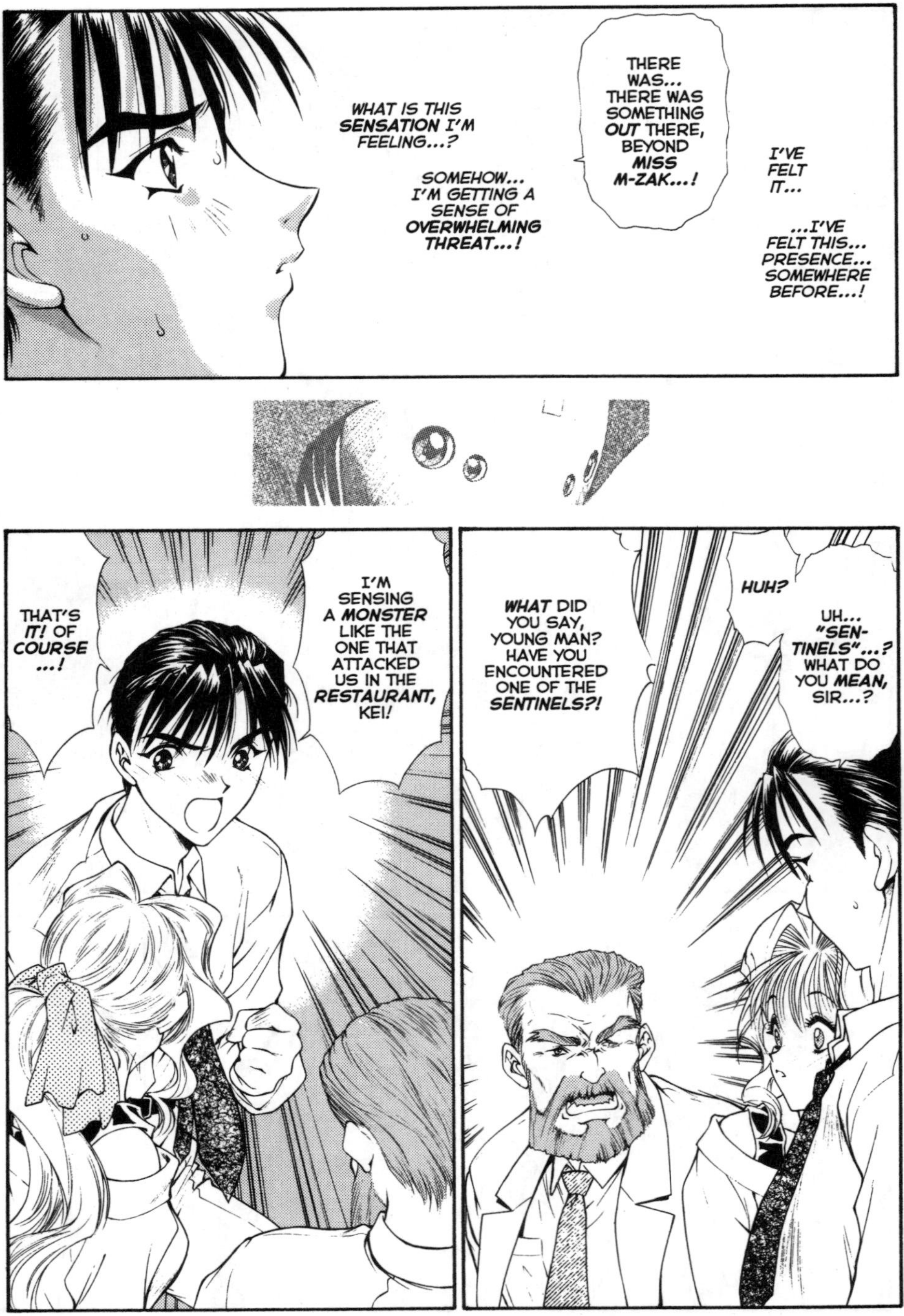
WHAT IS THIS SENSATION I'M FEELING...?
SOMEHOW... I'M GETTING A SENSE OF OVERWHELMING THREAT...!
THERE WAS... THERE WAS SOMETHING OUT THERE, BEYOND MISS M-ZAK...!
I'VE FELT IT...
...I'VE FELT THIS... PRESENCE... SOMEWHERE BEFORE...!
THAT'S IT! OF COURSE ...!
I'M SENSING A MONSTER LIKE THE ONE THAT ATTACKED US IN THE RESTAURANT, KEI!
WHAT DID YOU SAY, YOUNG MAN? HAVE YOU ENCOUNTERED ONE OF THE SENTINELS?!
HUH?
UH... "SEN- TINELS"...? WHAT DO YOU MEAN, SIR...?

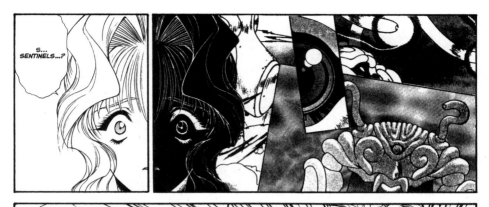

S...
SENTINELS...?

N-
NO...!

FMPP

SENTINELS...?
OH, GOD...
I *KNOW*
THEM...!

THEY
WERE THOSE
MONSTERS...
FROM...
FROM THE
STARSHIP!

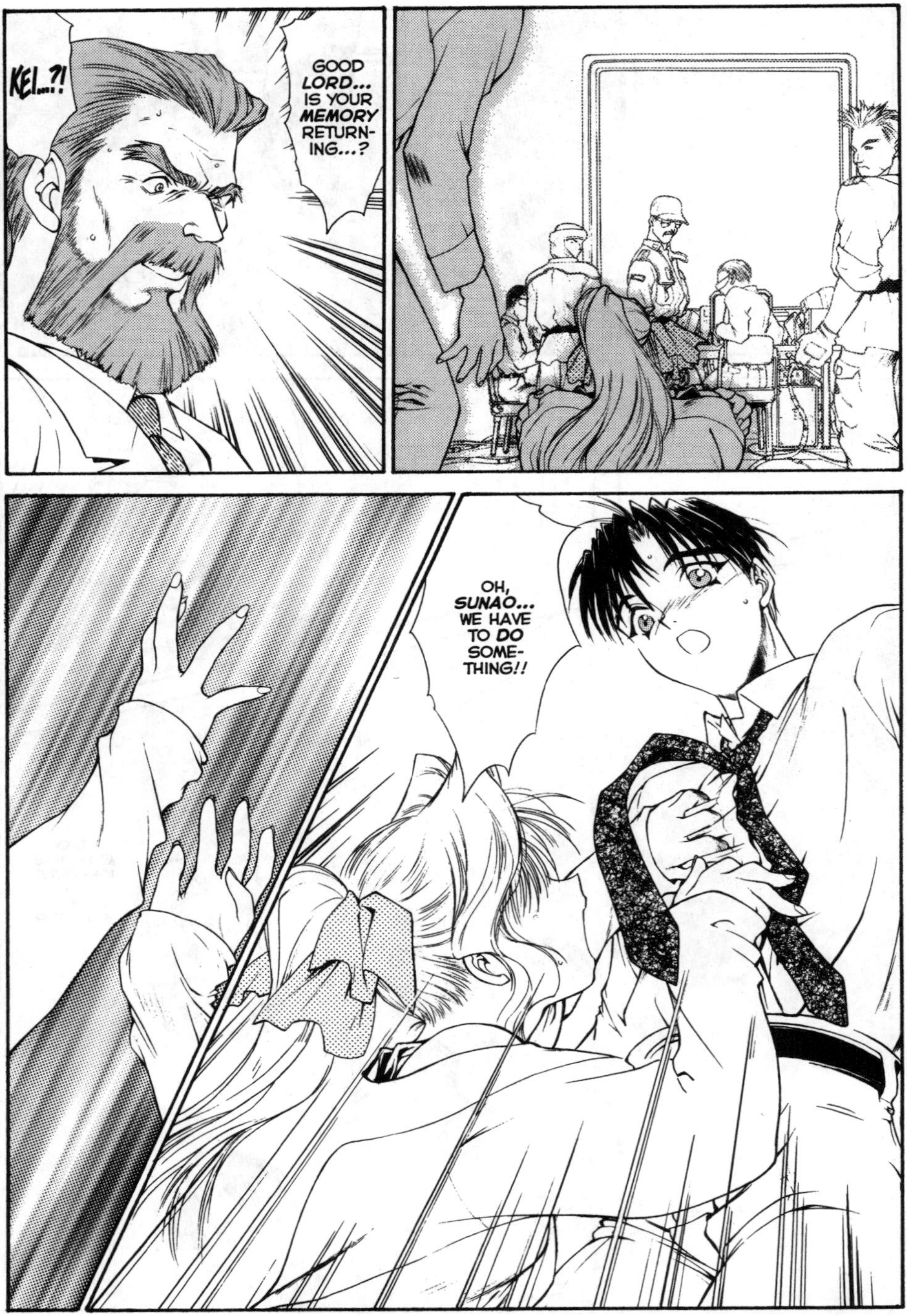
KEI...?!
GOOD LORD... IS YOUR MEMORY RETURNING...?
OH, SUNAO... WE HAVE TO DO SOMETHING!!

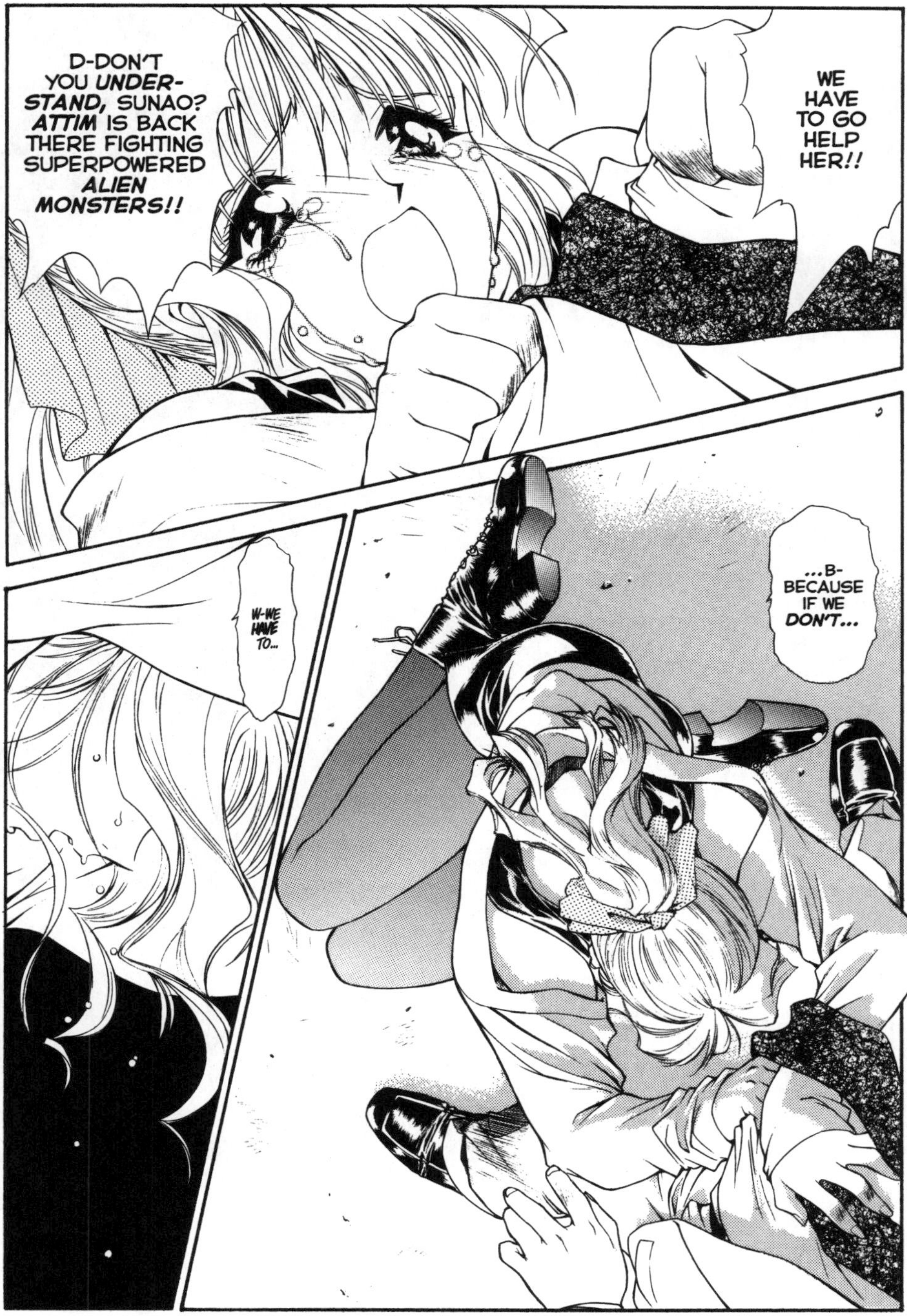
D-DON'T YOU UNDERSTAND, SUNAO? ATTIM IS BACK THERE FIGHTING SUPERPOWERED ALIEN MONSTERS!!
WE HAVE TO GO HELP HER!!
W-WE HAVE TO...
...B-BECAUSE IF WE DON'T...

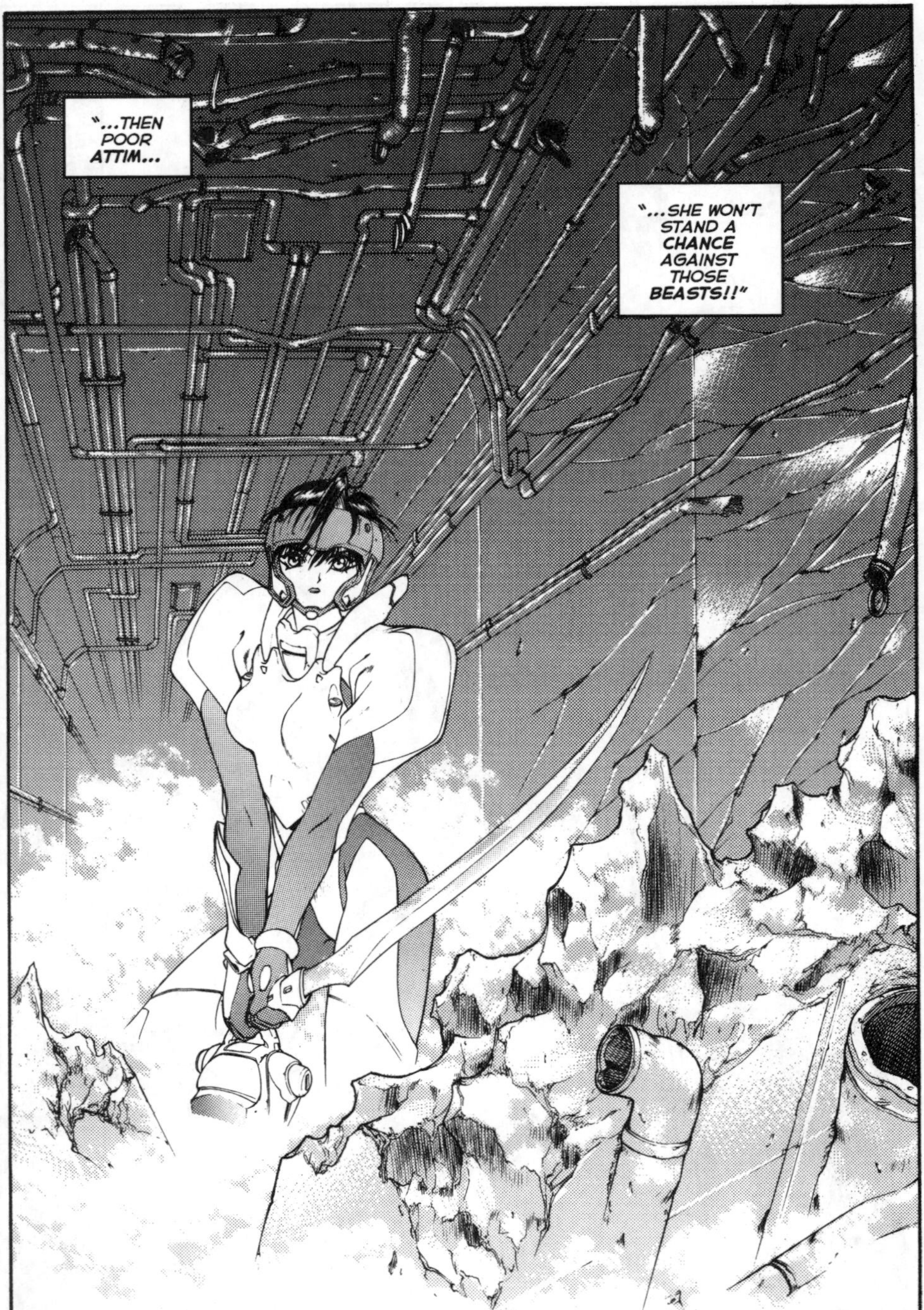
"...THEN POOR ATTIM...
"...SHE WON'T STAND A CHANCE AGAINST THOSE BEASTS!!"

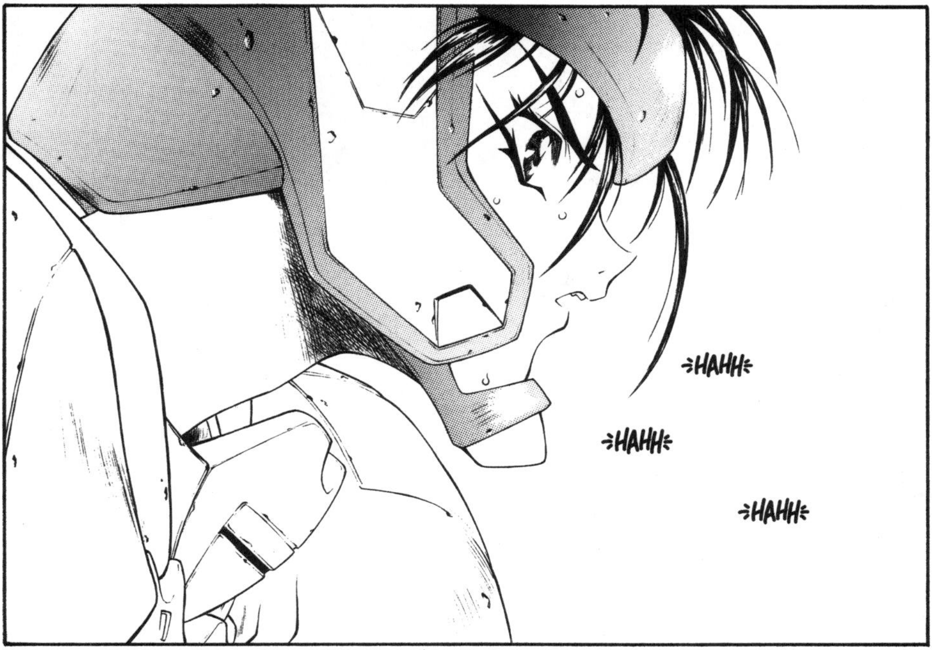
HAHH
HAHH
HAHH

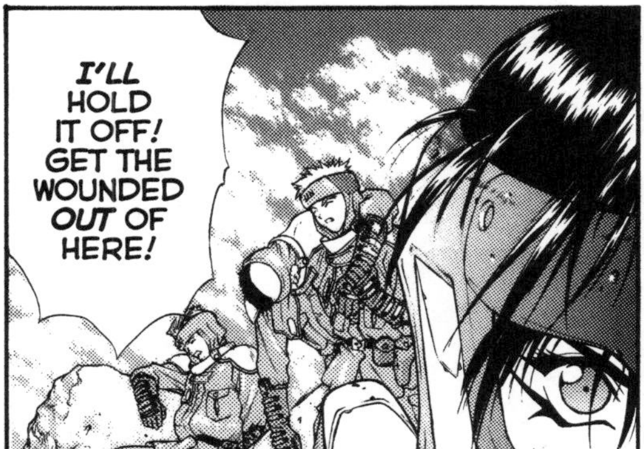
I'LL HOLD IT OFF! GET THE WOUNDED OUT OF HERE!

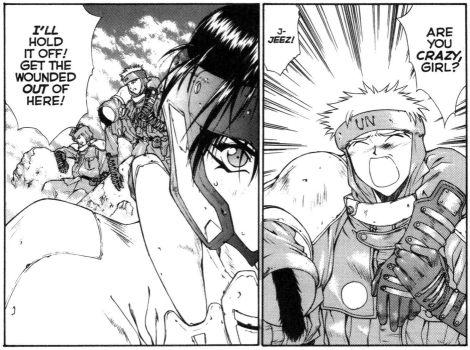

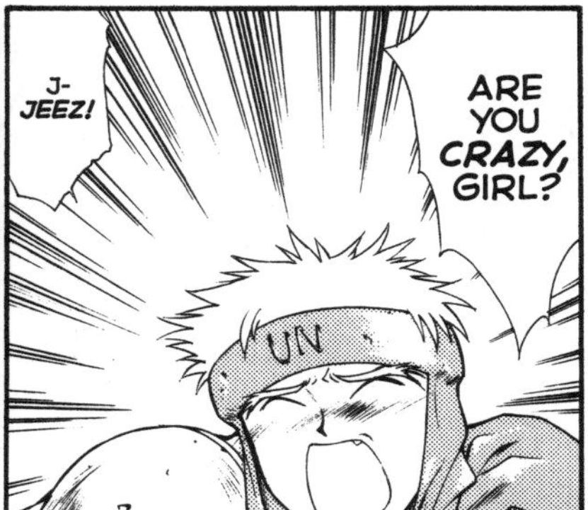
J- JEEZ!
ARE YOU CRAZY, GIRL?

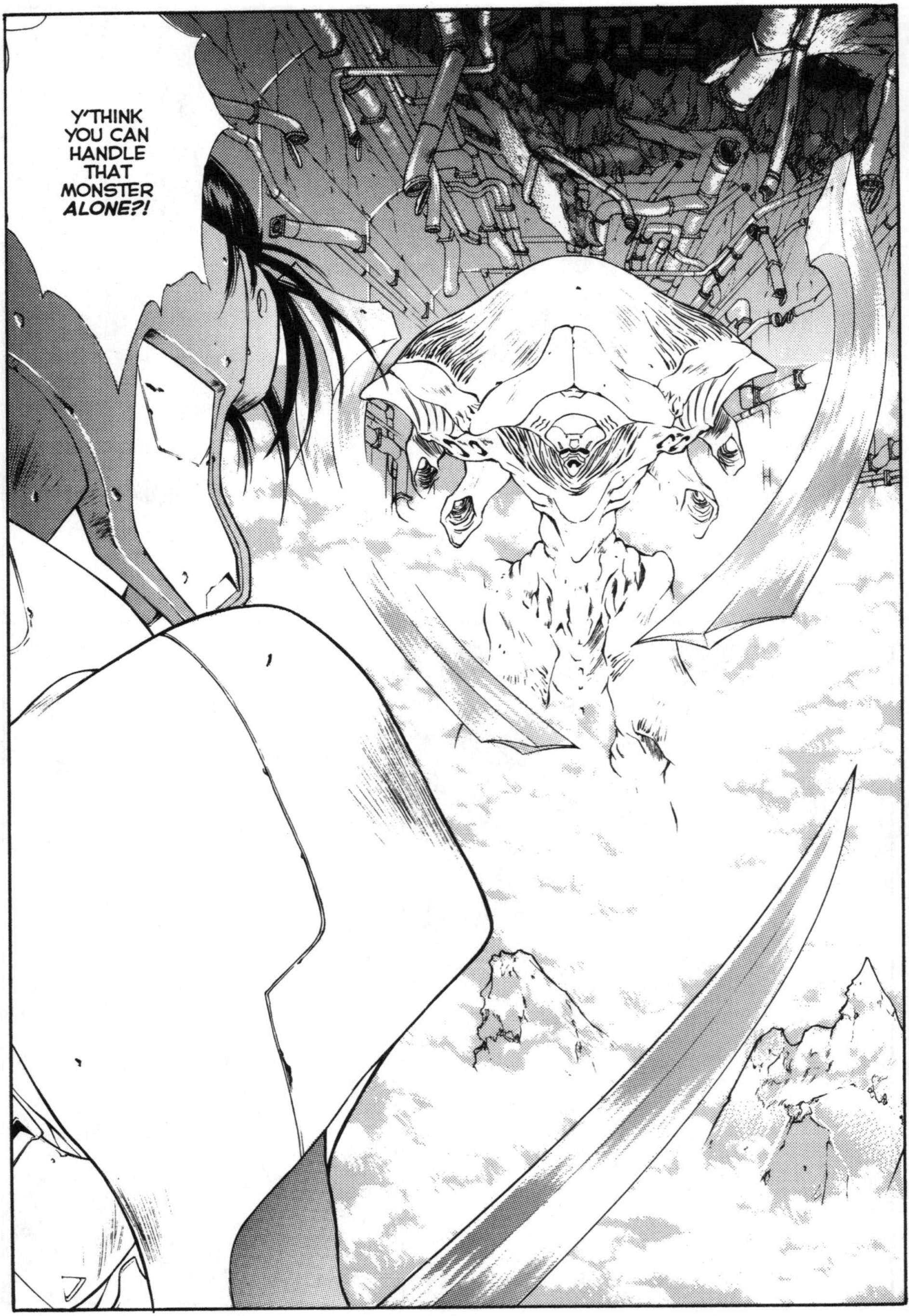
Y'THINK YOU CAN HANDLE THAT MONSTER ***ALONE?!***

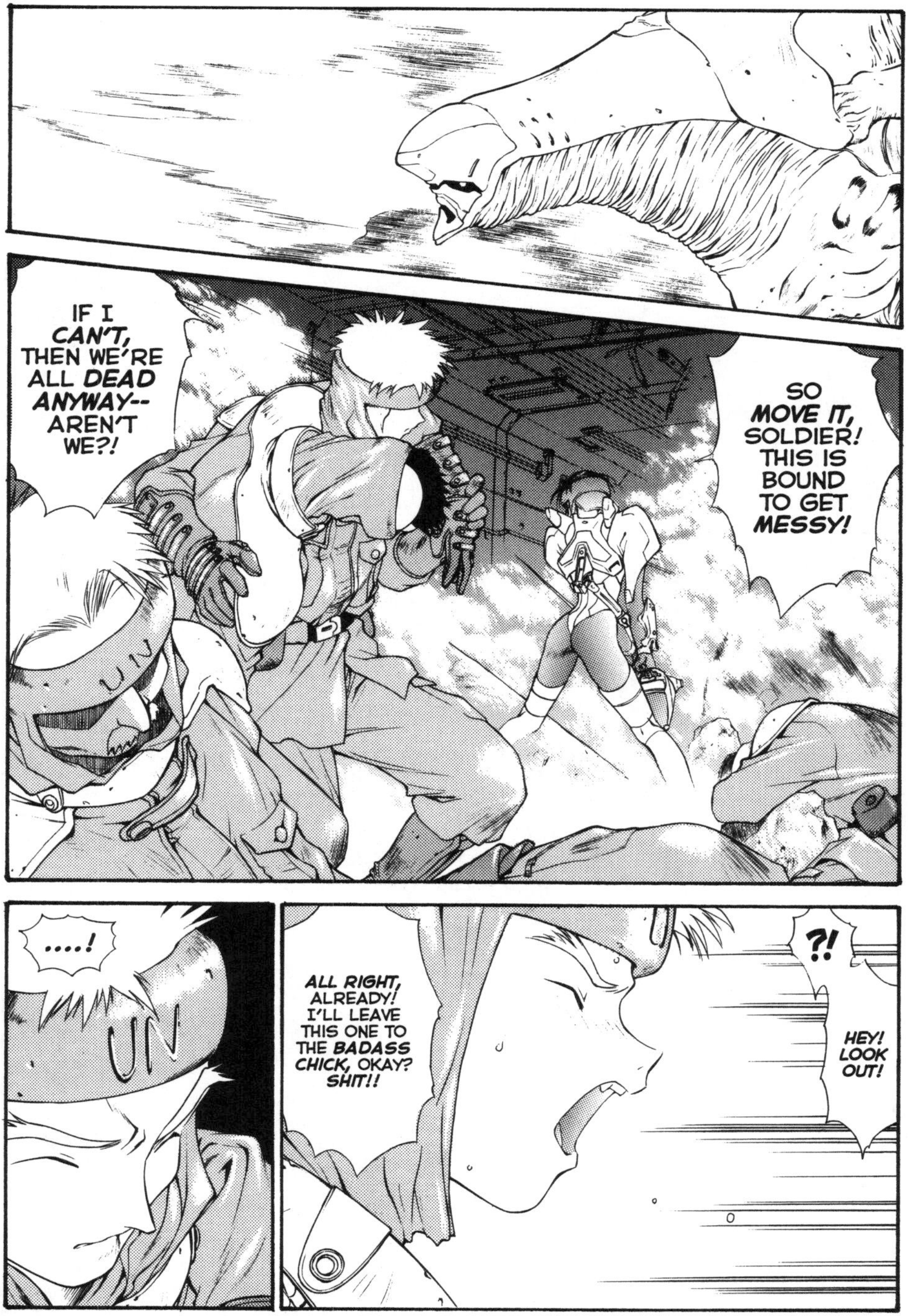
IF I CAN'T, THEN WE'RE ALL DEAD ANYWAY-- AREN'T WE?!
SO MOVE IT, SOLDIER! THIS IS BOUND TO GET MESSY!
....!
ALL RIGHT, ALREADY! I'LL LEAVE THIS ONE TO THE BADASS CHICK, OKAY? SHIT!!
?!
HEY! LOOK OUT!

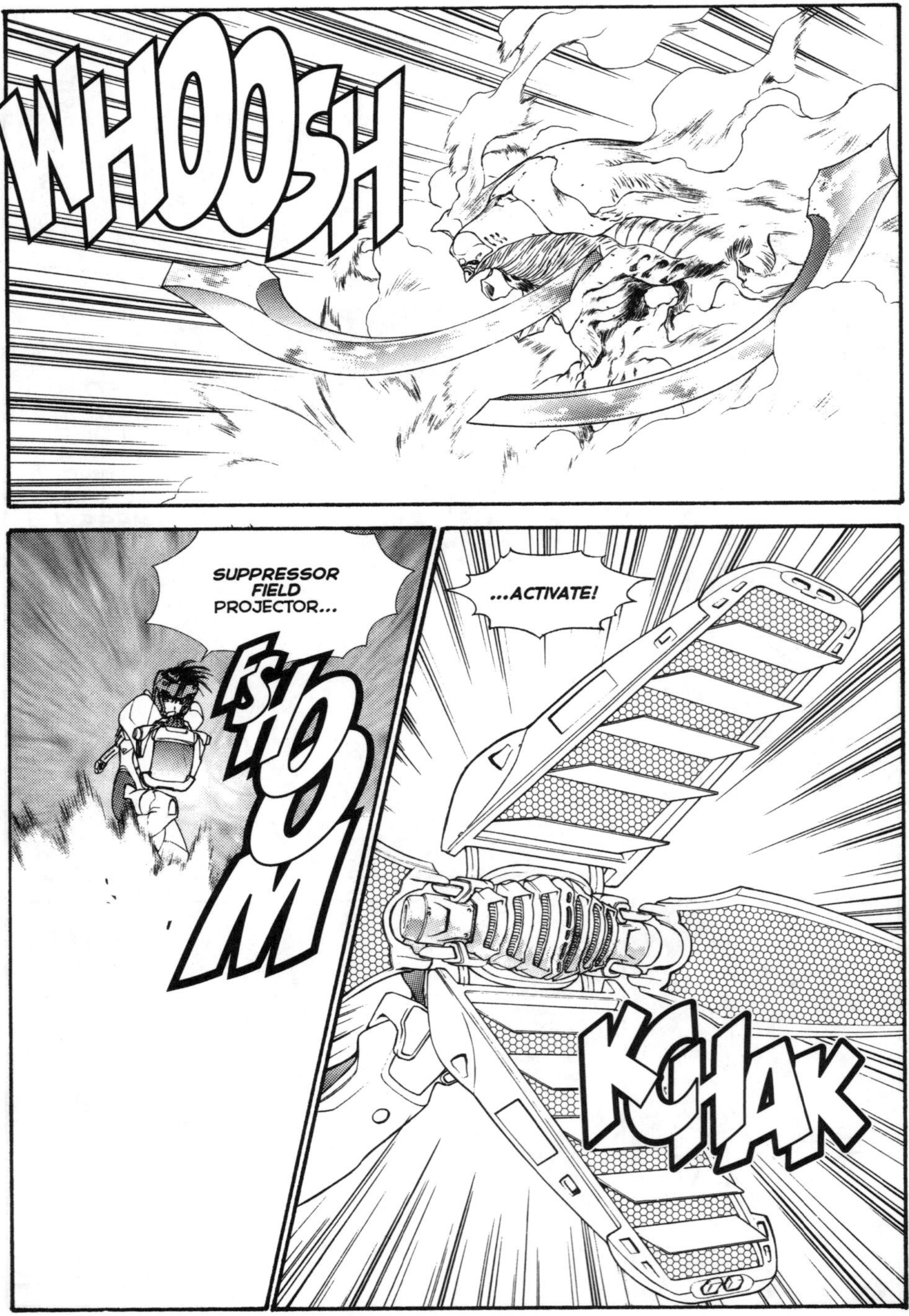
WHOOSH
SUPPRESSOR FIELD PROJECTOR...
FSHOOM
...ACTIVATE!
KCHAK

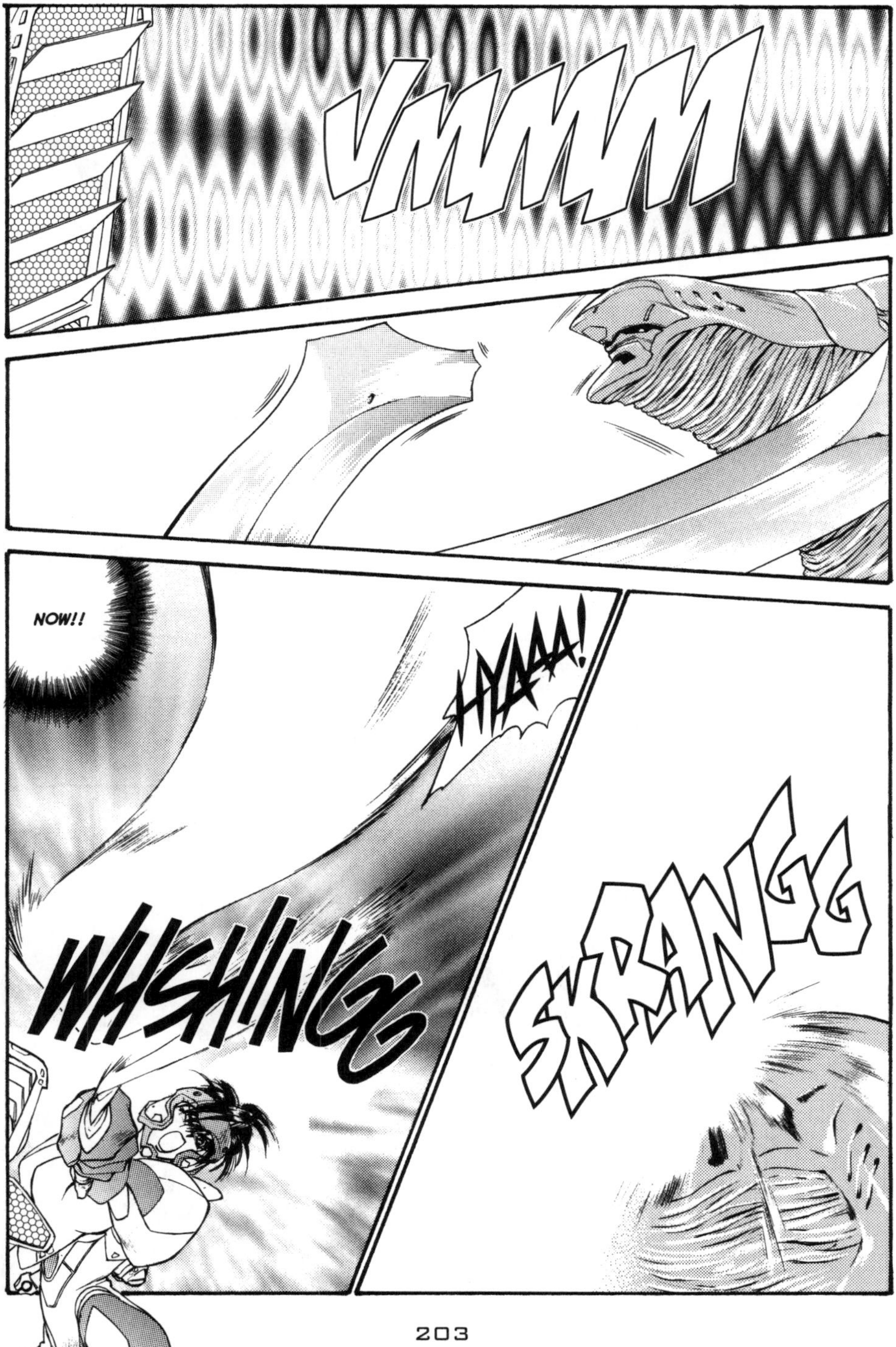
VMMMM
NOW!!
HYAAA!
WHSHING
SKRANGG

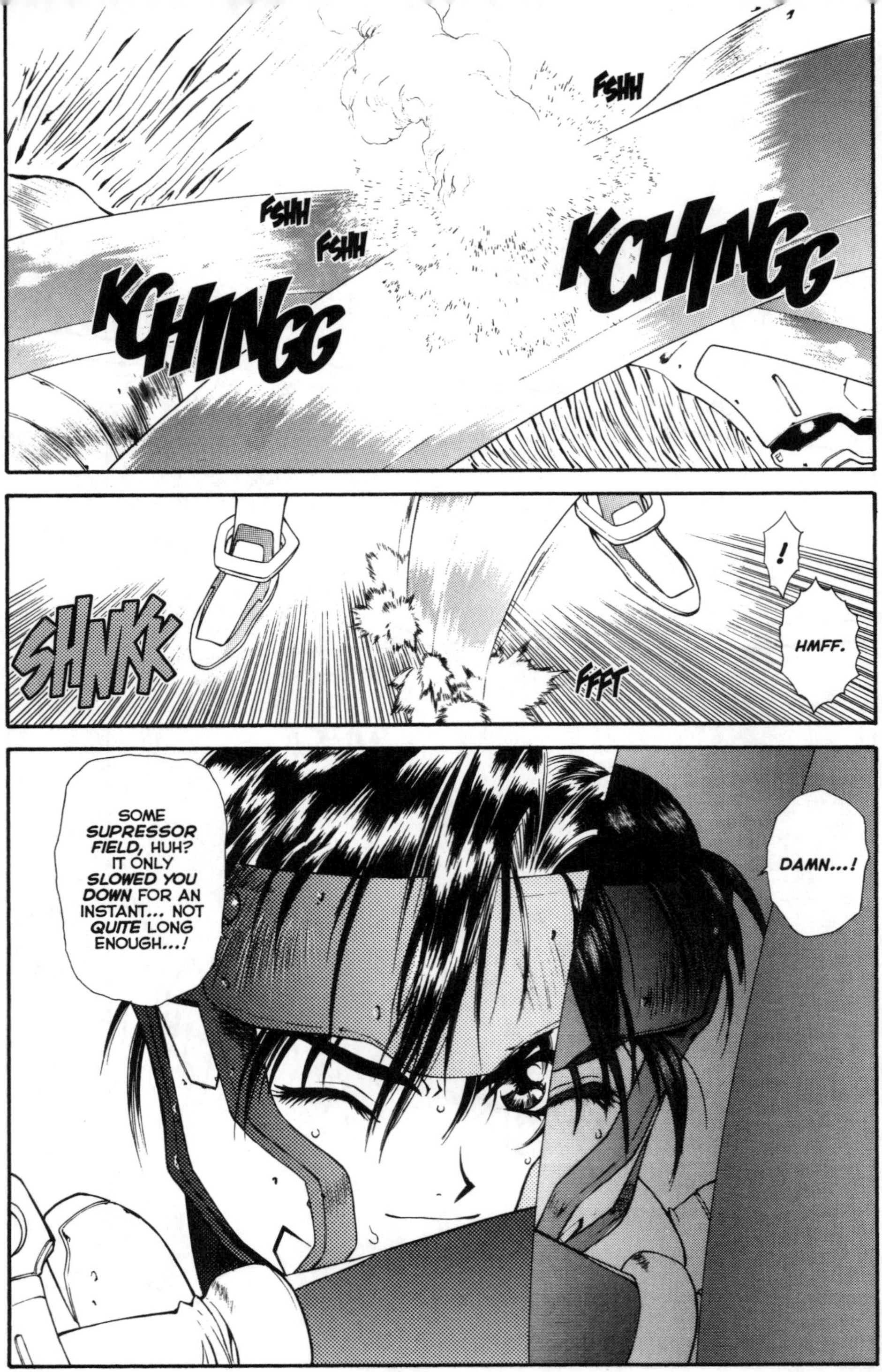
FSHH
FSHH
FSHH
KCHINGG
KCHINGG
SHNKK
FFFT
!
HMFF.
SOME SUPRESSOR FIELD, HUH? IT ONLY SLOWED YOU DOWN FOR AN INSTANT... NOT QUITE LONG ENOUGH...!
DAMN...!

ACT 27

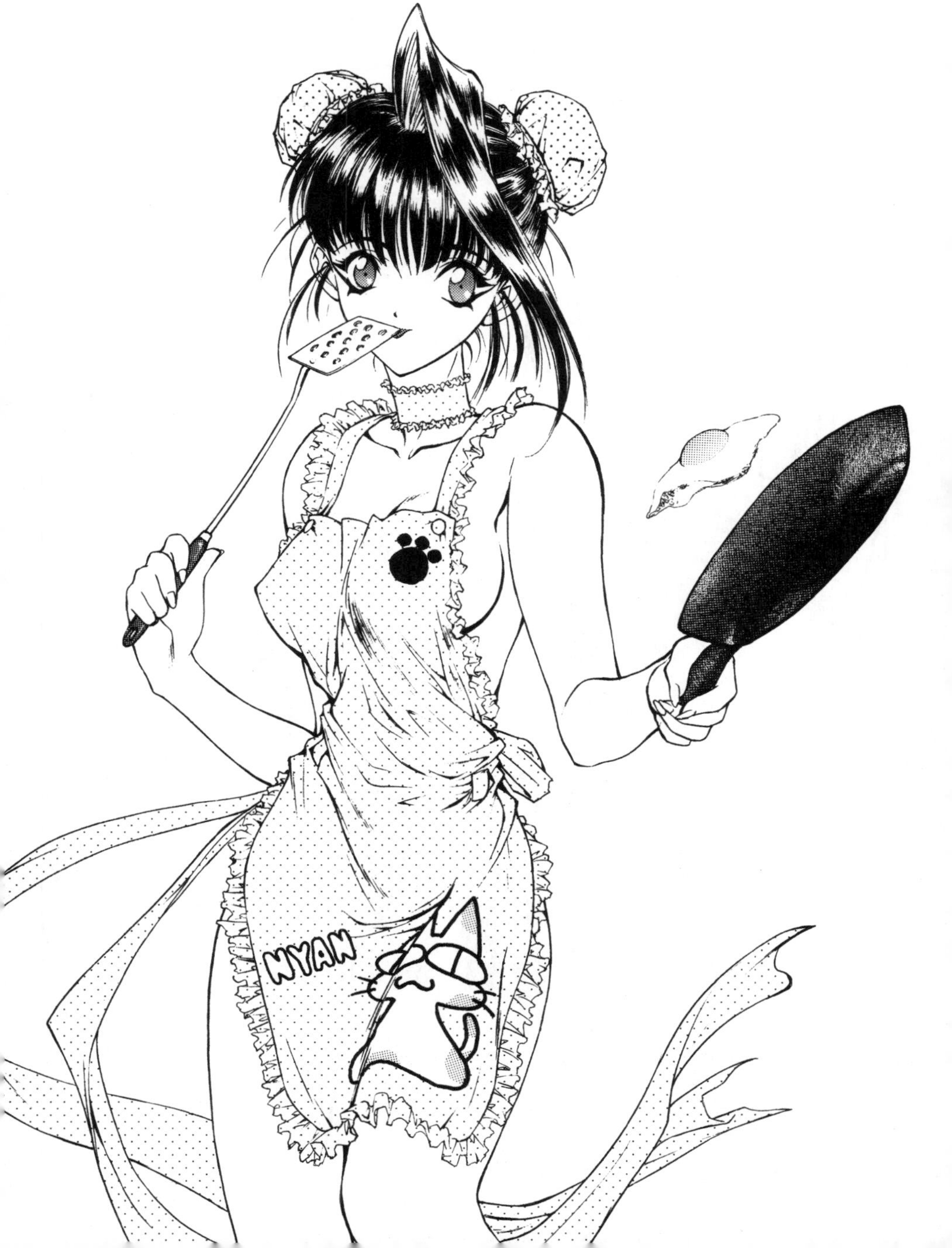
NYAN

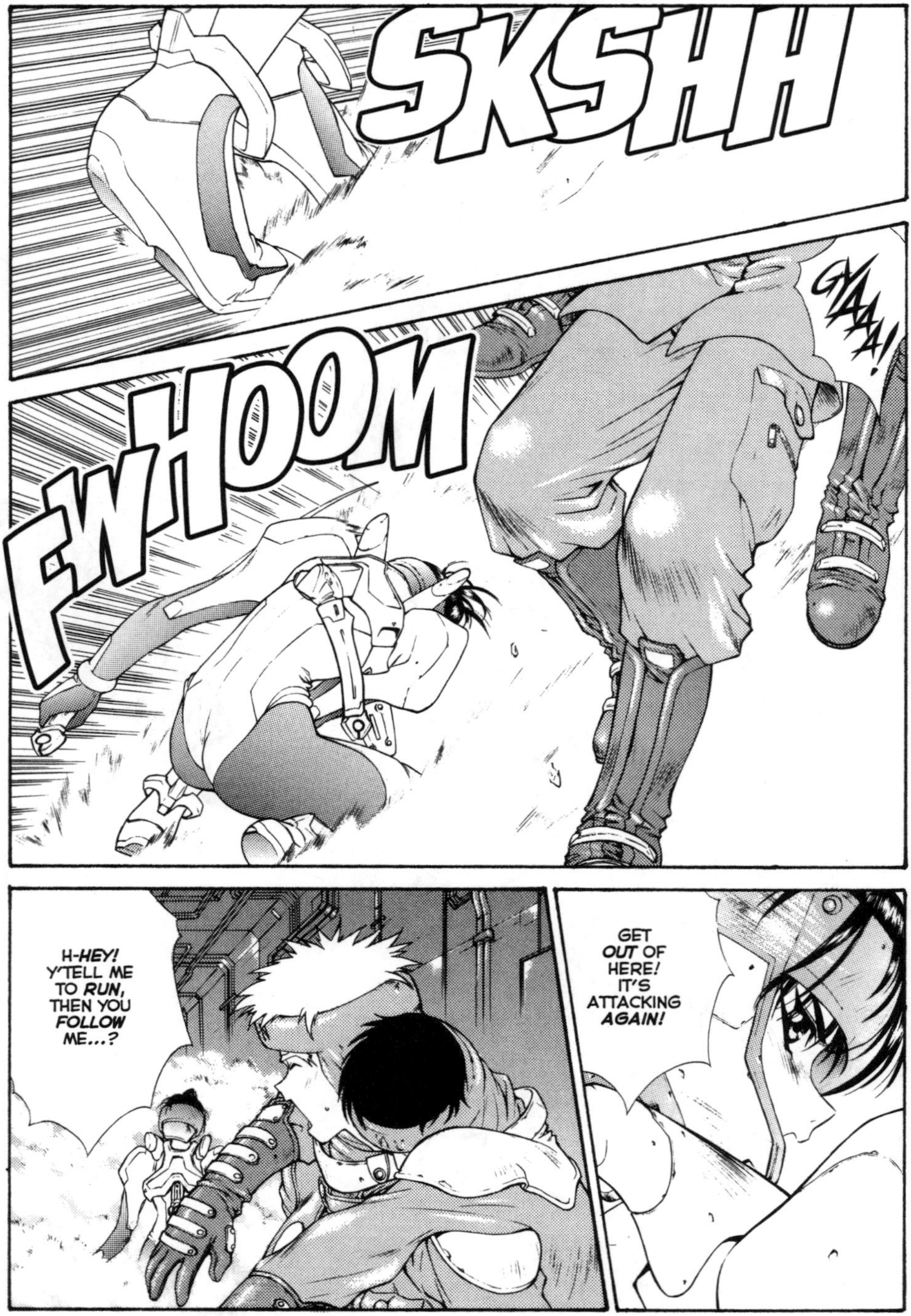
SKSHH
FWHOOM
GYAAAA!
H-HEY! Y'TELL ME TO RUN, THEN YOU FOLLOW ME...?
GET OUT OF HERE! IT'S ATTACKING AGAIN!

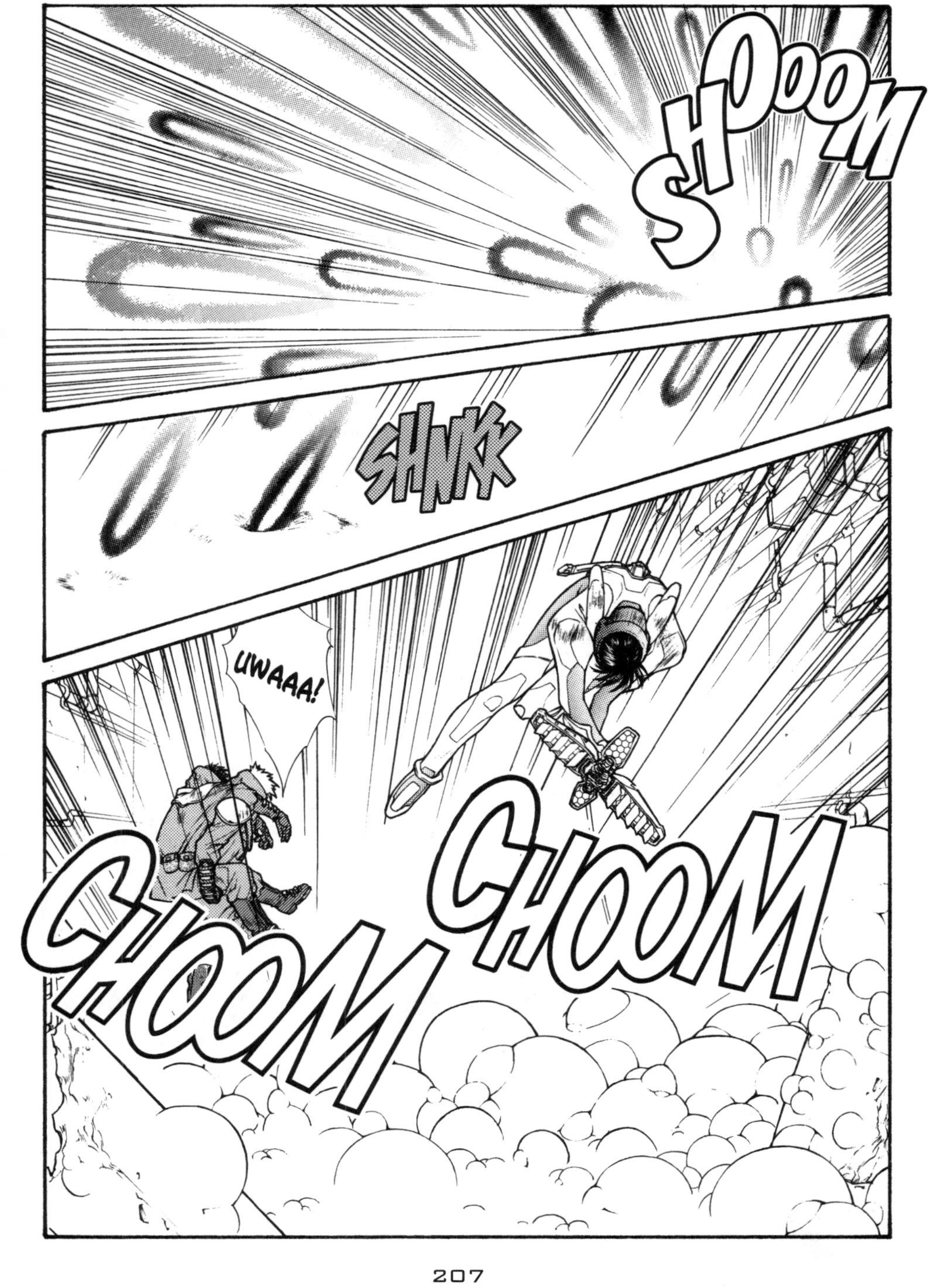
SHOOOM
SHNKK
UWAAA!
CHOOM
CHOOM

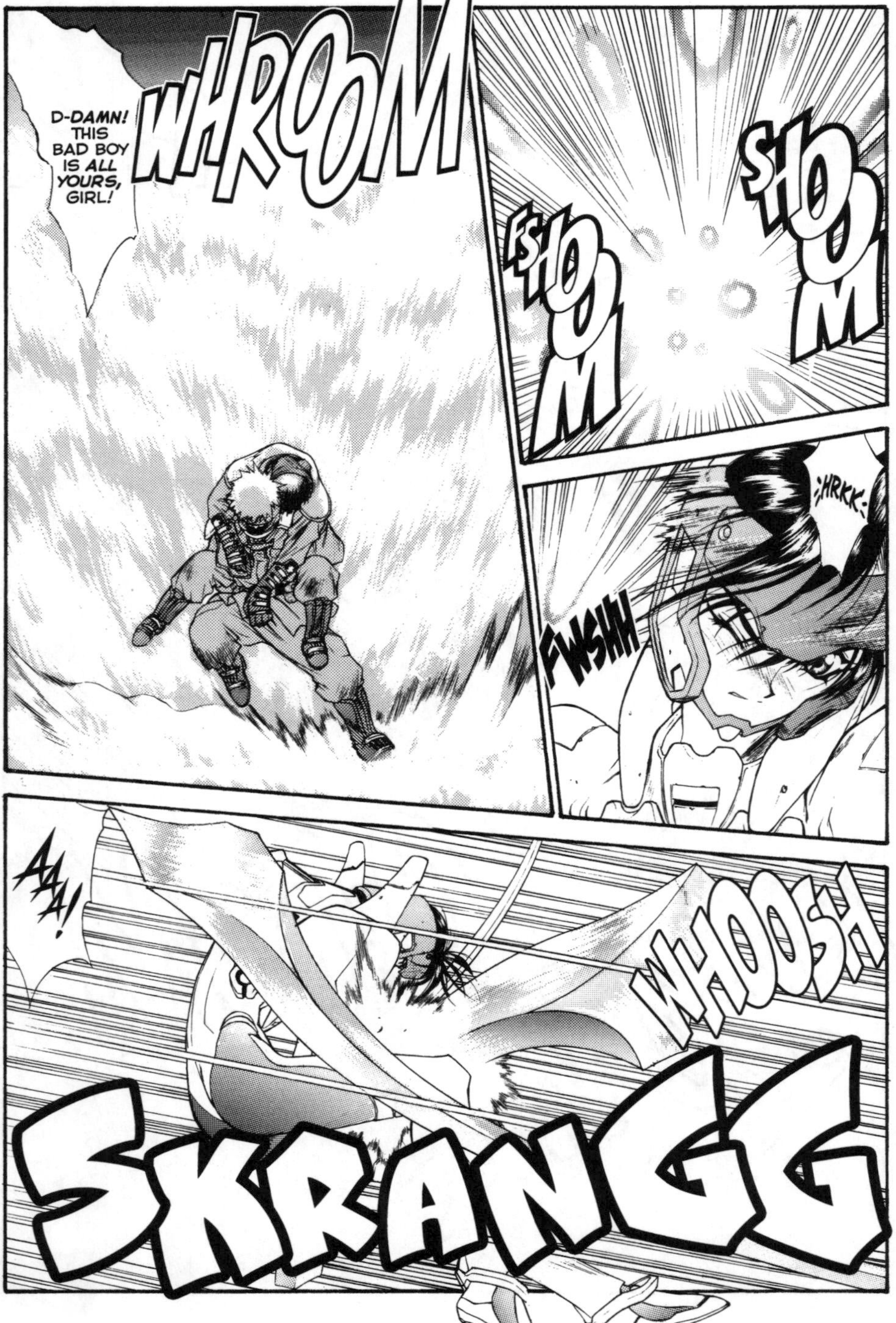
WHROOM
D-DAMN! THIS BAD BOY IS ALL YOURS, GIRL!
FSHOOM
SHOOM
HRKK
FWSHH
AAA!
WHOOSH
SKRANGG

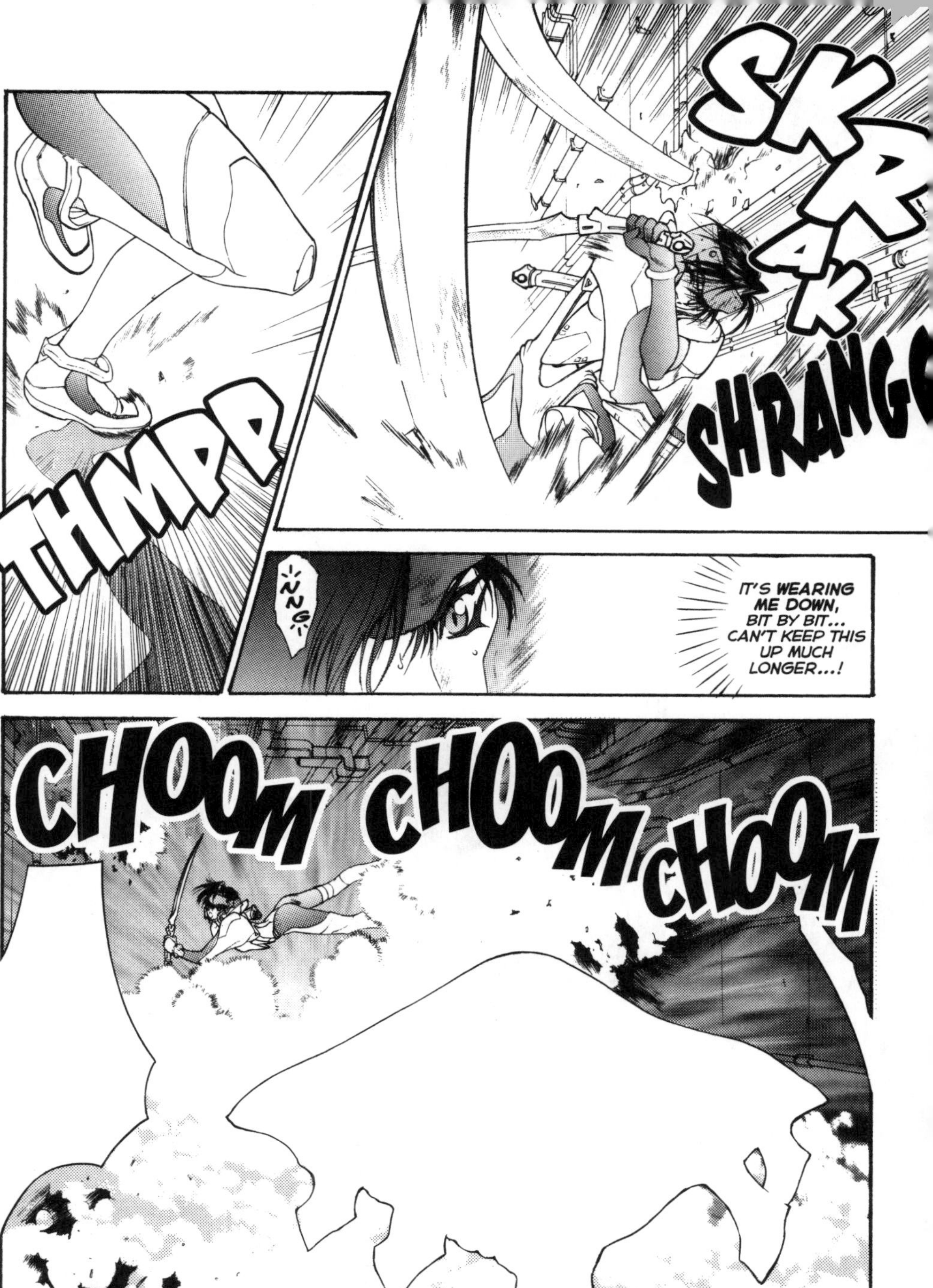
THMPP
SKRAK
SHRANGG
NNG
IT'S WEARING ME DOWN, BIT BY BIT... CAN'T KEEP THIS UP MUCH LONGER...!
CHOOM CHOOM CHOOM

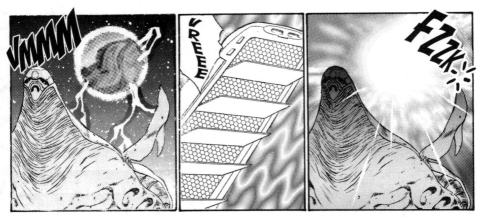

THAT *SUPPRESSOR-FIELD* PROJECTOR... A PRESENT FROM THE GOOD *DOCTOR HEIDEMANN,* I SUPPOSE?

HMFF.

STILL... *QUITE* A WOMAN, REALLY.

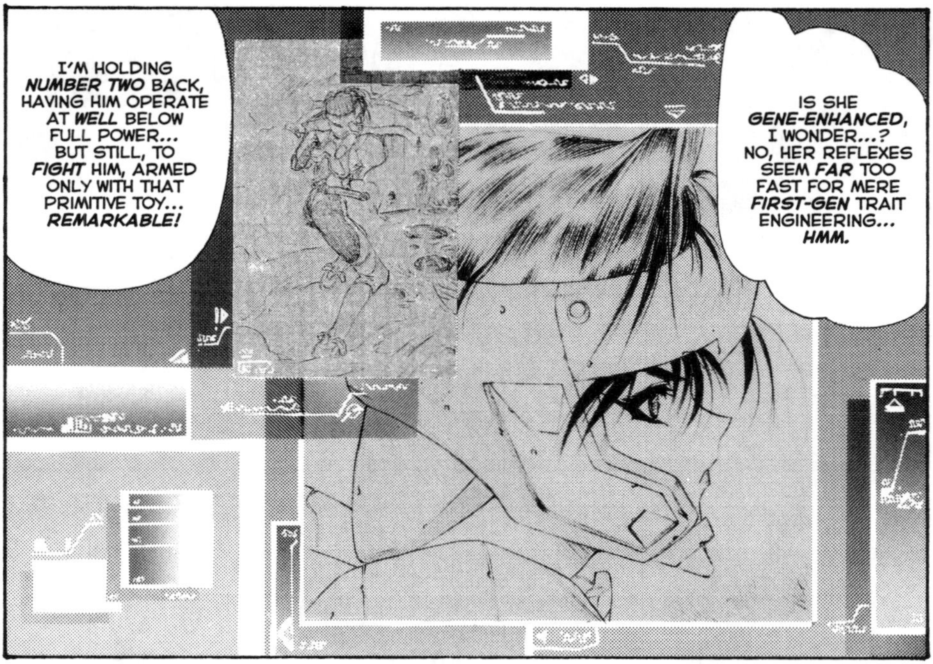
I'M HOLDING NUMBER TWO BACK, HAVING HIM OPERATE AT WELL BELOW FULL POWER... BUT STILL, TO FIGHT HIM, ARMED ONLY WITH THAT PRIMITIVE TOY... REMARKABLE!
IS SHE GENE-ENHANCED, I WONDER...? NO, HER REFLEXES SEEM FAR TOO FAST FOR MERE FIRST-GEN TRAIT ENGINEERING... HMM.
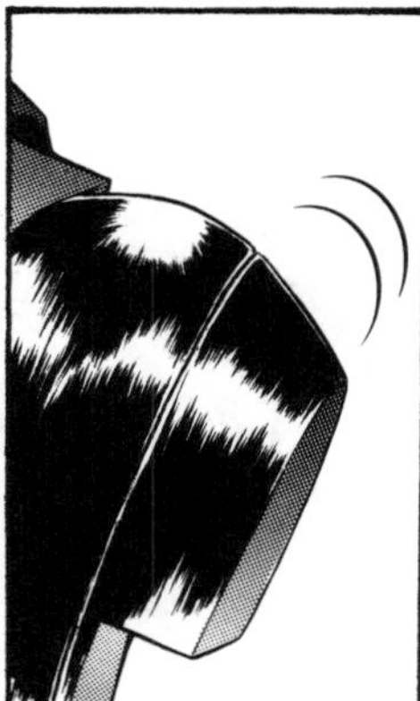
SHRKK
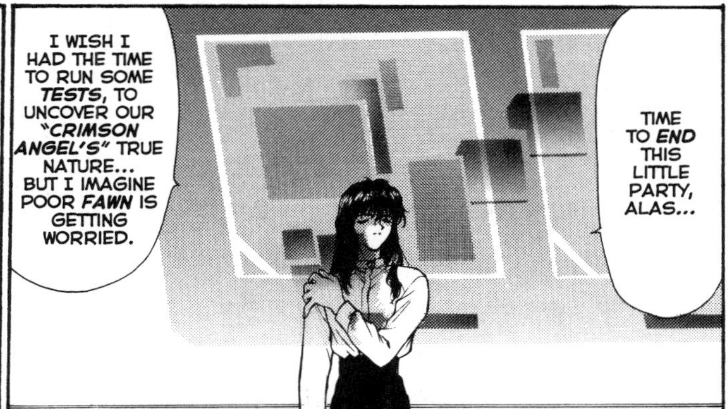
I WISH I HAD THE TIME TO RUN SOME TESTS, TO UNCOVER OUR "CRIMSON ANGEL'S" TRUE NATURE... BUT I IMAGINE POOR FAWN IS GETTING WORRIED.
TIME TO END THIS LITTLE PARTY, ALAS...

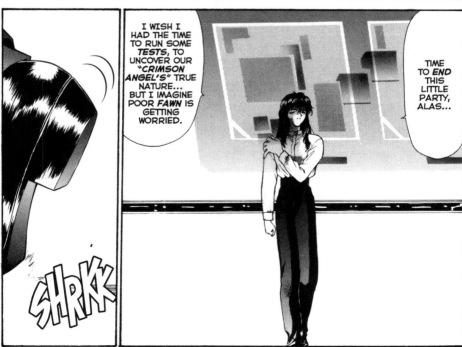

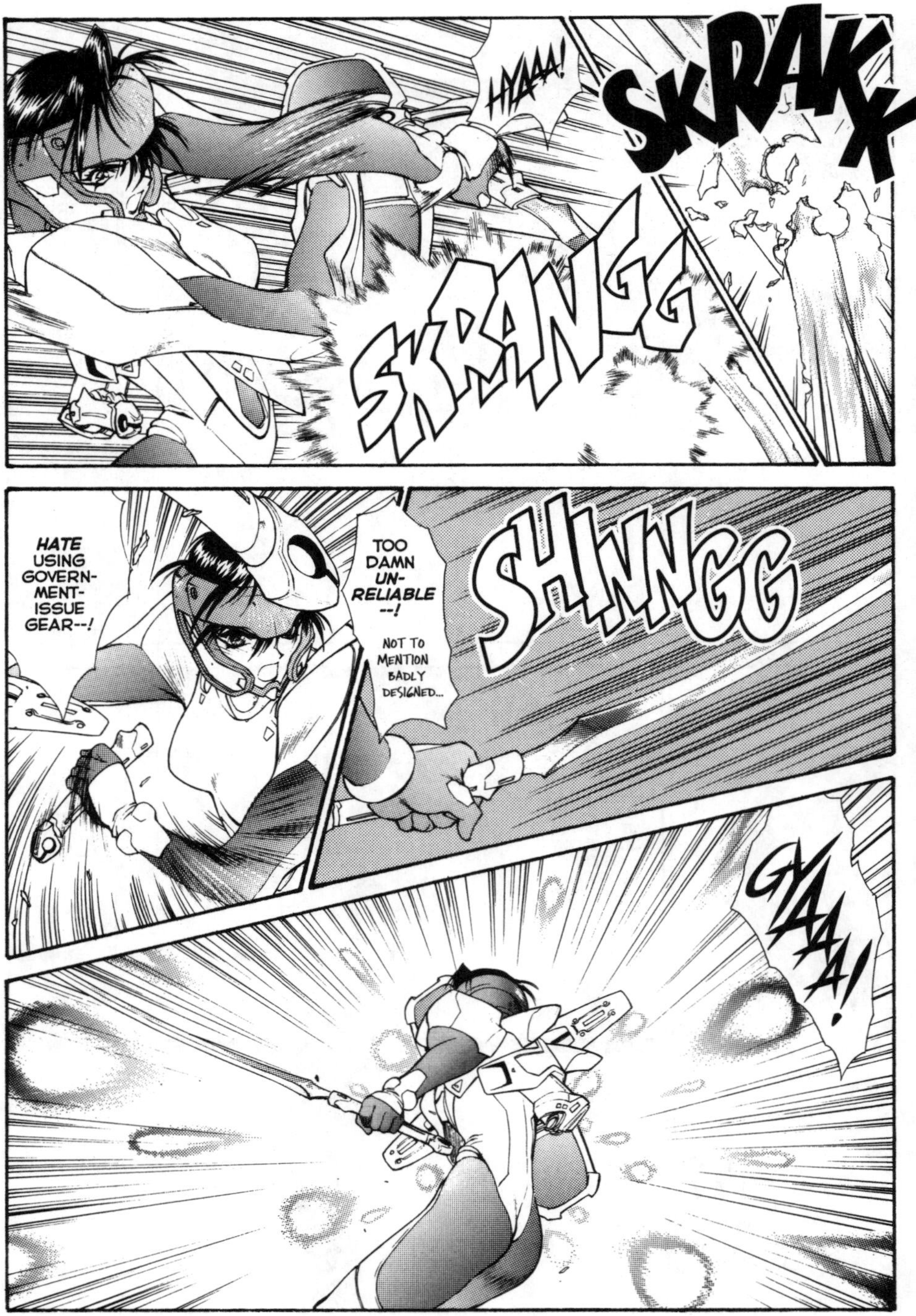
HYAAA!
SKRAKK
SKRANGG
HATE USING GOVERNMENT-ISSUE GEAR--!
TOO DAMN UN-RELIABLE--!
NOT TO MENTION BADLY DESIGNED...
SHINNGG
GYAAAA!

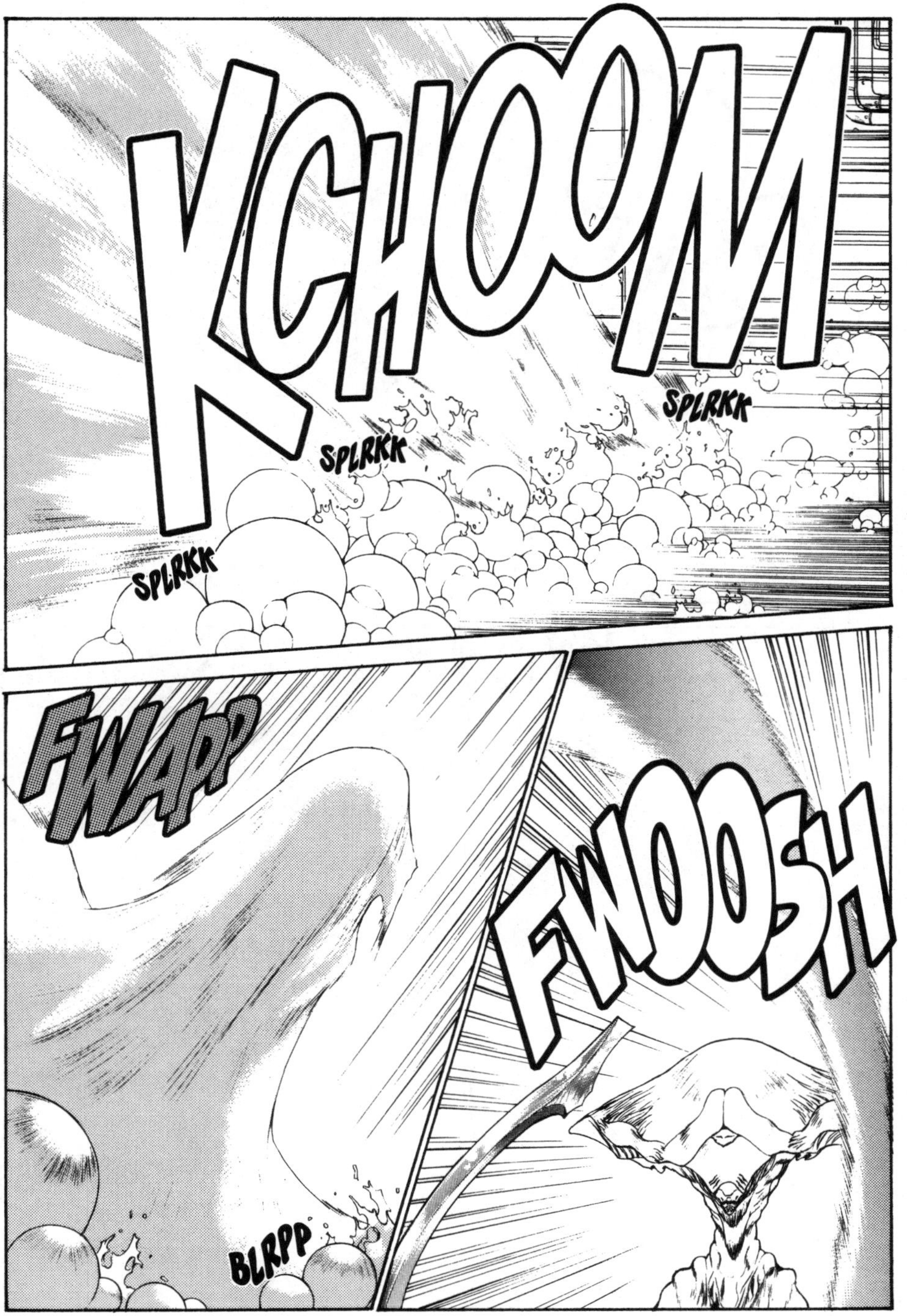
KCHOOM
SPLRKK
SPLRKK
SPLRKK
FWAPP
BLRPP
FWOOSH

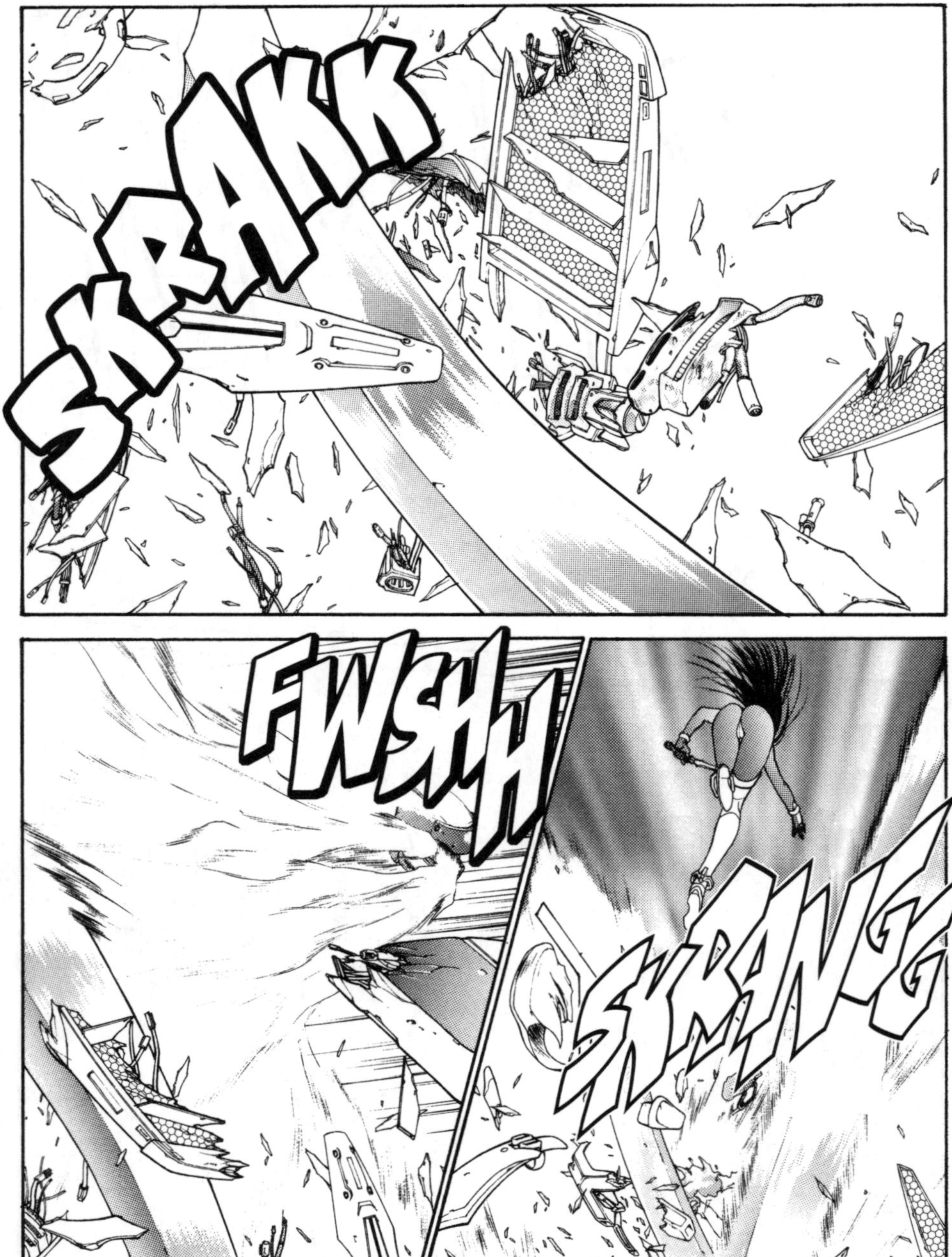
SKRAKK
FWSHH
SKRANG

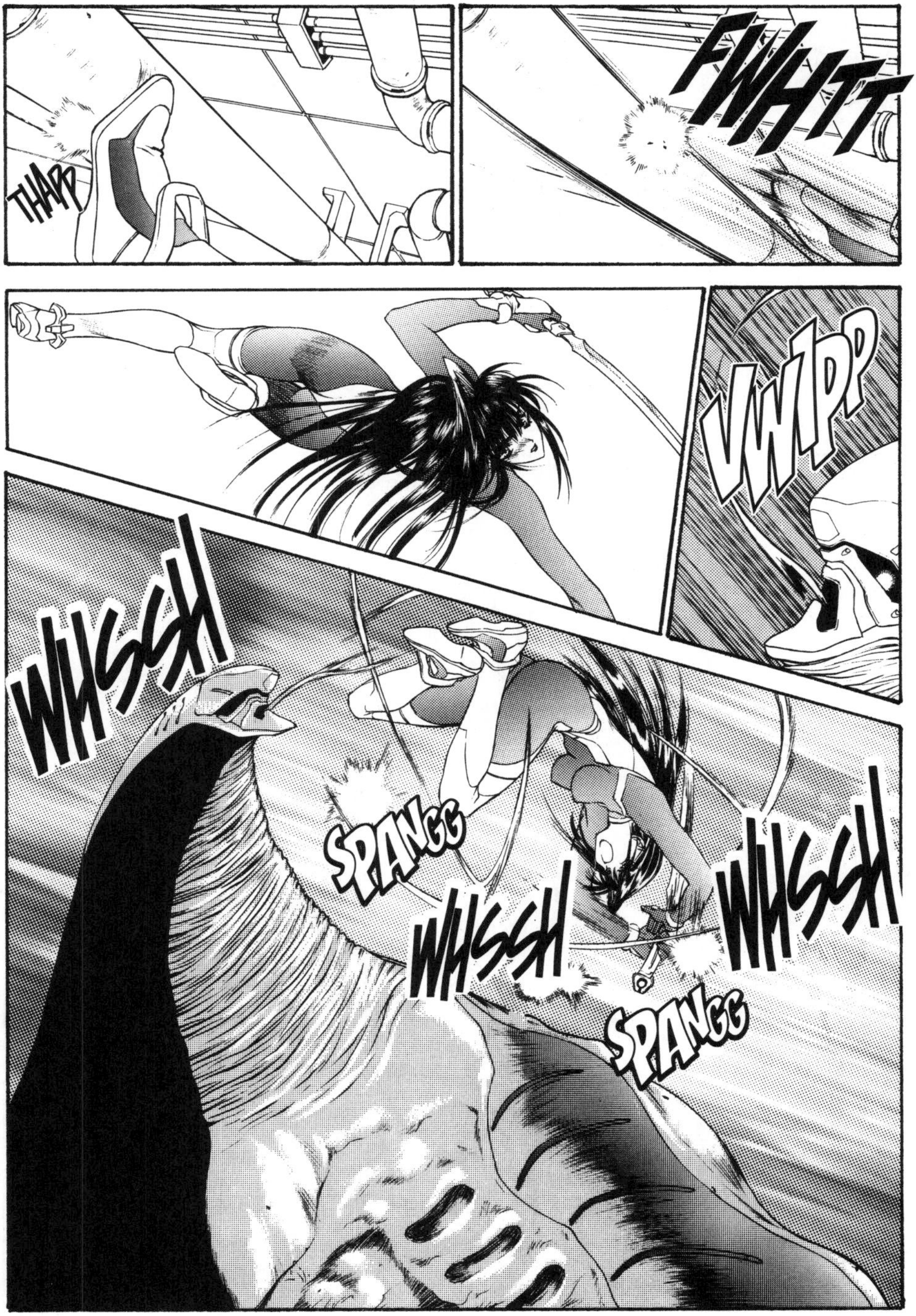
THAPP
FWHTT
VWIPP
WHSSH
SPANGG
WHSSH
WHSSH
SPANGG

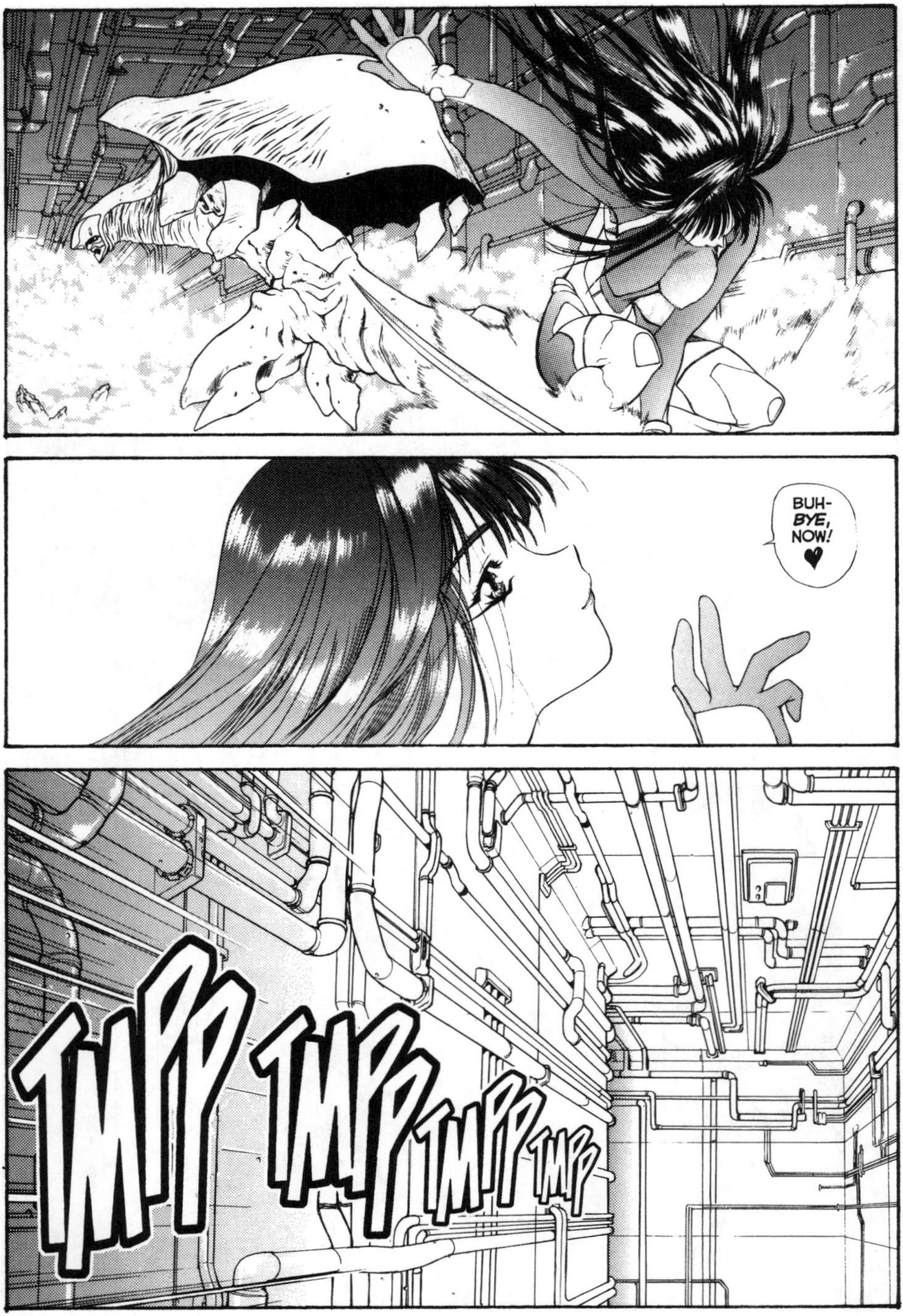
BUH-BYE, NOW! ♥
TMPP TMPP TMPP TMPP

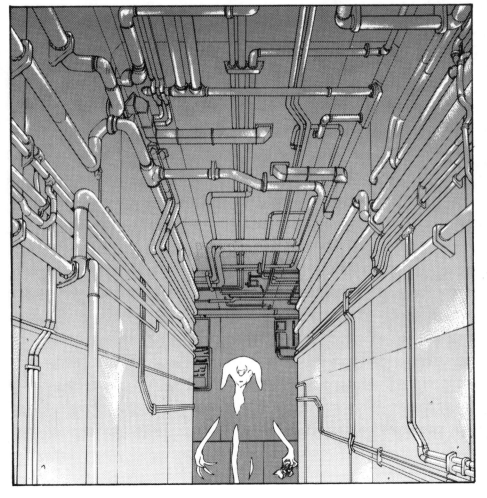

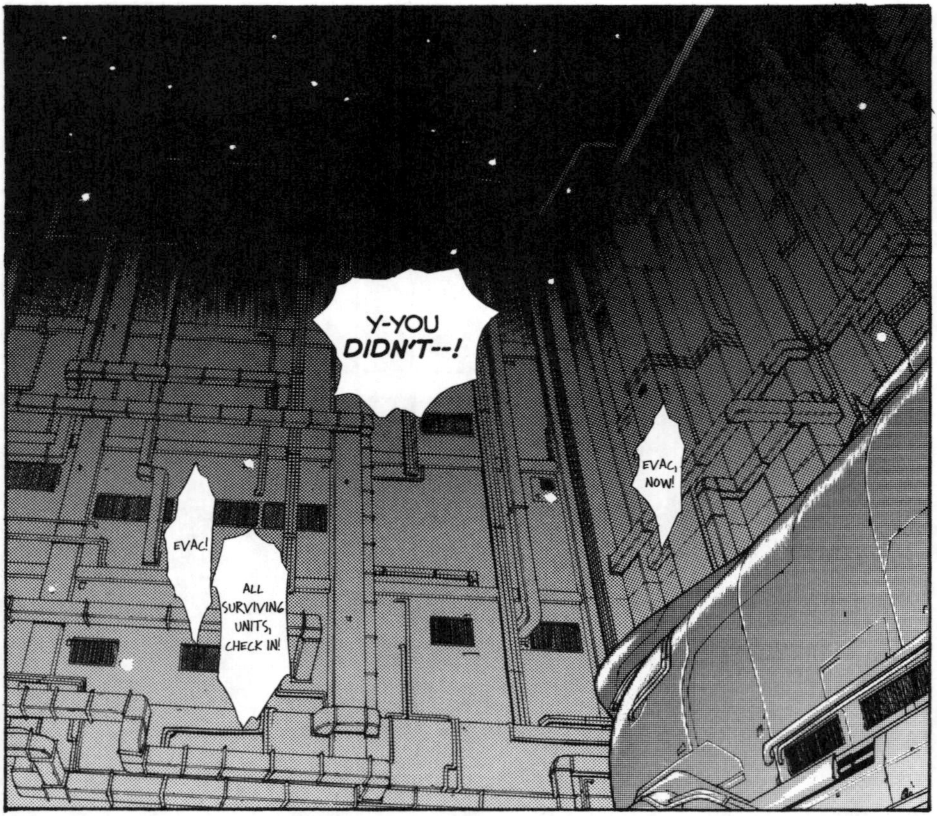
Y-YOU DIDN'T--!
EVAC!
ALL SURVIVING UNITS, CHECK IN!
EVAC, NOW!

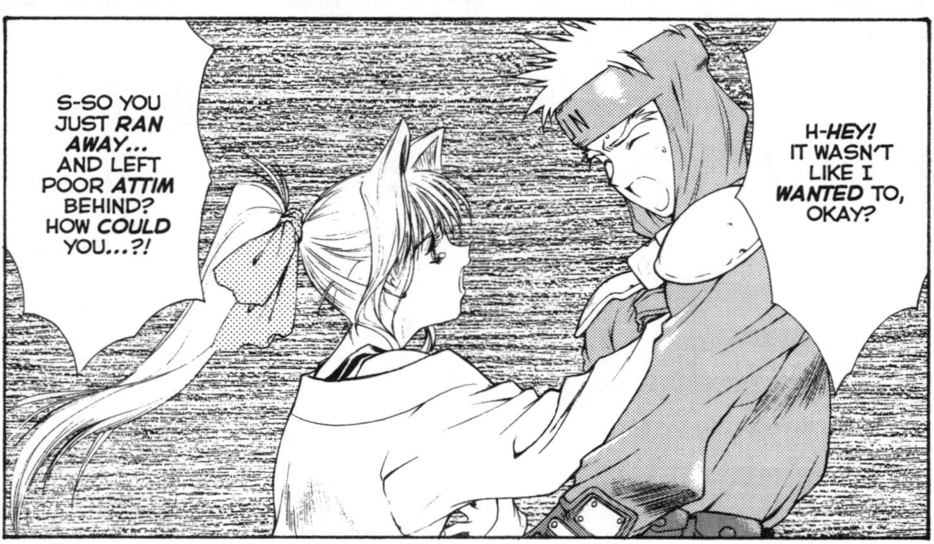
S-SO YOU JUST RAN AWAY... AND LEFT POOR ATTIM BEHIND? HOW COULD YOU...?!
H-HEY! IT WASN'T LIKE I WANTED TO, OKAY?

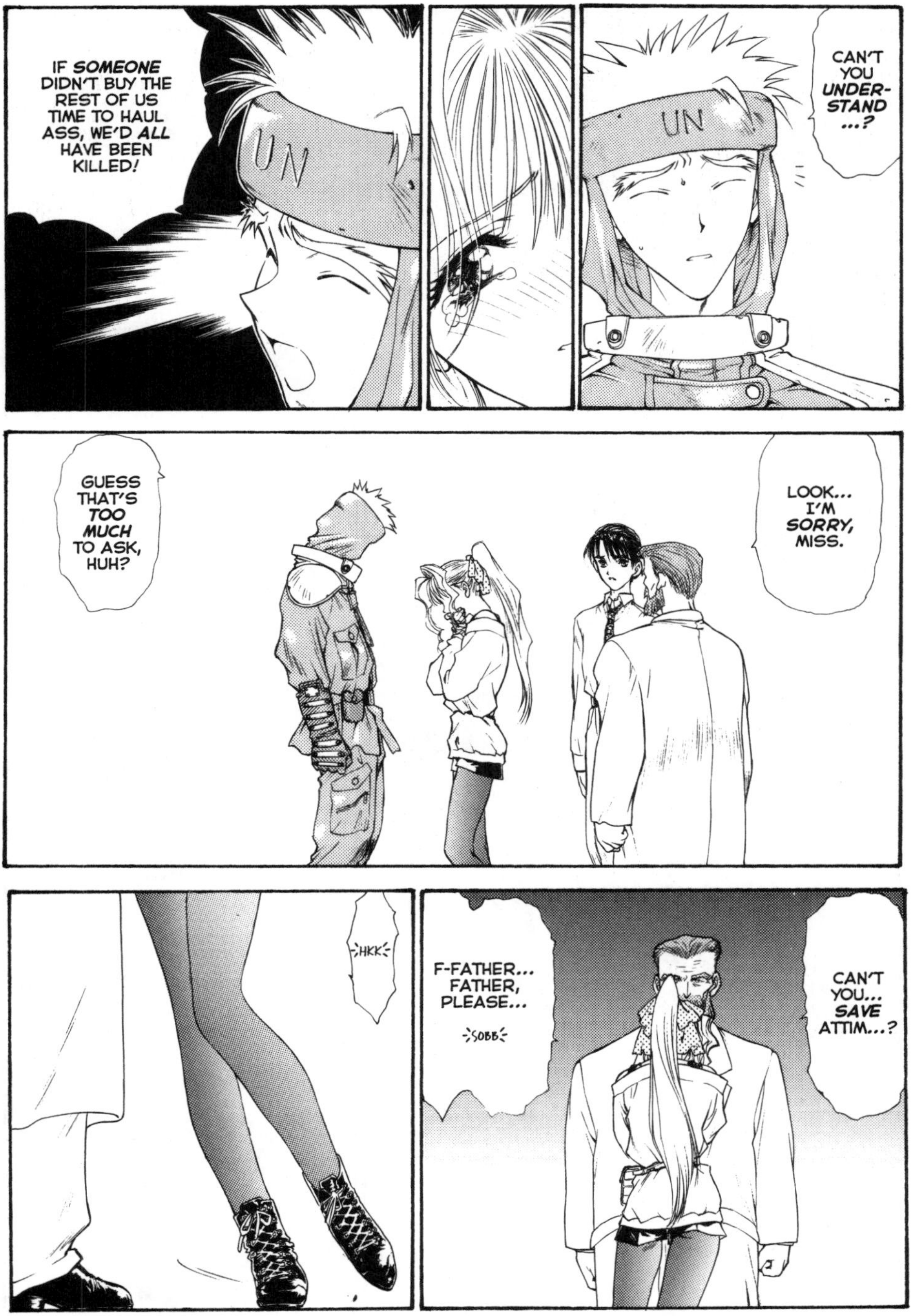
IF SOMEONE DIDN'T BUY THE REST OF US TIME TO HAUL ASS, WE'D ALL HAVE BEEN KILLED!
UN
UN
CAN'T YOU UNDERSTAND...?
GUESS THAT'S TOO MUCH TO ASK, HUH?
LOOK... I'M SORRY, MISS.
HKK
F-FATHER... FATHER, PLEASE...
SOBB
CAN'T YOU... SAVE ATTIM...?

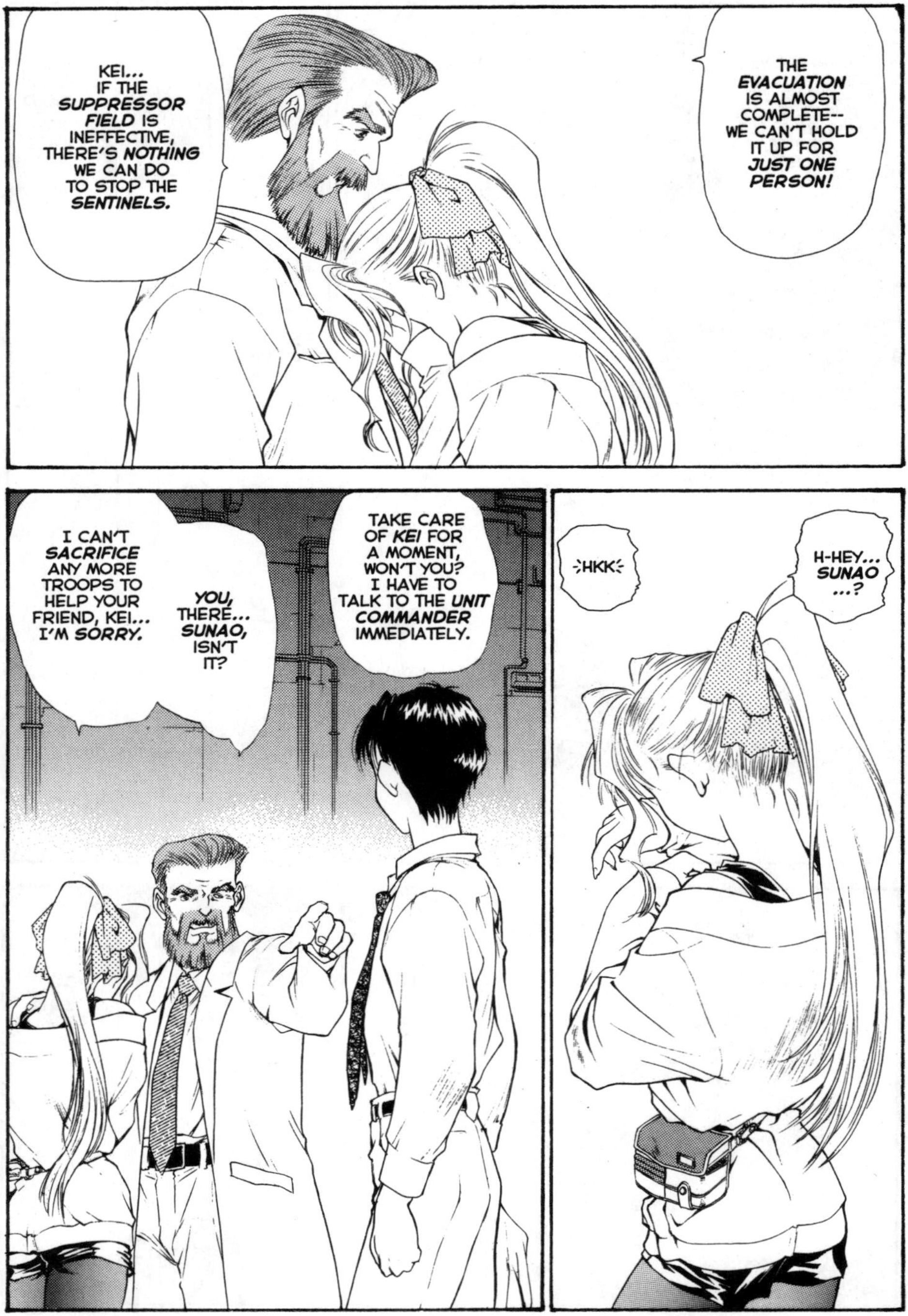
KEI... IF THE SUPPRESSOR FIELD IS INEFFECTIVE, THERE'S NOTHING WE CAN DO TO STOP THE SENTINELS.
THE EVACUATION IS ALMOST COMPLETE-- WE CAN'T HOLD IT UP FOR JUST ONE PERSON!
I CAN'T SACRIFICE ANY MORE TROOPS TO HELP YOUR FRIEND, KEI... I'M SORRY.
YOU, THERE... SUNAO, ISN'T IT?
TAKE CARE OF KEI FOR A MOMENT, WON'T YOU? I HAVE TO TALK TO THE UNIT COMMANDER IMMEDIATELY.
HKK
H-HEY... SUNAO ...?

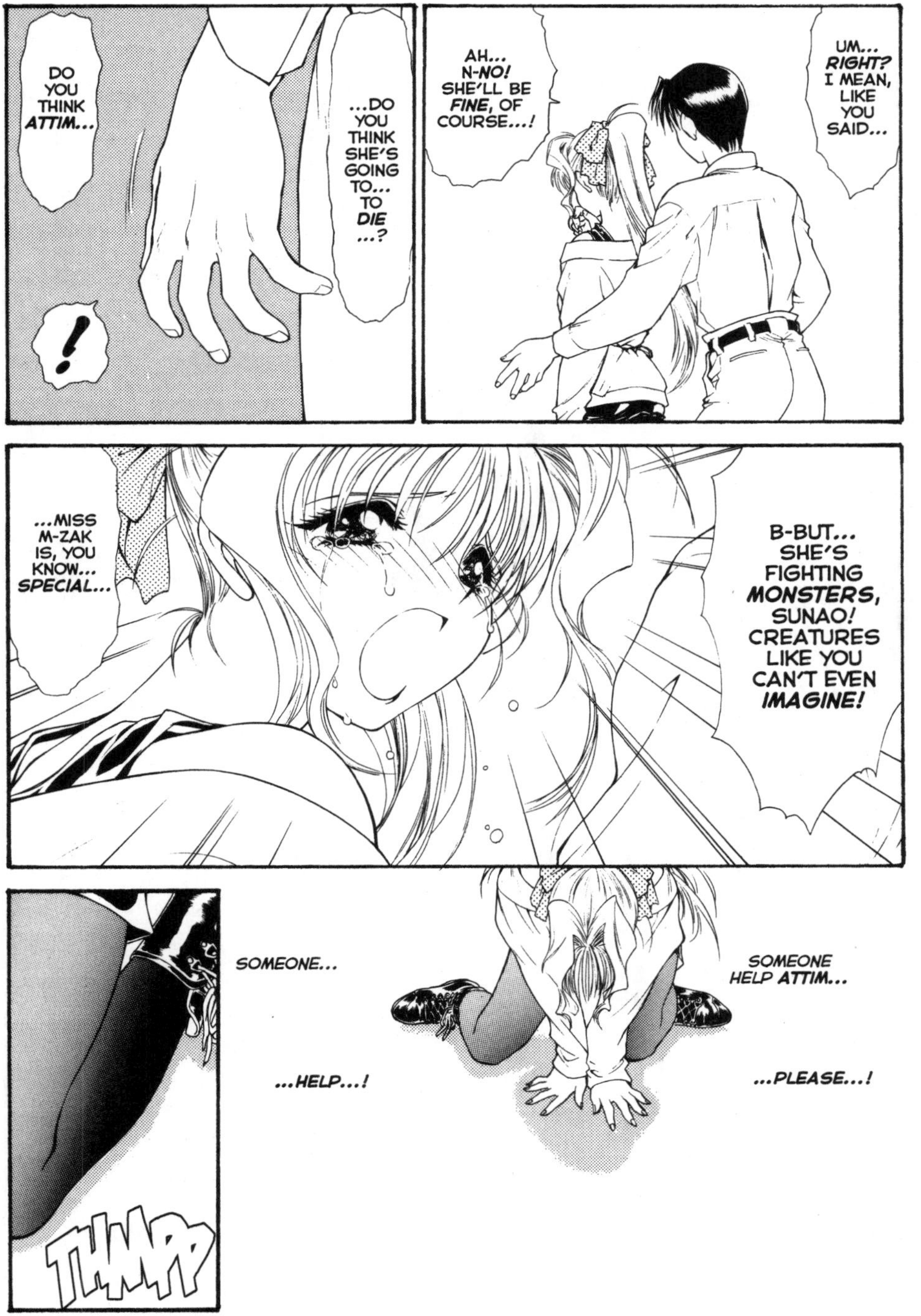
DO YOU THINK ATTIM...
...DO YOU THINK SHE'S GOING TO... TO DIE ...?
!
AH... N-NO! SHE'LL BE FINE, OF COURSE...!
UM... RIGHT? I MEAN, LIKE YOU SAID...
...MISS M-ZAK IS, YOU KNOW... SPECIAL...
B-BUT... SHE'S FIGHTING MONSTERS, SUNAO! CREATURES LIKE YOU CAN'T EVEN IMAGINE!
THMPP
SOMEONE...
...HELP...!
SOMEONE HELP ATTIM...
...PLEASE...!

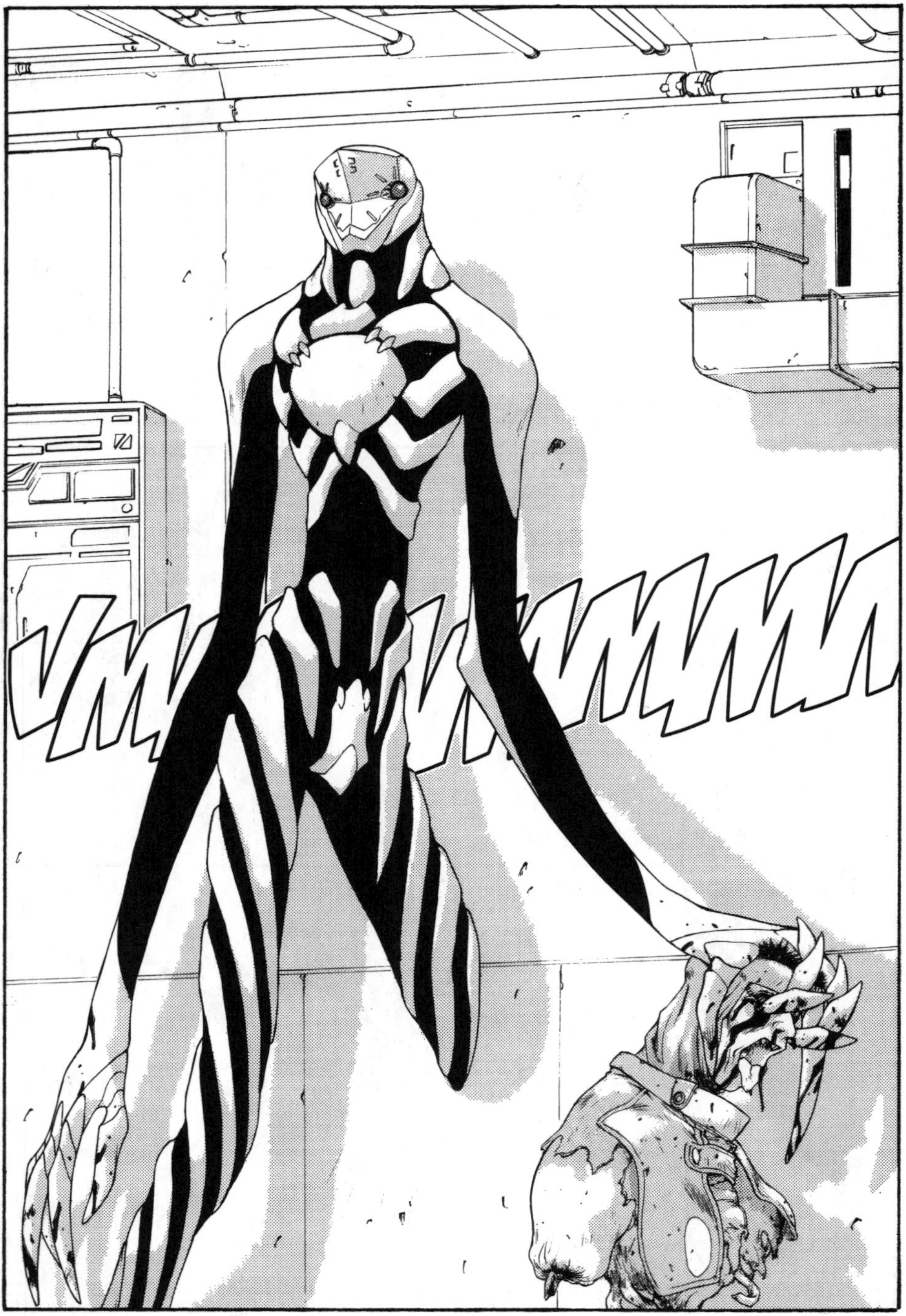

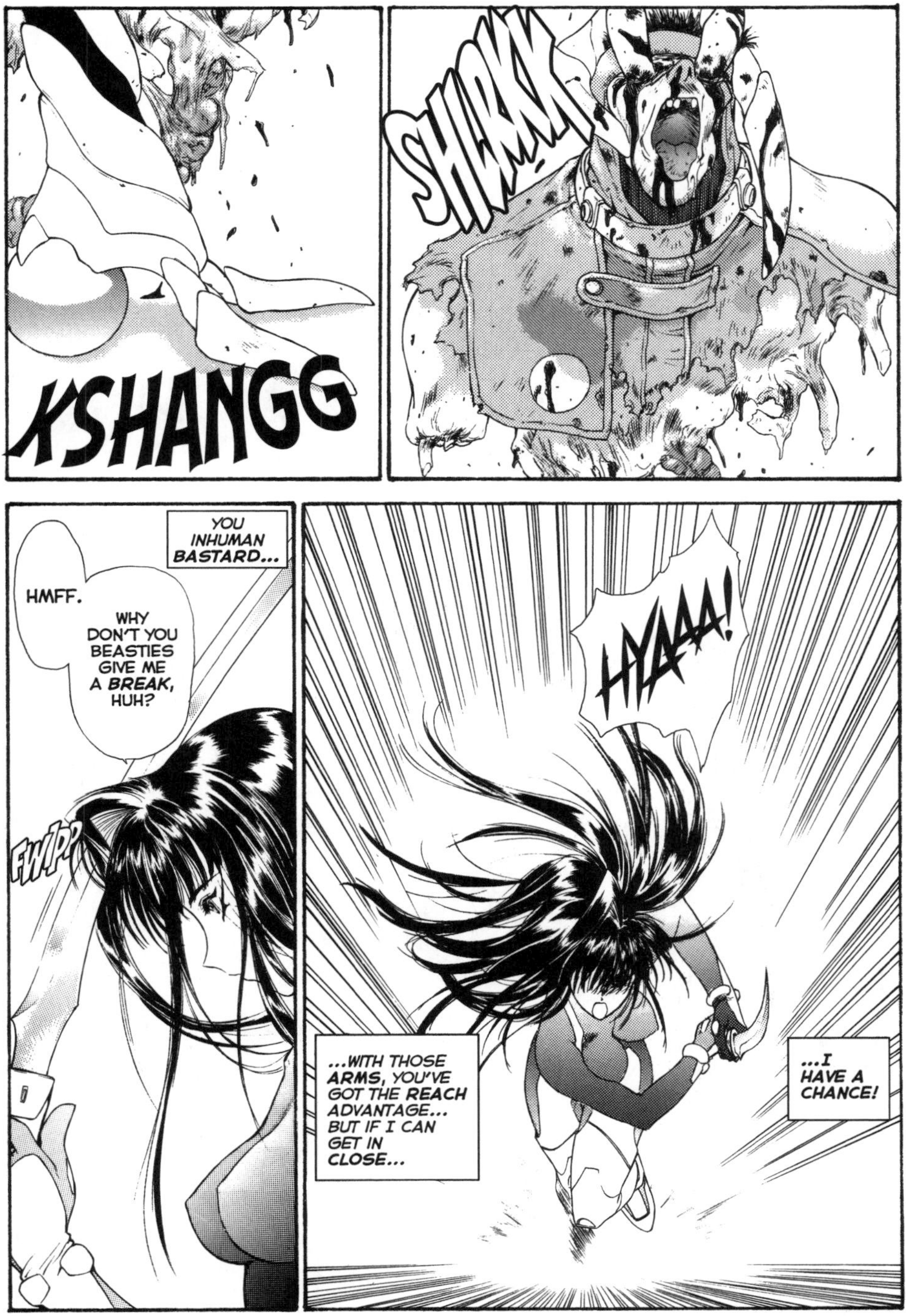
KSHANGG
SHRKKK
YOU INHUMAN BASTARD...
HMFF.
WHY DON'T YOU BEASTIES GIVE ME A BREAK, HUH?
FWIPP
HYAAA!
...WITH THOSE ARMS, YOU'VE GOT THE REACH ADVANTAGE... BUT IF I CAN GET IN CLOSE...
...I HAVE A CHANCE!

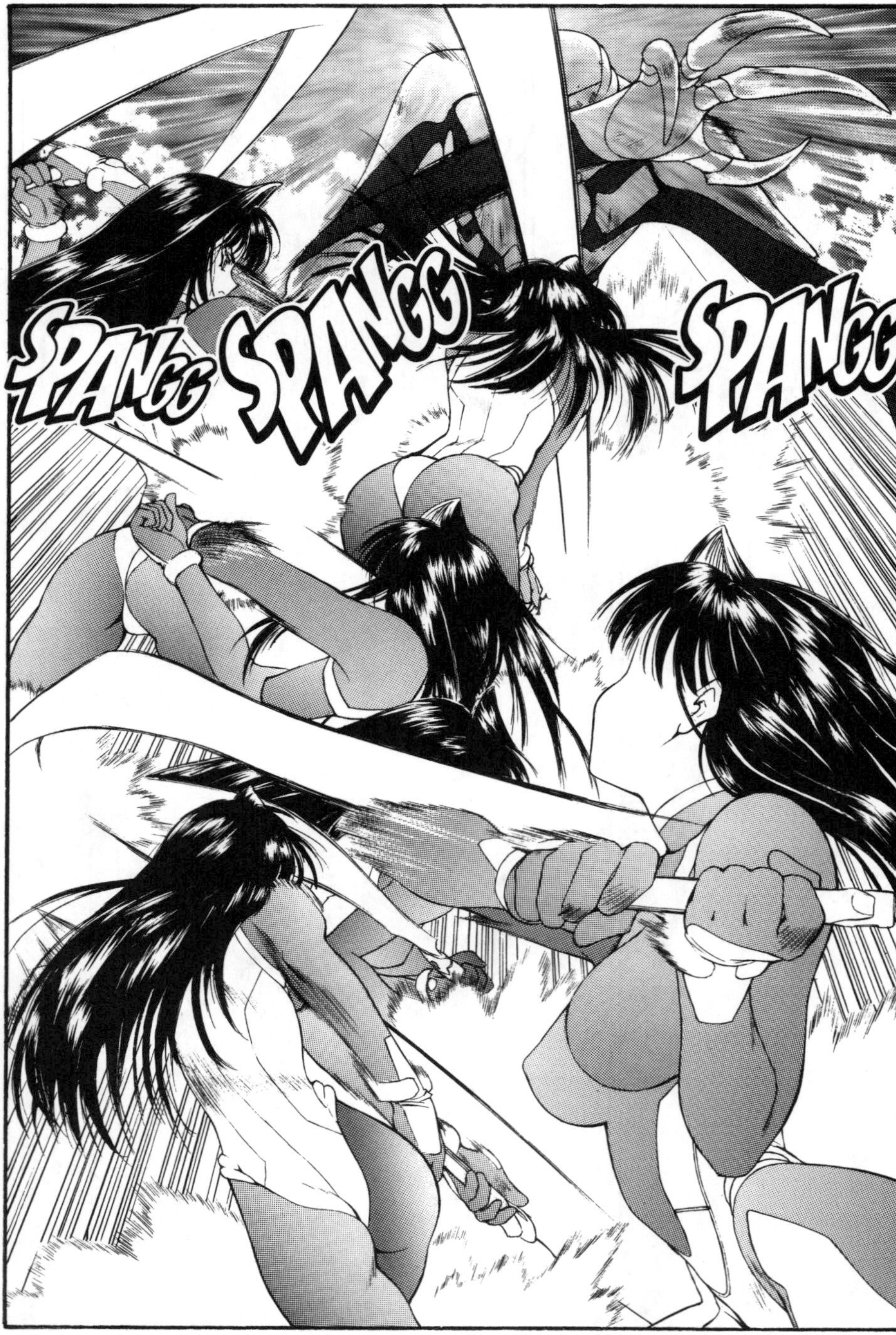
SPANGG
SPANGG
SPANGG

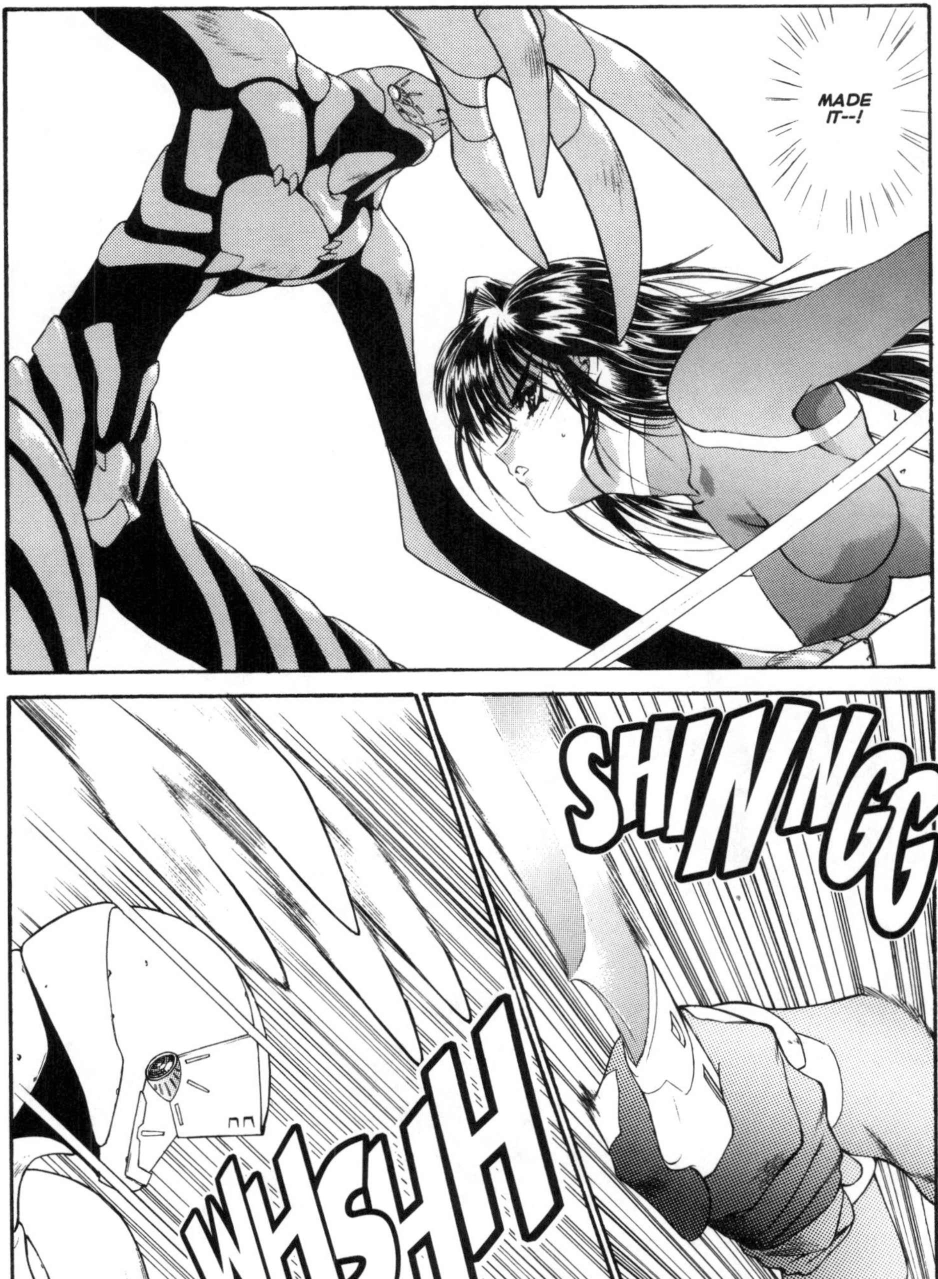
MADE IT--!
WHSHH
SHININGG

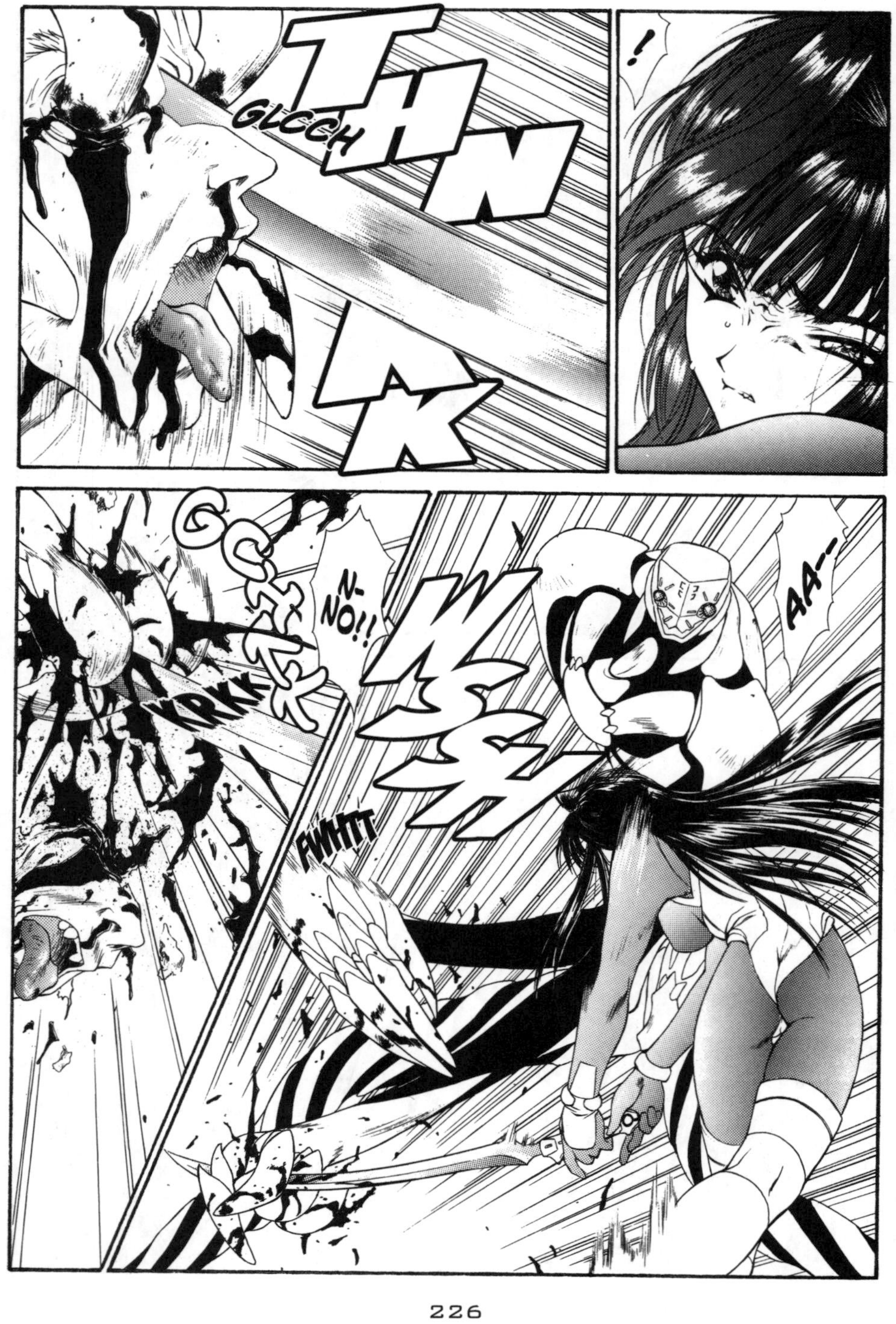
GLCCH
THNK
!
N-NO!!
KRKK
WSSH
FWHTT
AA--

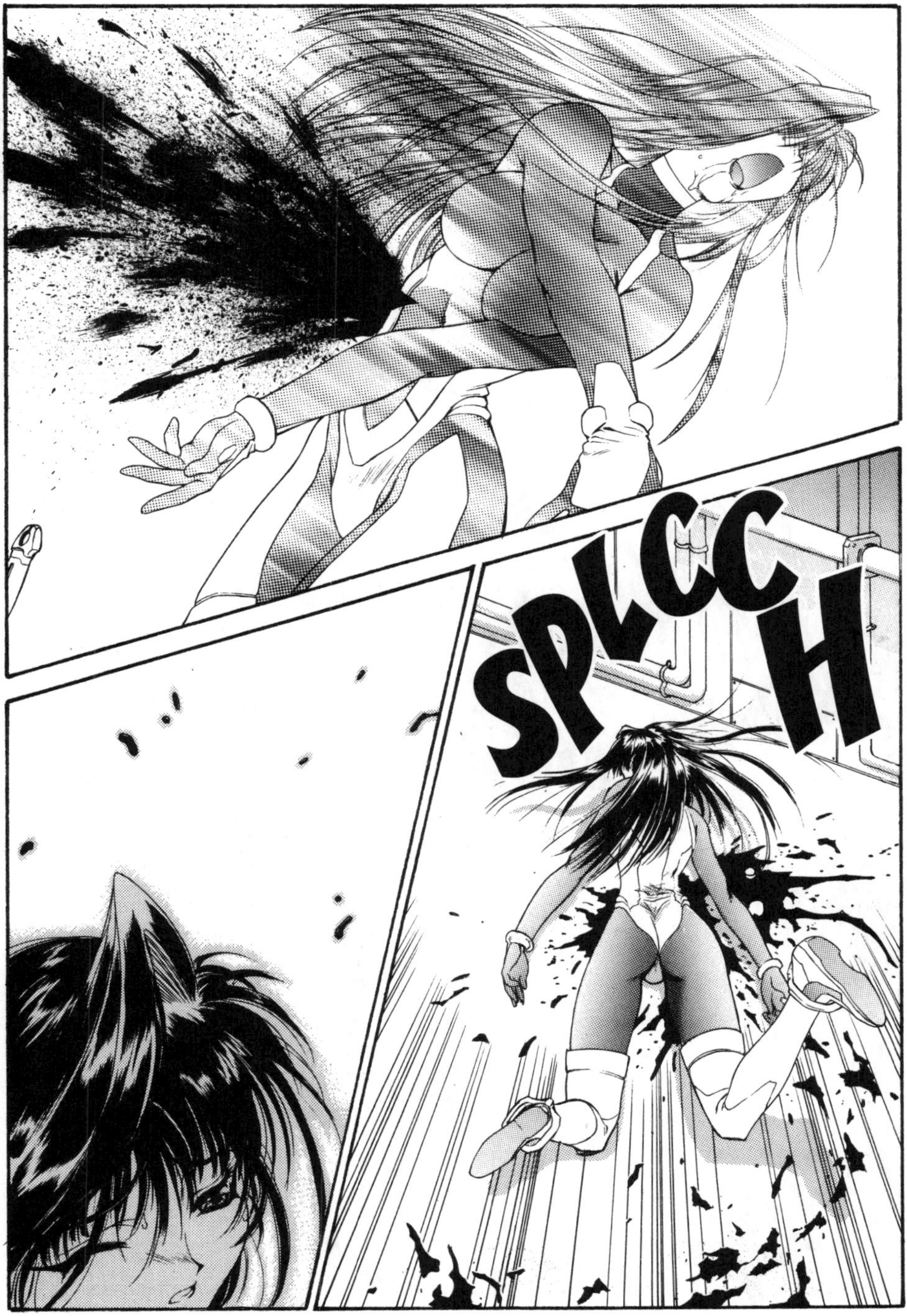
SPLCCH

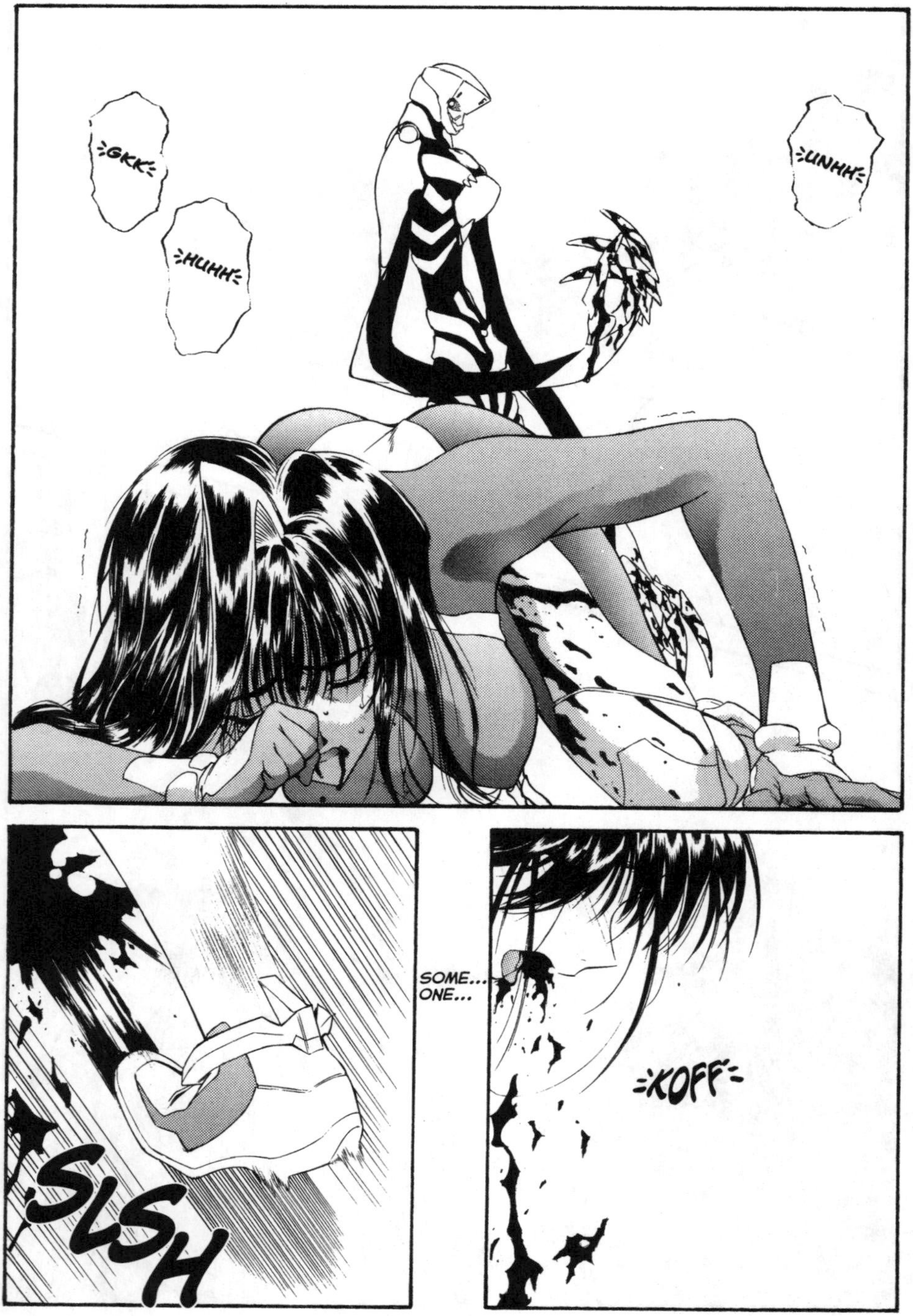
GKK
HUHH
UNHH
SLSH
SOME... ONE...
KOFF

...SOMEONE HELP...

...PLEASE... HELP HER...!

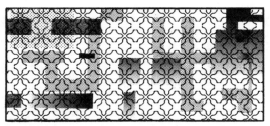

SOMEONE...

...PLEASE...

VREEEEE

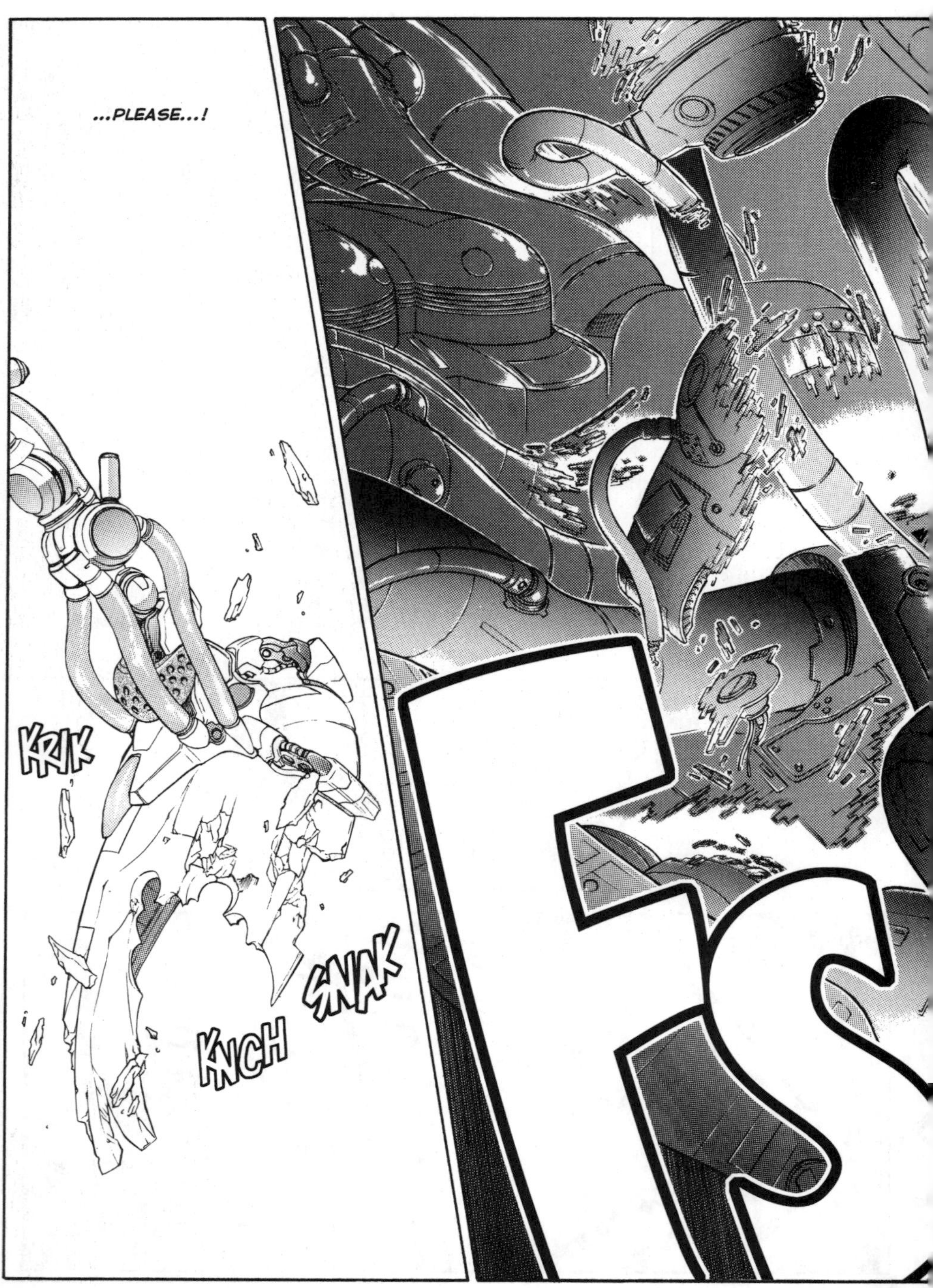
...PLEASE...!
KRIK
KNCH
SNAK

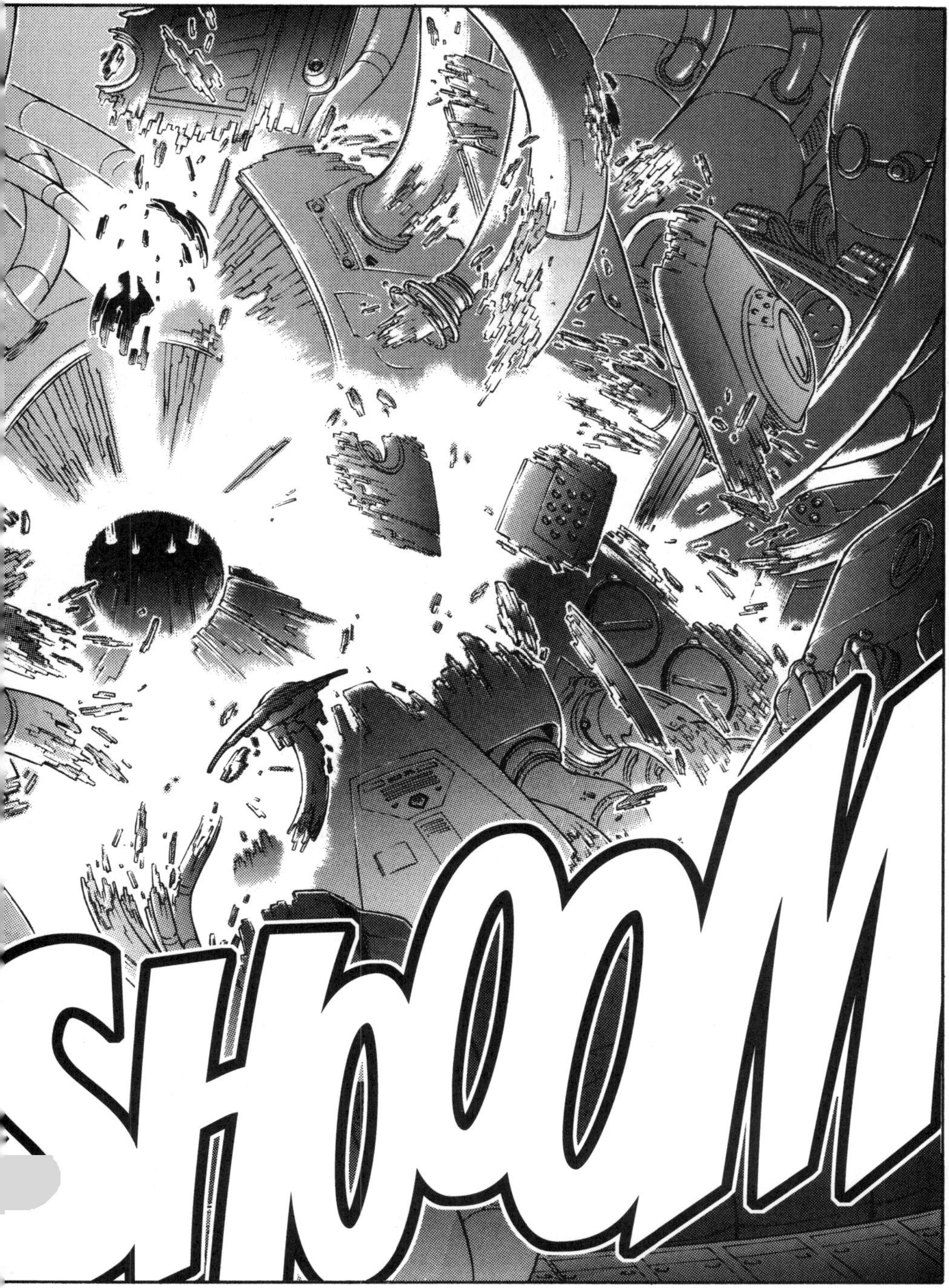
SHOOOM

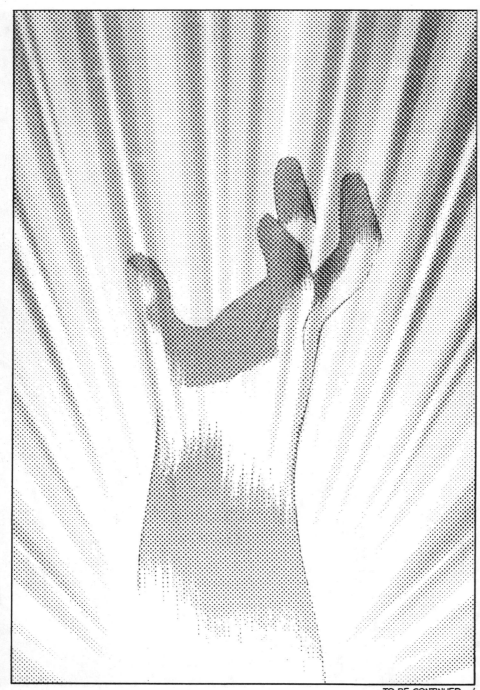

TO BE CONTINUED...!